D0866652

Accounting & Management

Accounting & Management
Field Study
Perspectives

HF
5657.4
.A25
1987

Edited by
William J. Bruns, Jr.
Robert S. Kaplan

Indiana
Purdue
Library
Fort Wayne

WITHDRAWN

Harvard Business School Press
Boston, Massachusetts

The paper used in this publication meets the requirements of the American National Standard
for Permanence of Paper for Printed Library Materials Z39.49-1984.
© 1987 by the President and Fellows of Harvard College
All rights reserved.
Printed in the United States of America
91 90 89 88   5 4 3 2

Library of Congress Cataloging-in-Publication Data

Accounting & management: field study perspectives / edited by William J. Bruns, Jr.,
Robert S. Kaplan.
p.   cm.
Proceedings of a colloquium held June 16–18, 1986, at the Harvard Business School.
Includes bibliographies and index.
ISBN 0-87584-186-4
1. Managerial accounting—Congresses. I. Bruns, William J.
II. Kaplan, Robert S. III. Title: Accounting & management.
HF5657.4.A25 1987
658.4'038—dc19   87-18373
CIP

Contents

Preface   vii

Introduction: Field Studies in Management
Accounting
William J. Bruns, Jr. and Robert S. Kaplan   1

PART I. **Adapting Management Accounting Systems to
Changing Environments**

1. Management Control System Change: The Adoption
    of Inflation Accounting
    Julie H. Hertenstein   17

2. Organizational Design versus Strategic Information
    Procedures for Managing Corporate Overhead Cost:
    Weyerhaeuser Company, 1972–1986
    H. Thomas Johnson   49

3. The Anatomy of an Accounting Change
    Krishna Palepu   73

PART II. **Designing New Information and Control Systems**

4. A Field Study of an Attempt to Change an Embedded
    Cost Accounting System
    William J. Bruns, Jr.   97

5. Tension in the Design of Formal Control Systems: A
    Field Study in a Computer Company
    Jeremy F. Dent   119

6. Organization, Information, and People: A Participant
    Observation of a MIS-Carriage
    Hein Schreuder   146

PART III. **New Directions for Cost Management Systems**

   7. Accounting for Labor Productivity in Manufacturing
       Operations: An Application
       Rajiv D. Banker and Srikant M. Datar   169

   8. How Cost Accounting Systematically Distorts Product
       Costs
       Robin Cooper and Robert S. Kaplan   204

   9. Adapting a Cost Accounting System to Just-in-Time
       Manufacturing: The Hewlett-Packard Personal Office
       Computer Division
       James M. Patell   229

  10. Accounting, Incentives, and the Lot-Sizing Decision:
       A Field Study
       Jerold L. Zimmerman   268

PART IV. **Measuring Management Performance**

  11. The Use of Relative Performance Evaluation in Orga-
       nizations
       Michael W. Maher   295

  12. How and Why Firms Disregard the Controllability
       Principle
       Kenneth A. Merchant   316

  13. Planning, Control, and Uncertainty: A Process View
       Robert Simons   339

      Contributors   363

      Index   367

Preface

On June 16–18, 1986, a colloquium on field research studies in management accounting was held at the Harvard Business School. Thirteen papers were presented to an audience of more than sixty business executives, consultants, and business school professors. The project started two years earlier when we invited selected accounting researchers from the United States and Western Europe to join faculty from the HBS Control Area in an innovative research project. The requirements for participation were that the researcher study an accounting issue within an actual organization (or organizations) and prepare a paper. Although recognized for their outstanding research accomplishments, some of the participants had never studied accounting problems in an actual organizational context. Nevertheless, almost all the people we asked to participate generously accepted our invitation so that they could learn more about field research methods and determine whether an organizational study could provide new insights for their teaching and research activities.

In January 1985, the entire group convened at Harvard to share ideas and plans for each research project and to learn more about the field research process. Three HBS professors with extensive experience in performing field research—Gordon Donaldson in Finance, David Garvin in Production/Operations Management, and Thomas Bonoma in Marketing—described the research processes they had

vii

used. Other HBS faculty in the Control Area, with extensive case-writing and clinical research experience (Charles Christenson, F. Warren McFarlan, and Richard Vancil) chaired a panel discussion on procedures for interviewing managers and collecting data in organizations. By the end of this two-day meeting, the researchers had received feedback on their projects and gained a degree of comfort and familiarity with field research procedures.

A second and briefer meeting occurred in August 1985 during the American Accounting Association annual meeting in Reno, Nevada. The researchers met for two hours to give progress reports on each project. Four HBS professors (William Bruns, Julie Hertenstein, Robert Kaplan, and Kenneth Merchant) then offered a full-day tutorial on field research methods to more than fifty AAA members. The goal was to disseminate even more widely the insights already gained on the benefits, techniques, and criteria for field research.

In January 1986, a third meeting was held at Harvard, and participants presented preliminary drafts of their papers. Two full days of active discussion clearly demonstrated the enthusiasm of the researchers for their projects and the considerable expansion of the topics under investigation. Being exposed to the realities of management accounting system design and implementation caused more of the projects to focus on political and organizational dynamics, rather than on technical design questions. Although each project was developed and researched individually, participants easily noticed many common strands across the seemingly diverse studies.

Participant enthusiasm and interest in their own studies also suggested that someone other than the researcher should present the paper at the colloquium; otherwise, too much time would be spent describing how the research developed over time, rather than the findings of the research itself. We were fortunate that four outstanding researchers—John Shank of Dartmouth, Anthony Hopwood of the London School of Economics, George Foster of Stanford, and Robert Swieringa, previously at Cornell and now a Member of the Financial Accounting Standards Board—agreed to present and critique the thirteen papers at the colloquium.

The colloquium itself was an exciting two-day experience. Academics in attendance, who had not participated in defining, describing, and executing the field research projects, frequently questioned the procedures used and inferences drawn in the papers. Experienced practitioners seemed to relate much better to the problems found and studied and to endorse, in general, the tentative conclusions drawn by the researchers. There was a constant tension between talking about research methods or the research process and about the substantive issues explored in each project.

At the conclusion of the colloquium and a half-day debriefing immediately following, there was general agreement that field research methods can, and should, be an important part of the repertoire for management accounting researchers. The challenge is to devise mechanisms—funding and publication—that will enable this particular research form to flourish. One of the more promising suggestions was for Harvard to continue supporting the process through periodic colloquia of the type held in June 1986. Thus, we hope that the present volume will prove to be not just an important document in its own right, but the first in a series of books on accounting innovations in organizations.

The Shell Companies Foundation, through the Division of Research at the Harvard Business School, provided substantial financial support for this project and the colloquium; we acknowledge their support with gratitude. At the same time we acknowledge our deep appreciation for the researchers who worked with us over two years to produce this volume. Without their commitment and endurance, this initial step would not have been possible.

Boston, Massachusetts   WILLIAM J. BRUNS, JR.
February 1987   ROBERT S. KAPLAN

Field Studies in Management Accounting

William J. Bruns, Jr., and Robert S. Kaplan

MANAGEMENT accounting creates information within the organization to facilitate managers' decision and control processes. Simple organizations whose main economic activity involves market exchanges with external entities do not require management accounting systems; their operations can be motivated and measured by the same system of financial transactions used in the conduct of external exchanges. The demand for management accounting information arises only when multiple activities are conducted within the organizational unit.[1] As organizations become more complex, more hierarchical, and more decentralized, the demand for effective management accounting systems increases.

Because management accounting information is created to plan, coordinate, motivate, and evaluate activities in complex organizations, research in the field must start with an excellent understanding of the management accounting processes in actual organizations. Many scientific fields, especially those in the natural sciences, can be studied experimentally in laboratories and other controlled settings. Physical, chemical, and biological laws maintain constancy, whether observed in laboratory settings or natural settings in the "real world." But since management accounting phenomena exist only in complex organizations, with their rich interaction of people, products, processes, markets, technologies, and cultures, it becomes extremely difficult to

1

study the subject except in actual organizational settings; management accounting systems *must* be studied in the settings where they have been developed and where they function.

This volume represents a major attempt to understand management accounting systems in actual organizations. While seemingly an obvious and straightforward project, in fact the research reported here represents a radical departure from the research typically performed by academic scholars in management accounting. Prior to this project, most management accounting research was conducted in researchers' offices and in university-based laboratories. The research took three basic forms: analyses, involving mathematical and economic models of simplified decision and control processes; experiments, studying the reactions of subjects—either students or cooperating managers—to alternative ways of presenting accounting information in well-controlled situations; or surveys, interpreting the responses of managers to questionnaires on a specific subject.

Several years ago, we concluded that these three traditional research methods were inadequate for understanding the richness of management accounting phenomena in contemporary organizations.[2] Rapid changes in organizations' environments were affecting the nature of competition and the sources of competitive advantage in fundamental ways. The changes included increased global competition, massive innovation in information processing and telecommunications technology, shorter life cycles for many product and process technologies, new procedures for organizing production processes, and major shifts in the regulation and deregulation of businesses. With these radical disruptions, it seemed unlikely that management accounting systems designed for relatively stable environments characterized by mass-produced, standardized products were still adequate in the current organizational environment. But the traditional research methods had no mechanism for learning about the new demands on management accounting systems and about the factors leading to the obsolescence of systems designed decades earlier.

Thus, the HBS colloquium had two principal objectives. First, the authors were to understand and document the management accounting practices of actual organizations. Some of the organizations would be captured in a process of transition: attempting, and occasionally succeeding, to modify their systems to measure, motivate, and evaluate operating performance. Other organizations were studied just to understand the system of measurement and control that had evolved in their particular competitive environment. For this first objective—documenting some contemporary practices—this volume offers perhaps the most wide-ranging view of actual management accounting practices ever reported.

A second, and even more important, objective of the colloquium was to begin the process by which field research methods in management accounting could be established as a legitimate method of inquiry. Academic researchers in accounting have extensive experience with deductive, model-building, analytic research; with the design and analysis of controlled experiments, usually in a laboratory setting; and with the empirical analysis of large data bases. This experience has yielded research guidance and criteria that, while not always explicit, nevertheless are widely shared and permit research to be conducted and evaluated.

Analytic, experimental, and empirical research methods score highly on internal validity; readers can understand what was done and judge whether the researcher's conclusions follow logically from the assumptions and methods used in the research. In principle, such research can be replicated by others and, when replicated, will lead to similar conclusions. But there is little assurance that these research methods have high external validity—that the phenomena being investigated, in the mathematical model or in the laboratory, bear any relationship to phenomena encountered by managers in actual organizations.

Field research methods, in contrast, tend to be high on external validity and low on internal validity. They are high on external validity because the researcher studies actual decision processes and actions taken by managers in real organizations. Thus, readers are better able to extrapolate the findings to similar organizations in similar circumstances. But the internal validity of field research studies will usually not be high. However many causes and explanations of the phenomena are noted by the researcher, the reader cannot be entirely confident that the researcher has identified the most critical and significant ones. The field research may be difficult, if not impossible, to replicate, and thus the reader must trust the clinical ability of the researcher to select the relevant explanatory variables and not overlook, or fail to report, significant alternative explanations.

The trade-off between research methods high in internal validity (deductive analytic models and laboratory experiments) and those high in external validity (field studies and case studies) exposes the conflict between rigor and relevance. There is a natural tendency in academic settings to prefer rigorous research methods; they are very effective when applied in fields where the phenomena to be explained are well documented and generally accepted by the research community. When applied to such phenomena, rigorous research methods can provide great insight and understanding and frequently suggest new experiments to test the limits of the emerging theory.

For fields where the phenomena are poorly documented, however, or where recent changes in the environment make even well-documented conventional wisdom suspect, it becomes important to opt for research methods that fully capture the relevant phenomena rather than to select methods that score high on internal validity. For immature fields, external validity or relevance assume more importance as criteria by which to judge research methods. One should not expect researchers to be able to use rigorous research methods when studying, describing, and classifying poorly understood phenomena.

This view was endorsed by the consultants and managers who attended the colloquium. One set of comments expressed this feeling particularly well:

The cost accounting, cost management, and investment planning techniques that are used by industry today are inadequate to the highly capitalized, automated, integrated manufacturing environment . . .

I was surprised that there was so much discussion concerning the validity of "field studies." It is almost axiomatic in other branches of research (in the physical or social sciences) that fieldwork is an essential part of the research process. I was further surprised that the presenters had done so little fieldwork in their careers. I would be chary of the relevance of a research project if it were not supported by field investigation. Fieldwork is more expensive, time-consuming, frustrating than theoretical studies, but that's the price of developing knowledge about the real world. All of the physical and social sciences face the same dilemma.

At a previous HBS colloquium, Professor Donald Schön of MIT discussed the dilemma of trying to achieve both rigor and relevance in studying professional practice:

Given the dominant view of professional rigor—the view which prevails in the intellectual climate of the universities—rigorous practice depends on well-formed problems of instrumental choice to whose solutions research-based theory and techniques are applicable. But real-world problems do not come well formed. They tend to present themselves, on the contrary, as messy, indeterminate, problematic situations. . . .

By defining rigor only in terms of technical rationality, we exclude as nonrigorous much of what competent practitioners actually do, including the skillful performance of problem setting and judgment on which technical problem solving depends. Indeed, we exclude the most important concepts of competent practice.

In the varied topography of professional practice, there is a high, hard ground which overlooks a swamp. On the high ground, manageable problems lend themselves to solution through the use of research-based theory and technique. In the swampy lowlands, problems are messy and confusing and incapable of technical solution. The irony of this situation is that the problems of the high ground tend to be relatively unimportant to individuals or to society at large—however great their technical interest may be—while in the swamp lie the problems of greatest human concern.

A professional who really tried to confine his practice to the rigorous application of research-based technique would find not only that he could not work on the most important problems but that he could not practice in the real world at all. Some professionals respond to this dilemma by choosing the swampy lowland, deliberately immersing themselves in confusing but crucially important situations. . . .

Practitioners who opt for the high ground confine themselves to a narrowly technical practice and pay a high price for doing so. . . . Some researchers have continued to develop formal models for use in problems of high complexity and uncertainty, quite undeterred by the troubles incurred whenever a serious attempt is made to put such models into practice. They pursue an agenda driven by evolving questions of modeling theory and techniques, increasingly divergent from the contexts of actual practice.[3]

This volume represents a deliberate attempt by researchers to immerse themselves in the important problems found in the swampland of management accounting practice, without regard to whether they could demonstrate "rigorous applications of research-based techniques" in the pursuit. But this immersion does not imply, as Schön suggests, that standards for excellent field research do not exist.

Because for the past several decades academic researchers in accounting have used, almost exclusively, research methods high in internal validity, there has been little experience with developing standards for field-based, clinical research. Recently, a group of faculty at the Harvard Business School, where field-based research methods are well ingrained, attempted to articulate their standards for excellent field research.[4] Out of their discussions, the following four criteria for good field research were generated and generally agreed upon:

1. Choice of Subject Matter.

The researcher chose a significant topic, asked good questions, and explored original themes. A good topic was recognized by its signifi-

cance to the management community and/or its potential for making
significant advances in the conceptual development of a managerially
relevant phenomenon. Originality occurred when the phenomenon
was previously undescribed or unexplained.

2. Research Design.

The choice of site(s) and research methods was appropriate for the
topic, especially in light of previous conceptual and descriptive work
on that topic (for example, one may not want to study general management processes on the shop floor of a factory). Careful site selection, sequence of inquiry, and choice of questions for interviews and
observation were critical to successful field research.

Site selection. Given limited resources, time, and existing theory, only
discrete, *focused* research sites made sense for in-depth investigation.
The selected sites exploited natural experiments when available (organizations in apparently similar circumstances following different
policies or using different systems); the sites were differentiated along
significant lines so that the structure of the sampled sites had face
validity.

Data collection. Rich, evocative data were included that described the
administrative dilemmas and the structural and environmental context of the managerial situation. Anecdotes were a powerful mechanism for communicating the organizational context of the study.

Triangulation. All kinds of available data were used to supplement
observation, including interviews, source documents, and questionnaires. Particularly for the study of management processes, unobtru-
sive observation often yielded the most valuable data.

Effective interviewing. Everyone involved in the topic was interviewed
thoroughly.

3. Data Presentation and Interpretation.

Face credibility of the data. The data had verisimilitude; for example,
executives were quoted in their own terms and not in edited, academic jargon. Informed readers recognized that the researcher under-

stood the territory being explored and was careful in interpreting the data and that each site was studied in sufficient depth.

Making sense of the data. The study was more than just raw description; the researcher developed or used previously existing concepts to organize the data and made them accessible and understandable to the reader, who was brought sufficiently close to the data to be able to imagine alternative diagnoses.

Data were related to theory. The data presentation was comprehensive; the knowledgeable reader did not find important dimensions of the problem undescribed. Good use was made of metaphor. The researcher's background in the discipline was applied to the data, and the findings were contrasted with existing theory and concepts. Thus, the structure of the reported data, and the concepts used to organize the data, connected easily to the established literature. Clinical research was most powerful when it showed that conventional models and wisdom did not apply in actual situations; used in this mode, clinical evidence could disprove hypotheses. Greater skill was required to use clinical evidence to establish new propositions and theories.

4. Practical Implications.

The findings from the research study were useful. The implications for practice were clear, and appropriate qualifications in light of the sample size and types of organizations studied, were noted. The validity of the description was supported by practitioner/experts who often made remarks like, "That's exactly the way it is; it's nice to have the problem articulated so clearly." The findings rang true to an informed reader, though practitioner/experts did not have to agree with the analysis, interpretation, or prescription offered by the researcher.

We have elaborated on these ideals to enable readers to assess each of the thirteen field studies presented in this volume. For a variety of reasons, most if not all of the studies fall short of these ideals. First, even though all the authors were experienced (and, in many cases, expert) researchers, many of them were doing field research for the first time. Second, the lack of previous field research in management accounting made the selection of hypotheses, topics, and sites for the research all the more difficult. Such topics as controllability, accounting method changes, and relative performance evaluation were being studied for the first time in actual organizations. Third, as an exploratory effort to learn more about the field research process, we wanted the researchers to gain in-depth experience with one firm (or, at most, a few firms), rather than to attempt a large-scale, comprehensive study, requiring several years to accomplish. Thus, the studies should be viewed as indications of what can be accomplished by serious field research but not necessarily as paradigms against which future efforts should be judged.

For example, as Professor George Foster of Stanford University pointed out in his discussion (at the colloquium) of the four papers on New Directions for Cost Management Systems (chapters 7–10), none described how managers reacted to proposed or implemented changes in their organization's cost accounting system. The papers succeeded in capturing the limitations of previous or existing cost systems, but the twelve-month time frame for the study did not permit the researchers to assess the consequences of a changed cost system, either through in-depth interviews of managers or by detailed analysis of cost data before and after a cost system was changed. Foster and other participants at the colloquium also noted that the site-selection process for many of the studies was opportunistic rather than the consequence of a well-thought-out process based on existing theory and hypotheses. At least one exception to this criticism was the study by Julie Hertenstein (chapter 1) of the internal adoption of inflation-adjusted information. Hertenstein was able to identify virtually all the U.S. companies that had successfully implemented inflation-adjusted accounting. (She was helped, in no small part, by the small number of them—fewer than a dozen.)

Many of the studies are snapshots of existing systems in companies rather than histories of the evolution and impact of evolving management accounting systems. Thus, they might best be called case studies rather than formal field research studies. Case studies are intensive examinations of a single organizational unit during a single time period; lacking variation over time or across organizational units, the researcher has little control over explanatory variables. Therefore, case studies can develop extensive information about a single entity and suggest hypotheses, but they cannot conduct formal tests on hypotheses, except perhaps to serve as counter examples. Case studies also may suffer if there are numerous interpretations that can be suggested for the phenomena described.

Some of the studies in this volume did manage to study management accounting phenomena either over time or across several organizations: for example, H. Thomas Johnson (chapter 2) documented the evolution of Weyerhaeuser's management control system over several decades in order to interpret recent developments; Kenneth Merchant (chapter 12) explored controllability issues across firms in several industries and competitive situations; and Robin Cooper and Robert Kaplan (chapter 8) drew upon previous case-writing experience in multiple firms to provide evidence on how traditional cost systems failed in several full-line producers.

But even the papers that analyzed only a single company at a particular time contributed to a cumulative record of evidence. The papers by William Bruns, Hein Schreuder, Rajiv Banker and Srikant Datar, and Jerold Zimmerman all showed the difficulty faced by organizations as they attempted to change their management accounting and control systems. Many of the authors independently concluded that their most surprising finding was the enormous resistance in organizations to major changes in their internal scorekeeping and measurement systems. In his discussion comments, Professor Anthony Hopwood of the London School of Economics emphasized that accounting changes are significant political events in an organization (this point also arose for Krishna Palepu, who found a corporation changing its external, financial accounting policies at least in part to implement significant internal structural changes). People think that accounting is a precise science; in fact, accounting is a politically charged process. Active debates occur over both the control and the adequacy of existing information. In several of our cases, proposed changes in accounting systems became the lightning rod by which managers, in a situation of high organizational ambiguity, played out power relationships. As suggested by Michael Jensen, proposed changes in accounting systems forced decision rights to be more clearly defined, thereby raising the stakes associated with accounting system changes.

The politics of accounting changes was not the explicit subject of any of the research initiated for the colloquium. Yet it emerged powerfully and independently in many of the studies and therefore created a research agenda for the future. The studies point to the necessity for future researchers to link their studies to the rich, existing literature on implementing organizational change. Thus, an aggregation of the single-company, single-period case studies provided insights and direction for significant new research.

Another theme reinforced by many of the papers was the divergence between authority and responsibility. Johnson's study of the Weyerhaeuser control system identified shifting managerial responsibility as the organization oscillated between promoting efficiency in functionally organized divisions and measuring and promoting profitability in diverse product-line groupings. Jeremy Dent, studying a leading European computer company, documented a new control system of overlapping responsibilities: both development managers and sales managers were held responsible for the profit on sales of products, development managers for the profit on products developed in their units, and sales managers for the profit on products sold in their regions. A similar control system was also found in an organization studied and reported on by Jensen and Richard Vancil, although this experience was not formally written up.

The divergence between authority and responsibility is consistent with the three studies on controllability presented by Michael Maher, Kenneth Merchant, and Robert Simons. These authors also found many situations in which managers were measured and held accountable for outcomes over which they had limited control and influence. Cumulatively, the studies documented that simple rules on manager accountability and control, which are frequently found in management accounting textbooks and writings, may hold only in limited circumstances. Their studies identify the need for much wider investigations to understand controllability issues in complex organizations, especially those that face high environmental uncertainty.

Several papers show the ambiguity of accounting measures. Palepu's study of a series of financial accounting policy changes by Harnischfeger describes how its senior managers believed that the new income-increasing methods would (1) help the company get new overseas business, (2) lower demands for capital investment within the firm, (3) support the company's more aggressive stance on competitive pricing, and (4) perhaps improve its image in equity and lending markets. Banker and Datar document how a newly instituted productivity gain-sharing program produced incentive payments to employees even though productivity may not have increased; the accounting measure used to compute incentive payments failed to control for potential environmental changes that would be confounded with productivity improvements. Zimmerman shows that when a manufacturing organization's accounting system omitted the important costs of creating and holding inventory, batch sizes seemed much larger than optimal, and customer service was impaired. Cooper and Kaplan's study describes how a simplistic cost allocation system that worked well for the financial accounting purpose of valuing aggregate inventory led to gross distortions in estimating the incremental costs of producing individual products, especially in an environment of high product diversity. These studies all show how the reality created by an artificial system—the management accounting system— changes managers' perceptions of their economic environment. The seemingly innocuous choices in the design of accounting systems can have profound and unexpected effects when these systems are implemented in complex environments.

The debriefing for academics, which was held immediately after the colloquium, yielded several insights into the field-study research process and identified issues that future researchers will have to deal with as they go into organizations. One of the most widely discussed was the time required to do research in the field. Several researchers, in describing their experiences, noted that field studies require more time than university-based research.

Simons stated that his data collection was costly, not because of the expense of travel, but because events and meetings had to be viewed in their original forms and sequence. Additional time was required to uncover and understand the hidden agenda surrounding events and managers' actions and descriptions. Datar suggested the need to think of a range of field study types that would match topic and coverage to the interests, needs, and time available to the researcher: some studies might be long-term, with the researcher essentially living on site or within one or more organizations; other studies might be short engagements in which a researcher seeks a complete but quick view of a problem or organization. Mindful that some of the studies had required more than a year of effort but still looked like "quick hits," the researcher's need to consider career, reappointment or promotion, and time criteria before embarking on a field study was a conclusion supported by everyone at the debriefing.

Professor Kim Clark of Harvard, an experienced field researcher in the production and operations management area, applauded the field research presented as a move toward better problem selection in the field of management accounting research. In his view, selection of the best research problems on which to devote time and effort, whether in the field, laboratory, or library, requires observation of what happens in organizations. Clark felt, however, that many of the colloquium's studies fail to reveal clearly enough the intellectual and selection processes that the authors went through as they observed and selected problems, gathered and interpreted data, and drew conclusions.

Professor Haim Falk of the University of Calgary felt that the studies partially met the original goals of the colloquium, which he interpreted as creating a data base for further management accounting research, developing theories and hypotheses for further exploration, and testing theories and hypotheses. However, he was concerned in particular about the use of interviews in the field research process. He argued that the best data for research are collected from original sources. Relying on interviews, with their potential for selectivity and bias, represents an important limitation of these field studies. Interviews also limit the chance for replication, since they cannot be repeated for confirmation or comparison.

The discussion about research methods and methodology led naturally to questions of whether field studies will be published by traditional research journals. Professor Ronald Copeland of Northeastern University indicated that unless such studies are published, they will have little impact on either practice or research. And he expressed the fear that the editorial criteria of research publications would lead to rapid rejections for most of the studies presented at the colloquium. Whether or not a new or different set of acceptance criteria can be developed or applied to field studies was discussed but the issue remains unresolved. Jensen, himself an editor of a respected research journal, proposed using criteria based on such questions as "Will the work be cited?" and "Will it move the field ahead?" This editorial approach may be essential if field researchers are to find access to research publications.

The debriefing ended with several unanswered questions to which the reader of this volume may wish to respond. If you agree that field studies are important to the development of management accounting, how can the quality of field studies such as those presented in this book be raised? How can the momentum that the colloquium project developed be maintained? What are the next steps that should be taken to understand management accounting in actual organizations? While every reader may answer these questions differently, if they are answered at all it will do much to bring more relevance to research in management accounting.

Two of the colloquium participants, John Shank of Dartmouth and Robert Swieringa, recently of Cornell and now a Member of the Financial Accounting Standards Board, offered their thoughts on field research. We close this introduction with excerpts from their comments. First, John K. Shank:

I believe there is a tremendous store of knowledge about management accounting practices and ideas out there in real companies. Academicians as a whole are far too ignorant of that knowledge. There are far too many reasons why it is possible for us to survive and prosper as academics without paying much attention to that data base.

Perhaps this colloquium is a breakthrough as academics begin to see the power of the thinking that exists in good companies and in the data base of case studies and commentaries that are used for teaching and illustration. When academics begin to see the relevance of this data base, perhaps generations of students will become more aware of its richness. Such awareness must precede any real progress on prescribing good management accounting for any given situation.

Next, Robert J. Swieringa:

These studies reflect the tension that naturally results from careful observation. To observe is to notice and punctuate events that are of interest. But which events should be noticed? Which events should be of interest? The answers to these questions are often grounded in the theories we use to do the observing and watching.

To observe is also to discover. The authors of these papers have provided descriptions of phenomena that are in need of explanation. These descriptions are presented as research findings. But to find something is also to discover something. Barton and Lazarsfeld note that "research which has neither statistical weight nor experimental design, research based only on qualitative descriptions of a small number of cases, can nonetheless play the important role of suggesting possible relationships, causes, effects, and even dynamic processes."[5]

The authors of these papers have observed interesting phenomena. We do not know how prevalent these phenomena are or under what conditions they exist or do not exist. But these studies suggest possible "relationships, causes, effects, and even dynamic processes" in the sense that Yogi Berra must have had in mind when he said, "Sometimes you can observe a lot just by watching."[6]

NOTES

1. Johnson, H. Thomas, and Kaplan, Robert S. *Relevance Lost: The Rise and Fall of Management Accounting.* Boston: Harvard Business School Press, 1987.

2. See Kaplan, Robert S. "The Role for Empirical Research in Management Accounting." *Accounting, Organizations and Society* 11, No. 4/5 (1986): 429–52.

3. Schön, Donald A. "The Crisis of Professional Knowledge and the Pursuit of an Epistemology of Practice." An essay prepared for the Harvard Business School 75th Anniversary Colloquium on Teaching by the Case Method, 1984.

4. Some of the studies cited for excellent research are listed below.

Simon, Herbert A.; Guetzkow, Harold; Kozmetsky, George; and Tyndall, Gordon. *Centralization vs. Decentralization in Organizing the Controller's Department.* New York: Controllership Foundation, 1954.

Donaldson, Gordon. *Managing Corporate Wealth: The Operation of a Comprehensive Financial Goals System.* New York: Praeger, 1984.

Garvin, David. "Quality on the line." *Harvard Business Review* (September– October 1983): 64–75.

Sultan, Ralph G. *Pricing in the Electrical Oligopoly.* Boston: Division of Research, Graduate School of Business Administration, Harvard University, 1974–1975.

Robbins, S. M., and Stobaugh, Robert. *Money in the Multinational Enterprise.* New York: Basic Books, 1973.

5. Barton, A. H., and Lazarsfeld, Paul H. "Some Functions of Qualitative Analysis in Social Research." In *Issues in Participant Observation,* edited by G. J. McCall and J. L. Simmons. Reading, MA: Addison-Wesley, 1969.

6. Attributed to Yogi Berra by Warren Buffet. See "Buffet's Complaint: He Can't Find Any Values." *Barron's,* 9 June 1986, 14.

PART I

Adapting Management Accounting Systems to Changing Environments

Management Control System Change: The Adoption of Inflation Accounting

Julie H. Hertenstein

INTRODUCTION

MANAGEMENT accounting systems have traditionally been based on the historical cost accounting model. This model does not reflect the current cost or current value of assets, nor does it provide information on the changing purchasing power of the currency unit. Rising inflation in the 1970s led to increased demand for alternative models, generally referred to as inflation accounting, to address limitations in historical cost accounting. Public reporting of certain accounting data adjusted for the effects of inflation became a requirement in the United States when in 1976 the Securities and Exchange Commission issued Accounting Series Release 190.[1] This standard was superseded in 1979 by Statement of Financial Accounting Standards No. 33 (FAS 33).[2]

With the advent of external reporting requirements for inflation accounting, it was hypothesized that inflation accounting would be useful to managers (Vancil 1976). Many potential managerial uses were identified for these data: to analyze product profitability (Dearden 1981; Webster et al. 1980); to set prices (Casey and Sandretto 1981; Schwarzbach and Swanson 1981); to improve asset utilization and management (Casey and Sandretto 1981; Webster et al. 1980); and to evaluate the real performance of a firm's products and businesses (MacAvoy 1980; Hussey 1976). While a great deal was published about the usefulness of inflation accounting data to external users such as stock market participants or security analysts, less was known about the actual managerial use of these data.[3]

Surveys were the primary source of information about the internal use of inflation accounting data (Seed 1981; Casey and Sandretto 1981; Schwarzbach and Swanson 1981; Frank et al. 1978).[4] Questionnaire responses indicated that relatively few firms used these data internally (Casey and Sandretto 1981; Schwarzbach and Swanson 1981). Even when questionnaire responses indicated that managers "used" these data, however, how they were used remained unclear. Did the respondents mean these data were the primary measurement system, or were they provided as a supplement to historical cost reports? Were current value or general price-level-adjusted data used internally? Were the data used for performance measurement and incentive compensation? Why were these data used, and what benefits and problems resulted from their use? Finally, since relatively few firms used these data, were their needs and uses idiosyncratic, or could this tool potentially be useful to a broader range of firms?

My research focused on a few firms to gain an in-depth understanding of their experiences with inflation accounting. The study was organized around four research questions:

1. How were management systems changed to incorporate inflation accounting data?
2. Why were the management systems changed?
3. How were the inflation accounting systems implemented?
4. What were the results of incorporating inflation accounting in the management systems?

Due to the lack of existing information describing in detail the internal managerial use of inflation accounting data, no specific expectations existed about the answers to these questions. Firms that undertook the effort to implement inflation accounting in their management accounting systems, however, did so because they anticipated advantages from the use of such systems; the advantages might accrue from the potential managerial uses identified earlier. Whether or not they achieved the advantages they anticipated, and how they made implementation choices for the inflation accounting systems, were areas to be explored through the research.

The results of the research suggest the following answers to the four preceding questions: (1) striking similarities existed in the choices made by firms among methods for inflation adjustments and in the accounting elements that were adjusted for inflation—even though the firms varied in the degree to which management systems incorporated the inflation accounting data; (2) these companies incorporated inflation accounting in routine operating reports to influence operating managers to improve financial performance, particularly in the management of assets; (3) not unexpectedly, the implementation of this significant change to management systems took a long time and required the backing of top corporate management; (4) whether or not these firms accomplished the intended results appeared to be a function of top management's ability to articulate the expected results and the amount of control that operating managers had over these result areas.

The remainder of this chapter is organized as follows. First, the research sites and methods are briefly described. Then, findings are presented for each of the four research questions. A summary of the research concludes the chapter.

RESEARCH SITES AND RESEARCH METHODS

Initially, a search was conducted to identify firms that were using, or had used, inflation accounting internally. The search began by reviewing the literature for references to such firms. In addition, some known users of inflation accounting were contacted to determine whether they could identify additional users. Corporate financial officers and controllers are frequently associated through organizations such as the National Association of Accountants and the Financial Executives Institute; thus, they form an informal network knowledgeable about management accounting practices at other firms.

Nineteen potential firms were identified. A preference for U.S. firms eliminated four firms; a preference for medium- to large-sized firms eliminated two small firms and one very large firm from the list. Firms were preferred that used inflation accounting in a meaningful way and did not simply circulate the unaudited inflation accounting section of the annual report to top management. The remaining twelve firms were ranked according to available information on their use of inflation accounting.

Eight firms were contacted, usually by an initial telephone call (sometimes preceded by a letter) to the chief financial officer or controller. A preliminary phone discussion was held to confirm that the firm was using or had used inflation accounting internally and to schedule a visit to the site. Of the eight firms contacted, one firm responded that these data were not used internally. Another firm was eliminated from the sample because, owing to a management turnover, the information was difficult to trace; thus, six firms remained for the study.

All these firms were large and diversified, except for one retailer (see Exhibit 1-1 for their lines of business). In 1985, the sales for five of the firms exceeded $3 billion; the remaining firm had sales of nearly a billion dollars.

Of the six firms studied, three still used their inflation accounting systems in 1986; they are referred to as retaining firms. Two other firms that had implemented inflation accounting systems had discontinued their general operating use, while retaining some data for limited corporate use. The sixth firm had initially implemented the inflation accounting system as a corporate requirement for all groups; subsequently it withdrew the corporate requirement for preparing these data, but some operating groups in the firm continued to use it. Because of the withdrawal of the corporate requirement, the sixth firm will be grouped with the discontinuing firms. Exhibit 1-2 identifies the retaining and discontinuing firms.

Interviews with managers were the primary source of data for this research.[5] In addition to interviews, such company documents as annual reports, internal memoranda, notes for speeches to management, budgets, reports of operating results, instructions for preparation of financial information, and training materials were reviewed. To assist in the data collection, a questionnaire was developed as a protocol (Yin 1984) for the interviews. This questionnaire, based on the four research questions cited earlier, contained sufficiently detailed subquestions to ensure that each of the four areas was explored adequately. The discussions were open-ended, however, and the questionnaire mainly served to guide the researcher.

RESULTS

Following the interviews and document reviews at the six firms, the development and use of inflation accounting at each firm

Exhibit 1-1 Lines of Business

Company A	Company B	Company C	Company X	Company Y	Company Z
Transportation products	Machinery: defense construction agricultural material-handling	Construction materials	Construction materials: residential commercial	Retailing: multiple formats—from department stores to specialty stores	Electronics
Building products		Chemicals			Defense
Air-conditioning products	Chemicals: industrial agricultural specialty	Metals	Transportation (automotive)		Transportation
Commercial printing		Oil and gas	Coatings		Energy products
			Resins		Industrial products
			Chemicals		

Exhibit 1-2 Status and Methods for Inflation Accounting

Status:	Company A	Company B	Company C	Company X	Company Y	Company Z
Retain / discontinue inflation accounting system as of 1986	Retain	Retain	Retain	Discontinue[a]	Discontinue	Discontinue
Implementation period for inflation accounting	1972–1982	1979–1983	1982– [b]	1974–1980	1979–1983	1977–1982
Primary/supplementary system of measurement	Primary	Primary	Primary[c]	Supplementary[d]	Supplementary	Supplementary
Specific/general price-level-adjustments	Specific	Specific	Both[e]	Specific	Specific	Specific

[a]The corporate requirement was discontinued; however, some operating groups retained.
[b]Implementation of inflation accounting in operating measures and operating reports began in 1982, although the firm had used some inflation-adjusted data, particularly for resource allocation, since the mid-1970s. The firm was actively expanding the inflation accounting system in 1986, and implementation was not complete.
[c]The firm was evolving toward using inflation accounting as the primary system of measurement, although they were still in transition from using historical costs.
[d]The inflation accounting data were supplementary, although they were contained in the primary report.
[e]Specific price-level-adjustments were used for inventories and cost of goods sold. General price-level-adjustments were used for fixed assets, although this was modified when the result was not consistent with current cost.

was described.[6] The six were then considered together to seek patterns and build explanations about the use of inflation accounting data. The results are presented below, as responses to the four initial research questions.

1. How Were Management Systems Changed to Incorporate Inflation Accounting Data?

Little evidence was available, prior to this study, on what managers meant when they said their firms "used" inflation accounting. At some firms, the inflation accounting data were the primary system of measurement (that is, they replaced historical cost data in routine budgets and reports of operating results); at others, they were supplementary and were provided in addition to historical costs (see Exhibit 1-2). Company A and Company B (two of the retaining firms) used inflation accounting as the primary system of measurement. Company C, also a retaining firm, was in transition, and inflation accounting had not fully replaced historical cost accounting; it was management's stated intention that inflation accounting would be the primary system of measurement, however, and the inflation accounting system was expanding at the time of this study. In the three discontinuing firms, the original intent had been for inflation accounting to be a supplementary system of measurement. At Company Y and Company Z, reports containing these data were separate from the primary historical cost operating reports. At Company X, the data were included in the primary operating reports but were considered secondary to the historical cost information also reported therein.

The six firms all selected specific price-level-adjustments, not general price-level-adjustments, for their internal management systems (see Exhibit 1-2 and 1-3). Company C appeared to be an exception to this since it used a general price-level-index (the GNP deflator) to adjust fixed assets for inflation. Company C managers, however, stated that they preferred specific price-level-adjustments, but used general price-level-adjustments because administrative precedents constrained them from using specific adjustments.[7] Further, general price-level-adjustments were used only when they produced results consistent with managers' estimates of the current cost of fixed assets; where general price-level-adjustments and estimates of current costs diverged significantly, alternative methods were used to produce values closer to current costs.

The six firms adjusted four accounting elements for inflation: cost of goods sold, inventories, depreciation, and fixed assets. Cost of goods sold and inventories were treated in one of two ways. The first used a current, or prospective, standard cost, including price changes expected throughout the year, to value both cost of goods sold and inventories. The standard was normally changed once a year, although more frequent changes were made if necessary. The second treatment valued cost of goods sold at LIFO and inventories at FIFO (or, equivalently, at LIFO plus the LIFO reserve).[8] Both treatments produced values that managers felt were sufficiently close to current costs.

Fixed assets were restated to current costs using specific indices such as producer price and construction price indices; the indices were frequently obtained from published sources. The indexed values were not as accurate as appraisals, but they were reasonably accurate and much easier to administer. When the indexed value of a particular asset or group of assets did not accurately represent its current cost, appraisals remained an option; appraisals were often the basis for revaluing property. Current cost depreciation was derived directly from the current cost of fixed assets. Initially, book lives used for historical costs were also used for current costs; as managers gained experience with inflation accounting, asset lives were often extended. Under historical costs, asset lives had often been quite short.[9] When the asset values were stated at current costs, short lives led to excessively high depreciation. As this became apparent, firms relied on engineering studies of expected asset lives and accounting records of asset acquisition and disposal to estimate new, more realistic, asset lives.

Two inflation accounting elements were not generally used in these internal management reports: holding gains and monetary gains.[10] None of the firms incorporated holding gains or losses on assets in their internal inflation accounting measures. As the manager of one company explained, "[The] holding gain is only realized if you don't replace the asset; otherwise you need to reinvest the holding gain to replace the asset." Only Company Z included monetary gains in operating measures for all business units; two firms computed monetary gains for subsidiaries operating in high-inflation countries. Several reasons were given for ignoring monetary gains in operating measures. First, they were viewed as being more complex and harder to understand than other adjustments; operating managers did not experience these gains in the same way they experienced price increases for nonmonetary assets. Additionally, most monetary assets and lia-

Exhibit 1-3 Elements of the Inflation Accounting System

Accounting Element	Company A	Company B	Company C	Company X	Company Y	Company Z
Inventories	Current standard cost[a]	Current standard cost[a]	LIFO + LIFO Reserve	LIFO + LIFO Reserve	FIFO	LIFO + LIFO Reserve
Cost of goods sold	Current standard cost[a]	Current standard cost[a]	LIFO	LIFO	LIFO	LIFO
Fixed assets	Specific, published indices	Primarily specific indices, also appraisals	General index (the gross national product deflator)[e]	Specific indices	Specific indices	Specific, published indices
Depreciation	Based on revalued fixed assets[b,c]	Based on revalued fixed assets[b,c]	Based on revalued fixed assets[d]	Based on revalued fixed assets[d]	Based on revalued fixed assets[b]	Based on revalued fixed assets[d]
Monetary gains or losses	Only for Brazil	Only for high-inflation countries[f]	No	No	No	Yes
Holding gains or losses on fixed assets or inventories	No	No	No	No	No	No
Asset charge	Yes[g]	Yes[g]	No	No	Yes[g]	No

[a] Standards were revised annually, and they included expected price changes for the year.

[b] Asset lives were modified following the implementation of inflation accounting.

[c] A depreciation charge for fully depreciated assets was instituted.

[d] Following the implementation of inflation accounting, the same book lives were used for fixed assets as were previously used for historical costs.

[e] Exceptions were made where the value of a division's general price-level-adjusted net fixed assets significantly exceeded managers' estimates of the true current cost of those assets.

[f] High-inflation countries were defined as those with a cumulative three-year inflation rate that exceeded 100%.

[g] The asset charge for Company A was 12% of net assets. The asset charge for Company B was 8% of average current cost capital employed. The asset charge for Company Y was 12% of *increases* in working capital.

bilities were corporate responsibilities, and operating managers had only limited influence over them. Finally, there were "risks associated with maximizing [monetary] gains; i.e., holding too much debt or liabilities."

In addition to the inflation accounting adjustments, managers at Company A and Company B made two additional changes to the management systems that they considered to be integral parts of the inflation accounting system. First, depreciation continued to be charged for fully depreciated assets; the managers believed that the current cost of all depreciable assets used should be charged, not just the current cost of those not yet fully depreciated. In addition, a capital charge was imposed. This charge, a percent of total operating assets, appeared as an expense on the operating income statement.[11] As discussed in the next section, these two additional changes were consistent with the emphasis of the two companies on the asset-management motivation for adopting inflation accounting.

Typically, both inflation-adjusted income statements and operating balance sheets were prepared. Summary performance measures included inflation-adjusted operating income and an inflation-adjusted return measure, such as return on net assets or return on capital employed (see Exhibit 1-4).

The inflation accounting data were distributed, usually monthly, to profit center managers, to their superiors (up to and including the chief executive officer), and to the respective staffs. From fifty to several hundred managers received the data (see Exhibit 1-5). It often took a year or more before the entire distribution was achieved; the system was often implemented at higher-level profit centers a year or two before it was implemented at lower levels.

All six firms prepared routine reports of inflation-adjusted results; however, the retaining firms also included these data in other management systems (see Exhibit 1-6). They used the data in budgeting and in measuring managerial performance; they also based short-term incentive compensation at least partially on inflation accounting measures, and they incorporated the data or similar data in their strategic planning systems. None of the discontinuing firms used inflation-adjusted data for strategic planning purposes, although some did prepare inflation accounting budgets.

Further, the discontinuing firms did not use the data in evaluating managerial performance or planning short-term incentive compensation; the two firms that attempted to use the data for short-term incentive compensation failed because of technical and communication problems and managerial resistance. None of the six firms used the data as a basis for awarding long-term incentive compensation.

2. Why Were the Management Systems Changed?

It is clear that inflation accounting represented a significant change for the management systems at the six firms, particularly at the three firms where inflation accounting was the primary system of measurement. Managers do not undertake significant change lightly; they must expect the benefits of a new system to outweigh the costs of implementation. Further, recognizing that the choice of measurements in a management control system influences behavior (Merchant 1985, 25), what behaviors were these managers trying to influence, and why?

Managers at each of the six firms linked the implementation of inflation accounting to problems with the firm's financial performance. Some identified problems with current financial performance; these ranged from a cash flow crisis to failure to measure up to the firm's publicly announced financial objectives. Others were anxious about long-term financial performance; they focused on the need to make appropriate resource allocations in order to ensure satisfactory future financial performance. All of the firms believed that historical cost accounting masked the effects of inflation and therefore failed to provide managers who could influence the firm's financial performance with the information necessary for appropriate decisions.

Specific goals related to financial performance provided the motivation for adopting inflation accounting: to improve long-term resource allocation, to improve operating performance, and to increase consistency between long-term (or strategic) measures and short-term measures of operating performance. Inflation accounting was viewed by managers as a tool to help them achieve these performance goals.

The need to improve resource allocation was frequently the initial motivation for using inflation-adjusted data within the firm. Five of the six firms (not Company Y) were diversified and had unrelated businesses (see Exhibit 1-1). The operating divisions had different capital intensities and owned assets of varying ages. Some of the businesses had been recently acquired and were less familiar to top management than traditional businesses; new acquisitions frequently had assets revalued to current values if purchase accounting had been used. This diversity of businesses and accounting data contributed to

Exhibit 1-4 Inflation Accounting Measures of Operating Income and Return

	Company A	Company B	Company C	Company X	Company Y	Company Z
Operating income	Sales − Current cost of goods sold − Current cost depreciation[a] − Capital charge − Other expenses[b] = Operating income	Sales − Current cost of goods sold − Current cost depreciation − Other expenses = Operating profit before taxes − Taxes = Operating profit after taxes − Capital charge = Net contribution	Sales − Cost of goods sold (LIFO) − General price-level-adjusted depreciation − Other expenses − Taxes (currently payable, not deferred) = Earnings	Sales − Cost of goods sold (LIFO) − Current cost depreciation[a] − Other expenses[b] = Pretax-preinterest earnings	Sales − Cost of goods sold (LIFO) − Current cost depreciation − Other expenses − Working capital charge = Real net income	Sales − Cost of goods sold (LIFO) − Current cost depreciation + Monetary gain on net monetary items + Monetary gain on corporate staff items − Other expenses = Real profit after tax
Return	(Operating income + capital charge)/ net assets	Operating profit after tax/current cost capital employed	Earnings/net assets	Pretax-preinterest earnings/total gross assets	(Real net income + working capital charge + interest component of leases)/real net assets	(Real profit after tax − monetary gain on corporate staff items)/average assets employed

Exhibit 1-4 (Continued)

	Company A	Company B	Company C	Company X	Company Y	Company Z
Investment base	Current cost inventory + Receivables + Current cost net fixed assets[a] − Current liabilities = Net assets	Current cost inventory + Other working capital + Current cost net fixed assets = Current cost capital employed	Inventory (LIFO) + LIFO reserve + Accounts receivable + General price-level-adjusted net property, plant, and equipment − Current liabilities = Net assets	Total current assets + Total gross fixed assets at current cost[a] + Total other assets = Total gross assets	Total current assets − Current liabilities (excluding notes payable and current portion of long-term debt) + Current cost net fixed assets (including the present value of capital and operating leases) + Other assets = Real net assets	Operating working capital + Current cost net fixed assets + Other assets = Assets employed

[a] The company refers to current cost fixed assets as replacement cost fixed assets and to current cost depreciation as replacement depreciation; however, the values are the same as those reported as current cost under FAS 33.

[b] Excluding taxes and interest.

Exhibit 1-5   Distribution of the Inflation Accounting Data

	Company A	Company B	Company C	Company X	Company Y	Company Z
Frequency	Monthly	Monthly	Monthly	Monthly	Monthly	Quarterly
Number of managers receiving data	Several hundred	Several hundred	50–100	50–100	50–100	Several hundred
Recipients	Board of directors	Board of directors	Board of directors	Board of directors	Board of directors	Board of directors
	Corporate executives and corporate staff	Corporate executives and corporate staff	Corporate executives and corporate staff	Corporate executives and corporate staff	Corporate executives and corporate staff	Corporate executives and corporate staff
	Global group managers	Group managers	Division managers and staff	Group managers and staff	CEOs and CFOs of retail companies	Sector managers
	Group managers	Division managers	Plant managers (proposed)	Business unit managers		Division managers
	Division managers	Plant or product-line profit center managers				
	Accounting reporting location managers					

Exhibit 1-6 Management Systems Incorporating Inflation Accounting Data

	Company A	Company B	Company C	Company X	Company Y	Company Z
Budgeting	Yes	Yes	Yes	Yes	Yes	No
Results reporting	Yes	Yes	Yes	Yes	Yes	Yes
Managerial performance evaluation	Yes	Yes	Yes[a]	No	No[b]	No[b]
Short-term incentive compensation	Yes	Yes	Yes[a]	No	No[b]	No[b]
Long-term incentive compensation	No	No	No	No	No	No
Long-term planning	Yes	No[c]	No[c]	No	No	No

[a] The use of inflation accounting for this purpose was limited due to its recent introduction; however, it was expected to become the primary measure.
[b] The firm unsuccessfully attempted to implement inflation-adjusted measures in management performance evaluation and incentive compensation systems.
[c] Strategic planning and resource allocation utilized other inflation-adjusted measures.

management's belief that existing accounting data were not comparable. As expressed by a Company B manager, "We had no common denominator with which to measure businesses." A common denominator was needed to ensure that resources were allocated to the most promising businesses or to help identify businesses for disposition. Inflation accounting provided a consistent means—a common denominator—for measuring these diverse businesses.

Major resource allocation decisions are made primarily by corporate, not operating, managers. Hence, firms could have used inflation accounting data at the corporate level for strategic or resource allocation purposes without changing routine operating measures or systems. Indeed, at Companies A, B, and C, inflation-adjusted measures were used extensively by corporate managers for these purposes prior to their implementation at the operating level. Use of the data for long-term resource allocation, however, contributed to the need for consistency as discussed below.

In addition to improving resource allocation, each firm identified a need to improve short-term operating performance. Because of the diversity of the firms' businesses, autonomous operating managers, who possessed local knowledge of their businesses, had to take actions to improve operating performance.[12] Top managers viewed inflation accounting as a means to communicate the need for improvements in operating performance; this is suggested by two statements made to operating managers:

First, awareness and understanding of inflation's impact are required. Then management can respond both operationally and strategically.

What is inflation doing to us? . . . Is the business earning adequate returns?

At some firms, primarily the retaining firms, top managers were quite specific about the actions expected from operating managers. These top managers strongly believed that their firms had excess assets, poorly utilized manufacturing capacity, outdated technology, and inefficient production processes, or were missing opportunities to raise prices. With the adoption of inflation accounting, they expected managers to dispose of excess assets, improve asset management, accomplish cost reductions, increase prices, improve productivity, and eliminate unprofitable product lines. Thus, a need to improve operating performance was the primary motivation for the implementation of inflation accounting data in far-reaching management systems and routine reports.

Finally, the desire for consistency among financial measures further influenced the adoption of inflation accounting in some firms. As previously discussed, three firms used inflation-adjusted measures for long-term resource allocation while simultaneously using historical cost accounting to measure operating performance. The inconsistency between short-term and long-term measures created credibility problems for the operating measures; recognized "limitations in the [operating] accounting data" had led to the development of the inflation-adjusted long-term measures. Operating managers were frustrated by this lack of consistency in measures, and top managers desired consistency in managerial action. As a Company B manager explained:

The company was not acting in a synchronized fashion between long-term corporate development and short-term operating performance. We were hoping for a better understanding of corporate objectives, and we wanted to get everyone on the same tune.

In summary, inflation-adjusted data were initially used for strategic planning and resource allocation needs; for these purposes, only limited corporate distribution of the data was required. The inflation accounting data were subsequently incorporated in routine, operating systems and reports for top managers to communicate the need for and to provide incentives for action by operating managers.

3. How Were the Inflation Accounting Systems Implemented?

Inflation accounting affected many managers and penetrated many management systems; implementing this management control system change was a major undertaking requiring a lengthy, evolutionary process. Company B's experience, shown in Exhibit 1-7, is representative of such processes. The impetus for adopting inflation accounting usually came either from the corporate controller (or another financial officer) or from higher officers in the organization, such as the chief executive officer or the board of directors.

Regardless of the source of impetus, the chief executive officer, the chief operating officer, and two or three other key senior managers made the decision to implement the system. The decision was not made by a single individual; the group had to reach consensus and to support the system. In addition, these top managers played important

Exhibit 1-7 The Process of Implementing Inflation Accounting at Company B

1978–1979	An inflation-adjusted strategic planning measure was studied and approved by top management.
1979	An inflation-adjusted measure was first used for strategic planning.
1979–1980	A committee was formed to define, develop, and install an integrated financial and operational information system, including a review of the measures used for evaluating operating performance. The committee concluded that existing historical cost measures masked significant inflationary impacts and that the routine operating financial control system needed to be consistent with the inflation-adjusted strategic planning measure.
1980	Current cost inventory and current cost of goods sold were adopted for locations using standard costs.
1981–1982	A corporate study team studied how to incorporate the effects of inflation in other operating measures and made recommendations to top management.
1982	Top management adopted (1) a simulated current cost inventory and current cost of goods sold for the remaining locations not on standard costs, (2) current costs for fixed assets and depreciation, (3) monetary gains/losses for foreign operations in high-inflation environments, and (4) a capital charge.
1982	The first inflation accounting budgets were prepared for budget year 1983.
1983	Operating results were first measured using inflation accounting. Current cost operating profit before taxes and current cost working capital were used as the basis for performance measurement and incentive compensation.
1985	The management performance and incentive compensation measure was changed to current cost net contribution, which was current cost operating profit, less taxes and less the capital charge.

roles following the introduction of the system. It persuaded operating managers of the need for the system; and it also used its authority and power to ensure that the system was effectively adopted and used.

The controller's organization was primarily responsible for working out the details of the system and for shaping it to fit the organization. The controller also planned and facilitated the introduction of the new system, first presenting the changes to the highest levels of management and then working down through successively lower levels of the organization. The controllers administered an extensive educational effort before and after the introduction of inflation accounting. To meet evolving managerial needs, they made changes to the system following implementation.

All of the firms implemented the inflation accounting system in stages similar to the four that are listed here:

1. Implement inflation-adjusted cost of goods sold and inventory before implementing inflation-adjusted depreciation and fixed assets.

2. Implement the inflation accounting system on a supplementary basis before implementing it as the primary system.

3. Implement inflation accounting at a more aggregate level (group) before implementing it at a disaggregate level (division).

4. Implement inflation accounting in budgets and monthly operating results before including these measures in management performance measurement and incentive compensation.

Firms often used a combination of these stages. For example, Company A implemented current cost depreciation for budgeting and results measurement at the group level before the division level; later, current cost depreciation was incorporated in the performance measurement and incentive compensation systems. The need for initial study and evaluation of inflation accounting, combined with the multiple stages of implementation, produced a lengthy implementation process: four or five years were common and as many as ten years were observed between the first serious consideration of inflation accounting and its final implementation.

4. What Were the Results of Incorporating Inflation Accounting in the Management Systems?

To identify and evaluate the results of adopting inflation accounting, it was first necessary to determine whether or not the firm's goals for inflation accounting had been achieved; then the problems, side effects, or additional benefits that occurred from adopting inflation accounting were considered. As noted, firms had three primary goals for using inflation-adjusted measures:

1. Improve long-term resource allocation decisions by identifying real performance and increasing the comparability of data among diverse businesses.

2. Support improvements in operating performance.

3. Increase consistency between long-term and short-term measures.

Managers in the retaining firms used the inflation accounting data for resource allocation and stated that inflation-adjusted measures facilitated comparisons across diverse businesses.[13] One firm demonstrated that it had, in fact, reallocated resources after examining the long-term inflation-adjusted return of its businesses.[14] Managers were convinced that this shift represented an improvement in the allocation of resources. The final results of such decisions, however, will not be evident for many years; so while inflation accounting may have contributed to consistency in resource allocation measurements, it is too early to reach conclusions about the quality of subsequent resource allocation decisions. The discontinuing firms did not find these measures to be useful for long-term resource allocation; they found that inflation accounting provided no additional information—this was especially the view of the undiversified retailer—and that the data were not consistent with corporate management's view of and goals for the business.[15]

The desired improvement in operating performance was the real reason for incorporating inflation accounting data throughout the management systems. In the companies retaining inflation accounting, the operating performance goals for adopting inflation accounting (e.g., improve operating margins or improve asset utilization) were clear to the operating managers who were interviewed.[16] Operating managers identified actions they had taken or were taking to meet these goals.[17] Examples included disposal of unproductive assets, consolidation of U.S. facilities, and moving some assets "back" to suppliers through increased external sourcing. The managers' beliefs that they had improved asset management and operating performance were supported by data at Company A and Company B indicating reduced asset levels and improved profitability in the years immediately following the adoption of inflation accounting (see Exhibit 1-8).

In the discontinuing firms, top managers perceived that they had not accomplished their operating performance goals largely because operating managers were unable to take actions suggested by the data. For example, top managers cited instances where negative operating income indicated a need to increase prices, but their markets were price competitive and their firm was not the price leader. Hence, operating managers were constrained from raising prices even though

Exhibit 1-8 Ten Years of Profitability and Asset-Turnover Data Surrounding the Adoption of Inflation Accounting at Company A and Company B

COMPANY A

	1971[a]	1972[a]	1973	1974	1975	1976[b]	1977	1978	1979	1980
Inflation Accounting Implementation stages		Capital charge	COGS[d]	COGS[e]	Depreciation[d]	Depreciation[e]		Inventory		
Profitability Income from continuing operations/sales	.009	.019	.027	.025	.028	.043	.049	.048	.054	.059
Inventory Turnover Sales/inventory	4.20	4.67	4.59	4.42	5.52	5.85	5.29	6.54	6.13	6.99
Total Asset Turnover Sales/total assets less cash and marketable securities	1.24	1.31	1.29	1.46	1.65	1.68	1.63	1.84	1.79	1.75

Exhibit 1-8 *(Continued)*

COMPANY B

	1976	1977	1978	1979	1980	1981ª	1982	1983	1984ª	1985ª
Inflation Accounting Implementation stages						COGSᵈ Inventoryᵈ		COGSᵉ Inventoryᵉ Fixed assets, Depreciation, Capital charge		
Profitability Income from continuing operations/sales	.054	.055	.048	.028	.041	.053	.043	.048	.068	.060
*Inventory Turnover*ᶠ Sales/inventory	5.41	5.55	5.38	6.52	6.85	6.94	7.63	12.34	13.70	14.08
Total Asset Turnover Sales/total assets less cash and marketable securities	1.33	1.26	1.43	1.42	1.39	1.34	1.43	1.55	1.51	1.29

ªSales declined from previous year.

ᵇAdopted LIFO inventory accounting for virtually all inventories for public financial reporting. Only a limited amount of inventory had been under LIFO previously.

ᶜThis ratio was computed using the primary publicly reported inventory value for each year (primarily LIFO after 1976). If the current cost (FIFO) inventory value had been used following 1976, however, the inventory turnover at the end of the period would still have been higher at the end of the 70s than it was at the beginning.

ᵈPartial implementation.

ᵉRemaining implementation.

ᶠThis ratio was computed using the publicly reported LIFO inventory value. An inventory turnover ratio was also computed using the current cost (FIFO) inventory value for 1975–1985; it showed essentially the same pattern.

the inflation accounting system had communicated the need for higher margins.

Progress had been made toward the goal of increasing the consistency between long-term and short-term measures, but it was not fully achieved. In some cases, the short-term measures of operating performance were still based on the accrual accounting model while the long-term measures were based on discounted cash flows. In other cases, different assumptions were made between the two (for example, in asset lives or choices of inflation indices). Yet, managers generally believed that the inflation accounting measures were more consistent with long-term measures than the prior historical cost accounting measures had been.

The adoption of this measurement system was not without problems or side effects even for firms retaining inflation accounting. The primary problem cited was the negative effect on the morale of operating managers. Managers were frustrated and demoralized when businesses that had been profitable under historical costs now reported losses. One manager described his situation as follows:

The main problem is that the negative operating income is very depressing. It is very discouraging, and makes dealing with subordinates difficult. . . . I have yet to find anyone among the group managers who says they find the system motivating. I think managers would be motivated better by positive numbers than being in the red all the time.

The negative effect on morale declined over time. When interviewed more than two years after the implementation of the system, fewer operating managers expressed such feelings. Although managers in some businesses had managed to improve from negative to positive operating income, even those managers whose businesses were still in the red were not so adamant about the negative effect on morale. Top managers also confirmed that morale had improved.

In addition to morale problems, inflation accounting generated numerous technical controversies, including disagreements about asset lives, arguments about appropriate indices, and discussions of whether or not certain assets should be accounted for on an inflation-adjusted basis at all. Such technical controversies are not unique to inflation accounting; controversies over asset lives, depreciation methods, inventory valuation methods, and so forth also arise in historical cost accounting. For the firms that retained inflation accounting, these technical problems were treated as routine; the benefits realized from using inflation accounting outweighed the technical problems.

Summary

Managers at the six firms did not agree on whether the inflation accounting data were useful. Inflation accounting data were intended for two distinct purposes:

1. To improve strategic planning and resource allocation decisions in order to improve long-term financial performance.
2. To motivate operating managers to improve the financial performance of their operations.

For strategic planning and resource allocation, the data were used primarily by corporate managers; they did not need to be incorporated into routine operating-level management control systems. Indeed, when several firms initially used inflation-adjusted data for these purposes, the data had limited corporate distribution. When asked why they had adopted the data for strategic planning and resource allocation, managers identified one or more of the following factors:

1. Businesses of subunits were in different industries or had assets of different ages; sometimes both conditions were present.
2. Many of the businesses were asset intensive, particularly fixed-asset intensive.
3. Some businesses were recently acquired.

In order to allocate limited resources, senior managers needed a basis for comparing the performance of diverse businesses. In their opinion, inflation accounting provided a way to measure different businesses that was more consistent and more representative of economic reality, particularly for fixed-asset-intensive businesses. Further, some managers responsible for resource allocation needed comparable performance measures because they lacked the firsthand experience to enable them to make intuitive adjustments to historical cost measures of business performance.

While these characteristics encouraged firms to experiment with inflation accounting, the data would be useful only if they provided incremental information that management could incorporate into their understanding of the businesses. If the data did not provide any new information, they were not perceived as useful. For example, at Company Z managers wondered, "What do the data tell us that we do not already know?" Under inflation accounting, they saw a large impact on the bottom line in their capital-intensive manufacturing businesses and almost no impact in their service businesses. But this was not new information, as managers expected these results simply because of the capital intensity of these businesses. If the information provided was inconsistent with widely held beliefs about the businesses, the data might also be rejected. For example, Company Y managers found it difficult to identify an inflation accounting method that produced results consistent with senior management's understanding of the relative performance of its various retail companies.

The second purpose of inflation accounting—to influence the behavior of operating managers—was the reason that these data were incorporated in such management control systems as routine budgeting and results reporting. Inflation accounting sent powerful messages to operating managers (particularly those in capital-intensive businesses with older fixed assets), about the need to improve asset utilization and to improve operating performance. It was clear, particularly in the retaining firms, that top management believed that such actions were not only needed, but overdue; managers indicated that their manufacturing technology was outdated and inefficient, that plant capacity exceeded current and expected demand, or that some business units had failed to increase prices sufficiently in markets where they could influence prices.

This purpose of inflation accounting was reflected in choices made about system design. Operating managers, responsible for ensuring that inventories and fixed assets were productively employed, needed to be aware of the current, relative costs of such assets. Specific price-level-adjustments were used because they were more credible to operating managers; they produced current cost values closest to those the operating managers experienced firsthand when acquiring new or replacement assets. Operating managers were responsible for operating assets, not for speculating on holding them; hence, they were not credited with holding gains. Reduction of assets was a top management goal; thus, rewarding operating managers for holding assets would have provided an inconsistent signal. The choice not to include holding gains in the inflation accounting system was consistent with top management's emphasis on asset reduction.

If, however, the operating managers could not take appropriate actions, they might conclude the data were not useful. In the case of the retailer, operating managers had little control over fixed assets (once the store was in place) or over prices, which were competitively set. Thus, there was not much the managers could "do" with the data;

that is, the data were not likely to change the managers' behavior. This need for controllability was also clear at Company X where the inflation accounting system was implemented by top management to emphasize the need for price increases. When the system was withdrawn at the corporate level, it was retained by only one of two lower groups. The retaining group, with more control over pricing, found that the inflation accounting data helped it improve performance; the other group, which had little control over prices because it was in highly price-competitive markets, discontinued inflation accounting.

The experiences of these firms suggest actions that managers can take to ensure that use of inflation accounting data is most effective. Implementing an inflation accounting system was a major organizational change; to accomplish it, managers used familiar approaches recognized for their success in changing organizations.

First, top managers strongly supported the use of the data before, during, and after implementation. Prestige, commitment, and authority, such as those of the CEO and other top officers, are recognized to influence positively the adoption of organizational change (Beer 1980; Dalton 1970). Not only did the top managers make speeches introducing and encouraging use of the data, but they also used the data as a basis for communication with operating managers. One operating manager described a presentation where he was told by the chief operating officer to remove vu-graphs from the projector because they contained historical-cost rather than inflation-accounting information.

Corporate support is strongest when inflation accounting data are not simply supplementary, but are the primary measurement system and are included in performance measurement and incentive compensation. Five out of six of the firms attempted to or did incorporate the data in performance measurement and incentive compensation systems; thus, it was clear that the companies intended the inflation accounting data to influence the behavior of managers. Changing the formal measurement system produced an effect on managerial behavior consistent with that observed for other changes in management structures (Beer 1980, 186). The firms that retained their inflation accounting systems are also the ones that were successful in making primary use of the data.

In addition to supporting the data and making them primary, top managers were quite specific about the actions they expected from operating managers as a result of using the data. When corporate management articulated such expectations, their message was understood by operating managers and translated into action. In those firms where corporate management was not as specific (for example, only saying that they generally wanted to "increase awareness"), operating managers were less responsive. Reinforcing inflation accounting with other measures (such as the capital charge), or other programs (such as productivity programs), clarified the desired goals for operating managers. Articulating and achieving understanding of the goals, however, was not enough. Operating managers needed leverage over variables that controlled or influenced their measured performance. For example, retail managers could dispose of a few fixed assets, such as fixtures, but they did not have significant control over most fixed assets; thus, they had little influence over fixed-asset utilization.

Finally, to prepare for a significant organizational change, top managers conducted extensive planning; such planning, prior to presentation to the organization, had been demonstrated to be crucial to the success of organizational change (Greiner and Barnes 1970; Lawrence 1958). The phased implementation process, described earlier, is also characteristic of effective organizational change. Changing accounting measures of operating performance from historical cost to inflation-adjusted can influence the behavior of managers, but the *process* by which it is accomplished is as important to the effectiveness of the accounting change in accomplishing management's goals.

Because of the nature and magnitude of inflation accounting adjustments, particularly fixed-asset adjustments, researchers have hypothesized that the data ought to be most "useful" to capital-intensive companies (Schwarzbach and Swanson 1981). The data in this study suggest that capital intensity may indeed be a factor in why firms choose to adopt inflation accounting, but it is not the whole explanation. The decision to adopt inflation accounting is not a simple one; a combination of factors contributes to the adoption decision and not all factors are present in the same degree in all cases. The current study supports the hypothesis that implementing the data in routine operating measures and reports is more useful to capital-intensive firms.[18] Further, a diversity of businesses in a corporation contributes to the usefulness of the data when managers lack enough firsthand experience to evaluate a business unit's performance intuitively, despite what the accounting measure indicates.

I argue, however, that not all diverse, capital-intensive firms will benefit from the use of inflation accounting. The data appear most useful at those firms where operating managers have significant opportunities to take the actions indicated by the data. For example, where inflation-adjusted returns are low, operating managers must be able to significantly influence the asset base by reducing the level of assets, or to influence the margins earned on that asset base through price increases, cost reductions, or productivity improvements. There are industries in which returns are low, but operating managers may not have much leverage to act. For example, in a commodity industry with low or declining growth and little expectation of significant technological improvements, and in which manufacturing processes are such that assets cannot be disposed of in small-to-medium increments, the data are not likely to encourage managers to take action.[19] Rather, operating managers are likely to be frustrated because they are constrained from taking the actions that are now so clearly needed.[20] This explains why capital intensity alone is not a sufficient reason for firms to adopt inflation accounting (Schwarzbach and Swanson 1981).

This research did not seek to explore why other diverse heavy manufacturing firms did not adopt inflation accounting. An earlier study, which included two nonadopting firms, suggests two tentative hypotheses: first, nonadopting firms may not experience the same pressure to improve their financial performance as adopting firms; second, nonadopting firms may place a lower priority on the management of fixed assets because other managerial issues require higher priority (Hertenstein 1984).[21] In addition, even though inflation accounting highlighted the need to manage fixed assets, other firms may have developed alternative means to emphasize fixed-asset management. Identification of alternative tools to motivate improvements in fixed-asset utilization, and the measurement of the relative costs and effectiveness of these tools, are research questions that were not addressed by this study.

Inflation accounting is one means to emphasize the need for improved asset and operations management in diverse capital-intensive firms; although the implementation of inflation accounting is not without costs, if management desires to improve asset and operations management, then inflation accounting is a powerful tool that can help accomplish these goals.

NOTES

1. Accounting Series Release 190, issued in March 1976, required supplementary disclosure of replacement costs for inventories, productive capacity, cost of sales, and depreciation.

2. FAS 33 (Financial Reporting and Changing Prices) was issued by the Financial Accounting Standards Board in September 1979. It required supplementary disclosure of both general price-level-adjusted data (constant dollar) and a version of specific price-level-adjusted data (current cost) different from the replacement cost data previously required by the SEC.

3. For the use of inflation accounting by stock market participants and analysts, see, for example, Berliner (1983), Baran et al. (1980), Beaver et al. (1980), Gheyara and Boatsman (1980), and Ro (1980).

4. A few studies described the use of inflation accounting data by individual firms. See, for example, Breden and DeMichiel (1985), Pearcy (1984), and Seed (1981).

5. In each firm, several managers were interviewed, including both corporate and operating managers. There were two exceptions: in one discontinuing firm only corporate officers and staff, not operating managers, were interviewed; in another discontinuing firm, one corporate officer was interviewed.

6. Detailed descriptions of the data gathered at each site are available from the author.

7. To prepare FAS 33 data on changing prices for external reporting, the corporate controllers at Company C first estimated the current cost of assets. They then sent these estimates to the field where operating managers, because of their more direct experience with these assets, were encouraged to make appropriate adjustments to better estimate current costs. Corporate managers were concerned that this precedent of adjusting corporate estimates by operating managers would be difficult to override when preparing data for the internal inflation accounting system; they further believed that internal use of these data might provide incentives for operating managers to manipulate the data. Thus, Company C managers used general price-level-adjustments to avoid such manipulation.

8. Some firms valued cost of goods sold at LIFO prior to adoption of inflation accounting. Because they believed that LIFO cost of goods sold already approximated current cost, these firms did not make additional adjustments to cost of goods sold; however, since inventories were understated on LIFO, they added back the LIFO reserve to restate the inventory value.

9. Some managers stated that short asset lives had intentionally been selected under historical costs to offset the understatement of depreciation resulting from inflation. Others explained that the historical-cost asset lives were merely consistent with prior practice, or with other accounting practices of the firm such as external reporting.

10. Holding gains are the increases in value resulting from holding nonmonetary assets during periods when their prices are rising. Monetary gains are the increases in purchasing power resulting from holding a net monetary liability position during a period when the general price level rises, and, hence, the purchasing power of the monetary unit declines.

11. Company Y also had an asset charge; it was applied only to *increases* in working capital.

12. Even Company Y had diverse retail formats, ranging from department

stores to specialty stores, which faced unique competitive conditions in distinct geographic markets.

13. Some of the inflation-adjusted measures for long-term resource allocation had been implemented prior to, and were somewhat different from, the inflation accounting measures of operating performance.

14. For example, in the four-year period following the adoption of inflation-adjusted measures, the proportion of the capital budget allocated to businesses with high potential returns had increased from 47 percent to 63 percent; the proportion allocated to businesses with low potential returns declined from 35 percent to 20 percent.

15. For example, a business considered to be a valuable cash provider could have negative operating results under inflation accounting. Top management perceived an inconsistency between their positive opinion of the business and their decision to retain it, and the negative view portrayed by inflation accounting.

16. Operating managers did not cite the goal of improving resource allocation; this may have been because it did not pertain to the job of the operating manager.

17. At Company C, the firm in the process of expanding the use of inflation accounting to the operating level, operating managers were able to identify the goals and to identify potential actions, but it was too soon to observe actions.

18. This conclusion is consistent with other observations that these data are not used in service industries (Archer and Steele 1984; Pearcy 1984).

19. Some commodity industrial chemical businesses may fit this profile.

20. Some top managers argue, however, that it is precisely this frustration that encourages operating managers to search further afield, to seek new, creative solutions, and to make innovative breakthroughs.

21. The nonadopting manufacturing firms studied had many assembly operations, and they purchased many components and subassemblies. Hence, the level of inventories was high relative to the level of fixed assets, and much managerial effort was focused on the management of inventories.

REFERENCES

Archer, G. S. H., and Steele, A. 1984. "The Implementation of SSAP 16, Current Cost Accounting, by U.K. Listed Companies." In *Current Cost Accounting: The Benefits and the Costs*, edited by Bryan Carsberg and Michael Page, 349–484. London: Prentice-Hall International, in association with The Institute of Chartered Accountants in England and Wales.

Baran, A.; Lakonishok, J.; and Ofer, A. R. 1980. "The Value of General Price Level Adjusted Data to Bond Rating." *Journal of Business, Finance and Accounting*, 135–49.

Beaver, William H.; Christie, Andrew A.; and Griffen, Paul A. 1980. "The Information Content of SEC Accounting Series Release No. 190." *Journal of Accounting and Economics* (August): 127–58.

Beer, Michael. 1980. *Organizational Change and Development: A Systems View.* Santa Monica, CA: Goodyear Publishing Company, Inc.

Berliner, R. W. 1983. "Use of FAS 33 Data by Financial Analysts." *Financial Analysts Journal* (March–April): 65–72.

Brandner, L., and Keal, B. 1973. "Evaluation for Congruence as a Factor in the Adoption Rate of Innovations." In *Innovations and Organizations*, edited by Gerald Zaltman, Robert Duncan, and Jonny Holbek. New York: John Wiley and Sons.

Breden, Denise, and DeMichiel, Robert. 1985. *Inflation and Managerial Decision Making.* Montvale, NJ: National Association of Accountants.

Casey, Cornelius J., and Sandretto, Michael J. 1981. "Internal uses of accounting for inflation." *Harvard Business Review* (November–December): 149–56.

Dalton, Gene W. 1970. "Influence and Organizational Change." In *Organizational Change and Development*, edited by Gene W. Dalton, Paul R. Lawrence, and Larry E. Greiner, 230–58. Homewood, IL: Richard D. Irwin, Inc.

Dearden, John. 1981. "Facing facts with inflation accounting." *Harvard Business Review* (July–August): 8–12.

Edwards, Edgar O. 1975. "The State of Current Value Accounting." *The Accounting Review* (April): 235–45.

Frank, J. W.; Kealey, T. F.; and Silverman, G. W. 1978. *The Effects and Usefulness of Replacement Cost Disclosure: Research Study and Report.* New York: Financial Executives Research Foundation.

Gheyara, Kelly, and Boatsman, James. 1980. "Market Reactions to The 1976 Replacement Cost Disclosures." *Journal of Accounting and Economics* (August): 107–26.

Greiner, Larry E., and Barnes, Louis B. 1970. "Organization Change and Development." In *Organizational Change and Development*, edited by Gene W. Dalton, Paul R. Lawrence, and Larry E. Greiner, 1–12. Homewood, IL: Richard D. Irwin, Inc.

Hertenstein, Julie H. 1984. "Innovation in Management Control: A Comparative Study of Inflation Adjusted Accounting Systems in Diversified Firms." DBA diss., Harvard Business School, Harvard University.

Hussey, David E. 1976. *Inflation and Business Policy.* London: Longman.

Lawrence, Paul R. 1958. *The Changing of Organizational Behavior Patterns: A Case Study of Decentralization.* Boston, MA: Division of Research, Graduate School of Business Administration, Harvard University.

MacAvoy, Robert E. 1980. "Strategic Planning." *Financial Executive* (June): 36–40.

Merchant, Kenneth A. 1985. *Control in Business Organizations.* Boston, MA: Pitman Publishing Inc.

Pearcy, J. 1984. "Some Uses of Current Costs in Management Accounting." In *Current Cost Accounting: The Benefits and Costs*, edited by Bryan Carsberg and Michael Page, 217–33. London: Prentice-Hall International, in association with The Institute of Chartered Accountants in England and Wales.

Ro, Byung T. 1980. "The Adjustment of Security Returns to the Disclosure of Replacement Cost Accounting Information." *Journal of Accounting and Economics* (August): 159–89.

Schwarzbach, Henry R., and Swanson, Edward P. 1981. "The Use of Replacement Cost Accounting Information for Decision Making During Inflationary Times." *Journal of Contemporary Business* 10, 2, 65–76.

Seed, Allen H. III. 1981. *The Impact of Inflation on Internal Planning and Control.* New York: National Association of Accountants, 1981.

Time Inc. "The *Fortune* Directory of the Largest U.S. Industrial Corporations." *Fortune*, 28 April 1986, 182–201.

"The *Fortune* Directory of the Largest U.S. Non-Industrial Corporations, *Fortune*, 9 June 1986, 122–52.

Vancil, Richard F. 1976. "Inflation accounting—the great controversy." *Harvard Business Review* (March–April): 58–67.

Webster, Frederick E.; Largay, James A.; and Stickney, Clyde P. 1980. "The Impact of Inflation Accounting on Marketing Decisions." *Journal of Marketing* (Fall): 9–17.

Yin, Robert K. 1984. *Case Study Research: Design and Methods.* Beverly Hills, CA: Sage Publications.

CHAPTER 2

Organizational Design versus Strategic Information Procedures for Managing Corporate Overhead Cost: Weyerhaeuser Company, 1972–1986

H. Thomas Johnson

MANAGING corporate overhead is among the most difficult problems that company executives face today. Direct evidence of overhead growth is not easy to find in the numbers that companies report in financial statements. But indirect evidence exists in public comments that executives make. For example, a recent poll of corporate leaders by *Fortune* magazine lists cost containment as top management's number one problem.[1] And business journalists frequently cite middle-management layoffs or corporate staff "unbundling"— examples of overhead reduction—as an immediate consequence of merger or takeover.

Most perplexing to managers is an insidious tendency for corporate overhead cost to rise steadily even though it is considered a fixed cost.[2] This tendency is apparent whenever an executive says, "We cannot seem to meet our profit targets even though we are meet-

I gratefully acknowledge the helpful assistance of many persons in the Weyerhaeuser Company, especially Charles W. Bingham, L. W. Christenson, Gary Healea, Donald J. Hopkins, Dennis A. Loewe, H. E. Morgan, Jr., Kenneth J. Stancato, and Herbert C. Winward. Helpful comments were made by Eli Berniker and by several participants at the June 1986 Harvard colloquium, especially Robin Cooper, Michael Jensen, Robert Kaplan, James McKenney, and John Shank. While thanking these individuals for their assistance, I hold them blameless for the conclusions, interpretations, and possible errors in this paper.

ing our marketing goals; somehow our programs to control costs do not seem to work."

Although "overhead creep" has long been recognized as a problem, successful solutions have not been forthcoming. The usual remedies—across-the-board budget and personnel cuts, mergers to eliminate redundant personnel, allocations of corporate overhead to stimulate cost-conscious behavior among managers—are seldom more than Band-aids. These remedies often reduce overhead in the short run, but there is no convincing evidence that they help managers control overhead in the long run.

Existing procedures do not help managers control corporate overhead costs in the long run because they do not attack the basic cause of overhead cost—the consumption of resources to manage diversity. As the next section of this chapter demonstrates, it was the historical growth in diversity of American industrial firms that caused overhead to become a pervasive management problem. Diversity confers many advantages on a firm, but it also increases the complexity. Managers could control the complexity of diversity directly if they had information about the particular resource-consuming activities that cause every dollar of corporate overhead cost. Until recently, however, the high cost of information processing has precluded managers' controlling overhead directly. Lacking information about the direct causes of corporate overhead, managers have resorted to controlling it with indirect procedures. The most common one is to design organizational structures that compartmentalize corporate activities according to more or less directly traceable cause-and-effect relationships. Corporate overhead, i.e., nontraceable systemwide costs, is then either managed by allocation or exhortation, or it is ignored altogether.

A case study of the conventional indirect approach to managing corporate overhead through organizational control procedures is provided by the particular effort of the Weyerhaeuser Company—a large forest-products company headquartered in Tacoma, Washington—to manage diversity since the late 1960s. A unique outcome of Weyerhaeuser's efforts, however, is its recent development of an accounting-based procedure for managing corporate overhead costs directly. Referred to by company personnel as a "charge-back" system, the procedure resembles allocation procedures for managing overhead that became popular in the 1970s.[3] But resemblance to these allocation procedures is deceptive.

Unlike allocations aimed at influencing managers' behavior indirectly—once considered an effective means of managing overhead costs—the new charge-back system gives managers direct decision rights over the use of resources that cause overhead cost. Indeed, Weyerhaeuser's charge-back procedure is akin to state-of-the-art methods of strategic cost management that have been applied recently in factory manufacturing settings.[4] The central idea in strategic cost management is that people cannot manage costs, they can only manage activities that cause costs. Weyerhaeuser's charge-back procedure extends this concept of strategic cost management to overhead costs that are incurred outside the factory. As the last two sections of this chapter indicate, this approach to strategic cost management may foreshadow increased use of information-based procedures and decreased use of traditional organizational control procedures to manage corporate overhead costs.

DIVERSITY AND OVERHEAD COSTS: AN HISTORICAL VIEW

Corporate overhead costs arise from resources that two or more activities (e.g., product lines or production processes) in one firm use in common.[5] Pooling of resources among activities occurs when firms diversify to capture either economies of scope—gains that result from jointly conducting two or more activities in one facility—or increased economies of scale—reductions in unit cost that result from increasing the rate of one activity in one facility. Diversification among product lines to capture economies of scope is often referred to as a strategy of horizontal integration, while diversification among marketing and production activities to capture scale economies is described as vertical integration. Increased diversity seems to be an inevitable fact of modern economic life. Moreover, a large literature describes the conditions under which diversity increases a business firm's profitability. But a central feature of twentieth-century American business history that most writers ignore is the task of managing and controlling the costs of diversity.

Managing diversity involves coordinating disparate parts of an organization into a smoothly functioning, effective whole. The conditions that require managers to control diversity have evolved gradually in the history of American industrial enterprise. In early nineteenth-century manufacturing firms, which usually focused on one activity and a homogeneous line of products, managers did not have to think about performance of the firm as a whole. If the separate parts of a factory ran efficiently and the flow of work among parts was carefully balanced, managers generally had done all they could to ensure profitable results in general.

Around 1900, when many manufacturers diversified vertically or horizontally, managers began to take conscious steps to ensure that efficient performance in a firm's diverse parts added up to profitable results overall. A few early vertically integrated firms, for example, devised the return on investment measure (a denominator of overall performance) to evaluate subdepartments that specialized in diverse activities such as purchasing, manufacturing, distributing, transporting, and financing. The use of return on investment data, perfected at Du Pont by 1915, remains a widely accepted method of managing vertically integrated industrial activities to this day.

Also at the turn of the century, some specialized manufacturing firms began to diversify their product lines. The firms, especially machine-making firms, attempted to manage diversity by tracing overall profitability to profits earned by separate products. They attempted to analyze each product's contribution to profit by tracing virtually all costs in the business to resources consumed by individual products. But processing such information in the early 1900s entailed high costs. Probably for that reason, after an initial flurry of interest from scientific management engineers in diversified machine-making firms, by 1914 this approach to managing product diversity fell out of favor.

Following World War I, some vertically integrated firms also began to diversify their product lines. They might have managed product diversity by tracing costs to the resources consumed in making products, as advocated before the war by scientific management engineers. But again, the high cost of labor-intensive information processing technology apparently precluded that possibility, not only in the early 1900s but for the first five or six decades of this century. So after World War I, giant industrial firms managed product diversity by creating multidivisional structures in which responsibility for the vertically integrated activities in each homogeneous product line was delegated to separate divisions. Referred to by economist Oliver Williamson as "American capitalism's most important single innovation of the 20th century," this M-form, or multidivisional form of organization, has remained a popular mechanism for managing diversity in large industrial firms.[6]

After World War II, some complex industrial firms implemented the matrix form of organization to help them manage diversity.[7] The matrix organization creates islands of specialization along both product (horizontal) and activity (vertical) lines. Unlike the M-form structure, it does not subordinate activities to product lines. Not widely used, the matrix structure has been applied most often in high-technology organizations where diverse professional specializations create value just as surely as diverse product lines do.

In seeking economies of scale and economies of scope through internal diversification, managed firms have created overhead expense by moving certain economic exchanges from the market into the firm. It was not inevitable that in the past century the search for opportunities to gain from economies of scope and scale would produce giant integrated and diversified hierarchies.[8] That it did suggests that the marginal cost of conducting some exchanges in certain industries was less in hierarchies than it was in markets during those years. Had the marginal cost of conducting those exchanges been less in the market than in those particular hierarchies, it is reasonable to assume that managers might have attempted to capture economies of scope and scale through "specialized firms contracting in the marketplace for the supply of common inputs."[9] Specialized firms do not incur corporate overhead costs when they contract in the marketplace for the supply of common resources, e.g., research and development, marketing expertise, legal counsel, accounting services, and engineering. Corporate overhead expense arose because firms acquired ownership and control over resources that were used in common by diverse activities. And diversified firms acquired this ownership and control presumably because they believed that by managing the productivity of common resources they obtained the output of those resources at costs lower than those for output purchased through the market.

Managing the productivity of company-owned common resources is, of course, equivalent to managing corporate overhead costs. And our discussion of the historical growth of diversity shows that industrial firms over the years have developed three procedures for managing corporate overhead. First, the M-form structure makes diversity manageable by decentralizing disparate product lines into islands of relative homogeneity. Top management, freed from managing diversity, can attend almost exclusively to the task of managing common resources. Second, vertically integrated and matrix firms centralize the task of coordinating disparate parts into a profitable whole. In those organizations top managers coordinate parts with carefully designed plans or budgets in which they denominate the local performance of diverse activities in terms of a common unit of overall performance such as ROI. Third, a method for managing diversity that until recently has almost never been put into practice is to trace all overhead costs to transactions (i.e., cost drivers) that consume resources. Cost information about transactions that involve the exchange of material or the exchange of information is analogous to the price information that directs economic exchange in the marketplace. Unlike the first two procedures for managing overhead, tracing costs to elemental transactions provides a *direct* means of managing overhead. Tracing overhead costs to elemental transactions that consume resources is the principle that underlies the Weyerhaeuser Company's new charge-back system.

MANAGING DIVERSITY AT WEYERHAEUSER, 1972–1986

Changes in management methods at Weyerhaeuser Company since the early 1970s provide an unusually good opportunity to study relationships among diversity, organizational structure, and the control of corporate overhead costs. These changes originated in the company's decision around 1950 to diversify beyond timber growing and lumber producing, the activities that comprised virtually all of Weyerhaeuser's business during the first half of this century.

The Decision to Diversify

Certainly by the 1950s, a strategic decision to diversify product lines was nothing new for an American industrial firm. Beginning with Du Pont and General Motors in the early 1920s, scores of integrated industrial firms had adopted a strategy of product diversification. Moreover, almost all these diversified industrial firms by the 1950s had adopted divisional forms of organization and profit-center systems for internal planning and control, following well-publicized precedents that Du Pont and General Motors had established in the 1920s.[10] At Weyerhaeuser Company, however, diversification led initially to a matrix structure, a form of organization that was not widely known when the company began to examine the organizational implications of diversification in the late 1960s. The matrix structure that was implemented at Weyerhaeuser Company in 1972 remained in place (with gradual modifications) until 1985, when it was replaced with a product-group structure that resembles the multidivisional form (M-form) of organization.

Like most companies that had already diversified, the Weyer-haeuser Company made its decision to diversify long before anyone in the firm had considered its implications for organizational design. The decision to diversify came around 1950, at a time when the company produced mainly one product line—timber and lumber. At midcentury, Weyerhaeuser was a mature company in a mature industry, facing long-run diminishing rates of growth and rising costs of production. The profitability of investing the company's substantial cash flows in further tree and lumber production could no longer be taken for granted; investment in traditional assets had to be balanced against other alternatives. Had there been no alternative uses for the company's traditional assets, it might have been wise at that time to delegate reinvestment decisions to the stockholders by repurchasing the company's shares. The company obviously rejected that course of action and chose instead, by diversifying, to invest in underutilized economies of scope. Weyerhaeuser had several advantages that offered opportunities to capture economies of scope: a nationally advertised name and reputation for quality; a national distribution chain; substantial research and engineering expertise; and, not least of all, the world's largest privately owned forest.

The company had started to diversify from the late 1940s to the early 1960s, apparently on an ad hoc basis. It was not guided by a systematic program to optimize potential economies of scope. Precedents for these moves were the company's 1931 decision to invest in sulphite pulp manufacture in Longview, Washington, primarily to provide an outlet for nearby stands of hemlock, which had little value in lumber production at the time, and the decision to purchase a paper mill in Springfield, Oregon, later in the 1930s, to add value to sawdust and chips from nearby sawmills. The pace of diversification quickened, however, after the late 1940s: a plywood mill opened in 1947, a containerboard plant in 1949, a paperboard mill in 1952, and veneer, hardboard, and particle board plants in 1953, 1954, and 1955. Major investments in 1956 and 1957 entailed the company's first purchase of timberlands in the southeastern United States and the acquisition of both the Kieckhefer Container Company and the Eddy Paper Corporation. Further investments in paper and box manufacture and considerable overseas investment continued through the first half of the 1960s.

After pursuing a strategy of diversification for just over a decade, the scope of Weyerhaeuser Company's activities in the early 1960s encompassed several new products that promised higher marginal returns than those attainable from timber or lumber. Although the company still regarded ownership and cultivation of forest land as a key source of competitive advantage, it had made an irrevocable decision to capture that advantage increasingly from end products other than trees and boards. But the array of potentially profitable new forest products posed a problem: namely, how to invest at an efficient minimum scale among the best available alternatives. The solution was an approach to long-term planning that began with the High Yield Forest (HYF) program in 1965 and became institutionalized in the Timber Asset Management Department (TAMD) in 1973.[11]

The HYF program was designed to select those diverse end products that optimized overall return to the company's timber stand; in effect, it was designed to maximize economies of scope from the company's vast timber holdings. Using a linear programming system to plan the optimal return to forest resources in each of the company's regions, the HYF plan matched simulations of potential long-term harvest from each region with various assumptions about long-run markets for wood fiber (e.g., pulp, paper, plywood, lumber) and about costs of production in each region. The plan identified long-term opportunities for new investment and specified an optimal short-term allocation of forest resources to facilities and markets in each of the company's regions. A Weyerhaeuser executive described the plan in a 1969 speech by saying that HYF "developed financial computer models that we could overlay on our biological simulations to tell us which of the alternative biological methods would result in the optimization of financial present value."[12] The company "made the assumption that 'each major forest property must be managed as a single unit containing a mix of investment opportunities.'"[13] The plan objective, quite simply, was to maximize the present value of net cash flows from the company's forest resources in each region of the nation.

The HYF program increased the average size and the diversity of the company's investment projects after the late 1960s. Increased size is partly reflected in the 1969 purchase of Dierks Forests Inc., a 1.8 million-acre complex of forest land and mills in Arkansas and Oklahoma that represented the company's largest single investment to that date. Then in 1973, the company announced a three-year nationwide expansion plan, totalling $2 billion, designed "to fully utilize the harvest on Company lands." The HYF planning program also increased the degree of diversity among products and among regions.

What had been as late as the 1950s a tree-growing and lumber-producing firm located largely in the Pacific Northwest had become by the early 1970s a diversified forest-products firm with heterogeneous timberlands and facilities located all over the United States and in many foreign nations. By sharply increasing the complexity of the company's activities, the HYF approach to planning prompted the company to reexamine the structure of its organization.

The Matrix Structure

The increased diversification and scale of Weyerhaeuser's activities heightened the complexity of problems that faced top management. But the HYF concept contributed a solution to the problem by opening the possibility of adopting a centrally directed matrix. Indeed, the linear programs and the simulations of HYF appeared to give top managers perfect tools for directing activities in the firm's diverse parts toward optimal overall results. With those planning tools in hand, top management in 1972 adopted a centralized matrix structure to run the company's internal affairs.[14]

As shown below, the gap between plan and actual results proved to be enormous. Although HYF provided well-defined central plans to guide the company, the accounting information used to control on-going operations could not satisfactorily disclose whether actual performance in one particular part of the firm diverged from overall corporate goals. Nevertheless, for nearly a decade the company managed diversity tolerably well with a matrix structure.

The 1972 matrix structure (see Exhibit 2-1) was built around two primary subunits: the Businesses and the Regions. Each Business within the Business subunit was responsible for sales, marketing, and long-term strategy for one of the company's five major product groups: land and timber (including the High Yield Forest plan), raw materials, wood products, pulp and paper, and containers. The Businesses subunit also managed the company's secondary manufacturing facilities—the box plants and milk carton plants that were strategically located with regard to customer markets. Responsibility for all production operations, from logging and reforestation of the timberlands to primary manufacturing in the mills, was assigned to the Regions, which was divided into eleven (eventually fourteen) geographic regions.

The matrix structure's management accounting and control sys-

Exhibit 2-1   Matrix Organization Structure circa 1973*

PRESIDENT, CEO	
Business Vice-presidents	*Region Vice-presidents*
One to manage strategy and marketing for product lines such as	Each in charge of a region's operations for
• Land and timber	• Reforestation
• Raw materials	• Logging
• Wood products	• Wood-product manufacture
• Pulp and paper	• Log and chip allocation
• Shipping containers	• Pulp and paper manufacture
• Box shop manufacture	

*This highly condensed organization chart includes only the subunits within the two primary axes of the matrix. Omitted are several corporate-level staff functions.

tem assigned ultimate responsibility for profits to the Businesses and responsibility for operating efficiencies to the Regions. To understand how that system worked, it is best to begin with the trees in the forest. Standing timber was sold by the land and timber Business to the raw materials Business at a market-based transfer price that was calculated on recent prices for trees on federal, state, and private lands. The land and timber Business recorded as profit the difference between that transfer price and the original stumpage cost recorded on the company's books. The land and timber Business was motivated to maximize that profit by selling those company trees that offered the highest present value according to the High Yield Forest plan. The raw materials Business paid forestry units in the Regions to fell trees and to deliver logs to users inside or outside the company. The raw materials Business transferred logs and chips to production mills in the Regions at a market-based transfer price. The raw materials Business also sold logs and chips to third parties. Production mills in the Regions transferred manufactured products to the pulp, paper, paperboard, wood product, and shipping container Businesses at cost. Those Businesses sold to outsiders through the company's various distribution networks and recorded a final profit.

This system allowed top management to monitor the separate profit of each group as it was recorded by the Businesses. The system, however, did not establish separate accountabilities for the contribution that each activity center in the Regions made to overall company profit. In the Regions, managers of forests and mills were not permitted to sell to or to source from outside third parties. Consequently, they could not be held accountable for profits in any meaningful sense. As managers of cost centers, they were held accountable only for operating efficiencies, not profit contributions. Loggers, mill workers, and regional managers worked against physical-output and manpower-efficiency goals, not profit targets. Consequently, incentives to achieve the profit goals of the High Yield Forestry plan were not as strong in the Regions as they were in the Businesses. This fact was noted in the following comment made to a Harvard case writer in 1974 by Gil Baker, manager of High Yield Forest Planning:

High Yield Forestry is accepted at the resource vice-presidential level, but operating foresters are taught to keep costs down and to ignore value and growth being created by the forestry industry. With High Yield Forestry, you have to buy the package. We committed to a whole at the top without much involvement at the forester level. Our strength is a weakness.[15]

People in the Regions were often content to follow operating rules that antedated the HYF program. Loggers, for example, might be content to cut the nearest trees and ship to the closest site, even though the high-yield simulation projected higher returns if logs were allocated in a different way. "The problem," according to another executive interviewed by Harvard case writers in 1974, "is that the loggers work for the manufacturing [Region], not for the land and timber [Business]. Woods procedure has been to look for the 'short haul' to keep logging costs down. However, a striking thing is the tremendous diversity of the asset. . . . We need economic understanding at [the woods] level."[16] Obviously a system was needed in the Regions to help minimize slack between actual results and the potential results that were spelled out in the long-range HYF plan. The system in place, however, offered little more than persuasion and education to convince the Regions to follow a plan that had little direct benefit to them.

In general, the management accounting and control system in the 1972 matrix structure did not give adequate visibility to the varied activities in which the company intended to achieve economies of scope and scale. The HYF plan outlined a clear program by which to capture underutilized opportunities for scope in the company's timberlands. But the accounting control system left open too many chances for slippage between plan and result. In the Regions, the system monitored actual operating costs of logging and manufacturing activities, but it failed to capture the opportunity cost of avoidable deviations from the plan. And the system, like most corporate management accounting systems, did not encourage efforts to manage the resources expended on corporate overhead activities such as (at Weyerhaeuser) forestry management, research and development, or engineering. Once a year, at most, top management simply allocated corporate common costs to the various Businesses. But decisions to expend resources on corporate overhead usually originated inside staff departments that lacked a clear sense of either the services they provided or the clients who benefited from those services. Not surprisingly, unanticipated growth in corporate overhead was often blamed when profits frequently fell below expectations.

Discontent with results of the matrix organization grew strong in the late 1970s. Causing particular concern in the company was a widespread feeling that the system did not establish proper accountabilities for profit and ROI.[17] This lack of accountabilities seemed not only to frustrate efforts to control outcomes of decisions, but also to engender a belief among employees that one's actions did not matter. Many felt that the company's management system had pushed too far in the direction of quantitative and analytic systems, with the result that decisions were often based on models too complex to comprehend. As one executive put it, their ability to optimize had exceeded their ability to execute. Moreover, complexity and the frustration of not being able to connect effort and results seemed to cause much lethargy and discontent.

To improve operating results and to restore lost employee enthusiasm, the company took several steps between about 1979 and 1983 to redesign their matrix structure. Those steps led to the appointment of an executive vice-president to coordinate operations in the Regions with marketing in the Businesses. The redesign also led to increased use of return on investment data to assess performance at lower levels in the organization. The stated purpose of these changes was to "manage better with fewer people."[18] As the new executive vice-president, Charles Bingham, said in an April 1982 speech:

We are in the midst of redesigning our organization to be sure that, given [current] economic and human value changes, we remain competitive in the 1980s. We are reducing layering and overlapping of responsibilities. We are pushing responsibility out of Tacoma and down the organization chain of command. We are redesigning jobs, and we are changing management behavior from that of supervise, check, and audit to that of counsel, lead, motivate, and trust. Total numbers of people will be somewhat fewer but those who are employed will have more responsible roles, a greater sense of personal ownership, and the security that comes from knowing their plant or logging site is the most competitive in the industry.[19]

The redesign still left Regions and Businesses in place as the organizational skeleton of the firm. It brought a change of emphasis, not a change in structure. Increased emphasis was placed on accountability for companywide goals at all levels in the organization. The intent of the redesign was "to use people, not optimizing models, more effectively" by reducing the need for complex information processing and decision making at high levels. Top management, therefore, reduced the former emphasis on centrally directed optimizing models; it delegated more decisions to people down the line. It was hoped that this would reduce the demand for supervisors and middle managers. As one executive put it, "Redesign forced the company to gamble that many small decentralized units making decisions far down in the organization might give better results than had been achieved by optimizing from the top down." The desired organizational outcome was frequently described as "unbundling" and "flattening."

An example of this redesign was the 1983 decision to decentralize the company's wholesale outlets for wood products: the Customer Service Centers (CSC).[20] The CSCs, about sixty in number, are a national chain of wholesale lumberyards that the company began to build at the time of World War I. Under the matrix organization in the 1970s, the CSCs were conduits for the output of the company's solid-wood manufacturing facilities. CSC managers had no control over what they sold; they simply sold what company mills shipped to them and were not permitted to source outside the company. The CSCs were accounted for as cost centers in the wood-products Business, making the manager of a CSC little more than a custodian for inventories of the company's finished wood products. To capture untapped potential for profits in these wholesale centers, the company in 1983 began to account for the CSCs as investment centers and to permit CSC managers to source from virtually any supplier. Although it is still too early to assess the results of the new policy, the company is aggressively recruiting and training CSC managers who, they hope, will manage product margins, operating costs, and asset turnover with an eye to company return on investment targets.

The early 1980s was a period of sharp recession in the American economy; it was a particularly hard time for firms in the forest-products industry. Weyerhaeuser had initiated efforts to redesign the matrix structure in the late 1970s, long before the onset of recession in 1981, and it is clear that deficiencies in the design of the company's internal structure, not external economic duress, had prompted the company to redesign the matrix structure. External shocks beyond the company's control—recession and deregulation—however, intensified the search for new ways (such as the reorganization of CSCs) to improve profitability throughout the company. Ultimately these external shocks caused the company to abandon the matrix. The severity of the recession and the impact of early-1980s' deregulation on construction, shipping, and export trade drove home the lesson that conditions in the Pacific Northwest timber-and-wood-products industry might never again be as healthy as they were in the 1960s and 1970s. For many people at Weyerhaeuser, already troubled about inadequate accountabilities and performance in the matrix organization, the sharp decline of wood-products markets after 1981 raised additional questions about the company's policy (implicit in the High Yield Forest program and the matrix structure) of basing strategy upon company-owned raw material and not on the market for company products.

The Divisional Structure

Concerned about making employees more sensitive to markets and more accountable for company performance, Weyerhaeuser's management rejected the matrix structure in 1985. The Regions and the Businesses were eliminated; they were replaced by a divisional structure comprised of three product groups, each led by an executive vice-president with full responsibility for the profits and activities (from raw-material acquisition to final customer sale) of a more or less homogeneous line of products (see Exhibit 2-2).

The rationale for Weyerhaeuser's 1985 reorganization rests on two very different considerations. One was the need to adopt the best possible structure for managing diversity, given the complexity already created by the firm's long-standing strategy of diversification. For divisions based on product lines, the M-form structure undoubtedly does better than the matrix to clarify accountabilities for performance at every level in the organization. The M-form reduces the cost at which the already diversified firm will capture economies of scope and scale through its internal activities. But another important reason for replacing the matrix with an M-form structure is to make it easier to evaluate the strategy of diversification per se. The M-form provides information more efficiently to judge whether it is best to

Exhibit 2-2 Divisional Organization Structure, early 1986

PRESIDENT, CEO		
Forest Products	Paper	Diversified Business
Executive VP	*Executive VP*	*Executive VP*
Business VPs*	Business VPs*	Presidents
Each manages strategy, operations, and marketing for product lines such as		
Reforestation	Pulp	Real estate
Logging	Paper	Mortgages
Wood-product	Containerboard	and GNA
mfg.	Newsprint	Diversified VPs
Wood-product	Shipping containers	Specialty VPs
sales	Bleached paperbd.	
Timber sales	Box shop mfg.	
Log sales		
Chip sales		

*Mill managers report to Business VPs.

seek economies of scope and scale by diversifying within the firm or to exchange in the market with separate specialized firms.

A sharp drop in the cost of market contracting since the late 1970s makes it especially important for diversified firms to evaluate their decision to capture economies of scope and scale within the firm rather than by contracting in the market. A technological revolution in communications and information processing has dramatically lowered the cost and improved the quality of market information over a wide spectrum of American markets. A sharp drop in the cost of market contracting, all other things being equal, lessens the advantage of capturing economies of scope and scale that a diversified firm has over "specialized firms contracting in the marketplace for the supply of common inputs."[21] Although there were advantages to conducting economic exchange in large-scale hierarchies rather than markets during most of this century, there is strong evidence, at least in many basic industries such as the forest-products industry, that the advantage has recently swung the other way.

If capital markets are reasonably efficient, then presumably the market value of a diversified firm will fall when the cost of contracting for economies of scope and scale in the market falls. To maintain their firm's market value, a diversified firm's managers at this point must decide either to increase the productivity of internally owned resources, or else break up the firm and sell some of those resources in the market.[22] If managers fail to take timely action, outsiders may do it for them. Indeed, it is gradually becoming understood that the gains realized by many takeover specialists in recent years are the result of splitting up diversified firms and selling their undervalued pieces at true market worth. Despite the belief of some journalists and politicians that these gains are unearned returns on dubious financial manipulations, it is reasonable to believe that they often reflect the sharp decline in recent years of the cost of contracting for economies of scope and scale in the marketplace.

Weyerhaeuser Company's new charge-back system helps managers evaluate the strategy of diversification by providing information to monitor the opportunity cost of common resources that provide economies of scope and scale. No longer are decisions to expend resources on staff services (e.g., research, development, legal, engineering, central accounting, information processing, telecommunications) made largely by suppliers of services rather than by users of services. Since 1985, all service departments *must* "charge back" all costs to users. These charge backs are no mere allocations; they attribute costs to the originating business's use of resources by carefully analyzing the activities that drive the consumption of common resources. And they prompt profit-oriented responses because users and suppliers are now free to acquire or sell the services of common resources outside the company.

An example of how the charge-back system works is provided by the Financial Services Department (FS), a staff unit that is responsible for all central accounting activities, including consolidations, general accounting, salaried payroll, accounts payable, accounts receivable, and invoicing.[23] At the start of a fiscal year, FS charges out its entire budget to forty-two user units in the company. The charges are based on specific transactions that give rise to the consumption of resources in FS. Chargeouts for accounts receivable costs, for instance, are made from two separate cost pools—one for the costs of handling and posting cash collections and another for the costs of invoicing and posting sales. To calculate user charges for cash and invoice posting, the system and personnel costs in each pool are divided by a relevant cost driver. For cash handling, the driver is invoice volume, and for customer file maintenance, it is the number of customers on the file. Information on the cost per unit of driver and on the user's expected driver activity gives managers of the units that use FS's accounts receivable service a very clear understanding of their costs in the coming year. Those managers, if dissatisfied, are free to challenge FS's charges by securing bids for comparable service from outside the company. Likewise, the manager of FS is free to sell services outside the company.

This system provides for rational management of the resource consumption that causes corporate overhead costs. The costs are not incurred at the discretion of the supplying service unit, without regard either to user demand or to alternatives available in the market. Charges to users are not cross-subsidized allocations, based on companywide denominators, that reward intensive users of overhead resources and penalize light users. Compare the charge for accounts receivable maintenance that a Weyerhaeuser Company division pays, for instance, with an allocation that is prorated over divisional revenues. In the latter case, divisions with thousands of small-volume retail customers—the divisions that likely cause the consumption of most of the accounts receivable resources in FS—are charged relatively much less for the service they receive than are divisions with small numbers of high-volume industrial customers. The Weyerhaeuser charge-back system mitigates the misuse of resources that is usually associated with such cross-subsidized allocations.

Dennis Loewe, manager of Financial Services, feels very positive about the results from one year's experience on the charge-back system. He believes that the analyses on which his charges and the users' challenges are based have increased communication throughout the company. Moreover, he feels that users who challenge FS charges develop a much deeper appreciation of the complications and costs involved in accounting. To date, no user unit in Weyerhaeuser Company has elected to take over any of the services that FS provides.

One staff-services unit that has suffered successful challenges to its charges is the Information Systems Department (IS). Built about ten years ago around a large mainframe computer system, IS provides central computing, programming, and systems-design services. Low-cost alternatives to its service, especially distributed microcomputer equipment, have appeared in the last few years, and challenges from users who can employ newer computing and telecommunications technology have forced IS to cut charges, to lay off a large number of its employees, and to embark on a major campaign to sell services to users outside the company (see Exhibit 2-3).

The charge-back system, while not without flaws, elevates the management of corporate overhead to a much higher level of sophistication than is usually found in most management accounting textbooks. Its value is limited in the face of interdependencies and insep-

Exhibit 2-3   Weyerhaeuser Company Newspaper Advertisements

Fortune 100 Company Secrets:

How to tap into our mainframe.

You need the power of a mainframe to run your business. Yet you don't have one now or you're at 100 percent capacity. The mainframe power/PC budget squeeze can actually hinder your company's growth.

The answer? Tap into the Weyerhaeuser Information Systems computer center. We put Fortune 100 company computing power at your fingertips using IBM, HP, DEC and Honeywell mainframes. And you only pay for the time you use.

Need on-line or batch processing? Use either your program or one of over 200 of ours. Need powerful utility software? Put our mathematics modeling, statistical analysis, graphics or other proven systems to work for you.

Call us today. We'll give you a free run-down on the best mainframe connections in the business. Right in your neighborhood. At a price you can afford.

(206) 924-4200, ext. 100

Weyerhaeuser
Information Systems
Tacoma, Washington 98477

Fortune 100 Company Secrets:

How to meet deadlines at 200 pages per minute.

It seems impossible. You've got 8,600 individual invoices, 9,300 statements and 2,200 separate earnings reports to get into the mail by Tuesday. Even your line printer can't handle the load. These documents have to convey quality.

Weyerhaeuser Information Systems can help. A Fortune 100 company knows what pressures like these require: high-volume laser page printing at 200 pages per minute and the technical expertise to fix the glitches that might arise.

Bring in your IBM, HP, DEC or Honeywell tapes and in a matter of hours, even the biggest jobs are complete. Or we'll pick up your tapes, back-up data, deliver the printed pieces—even mail them for you. Confidentially. On time. On budget.

Call us today. We'll give you a free estimate on your peak-load printing needs. And you'll meet those deadlines. Guaranteed.

(206) 924-4200, ext. 501

Weyerhaeuser
Information Systems
Tacoma, Washington 98477

Source: *Tacoma News Tribune*, 2 September, 1986.

arable joint costs. But it prompts managers to think of tracing corporate service costs directly to the consumption of resources, rather than allocating them as indirect costs. And with the power that company units have to buy and sell services on the outside, the system helps eliminate the concept of fixed overhead costs. In the near future, service units that cannot profitably sell services either in the company or on the outside may be forced to liquidate the company-owned resources that provide those services.

By providing information to monitor opportunity costs of corporate-level overhead resources, the charge-back system encourages managers and employees to assess internal performance against market-based targets. This assessment is no different, in principle, than that of an outsider bent on a corporate takeover. Equally important, in relation to the actions of a takeover specialist, is the influence the charge-back system has in directing the attention of personnel toward concrete *actions*—not vague dollar allocations—that will increase companywide profit.[24] By giving people a sharper sense for the results of their actions, charge-back information enhances the benefits of participation in an M-form firm. Indeed, the Weyerhaeuser Company's top management often justifies its decision to adopt an M-form structure by emphasizing the need for *participation* by people *at every level* in decisions that affect company results.[25] Participation is more likely to generate positive results the easier it is to compare individual efforts to overall company results. The desired outcome of the 1985 divisional reorganization, as expressed by Charles Bingham, is that "each person will be given more accountability, will have less supervision, and will be more a part of the team participating in a process to make choices and to help us all decide how things should be done better."[26] The charge-back system should increase the likelihood of that outcome by clarifying the connection between cause and effect.

By changing the locus of decision making from the top, where it was located during the 1970s in the matrix structure, to lower echelons, this emphasis on participation means that employees rather than central planners are being asked to identify what gives value to the company's resources. Moreover, employees have the opportunity to show how the company can capture that value by the decisions that they make. This is demonstrated not only by the charge-back system for corporate-level services, but also by top management's willingness to allow each product group and their respective mills to source input and to sell intermediate or final output anywhere they wish. In principle, each of the three product groups is viewed as a stand-alone company. This is not a new management idea, but Weyerhaeuser executives express the idea today with incredible force. Speaking of the new paper division of which he is head, Robert Schuyler said in mid-1985:

Although we proudly remain part of Weyerhaeuser, Weyerhaeuser Paper must now take responsibility for its own results and its own destiny. We will continue our relationship with Weyerhaeuser where this relationship makes good business sense, but a fully integrated concept is no longer suited for today's highly competitive environment. It's time to take a major step toward an independent paper company with clearly drawn objectives, sharply focused priorities, and involved employees.[27]

Managers of individual mills now have the freedom to choose sources of inputs and to negotiate market alternatives with people in charge of their marketing activities. This policy was expressed by Charles Bingham:

What we have to do is to get every plant competitive—competitive in the sense of an ability to manufacture and sell products and return a profit on the assets employed. We have some very good ideas at every plant on how that should be done. In many plants that requires fundamental changes in the way work is done, and in many plants it requires a reduction in the hourly wage rates. If those changes and reductions cannot be made, then those plants probably will not compete, and we'll have to redeploy those assets. . . . We're thinking about plant-specific solutions, rather than companywide solutions. And when we talk about unit accountability, that is precisely what we are going to have to insist upon.[28]

These policies are not evident from looking at the internal accounting information used at the group level to evaluate mills and product-group lines. Indeed, there apparently has been little change in the makeup of those reports. The pulp and paper mills, for example, submit profit and loss statements for their local activities that look much the same today as they did under the matrix system.[29] And a Business's profit and loss summaries that tied out with consolidated net income under the matrix system resemble the product-group profit and loss reports being prepared today. The similarities in these reports, however, do not extend beyond the outward form in which the numbers are compiled. Very different today is the freedom that local-level managers and employees have to make choices affecting the results shown in those reports.

Before the divisional reorganization in 1985, the Businesses had no responsibility for performance in the Regional mills and the Regions had no say in choosing the mix of products that they fabricated. The reorganization changed that by giving one individual in each product group a clear line of responsibility, from raw materials to final customer, for both efficiency (costs) and effectiveness (profits or RONA). Information about costs and revenues is still collected and compiled in much the same way as before, but accountabilities for results are sharpened and clarified. It is hoped that this sharpening of accountabilities will improve overall company performance by enabling people inside the organization to connect their efforts with results.[30] With a clearer sense of how their actions affect their overall company results, people undoubtedly respond more positively to internal and external incentives. And given a chance to participate in making choices, people inside the company now have a clear incentive to search for the best opportunities to create value for the customer and for the stockholder.[31] This incentive to "scan the market" was an idea that received much attention in efforts to redesign the matrix in the early 1980s. By making that idea an everyday reality, the Weyerhaeuser 1985 reorganization reinforced the shift in company policy from expanding basic capacity in the 1970s toward forward integration to markets in the 1980s.[32]

CONCLUSION

No matter what strategy or structure a company adopts, the object of the management accounting and control system should be to trace the consumption of resources to products or activities that give value to the customer and wealth to the owners. It is difficult, however, to achieve that goal in firms that diversify. Diversity complicates managers' attempts to link efforts unambiguously with outcomes. Historically, American industrial firms have coped with the complexity of managing diversity by designing organizational structures that either create decentralized islands of manageable homogeneity in a sea of diversity or provide for centrally planned coordination of diverse parts.

In the past sixty years, most American firms that pursued a strategy of diversification have adopted the classic product-line multidivisional structure to manage the complexities of diversity. The multidivisional structure simplifies and clarifies lines of communication, thereby enabling top managers to delegate the task of managing profitability to homogeneous subunits. In most multidivisional firms, moreover, decentralized profit centers report their performance using management accounting systems that emphasize accounting measures of results, not the transactions and economic events that give rise to those results. This accounting emphasis on control over decentralized operations has had an ironic result: the costs of inputs that generate economies of scale and scope—corporate overhead costs—are "out of control" in virtually all diversified industrial firms. Because these costs are typically viewed as outside the control of decentralized profit-center managers, they are reported "below the line" (if at all) in divisional performance reports. Therefore, the management accounting system establishes no direct control over the use of resources that cause corporate overhead costs.[33] It should be no surprise that the leading problem for CEOs of America's top 500 industrial corporations in 1986 is containment of costs.

Virtually no one has tried to manage diversity by tracing costs to transactions that consume resources. In large part this is because management accountants until recently had not developed cost-effective systems for tracing a company's profits unambiguously to resources consumed in the firm.[34] A new approach to strategic cost management, however, may solve the problem of controlling corporate overhead costs. Two central features of that new strategic cost management are accounting for all costs as long-term variable costs (i.e., dispensing with the concept of fixed costs) and focusing the management accountant's attention on cost drivers rather than costs per se.[35] Both features are present in the system for managing corporate overhead costs that is evolving within Weyerhaeuser Company's new divisional structure, although the system has evolved without any reference to ideas expressed by architects of the new strategic cost management. It is likely that other diversified industrial firms yet to be studied have recently developed management accounting and control systems similar to the new Weyerhaeuser system. The convergence of improved technologies for data processing and pressures to control corporate overhead costs seems to be leading American industrial firms toward a direct accounting solution to a management problem that for over sixty years has been resolved with indirect organizational solutions.

NOTES

1. *Fortune*, 28 April 1986, 29.

2. This tendency was noted by Charles T. Horngren in his *Cost Accounting: A Managerial Emphasis* (Englewood Cliffs, NJ: Prentice-Hall, 1982), 372.

3. See, for example, the following articles from the *Harvard Business Review:* John Dearden and Richard L. Nolan, "How to control the computer resource" (November–December 1973), 68–78; John L. Neuman, "Make overhead cuts that last" (May–June 1975), 116–26; and Richard L. Nolan, "Controlling the costs of data services" (July–August 1977), 114–24.

4. For more on strategic cost management see the following two Harvard Business School cases by Robin Cooper: "Cases in Product Costing: Overview," case 5-186-290 (1986) and "Schrader Bellows: A Strategic Cost Analysis," case 9-186-272 (1985).

5. General historical information in this section is based in part on material from H. Thomas Johnson and Robert S. Kaplan, *Relevance Lost: The Rise and Fall of Management Accounting* (Boston: Harvard Business School Press, 1987), chs. 2–6.

6. Oliver E. Williamson, *Corporate Control and Business Behavior* (Englewood Cliffs, NJ: Prentice-Hall, 1970), 175. The definitive study of the evolution of divisional enterprise in the United States is in Alfred D. Chandler, Jr., *Strategy and Structure* (Cambridge, MA: MIT Press, 1962).

7. A thorough discussion of the matrix concept is in Stanley M. Davis and Paul R. Lawrence, *Matrix* (Reading, MA: Addison-Wesley, 1977).

8. The view that economies of scope and scale can be captured through market exchange and do not require internal diversification in the firm is articulated in David Teece, "Economies of Scope and the Scope of the Enterprise," *Journal of Economic Behavior and Organization* I (1980), 223–47, and Oliver E. Williamson, *Markets and Heirarchies* (New York: The Free Press, 1975), ch. 5.

9. David Teece, "Economies of Scope," 225.

10. For details on management accounting developments at Du Pont and General Motors in the 1920s, see H. Thomas Johnson, ed., *System and Profits* (New York: Arno Press, 1980), and Johnson and Kaplan, *Relevance Lost*, chs. 4 and 5.

11. The HYF program and the TAMD are described in a series of Harvard Business School cases entitled "Weyerhaeuser Company Timber Management." Three cases were prepared under the direction of James L. McKenney: (B), 1-175-237, 1975; (C), 1-175-233, 1975; and (D), 1-175-235, 1975.

12. James McKenney, "Weyerhaeuser Company Timber Management (B)," 1.

13. Ibid., 4.

14. A question that deserves further study is why the company did not adopt an M-form structure to manage diversity in the early 1970s. It appears that once computer-based planning models made the matrix seem feasible, other factors made it seem desirable and perhaps even necessary. One factor was the great power held by regional mill managers, a legacy of the company's formative years. A product-line M-form structure, even one drawn along regional lines, probably would have diminished the power of mill managers.

15. James McKenney, "Weyerhaeuser Company Timber Management (B)," 3.

16. Ibid., 9.

17. The observations made in this paragraph are based on comments in conversations with and seminar presentations by the following Weyerhaeuser executives: Charles W. Bingham (29 August 1983 interview, 19 September 1983 correspondence, and 20 October 1983 seminar); Fred R. Fosmire (20 October 1983 seminar); Donald J. Hopkins and Herbert C. Winward (9 December 1983 seminar).

18. This goal was clearly outlined in a March 1982 employee orientation session on the purpose of organizational redesign.

19. Charles W. Bingham, "Speech to Aberdeen, Washington Rotary," 21 April 1982, 6.

20. The information about CSCs is based on several interviews in 1983 and 1984 with Herbert C. Winward and Donald J. Hopkins.

21. David Teece, "Economies of Scope and the Scope of the Enterprise," 225.

22. The "free cash flow theory of takeovers" explains why firms that issue large amounts of debt to buy back stock set up incentives for managers to not only promote organizational efficiency but also accept organizational retrenchment. An excellent discussion of free cash flow and its implications for mergers and takeovers is found in Michael C. Jensen, "Agency Costs of Free Cash Flow, Corporate Finance and Take-overs," Working Paper No. MERC 86-03 (February 1986), University of Rochester Graduate School of Management, and in abridged form in *American Economic Review* (May 1986).

23. This discussion of the company's charge-back system is based largely on an

interview with Dennis A. Loewe on 23 April 1986. For more details, see H. Thomas Johnson and Dennis A. Loewe, "How Weyerhaeuser Manages Overhead Cost," *Management Accounting* (August 1987).

24. The central idea here is that people cannot manage costs, they can only manage the things that cause costs. The emphasis on transactions that cause costs rather than on costs per se is a central theme of the "new" cost accounting that is articulated in the series of recently released Harvard Business School cases by Robin Cooper.

25. The company's strong commitment to the belief that participation favorably affects performance grew in part out of a 1980 experiment in one of the western lumber mills. Concerned that mill-level productivities under the centralized matrix structure had fallen below industry standards, the company gave full control over operations to the managers at one mill site. Within one year mill overhead was cut 32 percent, and the hourly work force was cut by 20 workers. These results gave great confidence that local participation in decision making could cause a substantial improvement in productivity.

26. *Weyerhaeuser Today* (July 1985).

27. Ibid.

28. Ibid.

29. Observations about internal performance reporting at the mill level, especially in the pulp and paper mills, are based on several interviews between November 1985 and April 1986 with L. W. Christenson (Federal Way) and Gary Healea (Longview).

30. An aspect of the company's 1985 reorganization not discussed here is the effort to tie compensation to operating performance at various levels in the organization. The company's effort to redesign management and mill-level compensation programs will be the subject of a future study.

31. Evidence of an intensified search for value since early 1985 is the increased attention that mill managers give to activities that drive long-term variable costs. At the paper company's Longview plant, for instance, regional controller Gary Healea is using a local data base on cost drivers to trace plant overhead to product lines. Plant managers find such information useful, of course, when they have the power to make decisions that affect profit outcomes.

32. See the letter from George Weyerhaeuser to stockholders in the *1985 Weyerhaeuser Company Annual Report*, 1–2.

33. Perhaps this explains, in part, the frequently made observation that American manufacturers are more concerned with managing the financial results of economic events, not with managing the events as such. CEOs, according to Harvard Business School's Robert H. Hayes, "seem more concerned with the results of solving problems, but not the problems themselves." Quoted in *Fortune*, 28 April 1986, 29.

34. For more on this thesis, see Johnson and Kaplan, *Relevance Lost*, chs. 3, 5, and 6.

35. See ch. 8 in this volume by Robin Cooper and Robert S. Kaplan.

CHAPTER 3

The Anatomy of an Accounting Change

Krishna Palepu

INTRODUCTION

GENERALLY accepted accounting principles allow companies a wide latitude in the choice of accounting policies. There is some evidence that firms often choose accounting policies to reflect managements' financial reporting strategy. After a firm chooses a set of accounting policies, current accounting rules also permit it to change from one policy to another at the discretion of the management.

Reported accounting numbers are used by all parties that have contractual and regulatory relationships with the firm. Investors use accounting information in assessing the investment potential of a firm's stock; lenders use accounting numbers in specifying debt covenant agreements; boards of directors employ accounting performance measures in determining top management compensation; and regulators and politicians use reported accounting numbers in enforcing existing laws as well as in the formulation of new laws. Given such a wide use of accounting data by various external parties, ac-

I am grateful to the management of Harnischfeger Corporation for help in gathering information for this chapter. I wish to thank Bill Bruns for help in the field research process, and Ray Ball, Robin Cooper, Paul Healy, Robert Kaplan, Ross Watts, and the participants of the colloquium for their comments.

counting researchers have posited that managements have incentives to choose accounting policies to influence the behavior of these parties.

Much of the empirical research dealing with accounting policy choice has analyzed large samples of firms, using conventional statistical methods. Here, in contrast, I examine in depth the case of one company that made major changes in its financial reporting strategy. The factors identified as important in this particular instance are compared with those proposed in the current accounting literature. By examining the case of one company in considerable detail, this study attempts to provide data that will help interpret the conclusions of the earlier studies. In addition, the study identifies avenues for further research.

This chapter examines a number of accounting changes made by Harnischfeger Corporation, a large New York Stock Exchange company. It appears that the factors hypothesized in the literature seem to have played some role in the company's decision to change its accounting policy. In addition, a variety of internal management considerations, and management's belief that it was costly (and perhaps impossible) for external users of accounting to adjust for differences in accounting policies across firms, seem to have been significant reasons behind the company's change in accounting policy. Since my analysis is based on a single case, the ability to generalize from these observations is seriously limited.

The first section of the chapter gives a brief overview of the accounting literature dealing with the determinants of accounting policy choice. This is followed by a detailed description of the case study. The last section compares the important factors in the case study with those hypothesized in the literature and discusses the implications of the similarities and differences between the two sets of factors.

ACCOUNTING POLICY CHOICE: A REVIEW OF THE LITERATURE

Early studies investigating the accounting policy choices of firms focused on the stock price behavior of firms that switched accounting policies.[1] These studies investigated whether the stock market is systematically misled by the effect of accounting changes on reported earnings. The studies attempted to discriminate between two competing hypotheses on how the stock market reacts to reported earnings: the "mechanistic" hypothesis, which states that the stock market reacts mechanically to changes in earnings due to accounting policy changes, and the "efficient market" hypothesis, which holds that the stock market does not react to changes in earnings due to accounting policy changes unless the accounting changes affect the cash flows of a firm (e.g., tax payments in FIFO/LIFO changes).

Among the accounting changes investigated by earlier studies were changes from accelerated depreciation to straight-line depreciation, from deferral of investment tax credits to flow through, and from FIFO inventory method to LIFO. Researchers studied the reaction of stock prices to earnings announcements immediately following a change in accounting policies. The evidence reported by these studies is generally inconsistent with the hypothesis that the stock market reacts mechanically to the accounting numbers by ignoring the effects of the accounting changes. Based on this evidence, some researchers have argued that it is unlikely that firms switch accounting policies to fool the stock market.

In light of the above conclusion, recent studies investigating the choice of accounting procedures by firms have examined the following question: If the stock market is not fooled by accounting changes, why do managers care about the accounting policies of their firms? This literature (the positive accounting theory literature) analyzes the use of accounting numbers by various parties that have contractual and regulatory relationships with firms: namely, bondholders, managers, and regulators. The proponents of the positive accounting theory hypothesize that if there are nonzero costs associated with writing and enforcing various contracts that use accounting numbers, managers have reasons to care about the policies used in defining and computing accounting numbers. This concern exists even if the stock market can "see through" the differences in accounting policies of a given firm across time and among different firms at any point in time.

The most frequently stated hypotheses in the positive accounting theory literature deal with the effect of the choice of management compensation plans, debt covenants, and political costs on accounting policies. Most management compensation plans make the awards contingent upon meeting or exceeding performance as measured by accounting numbers. Hence, it is hypothesized that managers have incentives to choose or switch accounting policies to affect their compensation awards. This, of course, assumes that the compensation committees of the boards of directors do not adjust the reported numbers for the effect of accounting changes.

Similarly, since debt covenant restrictions are often stated in terms of accounting numbers, it is hypothesized that firms have incentives to choose or change accounting policies to meet restrictions they would otherwise violate. Finally, it is argued that, since reported accounting numbers are used by politicians and other regulators, firms threatened with increased political costs (for example, the windfall profits tax levied on oil companies) choose policies that reduce current reported earnings and thus minimize political costs.

Empirical studies of the validity of the above hypotheses have analyzed statistically large cross-sectional samples of data. Simple proxy variables were used to represent each of the factors considered important. Among the variables used were debt/equity ratio, a 0/1 dummy variable for the existence of a management compensation plan tied to accounting numbers, and firm size (as a proxy for political visibility). There were two frequently found empirical regularities: firms with management compensation plans and high debt/equity ratios were most likely to choose liberal accounting procedures, and larger firms were likely to choose conservative accounting procedures.

But today's understanding of the determinants of a firm's accounting policy choices and changes is still limited. Interpretation of the empirical evidence is difficult because simple proxies have been used to test rich and complex hypotheses. For example, the debt/equity ratio is often used as a proxy to test the hypothesis that firms facing tight debt covenant restrictions are likely to choose liberal accounting policies. Holthausen and Leftwich (1983), in a recent review of this literature, state that "further progress depends on innovation in theory and empirical tests rather than continued application of the current state of the art." It is in this spirit that I undertook a descriptive analysis of a single company to gain further insights into the accounting policy decisions of firms.

REPORTING POLICY CHANGES AT HARNISCHFEGER: A CASE STUDY

This section describes the circumstances surrounding the major reporting policy changes that occurred at Harnischfeger Corporation and analyzes the reasons for the changes. The section begins with a brief description of the site-selection and data-collection processes. Following this, some background information on Harnischfeger's business and products is presented. Next, the financial crisis that the company experienced in 1982 and the subsequent management and strategic changes are described. Finally, I discuss the specific accounting changes that the company made and the management's stated reasons for instituting them.

Site Selection and Data Collection

The search for a site started with a NAARS data base listing of companies that made an accounting change in fiscal 1984. From among these companies, I chose Harnischfeger Corporation for two reasons. First, in terms of the number of changes, as well as their effect on the reported profits of the corporation, the accounting changes of Harnischfeger were far more significant than those of any other corporation on the list. Second, and equally important, Harnischfeger's management was willing to discuss the reasons for their accounting decisions and to provide access to the relevant data. Thus, the site selection was not random.

The data for the analysis presented in this chapter were obtained from two sources. First, public documents, including the company's annual reports, proxy statements, 10K statements, analysts' reports, and articles from the financial press, were used to gather information on the company's background and its accounting policy changes. Next, semistructured interviews with top management were conducted. Information gathered in these interviews was supplemented by internal documents obtained from the firm.

Company Background

Harnischfeger Corporation is an industrial machinery manufacturer based in Milwaukee, Wisconsin. The company was originally started as a partnership in 1884 and was incorporated in Wisconsin in 1919 under the name Pawling and Harnischfeger. Its name was changed to the present one in 1924. The company went public in 1929 and is currently listed on the New York Stock Exchange. In the fiscal year ending October 31, 1984, the company reported a net income after tax of $16 million from $489 million revenues and $640 million total assets (see Exhibit 3-1).

The company has two major operating segments: the P&H Heavy Equipment Group, and the Industrial Technologies Group. The heavy equipment group consists of the construction equipment

Exhibit 3-1   Harnischfeger Corporation

Consolidated Statement of Operations

(Dollar amounts in thousands except per share figures)

	Year Ended October 31,		
	1984	1983	1982
Revenues			
Net sales	$398,708	$321,010	$447,461
Other income, including license and technical service fees	7,067	3,111	5,209
	405,775	324,121	452,670
Cost of Sales	315,216	261,384	366,297
Operating Income	90,559	62,737	86,373
Less:			
Product development, selling and administrative expenses	72,196	85,795	113,457
Interest expense − net	12,625	9,745	18,873
Provision for plant closing	−	−	23,700
Income (Loss) Before Provision (Credit) for Income Taxes, Equity Items and Cumulative Effect of Accounting Change	5,738	(32,803)	(69,657)
Provision (Credit) for Income Taxes	2,425	(1,400)	(1,600)
Income (Loss) Before Equity Items and Cumulative Effect of Accounting Change	3,313	(31,403)	(68,057)
Equity Items			
Equity in earnings (loss) of unconsolidated companies	993	(3,397)	(7,891)
Minority interest in (earnings) loss of consolidated subsidiaries	(135)	170	(583)
Income (Loss) Before Cumulative Effect of Accounting Change	4,171	(34,630)	(76,531)
Cumulative Effect of Change in Depreciation Method	11,005	−	−
Net Income (Loss)	$ 15,176	$(34,630)	$(76,531)
Earnings (Loss) Per Common and Common Equivalent Share:			
Income (loss) before cumulative effect of accounting change	$ .35	$(3.49)	$(7.64)
Cumulative effect of change in depreciation method	.93	−	−
Net Income (Loss)	$ 1.28	$(3.49)	$(7.64)
Pro Forma Amounts Assuming the Changed Depreciation Method Had Been Applied Retroactively:			
Net (loss)		$(33,918)	$(76,695)
(Loss) per common share		$(3.42)	$(7.65)

Exhibit 3-1 *(Continued)*

Consolidated Balance Sheet
(Dollar amounts in thousands except per share figures)

	October 31.	
Assets	**1984**	1983
Current Assets		
Cash and temporary investments	$ 96,007	$ 64,275
Accounts receivable	87,648	63,740
Inventories	144,312	153,594
Refundable income taxes and related interest	1,296	12,585
Other current assets	5,502	6,023
Prepaid income taxes	14,494	14,232
	349,259	314,449
Investments and Other Assets		
Investments in and advances to:		
Finance subsidiary, at equity in net assets	8,849	6,704
Other companies	4,445	2,514
Other assets	13,959	6,411
	27,253	15,629
Operating Plants		
Land and improvements	9,419	10,370
Buildings	59,083	60,377
Machinery and equipment	120,949	122,154
	189,451	192,901
Accumulated depreciation	(93,259)	(107,577)
	96,192	85,324
	$472,704	$415,402
Liabilities and Shareholders' Equity		
Current Liabilities		
Short-term notes payable to banks by subsidiaries	$ 9,090	$ 8,155
Long-term debt and capitalized lease obligations payable within one year	973	18,265
Trade accounts payable	37,716	21,228
Employee compensation and benefits	15,041	14,343
Accrued plant closing costs	2,460	6,348
Advance payments and progress billings	20,619	15,886
Income taxes payable	1,645	3,463
Account payable to finance subsidiary	—	3,436
Other current liabilities and accruals	29,673	32,333
	117,217	123,457
Long-Term Obligations		
Long-term debt payable to:		
Unaffiliated lenders	128,550	139,092
Finance subsidiary	—	5,400
Capitalized lease obligations	7,870	8,120
	136,420	152,612
Deferred Liabilities and Income Taxes		
Accrued pension costs	57,611	19,098
Other deferred liabilities	5,299	7,777
Deferred income taxes	6,385	134
	69,295	27,009
Minority Interest	2,400	2,405
Shareholders' Equity		
Preferred stock, $100 par value — authorized 250,000 shares:		
Series A $7.00 cumulative convertible preferred shares;		
authorized, issued and outstanding 117,500 shares in 1984 and		
100,000 shares in 1983	11,750	10,000
Common stock, $1 par value — authorized 25,000,000 shares:		
issued and outstanding 12,283,563 shares in 1984 and		
10,133,563 shares in 1983	12,284	10,134
Capital in excess of par value of shares	114,333	88,332
Retained earnings	19,901	6,475
Cumulative translation adjustments	(10,896)	(5,022)
	147,372	109,919
	$472,704	$415,402

Exhibit 3-1 *(Continued)*

Consolidated Statement of Changes in Financial Position

(Dollar amounts in thousands)	Year Ended October 31.		
	1984	1983	1982
Funds Were Provided by (Applied to):			
Operations:			
Income (loss) before cumulative effect of accounting change	$ 4,171	$(34,630)	$(76,531)
Cumulative effect of change in depreciation method	11,005	–	–
Net income (loss)	15,176	(34,630)	(76,531)
Add (deduct) –			
Items included not affecting funds:			
Depreciation	8,077	13,552	15,241
Unremitted (earnings) loss of unconsolidated companies	(993)	3,397	7,891
Deferred pension contributions	(500)	4,834	–
Deferred income taxes	6,583	(3,178)	1,406
Reduction in accumulated depreciation resulting from change in depreciation method	(17,205)	–	–
Other – net	(2,168)	(67)	2,034
Decrease in operating working capital (see below)	7,039	11,605	72,172
Add (deduct) the effects on operating working capital of:			
Conversion of export and factored receivable sales to debt	–	23,919	–
Reclassification to deferred liabilities:			
Accrued pension costs	–	14,264	–
Other liabilities	–	5,510	–
Foreign currency translation adjustments	(6,009)	(1,919)	(5,943)
Funds provided by operations	10,000	37,287	16,270
Financing, Investment and Other Activities:			
Transactions in debt and capitalized lease obligations –			
Long-term debt and capitalized lease obligations			
Proceeds from sale of 15% Senior Notes and 12% Subordinated Debentures, net of issue costs	120,530	–	–
Other increases	1,474	–	25,698
Repayments	(161,500)	(760)	(9,409)
Restructured debt	–	158,058	–
Debt replaced, including conversion of receivable sales of $23,919, and short-term bank notes payable of $9,028	–	(158,058)	–
	(39,496)	(760)	16,289
Net increase (repayment) in short-term bank notes payable	2,107	(3,982)	(2,016)
Net increase (repayment) in debt and capitalized lease obligations	(37,389)	(4,742)	14,273
Issuance of:			
Common stock	21,310	–	449
Common stock purchase warrants	6,663	–	–
Salaried pension assets reversion	39,307	–	–
Plant and equipment additions	(5,546)	(1,871)	(10,819)
Advances to unconsolidated companies	(2,882)	–	–
Other – net	269	1,531	848
Funds provided by (applied to) financing, investment and other activities	21,732	(5,082)	4,751
Increase in Cash and Temporary Investments Before Cash Dividends	31,732	32,205	21,021
Cash Dividends	–	–	(2,369)
Increase in Cash and Temporary Investments	$ 31,732	$ 32,205	$ 18,652
Decrease (Increase) in Operating Working Capital (Excluding Cash Items, Debt and Capitalized Lease Obligations):			
Accounts receivable	$ (23,908)	$ (5,327)	$ 42,293
Inventories	9,282	56,904	26,124
Refundable income taxes and related interest	11,289	(2,584)	(6,268)
Other current assets	259	10,008	(439)
Trade accounts payable	16,488	(1,757)	(3,302)
Employee compensation and benefits	698	(15,564)	(3,702)
Accrued plant closing costs	(3,888)	(14,148)	20,496
Other current liabilities	(3,181)	(15,927)	(3,030)
Decrease in operating working capital	$ 7,039	$ 11,605	$ 72,172

and the mining and electrical equipment divisions; the industrial technologies group consists of the material-handling equipment and the engineering divisions.

Harnischfeger is a leading producer of construction equipment. Its products, bearing the widely recognized brand name P&H, include hydraulic cranes and lattice boom cranes. These are used in bridge and highway construction and for cargo and other material-handling applications.

Electric mining shovels and excavators constitute the principal products of the mining and electrical equipment division of Harnischfeger. The company has a dominant market share of the mining machinery market. The company's products are used in coal, copper, and iron mining. A significant part of the division's sales in recent years came from the sale of spare parts.

The material-handling division of Harnischfeger is the fourth-largest U.S. supplier of automated material-handling equipment. The division's products include overhead cranes, portal cranes, hoists, monorails, and components and parts. Since an increasing number of manufacturing firms have been emphasizing cost-reduction programs involving automation, the material-handling equipment business of the company appears to be a growth business.

Harnischfeger also provides engineering-systems services through its subsidiary, Harnischfeger Engineers. The subsidiary engages in design, custom software development, and project management for factory and distribution center automation projects. While revenues from the division accounted for only 12 percent of the total for the company in 1985, management expects this business to be a major source of the company's future growth.

Harnischfeger's operations extend worldwide through a number of subsidiaries, affiliated companies, and licensees. Export and foreign sales constitute a significant portion of the company's total revenues.

Financial Difficulties of 1982

The machinery industry experienced a period of explosive growth during the 1970s. Harnischfeger expanded rapidly during this period, with sales growing from $205 million in 1973 to $644 million in 1980. To fund its growth, the company relied increasingly on debt financing. The firm's debt/equity ratio rose from 0.88 in 1973 to 1.26 in 1980. The worldwide recession in the early 1980s caused a significant drop in demand for the company's products starting in 1981 and culminated in a series of events that shook the financial stability of Harnischfeger.

Reduced sales and the high interest payments led to poor profit performance; a loss of $77 million was reported in 1982. Management commented on its financial difficulties in the 1982 annual report.

There is persistent weakness in the basic industries, both in the United States and overseas, which have been large, traditional markets for P&H products. Energy-related projects, which had been a major source of business of our Construction Equipment Division, have slowed significantly in the last year as a result of lower oil demand and subsequent price decline, not only in the U.S. but throughout the world. Lack of demand for such basic minerals as iron ore, copper and bauxite had decreased worldwide mining activity, causing reduced sales for mining equipment, although coal mining remains relatively strong worldwide. Difficult economic conditions have caused many of our normal customers to cut capital expenditures dramatically, especially in such depressed sectors as the steel industry, which has always been a major source of sales for all P&H products.

The significant operating losses recorded in 1982 and the credit losses experienced by its finance subsidiary caused Harnischfeger to default on certain covenants of its loan agreements. The most restrictive provisions of the company's loan agreements required it to maintain a minimum working capital of $175 million, consolidated net worth of $180 million, and a ratio of current assets to current liabilities of 1.75. On October 31, 1982, the company's working capital (after reclassification of about $115 million long-term debt as a current liability) was $29.3 million, the consolidated net worth was $142.2 million, and the ratio of current assets to current liabilities was 1.12. Harnischfeger Credit Corporation, an unconsolidated finance subsidiary, also defaulted on certain covenants of its loan agreements; this was largely due to significant credit losses related to the financing of construction equipment sold to a large distributor. Because of these covenant violations, Harnischfeger's long-term debt of $124.3 million became due on demand, the unused portion of its bank revolving credit line of $25.0 million became unavailable, and the unused short-term bank credit lines of $12.0 million were cancelled. In addition, the $25.1 million debt of Harnischfeger Credit Corporation also became immediately due. The company stopped paying dividends and began negotiations with its lenders to restructure its debt to permit the company to continue to operate. Price Waterhouse, the company's audit firm, issued a qualified audit opinion in the company's 1982 annual report.

Corporate Recovery Plan

Harnischfeger responded to its financial crisis by developing a corporate recovery plan. The plan had four elements: (1) changes in top management, (2) cost reductions to lower the break-even point, (3) reorientation of the company's business, and (4) debt restructuring and recapitalization. The company's actions in each of these four areas are described below.

Following the advice of a reputable management consulting firm, Henry Harnischfeger, then chairman and chief executive officer of the company, created the position of chief operating officer. After an extensive search by Harnischfeger, William Goessel, who had considerable experience in the machinery industry, accepted the position in August 1982. Jeffrey Grade was another important addition to the management team; he joined the company in 1983 as senior vice president of finance and administration and chief financial officer. His appointment followed the early retirement in 1982 of the previous vice president of finance. The engineering, manufacturing, and marketing functions were also restructured to streamline the company's operations.

At the time he joined the company, Goessel was aware of the financial problems facing Harnischfeger. He knew, however, that the company had a strong market position in several of its businesses and felt he could manage the company out of its difficulty. To deal with the short-term liquidity squeeze, the company initiated a number of cost-reduction measures. These included (1) reducing the workforce from 6,900 to 3,800; (2) eliminating management bonuses, reducing benefits, and freezing wages of salaried and hourly employees; (3) liquidating excess inventories and stretching out payments to creditors; and (4) permanently closing the company's construction equipment plant at Escanaba, Michigan. These and other related measures improved the company's cash position considerably and helped reduce the rate of loss during fiscal 1983.

Simultaneously with these cost-reduction measures, the new management made some critical strategic decisions to reorient the company's businesses. First, it entered into a long-term agreement with Kobe Steel, Ltd. of Japan. Under this agreement, as Harnischfeger phased out its own manufacture of cranes, Kobe agreed to supply it with construction cranes for sale in the United States. This step was expected to reduce significantly the manufacturing costs of Harnischfeger's construction equipment, enabling it to compete effectively in the domestic market. Second, the company decided to emphasize high-technology markets by targeting the material-handling equipment and systems businesses for future growth. To facilitate this strategy, the company created a new group called the Industrial Technologies Group. As part of this new emphasis, the company stated that it would develop or acquire new products, technology, and equipment to expand its abilities in providing computer-integrated solutions to material-handling, storing, and retrieval applications hitherto not pursued by the company in industries such as distribution warehousing, food, pharmaceuticals, and aerospace.

As the company was implementing its turnaround strategy, it was also engaged in complex and difficult negotiations with its bankers. On January 6, 1984, the company entered into agreements with lenders to restructure its debt obligations into three-year term loans secured by fixed as well as other assets, with a one-year extension option. The agreement specified, among other restrictions, minimum levels of cash and unpledged receivables, working capital, and net worth.

The company reported a net loss of $35 million in 1983, down from the $77 million loss the year before. Based on the actions taken during the year, management expressed confidence that the company would soon return to profitability. The 1983 annual report stated this belief:

We approach our second century with optimism, knowing that the negative events of the last three years are behind us, and with a firm belief that positive achievements will be recorded in 1984. By the time the corporation celebrates its 100th birthday on December 1, we are confident it will be operating profitably and attaining new levels of market strength and leadership.

During 1984, the company reported profits during each of the four quarters, ending the year with a pretax operating profit of $5.7 million and a net income after tax and extraordinary credits of $15 million (see Exhibit 3-1). During the year, the company raised substantial new capital through a public offering of debentures and common stock. Net proceeds from the offering, which totaled $150 million, were used to pay off all the company's restructured debt.

Changes in Financial Reporting Policies

While Harnischfeger Corporation was undergoing significant operational and financing changes, its management also changed financial reporting policies. These included changes in accounting principles as well as changes in accounting estimates. Collectively, these changes accounted for most of the reported profits of the company in 1984 and, more important, changed significantly the reporting philosophy of the company. The accounting changes will likely affect the company's reported numbers in all future periods.

During fiscal years 1984 and 1985, the company made the following major accounting policy changes:

1. The depreciation method was changed from accelerated to straight line, applied retroactively to all assets. The cumulative effect of this change, not including the reduction in the current year's depreciation expense, increased net income for 1984 by $11.0 million; this was reported as a one-time gain on the income statement. The company reported that the impact of the new method on the depreciation expense for 1984 was insignificant.

2. The company also changed its estimated depreciation lives for certain U.S. plants, machinery, and equipment and the estimated residual values on certain machinery and equipment effective the beginning of the fiscal year 1984. This change increased the pretax reported profit by $3.2 million.

3. In 1984, the company changed its rate of return assumption for determining pension expense. The rate assumed was 9 percent, compared to 8 percent in 1983 and 7.5 percent in 1982. During the year, the company also restructured its pension plan. The effect of the changes in the rate of return assumption for the pension plans, and the plan restructuring, reduced the pension expense by approximately $4.0 million in 1984. In addition, the company recaptured $39.3 million in excess plan assets from the pension-plan restructuring. This $39.3 million cash gain was treated, as required by accounting rules at that time, as an actu-

arial gain; it is being amortized over the ten-year period that commenced in 1984. This led to a $3.93 million pretax gain in 1984.

4. Effective fiscal 1984, for certain foreign subsidiaries the company changed the financial year ending from July 31 to September 30. Thus the 1984 consolidated income statement of Harnischfeger included the results of fifteen months of operations for these subsidiaries. This action increased 1984 net sales by $5.4 million; the profit effect of this change was reported to be immaterial.

5. During 1985, the company changed its accounting for durable patterns and tooling. Previously, the cost of patterns and tooling was expensed in the year of acquisition. Under the changed method, these assets are capitalized and their cost amortized over their estimated useful lives. The cumulative effect of the change on fiscal years prior to 1985 increased the 1985 net income by $2.85 million. The impact of the change on the annual expense in 1985 was not disclosed, but was described as "insignificant."

6. In 1985, the company also changed the pay increase assumption used for computing the pension expense from 6.5 percent to 5.5 percent. This change reduced the 1985 pension expense by approximately $0.4 million.

A number of points related to these changes are worth mentioning. First, the cumulative effect of the decisions accounts for most, if not all, of the reported 1984 profits. Second, all the changes affect reported profits not only in the year of the accounting change but also in several future periods; given the current disclosure requirements, it is quite difficult to estimate these future effects. Third, the only accounting changes among the above that had a direct cash-flow effect were the pension accounting changes.

Management's Reasons for Accounting Changes

The impetus for the changes in Harnischfeger's accounting policies seems to have come from two major events: the financial crisis of 1982 and the change in top management. Within the company, the accounting policy-change process was initiated by the chief financial officer, who first consulted the external auditors on whether the proposed changes would be acceptable to them. After the external auditors gave their approval, the rest of the top management of the firm was informed of the proposal. The role of the audit committee and the rest of the board of directors was quite limited. The board's primary concern was apparently to make sure that the external auditors approved of the proposed change. The auditors pointed out that the changes represented a shift in the company's reporting philosophy, but they were willing to recommend them, given the circumstances of the company.

In explaining the decision to change its depreciation policies, the company disclosed (in a footnote to the financial statements) that "the changes in accounting for depreciation were made to conform the corporation's depreciation policy to those used by manufacturers in the corporation's and similar industries and to provide a more equitable allocation of the cost of plants, machinery, and equipment over their useful lives." Similarly, the company explained its decision to capitalize the tooling and patterns costs by stating that "the change was made to recognize the corporation's investment in these assets and to provide a better allocation of their cost over their useful lives." The company did not disclose the reasons for its other accounting changes.

During my visit to the company, management gave three specific reasons for the accounting changes: the management's belief that external parties could not fairly compare Harnischfeger's performance with that of its competitors; the firm's recent experience with its debt covenant requirements, which were based on reported accounting numbers; and the internal management consequences of accounting policies chosen for external reporting purposes. These three reasons are discussed below in detail.

Prior to the recent changes, most competitors had used more liberal accounting policies than Harnischfeger. The company listed its significant competitors as Dresser Industries, Caterpillar, Eaton, Bucyrus-Erie, Marion Power Shovel, and Litton Industries. With the exception of Caterpillar, all these companies used straight-line depreciation in 1983. Similarly, with the exception of Dresser Industries, which assumed an 8 percent rate of return in determining its pension expense, the others assumed a return of 7.5 percent or less. Harnischfeger's management felt that because of its conservative accounting policies, the company had been consistently reporting lower profits than its competition. The chief financial officer of the company emphasized that, given the current disclosure requirements, he believed external users did not make appropriate adjustments for accounting differences. He pointed out that no clear evidence existed to show that external parties adjusted reported accounting numbers for accounting policy differences. Given this belief, Harnischfeger's management felt that its conservative accounting policies had impaired the company's ability to compete effectively with other firms for capital, customers, and talented employees. In fact, management felt that the implementation of major strategic changes for the survival and growth of the company would not have been possible under its previous financial reporting policies.

As mentioned above, a major part of the company's recovery plan was to issue fresh debt and equity to retire the restructured debt, which carried very strict covenants and a very quick repayment schedule. In 1984, the company issued $150 million in senior debt, subordinated debentures, and common stock. Just before these public issues, the company announced its return to profitability after the substantial losses reported in the prior two years. While management attributed its success in raising substantial new capital to the sound strategic changes made in the company's operations, it nonetheless strongly believed that its efforts had been greatly aided by the company's return to profitability.

The management of Harnischfeger did not believe that it was fooling the stock market through its accounting changes. On the contrary, the company took a proactive role by explaining its accounting policy changes to the analysts. The company knew that the analysts would adjust the company's reported numbers for the effect of the accounting changes in the year of the change. But given the difficulty in tracing the effects of these changes in subsequent years, management did not believe that profits in subsequent years would be adjusted. In fact, it was this belief that had initially made management worry about the ability of investors to compare Harnischfeger with its competitors on a fair basis.

Management's accounting changes were also influenced by its experience with the recent violation of debt covenant restrictions and the consequent financial crisis. Management felt that during its financial difficulties the company had not received any special beneficial treatment from its lenders when they enforced the debt covenant restrictions—even though the company had used conservative accounting policies. The traumatic experience resulting from the consequences of violating these covenants, made the company determined to avoid any future violations. To this end, management felt that violations were less likely if more liberal accounting policies were adopted.

Some internal management factors also appear to have influenced the company's accounting decisions. The company had used the same accounting rules for external reporting and for internal management accounting. The company's pricing was based on fully allocated product costs, and therefore its accelerated depreciation policies apparently caused its products to be overpriced relative to competition.[2] In addition, the higher depreciation charges led its divisions to demand increased capital reinvestment for maintaining and replacing fixed assets.

A similar internal management reason was cited as a factor in the decision to capitalize the company's tooling and patterns expense. Under the company's previous capital-budgeting system, capitalized costs were subject to top management approval, whereas decisions regarding other costs were decentralized. Since tools and patterns were expensed, these costs were not controlled by the top management even though they accounted for a significant amount of investment. As part of its overall cost-control effort, the new management felt that it needed better control over tooling and patterns costs. The most practical way to accomplish this objective was to start treating the item as a capital expenditure. Once this treatment was adopted for internal purposes, the company believed that it should use similar treatment for external reporting as well.[3]

In sum, a belief about the inability of the external users of accounting data to adjust for Harnischfeger's conservative financial reporting, the unpleasant experience with its debt covenant restrictions, and the interaction between management accounting and external reporting were the major reasons for the company's change in its accounting policies.

Underlying all the accounting changes was a reporting philosophy outlined by the chief financial officer (now president) of the company:

In accounting, there is no such thing as absolute truth. The same underlying reality can be accounted for using a range of assumptions. The earlier philosophy of this company was to choose the conservative alternative whenever there was a choice. Now we have decided to change this. We would like to tell the world that we are alive and well. We wish to tell the truth but do not want to be overly conservative in doing so.

When the outside world compares our financial performance with that of other companies, they may or may not take the time and effort to untangle the effects of the differences in financial policies that various companies follow. My own belief is that people adjust for the obvious things like one-time gains and losses but have difficulty in adjusting for ongoing differences. In any case, these adjustments impose a cost on the user. If people adjust for the differences in accounting policies when they compare us with other companies, then it should not matter whether we follow conservative or liberal policies. But suppose they do not adjust. Then clearly we are better off following the more liberal policies than conservative policies. I am not sure whether people make the adjustments or not, but either way we wish to present an optimistic version of the picture and let people figure out what to do with those numbers.

As a company you have to put the best foot forward if you want to raise capital, convince customers that you are a viable company, and attract talented people to work for the company. I feel that the financial reporting should help rather than hinder the implementation of our operating strategy. In my opinion, the changed accounting format highlights the effectiveness of our strategy better than the old policies do.

Role of Accounting Literature Hypotheses

As I mentioned earlier, the positive accounting theory literature hypothesizes two primary factors leading to income-increasing accounting changes of the type made by Harnischfeger: debt covenant restrictions and management compensation plans specified in terms of accounting numbers. In Harnischfeger's case, these two factors seem to have played only a minor role in the company's accounting policy decisions.

Harnischfeger did not change its accounting policies to avoid an anticipated violation of debt covenant restrictions. Rather, the changes were a reaction to the painful experience of having violated such covenants. Management felt that the company's lenders had not distinguished between conservative and liberal accounting policies in specifying and administering debt covenant restrictions. It also knew, however, that an accounting policy change, solely made to avoid debt covenant restrictions, would be detected by the lenders who would then take appropriate action. By choosing to change its accounting policies when the company was not in immediate danger of violating any restrictions, the management felt it could avoid future problems.

Although Harnischfeger has an executive incentive plan under which senior executives of the company are awarded bonuses based on accounting earnings, the desire to achieve short-term profit targets for bonus purposes does not appear to have been a factor in management's accounting policy changes. The company's bonus awards had been linked to the achievement of profit budgets specified annually at the beginning of the year. Since all the accounting policy changes documented in this study were made at the beginning of the year, the profit budget for each year was prepared using the same accounting policies as the ones employed in calculating the actual profits. This led to an automatic adjustment of the profit performance for the effects of the accounting policy changes in the determination of the management bonus awards.

Harnischfeger's management did expect to receive an indirect (and in its view, a legitimate) benefit from its accounting decisions. It felt that the accounting changes would enhance the company's ability to raise the resources necessary to implement its new operating strategy. The company's shareholders would benefit from the improvements in the company's long-term profitability. Management clearly expected to be rewarded for this achievement.

SUMMARY AND DISCUSSION

As noted, the analysis presented in this chapter, being based on a single case study, cannot be uncritically generalized. The following discussion therefore focuses on identifying areas for further research rather than on drawing definite conclusions.

The single most important reason for Harnischfeger's financial reporting philosophy appears to be management's belief that it is costly, if not impossible, for the external users of accounting data to adjust for the effects of accounting policy differences across firms. Despite the substantial evidence on the efficiency of the capital markets, the managers I talked with at Harnischfeger were unconvinced of the stock market's ability to "see through" accounting policy differences.[4]

The efficient capital markets literature is by no means conclusive on the nature of the relation between accounting earnings and stock prices. Much of the research deals with stock returns and not the levels of stock prices.[5] Also, the studies that analyze the stock price reaction to accounting changes do not examine the recurring earnings effects of these changes. Instead, they examine the stock price behavior only in the year of the accounting change—the period in which the earnings effects can be ascertained most easily. There is a clear need for additional research in this area. Without such research, it is difficult to present convincing evidence to managers as to whether their current beliefs are valid or not.

Even if the stock market sees through the effects of pure accounting decisions, there still may be other reasons for managers to care
about their accounting policy choices when dealing with public capital markets. Auditors, underwriters, and trustees in bond offerings
have reasons to prefer dealing with profitable firms, all else being
equal. For example, the trustees in a bond offering may believe that
they have a better chance to defend themselves successfully against
potential law suits if the offering company is profitable.[6] This may
explain why the management of Harnischfeger felt that it was quite
necessary for the company to report a profit, however modest, before
the firm could successfully issue public debt and equity offerings.
(This line of argument, of course, assumes that the legal system does
not see through the complexities of financial reporting as easily as the
capital markets do.) We currently have little understanding of the influence of the financial intermediaries on the accounting decisions of
firms, and further research in this direction would be quite useful.

It may be appropriate to reexamine whether managers do make
accounting decisions believing that capital markets are fully efficient.[7]
Many managers, in fact, seem unconvinced by the impressive evidence academic literature has compiled on stock market efficiency.
The question then is whether there are significant penalties for a manager who makes an accounting decision with an erroneous belief about
its impact on the firm's stock price. If such penalties exist, sooner or
later managers will learn what the penalties are. Otherwise, they may
continue to believe (correctly or not) that the capital markets cannot
see through the effects of pure accounting decisions and may make
decisions accordingly. At present, we have little empirical evidence to
show whether penalties exist for such behavior.

A second factor that influenced Harnischfeger's accounting policy decisions was the link between accounting policies used for external reporting and those used for internal planning and control purposes. Whether such linkage between financial and managerial
accounting systems is a good practice is debatable. But given that it
exists, the factors that affect the choices for one system are likely to
be important for the other system.[8] The opportunity therefore exists
to explore the linkage of financial reporting policy choices with management accounting and control systems.

Debt covenant restrictions and management compensation plans
seem to have played only a minor role in Harnischfeger's accounting
policy decisions. One explanation for this is that the links between
opportunistic accounting decisions and debt and compensation con-

tracts may be more valid for accounting accrual decisions than for the highly visible accounting policy changes.[9]

In summary, a variety of internal management considerations, and management's belief that it is costly for external users to adjust for the recurring effects of accounting policy differences across firms, seem to have been the significant reasons for Harnischfeger's accounting policy changes. While other researchers have also noted the importance of such factors in accounting decisions, further research is needed to better understand their role.

NOTES

1. See Watts and Zimmerman (1986) for a comprehensive review of the literature.

2. See Cooper and Kaplan (1986) for a discussion of the prevalence of this practice.

3. Internal management factors were also cited by another company that I visited as a reason for a recent change in its depreciation policies for equipment leases.

4. A recent article, entitled "Manipulating Profits: How It's Done," *Fortune*, 25 June 1984, indicates that this belief is widespread among managers.

5. See Lev and Ohlson (1982).

6. I am grateful to Ross Watts for this example and this general hypothesis. See Watts (1977).

7. Wyatt (1983) provides a similar argument.

8. Watts (1977), Zimmerman (1979), Ball (1985), and Watts and Zimmerman (1986) also point out this possibility.

9. See Healy (1985).

REFERENCES

Ball, R. 1985. "Accounting, Auditing and the Nature of the Firm." Manuscript, Australian Graduate School of Management, Sydney, Australia.

Cooper, R. C., and R. Kaplan. 1987. "How Cost Accounting Systematically Distorts Product Costs." Ch. 8 in this volume.

Healy, P. 1985. "The Impact of Bonus Schemes on the Selection of Accounting Principles." *Journal of Accounting and Economics* 7, 85–107.

Holthausen, R. W., and R. W. Leftwich. 1983. "The Economic Consequences of Accounting Choice: Implications of Costly Contracting and Monitoring." *Journal of Accounting Economics* 5:2, 77–117.

Lev, B., and J. A. Ohlson. 1982. "Market-Based Empirical Research in Accounting:

A Review, Interpretation, and Extension." *Journal of Accounting Research* 20, Supplement, 249–322.

Watts, R. L. 1977. "Corporate Financial Statements, A Product of the Market and Political Process." *Australian Journal of Management* 2, 53–75.

Watts, R. L., and J. L. Zimmerman. 1986. *Positive Accounting Theory.* Englewood Cliffs, NJ: Prentice-Hall.

Wyatt, A. R. 1983. "Efficient Market Theory: Its Impact on Accounting." *Journal of Accountancy* (February), 56–60.

Zimmerman, J. L. 1979. "The Costs and Benefits of Cost Allocations," *Accounting Review* (July), 504–21.

PART II

Designing New Information and Control Systems

A Field Study of an Attempt to Change an Embedded Cost Accounting System

William J. Bruns, Jr.

CALLS for changes in management systems are common conclusions to organizational analyses by academics, consultants, and managers. Recently, cost accounting systems have received prominent attention in such calls. Managers have been asked whether their cost accounting is up to date, told that yesterday's accounting undermines production, and promised that there is a cost accounting revolution in the making.[1] But there is little evidence that the revolution has begun. Despite a search among companies and divisions that were "chosen because they were innovative manufacturers and therefore offered the best hope for finding . . . new management accounting features," Robert Kaplan was forced to conclude that changes in accounting and control systems are lagging far behind changes in the real production phenomena they are supposed/purported to represent.[2]

There are at least three possible explanations for the lag in developing cost accounting systems more appropriate for today's environments. First, present cost accounting systems may actually meet many of managers' needs, even though outsiders conclude that new systems would meet those needs better. Second, cost accounting systems become embedded in organizations, making change very difficult or impossible. Third, because cost accounting systems are seldom

97

changed, managers simply may lack knowledge or experience on how to change from one system to another.

In addition to, and supporting, these possible explanations are hypotheses about how organizations decide to make changes in management systems. For example, Miller and Friesen have developed a "revolutionary quantum view of structural change" in which organizations need to maintain harmony among their elements of structure and therefore must adjust their structures as environment and strategies change.[3] They hypothesize a cost (C_1), when the structure is out of kilter with the environment or strategy, and a cost (C_2) of destroying or resurrecting complementarities among structural elements. Because C_2 costs will often be high, quantum structural change must often be delayed until anticipated C_1 costs are larger than C_2 costs.

In an effort to learn which of these explanations and hypotheses is most credible (or how they may all interact), I made a field study in a company that had decided to develop and implement a new cost accounting system. The study focused on the reasons why managers decided a new system was needed, the processes they selected to design and implement a new system, and the effectiveness of those processes. The field study is being continued in hopes of learning the extent to which the new system improves performance and management processes and meets the objectives management has for it.

DESCRIPTION OF THE FIELD STUDY SITE

In order to study and document the reasons why managers initiated processes to develop new accounting systems and what happened when they did, it was necessary to find a company that was already caught up in those processes. The possibility of selecting a company at random and waiting to see if and when it might initiate such changes was never seriously considered. In fact, the company selected initially presented itself for study because of internal questions growing out of (and related to) the processes and results of changing its cost accounting systems. Thus, the description of factors behind the decision to change systems is retrospective; the company had already made the decision, and the descriptions, documents, and corroborating data supporting their decision were determined by events that had already taken place. On the other hand, the interviews, observations, and interpretations were contemporaneous with much of the process of changing cost accounting systems.

A short description of the research site provides insight into the nature of the company and the stage of the process at the point my interviews and observations began. Baker Division—the object of this study—is a highly integrated production organization for a major consumer, industrial, and commercial supplier of specialized, trade-marked products.[4] Because of unique, patented, and proprietary processes, a high proportion of all the manufacturing operations of Baker's parent company, Baker Corporation, resides in Baker Division. And although Baker Division has manufacturing operations in several plants at separate locations around the world, those located in a single complex in the industrial city where the parent company was founded dominate all other locations; they produce over 70 percent of Baker Division's output. Substantially all of more than 40,000 separate products are manufactured at this complex, while other locations produce more limited lines of high-volume products.

Baker Corporation grew into a highly centralized, integrated company. Company philosophy favored extensive vertical integration. High market share, margins, and company profitability were thought to follow directly from an emphasis on quality and from consumer recognition of the Baker name and trademarks. Strategic direction and decision making were highly centralized during a growth period extending over the first eighty years of this century. Baker Division produced the products, and Baker Corporation distributed and sold them through other highly integrated and centralized sister divisions.

By the mid-1970s, however, new competitors began to change the competitive environment of Baker Corporation. Attempts to extend the Baker trademark into new areas met both technological and competitive problems. Market share, product superiority, and consumer preference all began to slip. Management reactions were varied, but they focused on restoring market position and corporate profitability. Calls for cost reduction and budgetary cost control were frequent and loud. These affected Baker Division and all other parts of the company, but their responses were ineffective in the eyes of centralized corporate management. Because of its size and its location in the headquarters city, Baker Division was a prime target for cost cutting. As calls for cost reduction became louder, the cost accounting systems of Baker Division came under greater scrutiny, both inside and outside the division. The cost systems had been developed and installed in the 1950s when manual cost accounting processes were adapted to punch-card and machine-aided systems. By the late 1970s, these systems were virtually all computerized.

The absence of a single cost accounting system in Baker Division stemmed from the nature of the division itself. While management functions in Baker Corporation were quite highly centralized, those in Baker Division were not. The diversity of processes and products, and the size and dispersion of the manufacturing complex, had allowed some autonomy to many subparts of Baker Division. Through time, these had led to specialized variations of basic, standard, full-cost accounting systems, so that by the 1980s accountants could identify many separate but interrelated systems (perhaps as many as 180) in place in the division. But despite this diversity, these systems worked in the sense that they produced costs of product for inventory purposes, and costs of operations, on a regular basis.

Nevertheless, changes were occurring, and forces were such that by mid-1984, major changes in the cost accounting systems at Baker Division were clearly under consideration, if not already underway. By the time my field study began in January 1985, Baker Division was deep into the process of changing its cost accounting systems. Managers would claim today that they are still far from being satisfied with what they have done, and they would protest that they are so unique that the lessons from their experience are of little help to others. But Baker Division is a good example of a firm in which cost accounting systems were firmly embedded in the experience and culture of the organization and its managers. This field study sought to investigate why managers at Baker Division decided to change systems, how they attempted to introduce changes, and what could be observed of the process of changing cost accounting systems.

THE FIELD STUDY PROCESS

Following an initial contact with Baker Division in January 1985, I gathered background information on Baker Corporation from annual reports and library references before I started my fieldwork. I first visited the field site in February 1985. Subsequent visits were made at approximately three-month intervals through September 1986, by which time more than twelve full days of interviews, meetings, plant tours, and review of documents had been completed.

Additional background information on the histories, products, competitive positions, personnel, and management of Baker Corpora-

Exhibit 4-1 Summary of Interviews and Time on Site

Management Level	Number of Persons	Total Interview Time (hours)
Division general managers	3	13
Division assistant general manager	1	1
Division department managers	4	5
Materials managers	4	7
Division controllers	2	9
Division director of accounting	1	16
Project manager—new cost accounting	1	13
Cost specialists, staff accountants	5	21
Outside consultant (academic)	1	3
Corporate financial planner	1	1
Plant tours		3

tion and Baker Division was collected through interviews with senior managers. The production processes employed in manufacturing were observed and studied. Information on the conceptual and computational design of existing cost accounting systems came from interviews and meetings with accountants and from reports and other documents. Interviews with managers from staff accountant to division management levels probed the degree to which managers understood the cost accounting system, the degree to which they were (or felt) served by it, and the extent to which they needed cost data in their work. Interview protocols were used, but the protocols were never allowed to interfere with the ideas, insights, or problems each manager wanted to discuss. Exhibit 4-1 gives a summary listing of managers interviewed and time spent in interviews through September 1986.

The focus of interviews differed somewhat according to the management level of the interviewee. At top management levels, the focus was most often on competitive position, organizational matters, and perceived needs for improved performance. Top managers made little mention of the use of cost accounting information in their work. Department and materials managers focused on the need for better, more timely information, and on the failures of the existing systems. The controller and accounting level interviews usually focused on the technical details of systems, existing and proposed, and on the steps under way to develop and change systems. Wherever possible, complaints or statements about the systems by managers at one level were verified or discussed with managers in other jobs or at other levels. For example, if a manager said certain information was available with a three-week delay, that statement was checked with accounting staff. Whenever possible, copies of documents referred to in interviews were taken for later study.

I conducted approximately one-half of the interviews, assisted by an associate taking notes. In the remainder, I was alone, but took notes. In either case, a full, dictated summary of all interviews was made as soon as possible after site visits were completed and usually within a few hours. The next four sections summarize the data collected in the field study process.

EXTERNAL FORCES AFFECTING BAKER CORPORATION

For much of this century, Baker Corporation dominated its competitors in product development, production technology, market share, and customer recognition. Specialized knowledge and protective patents restricted attempts by competitors to enter Baker's markets even if the potential competitors were larger and technically capable. Competitors had little choice but to seek specialized niches in markets dominated by Baker. Technological superiority, an image of high quality, near worldwide distribution, and heavy promotion made Baker a formidable competitor.

The consequences of this enviable market position were predictable. Company growth, supported in part by continuous new product development, was fairly steady. Profit margins were ample, and Baker had a reputation as a "very comfortable company" (company executive's description) with "a history of providing generous bonuses and lavish benefits. A job at [Baker] has been a job for life, with managers counting on orderly if measured progress up the ranks."[5]

But by the beginning of this decade, the competitive environment had changed. Baker was being challenged both technically and managerially by firms large enough to inflict damage on product profit margins in selected markets. In particular, significant competition began to develop abroad, particularly from Japan. Competitors threatened on two dimensions: quality and cost. By 1985, the president of Baker Corporation told a reporter from *The Wall Street Journal*, "We've come out of an environment where we were the single world leader, we had a technology that nobody else could really match, and we were able to dominate that field. The world doesn't allow companies

Exhibit 4-2 Baker Corporation: Performance Measures, 1974–1985

	Index of Sales 1974 = 100	Index of Earnings 1974 = 100	Earnings as Percent of Sales	Earnings after Taxes as a Percent of Shareholders' Equity
1974	100	100	13.7	19.2
1975	108	97	12.4	17.2
1976	119	103	12.0	16.8
1977	130	102	10.8	15.4
1978	153	143	12.9	19.6
1979	175	159	12.5	19.5
1980	212	183	11.9	20.2
1981	226	197	12.0	19.2
1982	236	184	10.7	16.2
1983	222	90	5.6	7.5
1984	231	147	8.7	12.6
1985	232	53	3.1	4.8

to do that anymore. We've got to change, and that's a very hard lesson to learn."[6]

The effect of these external forces on reported company performance was significant. Exhibit 4-2 details the changes in sales, earnings, profit margins, and return on shareholders' equity from 1974 through 1985. What these data reflect is a decline from Baker Corporation's historic annual growth rate of 8–10 percent (which it had been for decades) to one nearer to 4 percent; at the same time competitors were gaining market share, and new technologies were emerging.

As the principal source of products for Baker Corporation, Baker Division came under pressure as early as 1982 because of the changing competitive environment. The general managers of Baker Division called for a major program to reduce costs. Known as "The Effectiveness Program," it sent a new message to the entire staff about the importance of understanding and managing costs. Workforce reductions through early retirements and separations—supported by incentives—and layoffs made it clear that the company was serious about achieving significant cost reductions. Baker Corporation cut its U.S. workforce by 8.5 percent in 1983.

These data and events support the Miller and Friesen view of organizational change. By the early 1980s, external forces were raising C_1 costs—those costs related to possible mismatches of structure to environment or strategy; as a result, such costs may have been perceived by Baker management as exceeding C_2 costs—the costs of destroying complementarities between structural elements that had been effective in earlier years. According to Miller and Friesen, this condition is sufficient to motivate managements to create new structures, such as a new cost accounting system.

ORGANIZATIONAL CHANGES AND THE OBSOLESCENCE OF EMBEDDED COST ACCOUNTING SYSTEMS

After its founding, Baker Corporation developed and maintained a highly centralized functional organization. Manufacturing and marketing organizations developed independently, and a central executive office made all strategic decisions and coordinated the two functions as necessary. In essence, manufacturing's primary objective was to produce products as needed. Support systems, such as cost accounting, were developed by manufacturing, subject only to the requirement that they provide data needed for planning, coordinating, and consolidating corporate performance.

Although other manufacturing locations were established before 1900, Baker Division's complex in headquarters city has always been the largest, most integrated, and most important manufacturing site for Baker Corporation. Its size and versatility, as well as its location near corporate headquarters, made it a key element in corporate strategy. Little happened in Baker Corporation that did not involve or affect Baker Division and the complex, and vice versa. The corporation's high-margin products were in great demand, and Baker Division was entrusted with assuring that high-quality products were always available.

By the late 1970s, Baker Corporation had established eight manufacturing locations in seven different countries, but the Baker Division complex in headquarters city remained the dominant manufacturing location. No other plant matched the production levels of the Baker Division complex, and none produced such a variety of products. Because of its size and importance, the Baker Division complex was a key element in centralized operations.

By the early 1980s, competitive pressures and corporate size led Baker Corporation executives to conclude that their functional organization was no longer effective. After studying the problem they decided to decentralize operations and establish a multidivisional organization to be designed around seventeen line-of-business units, each with profit responsibility for a group of related products or customers. This line-of-business organization was expected to enable Baker Corporation to compete more effectively in all product markets; the organizational change was announced in the last months of 1984.

Baker Division could not be divided or assigned to any of the new business units. Its integrated nature and size precluded even arbitrary division. Because it did not deal directly with customers, it was not made a line of business itself. Instead, Baker Division was made a "shared resource," and it was instructed to continue doing what it had always done—produce products in sufficient quantity to meet demand.

The organizational changes, however, brought a new twist to the mission of Baker Division. Products were now transferred to the newly created line-of-business units at cost, and the cost of each product became a critical element in the performance measurements of the line-of-business managers. Furthermore, line-of-business managers now were concerned about whether their product orders were filled by production in Baker Division complex or at another manufacturing unit because the costs differed depending on where manufacturing was done. The old cost accounting systems at Baker Division were not prepared to supply the cost information that the line-of-business managers demanded.

During this period of corporate reorganization, Baker Division was also changing. Pressures to increase efficiency and reduce costs mounted as competitive pressures increased. While Baker Corporation had developed as a centralized organization, Baker Division had developed as a decentralized manufacturing complex. Products and processes were the basis for departments whose activities were coordinated by division management, but department managers had considerable autonomy. Each department was free to develop its own technical staff and many of its own support functions.

As part of The Effectiveness Program of 1983, the division general manager called for total centralization of Baker Division. Similar processes in product-oriented manufacturing units would be combined for management purposes. Exhibit 4-3 presents a highly simplified, schematic organization chart for Baker Division and its product flows. After the reorganization was complete, the process organizations dominated departments, and technical staff and support became part of the process organizations. Redundant staffs were com-

Exhibit 4-3   Baker Division
Schematic Organization and Product Flows (simplified)

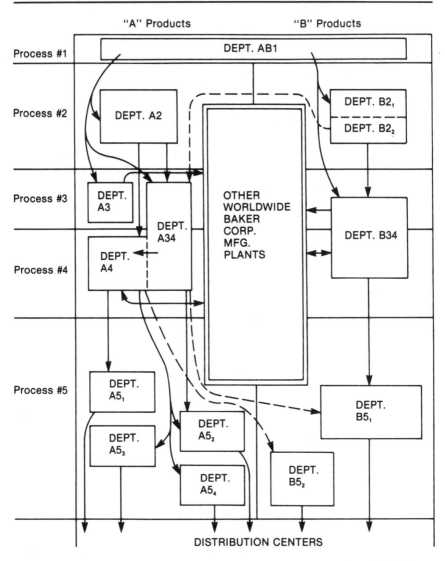

Note: The actual number of departments and subdepartments is substantially greater than depicted here. Solid lines represent major material and product flows; dotted lines represent product flows for "B" products requiring some of the same processing as "A" products.

bined and streamlined. The result was a more integrated organization that could be managed much more easily at the division manager level.

After the reorganization of Baker Division, however, the cost accounting systems remained focused on the old departmental organization. Each department received periodic cost reports on its activity, efficiency, and variances from standard costs. Each reporting period was approximately one month long. After almost thirty years of tailoring each of these systems for the particular department, the systems did not lend themselves to being easily refocused on the new process organization. Yet the departmentally oriented systems did not produce product costs of the type needed by the line-of-business unit managers of Baker Corporation.

Much evidence supports the conclusion that there was no absolute failure of the cost accounting systems in Baker Division. Costs were collected and reported to departments. Overhead was allocated to departments as it always had been. Reports were still prepared, and the information needed for shareholder and tax accounting was gleaned from the systems. The systems were working as they had for more than thirty years; but they had been made obsolete by the corporate and division reorganization at the very time external forces were intensifying the need for better management information. External competitive forces had driven Baker Corporation and Baker Division managers to change the organization in hopes of improving performance, but the cost accounting needs of the new organization form had not been adequately considered.

NEEDS, SYMPTOMS, AND THE USES
OF INFORMATION ABOUT COSTS

It is difficult to pinpoint exactly when it became obvious to managers at Baker Division that a new cost system might be needed; over many years obsolescence seems to have crept into the division's experiences. For example, by 1981 it became clear that the general ledger system was no longer large enough, or flexible enough, to accommodate the demands being made on it. Thus, the accounting systems themselves were signaling the need for change, and management initiated a project to find or develop a new general ledger. (More than four years later, in January 1986, a new general ledger system went into use; it will link up with new cost systems as they are developed.)

But the general ledger project predated widespread recognition that new cost systems were needed.

In 1983, a Performance Measurement Committee, headed by one of the division general managers of Baker Division, grappled with complaints by manufacturing managers that existing systems yielded inadequate reports, yet they were still being used as a report card on their performance. The committee sought to establish performance measures for all departments in Baker Division and especially for Baker Division complex. Identifying performance measures for departments that manufactured materials and products was relatively easy; physical measures could be related to the cost of inputs and outputs. But performance measures for important support activities such as maintenance, engineering, and technical support proved much more elusive. The committee's work did not lead to major changes in cost reports.

The clearest evidence of official recognition of the need for new systems appeared in May 1984 with the creation of a twelve-member Accounting Resource Committee. Consisting of department managers, superintendents, a division assistant general manager, and staff personnel, the Accounting Resource Committee worked under the following mission statement:

The mission of the Accounting Resource Committee is to specify the outputs of a [Baker Division] reporting system that includes financial and nonfinancial information to be used by all levels to manage the business. The reporting system should be flexible, timely, enduring, understandable and a model for worldwide use.

The division director of accounting served as chairman. The committee met twenty-four times over a period of twelve months.

An outline of a draft final report of the Accounting Resource Committee gives some clues as to needed changes and symptoms of dissatisfaction with the status quo. The following are quoted in entirety from the draft outline.

Performance should be measured relative to some estimate (i.e., standard).

Need two standards as routine features of the new cost systems—annual standard and current standard.

Provide mechanics for other types of "standards" that would facilitate quick special analyses but would not be routinely reported (e.g., ideal standards, stretch goals, past actuals).

Greater emphasis, where appropriate, on the magnitude of a cost as opposed to a dollar or percent variance (e.g., waste, cost of a particular material).

Greater emphasis in general on the control of the "hidden" as well as the obvious costs of material (e.g., inventory costs).

Promote, if not require, much more active participation by operating personnel in presentation of cost meetings.

More rigorous use of the concept of exception reporting.

Need faster and more timely reporting of costs and variances. Aim should be five to seven working days after the close of the period for divisional cost reporting.

A quality cost reporting system should be implemented for 1986.

Implement greater use of nonfinancial data and measurements to quickly judge operating performance, trends, etc.

Use data base concepts combined with more flexible systems to enhance "what if" analysis by not only financial personnel but also operating people if so inclined.

In an interview the division director of accounting summarized his feelings about the management needs uncovered by the committee as follows:

They want to participate.
They want to explain deviations in performance.
They want a system that will allow them to make predictions.
They want more attention on the use of material.
They want to know actual costs.

By implication, these user needs were not being adequately met by the existing cost systems.

As noted, despite the time and effort spent by the Accounting Resource Committee, there is no evidence that it had any success or impact. No final report was ever prepared, nor was any presentation of its conclusions ever made to Baker Division management outside of the accounting group. Although the division director of accounting discussed the committee's work and conclusions with the division controller, the effort seems to have lacked any impact because there was no process to translate what was learned into actions to improve reporting systems.

By May 1985, when the Accounting Resource Committee stopped meeting, at least three groups of managers had made it clear that better cost information was needed. These included the newly appointed line-of-business managers (whose costs would be determined in part by Baker Division), the management of Baker Division itself, and a small group of liaison managers, known as Managers, Manufacturing-Materials, who operated at the interface between Baker Division and the line-of-business organizations (the role of the Managers, Manufacturing-Materials group is explained more fully below).

Line-of-business managers sought reliable supply from Baker Division at lowest possible cost. They wanted to know actual costs in advance so that they could make pricing, product mix, and promotion decisions. Standard costs were available, but the actual costs that would be charged were not known until after goods were manufactured. Furthermore, the level of actual costs charged varied from period to period owing to different levels of operations, spoilage and waste, and overhead allocations. Line-of-business managers would have been happy with a "contract price," but that option had been rejected by Baker Corporation management. In the absence of a change in transfer price policy, line-of-business managers felt frustrated because they could not predict, control, or explain the level of their product costs.

Baker Division management needed cost information on the efficiency of manufacturing processes to assess current performance and to plan efficiency improvements. In particular, the cost of spoilage and waste seemed obscured by the present cost accounting methods. A significant and unfavorable accounting adjustment caused by unabsorbed overhead costs at the end of 1985 surprised division management. Faced with new calls from Baker Corporation management for significant cost reductions in 1986, Baker Division managers were frustrated because the existing systems only gave them infrequent, inconsistent clues on how to reduce costs further. And the absence of product costs in which management had confidence made comparisons with competitors' cost information suspect.

Baker Division management felt that it might be better to purchase internal services such as plant engineering, maintenance, and laundry from outside vendors. But the cost information available was insufficient to support meaningful make-or-buy analyses. Allocations of overhead and common costs by the cost accounting system made it difficult to isolate the separate costs of some activities, and any comparison of outside bids against internal costs was viewed with suspicion because there was little confidence in the cost accounting system.

The Managers, Manufacturing-Materials (materials managers) were a small group of staff specialists in the manager's office of Baker Division. Technically trained, and with long experience in manufacturing, they acted as a liaison with the line-of-business organizations. While they had no staffs of their own and no direct authority over manufacturing operations, they strongly influenced (and sometimes decided) which products would be produced in Baker Division and which by the six manufacturing plants in other countries. They dealt with product quantity and quality, and with manufacturing problems and also worked with line-of-business managers on pricing, product policy, and supply problems.

Because of their role, the materials managers wanted to be able to compare cost of product produced in the different facilities of Baker Division to those in other Baker Corporation plants. Furthermore, they wanted to understand the effects of such variables as run length, waste, and product specification on cost of product. In interviews these managers repeatedly said they needed actual costs, not just standard costs, to perform their function. Variances at the process department level were calculated in each operating period, but variances at the product level were available only quarterly and only after considerable delay (often more than two months). A variety of cost-distribution methods were used to associate process variances with products. Differences in cost accounting systems used by non-U.S. plants also compounded the problems cited by these managers.

To bridge some gaps between the official cost accounting systems and the managerial needs for cost information, members of the controller's staff organization in Baker Division were appointed to work with each of the materials managers. They responded to questions raised in materials management by conducting searches in cost records and performing other special analyses. In addition, a financial services group from Baker Corporation sponsored development of a computer-supported cost-modeling system that was available to the materials managers (unfortunately, it supported fewer than fifteen products). Furthermore, the cost information produced by the cost-modeling system was hypothetical because it was not linked to any actual plant cost or current operating conditions. Computer-generated options cautioned against using the information for certain kinds of decisions because of recognized imprecision.

The information needs of the materials managers were highly visible to the division manager of Baker Division; his office was near theirs, and they conferred with him regularly. As the link between the shared production resource of Baker Division and the line-of-business units, materials managers were viewed as advocates of strategies for change in manufacturing.

Since so many managers complained of unavailable or unusable information on costs, the Baker Division controller proposed development of new cost accounting systems. So far as can be determined, there was no single event or obvious decision date that triggered this proposal. The old cost systems were working in that they supported periodic reports to departments, provided product costs for inventories, and linked to financial reports for shareholders and tax purposes. But competitive pressures on Baker had increased the need for better cost data, and organizational changes had made managers responsible for decisions that required they have it.

As Simon et al. have discovered, managers use accounting information to ask three different kinds of questions.[7]

Scorecard questions: "Am I doing well or badly?"
Attention-directing questions: "What problems should I look into?"
Problem-solving questions: "Of the several ways of doing the job, which is best?"

At Baker Division, the old cost accounting system focused on keeping score; but after the organizational changes, managers needed to direct attention and solve problems to a larger degree than had been required in earlier years. A new system looked like the answer to these needs.

DEVELOPING NEW COST ACCOUNTING SYSTEMS AT BAKER DIVISION

Two steps in the process of developing new cost accounting systems have already been mentioned. The first step was the development of a new general ledger system (the data base for new cost systems); it was begun in 1981 and completed in 1986, one year later than scheduled. Budgeted to cost $1.7 million, the development and installation is now estimated to have cost over $3 million. The new general ledger system has been in use since January 1986.

The Accounting Resource Committee represented the second step toward a new system. Opinions differ about its contribution to the process. A committee member from the controller's staff felt that the committee's inputs were useful as a forum for criticism of the existing cost accounting system, even though few, if any, answers emerged to the problems. Another member, however, told us the committee was not effective because it discussed the same issues again and again, wasted the time of its members, and accomplished very little. He reported that the committee never discussed or developed any process for putting together a new cost accounting system.

By late 1984, the controller's organization had begun to write definitions for a new system (a dictionary) and to write a book on a generic cost system for cost centers. Between two and four persons worked on the two projects, which were completed in July 1986. Efforts were slowed by a corporate decision to adopt a new materials planning system in manufacturing and by discussions with corporate management about the possibility of worldwide cost accounting compatibility. The materials planning system (AMAPS) is still under study to determine how the new cost system might link up with it and whether AMAPS can provide the data to support a new cost system. Baker Division is working with other plants and corporate financial staff to see if worldwide compatibility can be attained.

The book on the cost model for the generic cost system gives financial staff the conceptual basis of the new system. Exhibit 4-4 shows a cost system development time line prepared in December 1985, but the steps scheduled for completion by the end of 1985 were not finalized until mid-1986. Division management outside of the controller's staff had not reviewed any elements of the new system at the time of my study, and several persons indicated they felt the timetable was too optimistic, given current staffing and support levels. Much work remained to be done, and there was little evidence of top management support or understanding of the effort and time required.

Finally, because of cost and personnel reduction goals, the corporation offered in 1986 a program to stimulate early retirements. The director of accounting (who chaired the Accounting Resource Committee and is credited by many for initiating the idea of a new cost accounting system) retired at the end of March 1986. The Baker Division controller accepted early retirement on May 31, 1986; he was replaced by a new division controller who had not previously been part of the decision or implementation processes concerning the new cost accounting system.

INTERPRETING THE DATA

Complexity is perhaps the most notable feature of the cost accounting systems in use at Baker Division, and because of the inter-

Exhibit 4-4   Baker Division
A Cost System Development Time Line

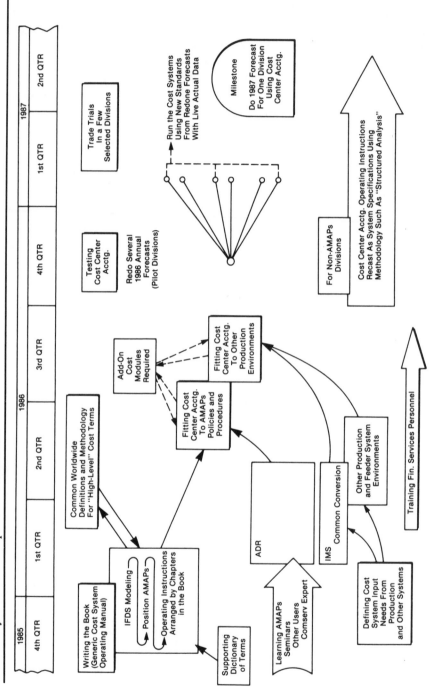

related nature of complex production and product problems, any new cost accounting system is likely to be complex and complicated to design. But whether a new system will prove to be worth its cost, and whether efforts to design a new system have been well managed, are issues that are impossible to determine at this time.

The role of external events in stimulating managers to begin working on a new system has clearly been important. The decline in corporate performance, due in part to competitor aggressiveness, is obvious to everyone at Baker Corporation. It has focused attention on cost reduction, and this prompted the management of Baker Division to reorganize in ways that were inconsistent with the design of the embedded cost accounting systems. Competition also stimulated top management to reorganize from a centralized functional organization to a line-of-business profit-center organization, and this created new demands for information on product cost and profitability. These events are consistent with Miller and Friesen's view: Change takes place only when its costs are exceeded by the costs of not changing. All of the reasons Baker managers gave for favoring a new system were directly traceable to pressures from external forces or to the organizational changes that were made in response to those forces.

Of particular interest is the absence of top management sponsorship for the new cost accounting system project. The general managers of Baker Division are concerned with producing high-quality product at the lowest cost possible. Their technical backgrounds and experience focus their attention on technical problems. They hear about and speak of the need for better cost information; but they did not initiate the development of a new cost accounting system or support it with either their personal sponsorship or with significant corporate resources. The controller and cost accountants are the primary sponsors of the new cost accounting system.

Accountant sponsorship of a new accounting system seems to have had an interesting effect at Baker Division. The cost accountants have great pride in the existing system, which produces reports on a regular basis for complex sets of departments and product inventories. Hence, their specifications for a new system are very high— "state-of-the-art" process control linked with worldwide compatibility. The old system still works (for them at least), and therefore if it is to be replaced, they wish to do it as perfectly as possible.

These latter views keep the system designers from acquiring a new system from outside suppliers. ("Baker is too unique to use a standard cost accounting system package.") They also create doubts about whether an outside consultant can be helpful; so the design task moves slowly ahead with limited resources borrowed from a staff group under severe cost constraints. The project has repeatedly lagged behind schedule. Designing and implementing any major new system is always a time-consuming process, but it takes even longer when top management is not the sponsor, the design group seeks perfection but feels little pressure to proceed quickly, and resources applied to the design effort are meager.

Managers at Baker Division apparently fail to see the diversity of demands they place upon a cost accounting system. There are many different questions that the present system cannot readily answer on a regular report, or request, basis; they concern current operating efficiencies, product costs for special orders and pricing, design costs of product specifications, the costs of quantity changes, and so forth. Each unanswered question is cited as a failure of the existing cost accounting system that needs to be overcome by "the new system." It seems obvious that too much is expected. A new cost accounting system will answer some scorecard questions that now go unanswered at Baker Division, but many of the current complaints about cost accounting are concerned with attention-directing and problem-solving issues. Recognizing that systems never serve all needs equally well, Simon et al. concluded that their study indicated ". . . *that further development of staff and facilities for special studies is a more promising directing of progress than elaboration of periodic accounting reports*" (emphasis in original).[8] The idea that special cost analyses by people who understand the present cost accounting system can answer many of the questions being raised by materials managers and line-of-business managers has apparently been overshadowed by the search by cost accountants for a system that does everything.

CONCLUSIONS

Field study at Baker Division sheds some light on the question of why developments in cost accounting systems often lag the real production phenomena they should represent. At Baker, the lag is recognized by many managers and accountants; external forces and organizational responses to those forces have made the need for a better cost accounting system obvious. But the existing cost accounting system is heavily embedded in the organization, and the task of changing the system has been left to the accountants to pursue, with limited resources, while they continue to operate a system that does meet accounting needs for external and tax reporting.

Division managers at Baker Division have not involved themselves in the effort to create a new cost accounting system. None of them is trained or experienced in accounting or financial management, each having been appointed a division manager because of specialized technical and manufacturing training and skills. Amid calls for cost reduction, the idea that more resources be devoted to developing cost accounting seems to have received little consideration. No one from the controller's organization has argued that more personnel would speed the process, and thus that organization has been reluctant to suggest that any outsider (a consultant, for example) can do the work faster or more effectively than they are doing it.

Based on our observations of progress to date, it seems as if changing the system at Baker Division requires either greater support and involvement by top management or the added help of a change agent such as a consultant. More resources than have been expended to date are required. This suggests that objectives for a new system should be very carefully drawn up, so that a successful design and implementation effort does not result in too extensive or too limited a system. Whether a firm that changes systems only once every thirty years or so can develop managers to move such a project along seems doubtful.

The embedded nature of cost accounting systems and the inexperience of managers at changing them may be the reason we find so few up-to-date systems in use, even though the need for better systems seems obvious to many managers and outside observers alike.

NOTES

1. Robert G. Eiler, Walter K. Goletz, and Daniel P. Keegan, "Is your cost accounting up to date?" *Harvard Business Review* (July–August 1982): 133–39.

Robert S. Kaplan, "Yesterday's accounting undermines production," *Harvard Business Review* (July–August 1984): 95–101.

Robert S. Kaplan, "Cost Accounting: A Revolution in the Making," *Corporate Accounting* (Spring 1985): 10–16.

2. Robert S. Kaplan, "Accounting Lag: The Obsolescence of Cost Accounting Systems," in *The Uneasy Alliance: Managing the Productivity-Technology Dilemma*, edited by K. Clark, R. Hayes, and C. Lorenz (Boston: Harvard Business School Press, 1985), 195–226.

3. Danny Miller and Peter H. Friesen, *Organizations: A Quantum View* (Englewood Cliffs, NJ: Prentice-Hall, 1984), 209.

4. The company name and research site are disguised to avoid disclosure of certain information to competitors and to encourage candid disclosures by selected managers in the research process.

5. *The Wall Street Journal*, 1985. (Reference truncated to preserve company disguise.)

6. Ibid.

7. Herbert A. Simon, Harold Guetzkow, George Kozmetsky, and Gordon Tyndall, *Centralization vs. Decentralization in Organizing the Controller's Department* (New York: Controllership Foundation, 1954), 3.

8. Herbert A. Simon et al., *Centralization vs. Decentralization*, 4.

REFERENCES

Eiler, Robert G.; Goletz, Walter K.; and Keegan, Daniel P. "Is your cost accounting up to date?" *Harvard Business Review* (July–August 1982): 133–39.

Kaplan, Robert S. "Yesterday's accounting undermines production." *Harvard Business Review* (July–August 1984): 95–101.

———. "Accounting Lag: The Obsolescence of Cost Accounting Systems." In *The Uneasy Alliance: Managing the Productivity-Technology Dilemma*, edited by K. Clark, R. Hayes, and C. Lorenz. Boston: Harvard Business School Press, 1985.

———. "Cost Accounting: A Revolution in the Making." *Corporate Accounting* (Spring 1985): 10–16.

Miller, Danny, and Friesen, Peter H. *Organizations: A Quantum View.* Englewood Cliffs, NJ: Prentice-Hall, 1984.

Simon, Herbert A.; Guetzkow, Harold; Kozmetsky, George; and Tyndall, Gordon. *Centralization vs. Decentralization in Organizing the Controller's Department.* New York: Controllership Foundation, 1954.

The Wall Street Journal. 1985. (Reference truncated to conceal company identity.)

CHAPTER 5

Tensions in the Design of Formal Control Systems: A Field Study in a Computer Company

Jeremy F. Dent

INTRODUCTION

THE quest for new administrative structures to promote flexibility and innovation is a recurring theme in contemporary management literature. Apparently many large organizations find their systems and procedures ill matched to today's changeful, competitive environment.

This chapter is concerned with design of formal control systems in complex organizations. More specifically, it is concerned with the question of appropriate *principles* or *precepts* underlying the design of such systems. What criteria and value judgments can managers apply in appraising the viability of alternative designs? What principles are appropriate in today's uncertain business environment?

Theoretical approaches to the design of formal control systems have developed through various stages. Early prescriptions were introverted (e.g., Anthony 1965); they were premised on the primacy of stability and efficiency in the accomplishment of given organizational tasks (Dunbar 1981). Later theorists were influenced by organization-environment dependencies (e.g., Lowe and McInnes 1971; Ansari 1977, 1979). Their prescriptions sought to introduce a more extroverted orientation, pivoting control-systems design around the task of adapting organizational activities to environmental changes. More recently, contingency theories have been advanced (e.g., Waterhouse and Tiessen 1978; Ginzberg 1980), with the implication that optimal design characteristics depend on an organization's particular circumstances: for example, the degree of change in the organization's environment, the organization's size, and the complexity and interdependence of organizational activities.

These developments have advanced our appreciation of the breadth of issues to consider in designing formal control systems. The point of departure for this chapter is, however, a concern that the prescriptive content of mainstream theory is still remarkably conventional; it relies on neoclassical bureaucratic principles of "rational and efficient organization" (Weber 1947). Order and coherence is seen as "good," disorder and chaos as "bad." Confusion and ambiguity indicate poor management, a facet of organizational life to be suppressed. Actions should be intensively analyzed before they are implemented. Responsibilities for task execution should be uniquely defined through monolithic administrative structures. Increasing turbulence, hostility, and uncertainty should be countered by more efficient structures and tighter controls.

Over the last decade or so, an "alternative" theory has emerged to challenge the wisdom of this approach. The theory suggests that the principles of rational bureaucratic organization are ill-founded in all but the most simple and stable contexts, for they have the potential to insulate organizational members from inherent uncertainties and change in their environments and to promote inflexibility (Brunsson 1985). Alternative principles are proposed. Ambiguity and foolishness are advanced as intelligent bases for decisions and choice (March 1976). Individuals and organizations are encouraged to experiment, to be skeptical, to act on intuition, and to pursue incompatible goals; for through such behavior they discover their preferences and learn about their environments (Jonsson and Lundin 1977; Starbuck 1982). Incoherence and insecurity are promoted to counter tendencies toward inertia and perpetuation of the past. Formal control systems should be designed to stimulate curiosity (Hedberg and Jonsson 1978). They should promote latent tensions, so that they become explicit motivators for action (Hedberg, Nystrom, and Starbuck 1976). Degrees of confusion, overlap, and ambiguity are advocated to activate dynamics and discovery in organizations.

Considerable circumstantial evidence has accumulated to suggest that overreliance on bureaucratic principles is not always constructive. For example, Grinyer and Norburn's (1975) study of a sample of U.K. firms found no correlation between the sophistication of formal planning and control practices and the firm's financial performance. Instead, they found that higher-performing firms tended to rely more on informal communications. Similarly, Haka, Gordon, and Pinches's (1985) study of sample U.S. firms found that the adoption of sophisticated capital-budgeting techniques was not, of itself, reflected in superior stock market performance.

Adopting more contingent perspectives, Burns and Stalker's (1961) studies of British electronics firms found bureaucratic principles to be inappropriate in changing contexts. Changing contexts apparently favor more organic practices: low structural-formalization, fluid administrative arrangements, and minimal hierarchical control. Indeed, Burns (1966) refers to bureaucracy as a pathological tendency for firms in these contexts. Similarly, Miles and Snow (1978) question the relevance of bureaucratic principles for "prospector" firms pursuing strategies of product/market innovation. Their case analyses lead them to the proposition that effective prospector firms act before they plan, continually experimenting with incomplete information. These firms exhibit a fluidity similar to Burns and Stalker's organic forms.

Thus, contemporary literature and research suggests two "generic" approaches or principles for the design of formal control systems. Bureaucratic principles emphasize efficiency in task accomplishment; the alternative principle focuses more on the activation of dynamics for change. Alternative theory, with its emphasis on curiosity and experimentation, stands in opposition to accepted bureaucratic principles. The implication is that organizations face choices between designs for order or for disorder, for coherence or for confusion, and for continuity or for change. To an extent, this dichotomy is perhaps false. Polarities are drawn and arguments overstated. Katz and Kahn (1978) note that organizations possess both *maintaining systems*, which insulate them from change and uncertainty and perpetuate the status quo, and *adaptive systems*, which stimulate innovation and experimentation. Large organizations, in particular, may need degrees of structure and order. Simultaneously there may be a need to foment pressures for change. Arguably, design options are best seen as ranging across a continuum, affording varying emphases to each of the approaches. This suggests an essential tension in designing formal control systems. It focuses attention on the question of an appropriate balance between *both* principles in systems design.

This chapter explores the way in which tension between the two principles is worked through in practice. Its empirical content is drawn from a detailed study of the design and operation of the formal control systems in a medium-sized computer company. The study uses a qualitative research method. In fact, the research falls within the interpretive tradition in the social sciences in general (Burrell and Morgan 1979) and in anthropology in particular (Geertz 1973). The researcher sought to get beyond mere description to develop an appreciation of subjects' perceptions of the influence of the formal control systems on individual and organizational actions. The data consist of subjects' accounts and reflections, together with the researcher's observations of organizational practice.

The chapter is structured as follows. The next section traces out some theoretical constructs and explains why the computer company was selected for study. The following section describes the research method. Thereafter, a section documents the study itself. Initially, it gives an overview of the organization and the design of its formal control systems. Subsequently, it presents an interpretation of their effect on action. Afterward, the findings of the study are discussed. The final section provides a conclusion.

In brief, the findings of this study point to a fascinating dialectic between the two principles. In some respects this organization's formal control systems adhere to concepts of "rational and efficient organization." In other respects, these concepts are systematically violated. It appears that the organization has, consciously or unconsciously, structured a degree of ambiguity and disorder through the design of its systems. This is interpreted in the light of the particular context of this organization. Although no claim to generality is made for the findings, I note that several other companies in the same industry appear to have adopted similar practices. An implication is that in this context, at least, the alternative design principle has some empirical validity.

FORMAL CONTROL SYSTEMS, ORGANIZATIONAL CONTEXTS, AND ORGANIZATIONAL PROCESS

For the purposes of analysis, formal control systems may be thought to consist of various interrelated elements.

1. *Structures of accountability*, which reflect patterns of responsibility for task performance within an organization (the "responsibility

structure"). These define the subset of organizational activities for which each individual is held accountable.

2. *Planning and budgeting procedures*, which define a set of formal systems through which individuals' proposed activities may be brought into alignment. These may result in (formal or informal) commitments to undertake specific tasks and to achieve designated performance levels.

3. *Reward structures*, which reflect the way in which extrinsic sanctions and rewards are administered within organizations. Rewards and sanctions may, or may not, be contingent on performance.

These elements are overlaid on

4. *Structures of authority* (the "organization structure"), which denote the subset of organizational activities falling within each individual's formal authority to direct and control. These activities may, or may not, be consistent with the activities for which the individual is held accountable.

By common agreement, much diversity exists across organizations in the design of their formal control systems. The contingency framework suggests that this diversity is attributable, in part, to differences in organizations' contexts. To paraphrase Galbraith (1973), there is no one best design for formal control systems: the best design depends on the situation.

Situational variables have been variously defined to include organizational size, the interdependence and (non) routineness of organizational tasks, and aspects of organizational environments: e.g., the degree of environmental hostility, dynamism, market complexity, and diversity (Mintzberg 1979). These situational variables are held to determine appropriate administrative arrangements for an organization, with the implication that *matching* the design of organizations' structures and control systems to the situational variables leads to organizational effectiveness. (For fuller accounts of contingency research in accounting, see Dent 1986.)

The contingency framework is open to criticism on a number of counts. It suggests situational "imperatives" in the design of administrative arrangements, underplaying the significance of strategic decisions in the shaping of organizational contexts (Child 1972). It implies that managers have no degree of freedom in their choice of administrative arrangements. Theories are typically underspecified.

In general, empirical support is weak (Dent 1986), and conclusions are sometimes elusive (Starbuck 1981; Mohr 1982).

As a consequence, few organizational researchers now believe the implications of contingency theories to be as definitive as was thought by early proponents (e.g., Pugh et al. 1968; Pugh 1981). Nevertheless, a legacy survives in a number of more or less empirically grounded propositions that inform postcontingency research.

One proposition concerns *organizational size*. Apparently, increasing size leads to task specialization, especially where economies of scale are available. This in turn creates task interdependence and pressures for the emergence of bureaucratic planning procedures to facilitate coordination (Mintzberg 1979).

Other propositions concern *environmental context*. Market complexity tends to lead to decentralization of decision making, giving discretion to those with specialized market knowledge; while changefulness (dynamism) is best managed through fluid, organic arrangements (Mintzberg 1979).

Further propositions concern *task unpredictability and nonroutineness*. Individuals or groups who demonstrate unique competences in coping with unpredictable, nonroutine tasks tend to acquire increasing influence and autonomy (Crozier 1964; Thompson 1967; Hickson et al. 1971). Task unpredictability and task interdependence in combination call for coordination procedures that promote mutual adjustment between units as circumstances unfold through time.

When situational variables take on the characteristics described above, theory predicts that organizations will experience difficulties in designing formal control systems. The variables suggest conflicting implications. On the one hand, size and task interdependence favor bureaucratic formalization; on the other hand, the uncertain nature of the task, and the complex, changeful environmental context, call for fluidity and flexibility in management practice. Organizations in such situations are likely to experience tensions between the principles or approaches mentioned earlier. There will be pressures for structuring and order. At the same time, degrees of confusion and ambiguity may be needed to foment organic dialogue, mutual adjustment, and adaptation.

My study is concerned with the way in which such tensions are worked through in practice. I selected a medium-sized computer company as a research site. A priori, such an organization may be expected to experience these tensions acutely: computer companies are relatively large by general standards, the industry is very competitive, and the availability of economies of scale in nearly all functions leads to functional specialization. Size and task interdependence combine to create pressures for formalization. At the same time, computer firms operate in a dynamic, fragmented market. The industry is characterized by a high rate of technological change, and customers have widely differing information-processing requirements. Typically, companies depend on decentralized knowledge and expertise. Thus, the nature of the task and the environmental context favor continuous interaction to promote adaptation as events unfold.

Implicit in the above description is the issue of an appropriate focus for the matters to be explored: the question of structure versus process. A structural approach to the analysis of formal control systems would focus on such issues as the formal, observable properties of planning and control procedures, on the relative influence of managers at different levels in the organizational hierarchy, and on the techniques used to measure and reward managerial performance. The perspective is static. In contrast, a processual analysis emphasizes more the way in which interpretations, beliefs, and actions emerge through interaction and dialogue surrounding planning and control activities; it focuses on the dynamic, evolving nature of participants' perceptions and actions.

Contingency research in control systems design overemphasizes the structure of control systems to the neglect of the emergent process. To redress this imbalance, it is tempting to concentrate on dynamic, processual aspects to the exclusion of structure. But to the extent that formal control systems are not, in practice, uncoupled from action and behavior, it is useful to recognize a degree of interaction between structural attributes and organizational process. Control systems are instrumental in the creation of structure. This structure provides a context in which interaction occurs. Rather than concentrating on structure or process as alternatives, I attempt to explore the way in which the structuring of formal control systems is implicated in the creation of ongoing dynamic interaction through which organized action emerges.[1]

Control systems may be structured to create interaction in a number of ways. By way of example, take the thorny problem of cost allocations, whereby costs incurred in one organizational unit are allocated to others. There are arguments that cost allocations should be avoided in performance measurements. These arguments rest on the premise that managers should be evaluated on that which falls within their control. Yet it is well known that, in practice, cost allocations occur frequently in performance measurements. Different explanations exist, but Vancil (1979), in particular, has argued that this practice may be constructive in fostering interaction and process. Implicitly, recipients of cost allocations are informed that other units' costs are their own legitimate concern. This creates a tension. Dialogue may ensue.

More boldly, managers may be held accountable for the performance of functional activities quite outside their formal control. A manufacturing manager may be held responsible for profit (and not just costs, for example), although revenue generating activities may formally fall under a separate line of authority. Again, this creates a tension that may lead the manager to interact with marketeers to ascertain and satisfy market requirements. Such a design would be quite far removed from convention. Managerial responsibility exceeds formal managerial authority. But it can be understood through the principle of structuring formal controls to create organizational process.

RESEARCH METHOD

My study is qualitative, falling into the generic category of "naturalistic" research (Abdel-Khalik and Ajinka 1979). Further, it is informed by "interpretive" methodology (Burrell and Morgan 1979). I have tried to develop an appreciation of events and actions from participants' points of view.

This approach requires a research method that allows participants' understandings to surface. Extensive exposure to the research setting is necessary so that the researcher may develop an empathy with people in the organization. Emerging appreciations have to be continually checked against available data to ensure that the account is a faithful representation.

The legitimacy of qualitative research has been the subject of debate in the accounting literature (Abdel-Khalik and Ajinka 1983; Tomkins and Groves 1983). Opinions are divided. In this, they mirror the controversy in organizational theory, and in social science in general (e.g., Kimberly 1981). Although closure of the debate is unlikely to be forthcoming, there are grounds for elevating the status of this kind of research. Qualitative inquiry is conducive to a richer appreciation of the way in which control systems may be implicated in action and behavior, and it allows interesting processual issues to emerge (Dent 1986). Qualitative methods are well developed.

The research proceeded as follows. Initially a number of companies were approached with broad details of the project. Responses suggested that several companies would be interested in participating. Initial discussions were held with senior managers in these companies. One company was selected for further analysis. It agreed to provide access to the researcher.

Data on the company were collected in stages. The first concern was to develop a familiarity with the design of the company's formal control system. Documentation was sought. Unstructured interviews were held with senior finance, planning, and personnel staff.

The next stage of the research elicited from line managers their perceptions of the operation of the control systems and their impact on managerial actions. Unstructured interviews were held with twenty-eight senior managers (or their assistants), covering the breadth of functional responsibilities. These interviews were tape recorded and subsequently transcribed. In addition, access was gained to a series of organizational development meetings. These typically involved groups of twenty middle managers drawn from across the organization. At these meetings time was made available for participants to discuss the control systems and their effect.

The final stage of the research involved making sense of the data. Transcripts of many hours of interviews were available, as were voluminous notes from the organizational development meetings. These transcripts and notes contained a wide variety of material touching on many aspects of the organization's operations. I have extracted certain underlying strands for presentation here.

EUROCORP

The company participating in this study is Eurocorp.[2] The company develops, manufactures, and distributes a wide range of computing products. Hardware extends from personal computers to mainframes; software covers an extensive range of business applications. The company operates in seventy countries around the world. Its turnover in 1986 was in the region of US$ 2 billion. It employs approximately 20,000 people.

Organization

Broadly speaking, patterns of formal authority in Eurocorp reflect functional specialization. Manufacturing, development, and sales ac-

Exhibit 5-1   Eurocorp's Organization Structure

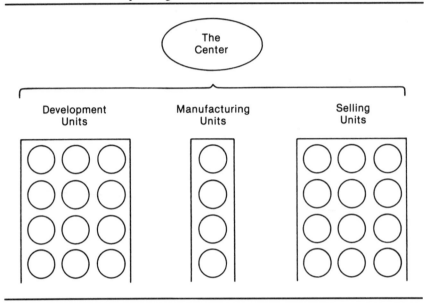

tivities are distinguishable in organization charts: sales operations are organized by territory, and manufacturing by plant. Development operations are carried on in a series of product-dedicated units. Exhibit 5-1 illustrates the patterns of authority in the organization.

Manufacturing operations are relatively small. Only hardware products are manufactured, and many of these are composed of purchased subassemblies. Typically, for medium-sized companies in this industry, manufacturing operations account for less than 20 percent of the total headcount. Development activities are more extensive than in many other industries, involving the design and engineering of hardware and software products. Some products are generic or multipurpose. Others are systems specific to particular customer types. Systems, in particular, are complex to develop, often involving many generic products and customized software. Products are continually upgraded as competitors introduce new offerings and technological advances open up new potential. Development units have staff with expertise in market analysis as well as in technology. Selling units are involved in all field-related activities: interacting with customers, installing systems, performing additional customization, and providing subsequent service and product support.

Planning and Budgeting

Eurocorp operates on an annual planning cycle. The cycle starts with a conference at which managers discuss broad competitive issues and confirm or revise existing corporate priorities. Following this, strategic plans are prepared. These document and evaluate relevant market opportunities, looking ahead up to five years, and detail necessary development, marketing, and manufacturing initiatives. Subsequently, shorter-term operating plans and budgets are prepared, expanding the first years of the strategic plan into specific operational detail.

Strategic and operational planning activities follow similar sequences. Initially, sales, development, and manufacturing units document opportunities and intended actions, and the costs and revenues associated with each. The plans are circulated to other units and forwarded to the corporate center (the head office). Head-office planning and finance staff corroborate units' intentions against central market intelligence, putting the plans together to check for consistency of intended actions and overall support for the corporate priorities. Inconsistencies between units are pointed out to the respective units by the corporate center so that differences can be resolved through direct bilateral negotiation. Each sequence concludes with review meetings at which units present their plans to a management committee for approval. These plans identify specific financial and nonfinancial objectives for each unit.

Accountability and Performance Measurement

Manufacturing is a cost center. Sales and development units are treated as profit centers. Finance operates a multidimensional accounting system, a "cube", whereby costs, revenues, and profit can be extracted in different ways. Sales territories are held accountable for profit by region (across all products). Development units are held accountable for profit by product (across all regions). Manufacturing is accountable for production costs. Budgets are integrated into the cube, so that budget, actual, and variance figures are routinely available. Exhibit 5-2 illustrates the cube.

Financial measurements are supplemented with operational measures that reflect performance against the nonfinancial objectives established in the planning cycle. Nonfinancial objectives differ among

Exhibit 5-2   The "Cube"

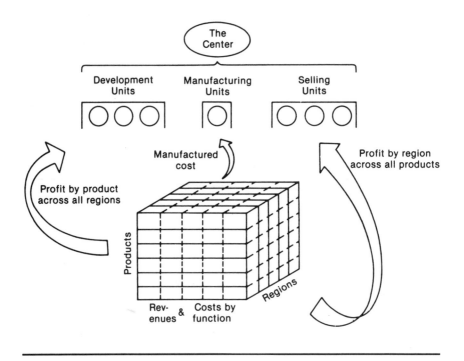

units, but they might include physical sales volumes and market shares in designated segments, quality targets both for software and hardware products, and due dates for key events such as product introductions or the securing of major orders.

The performance of each unit is reviewed each quarter by the management committee. Actual or potential problems are discussed with the unit manager, and corrective actions are evaluated.

Compensation Schemes

Unit managers receive bonuses for meeting or exceeding their unit's planned objectives. Specific arrangements differ according to the role of each unit in the overall corporate strategy; they are formula based. Unit managers have a degree of discretion in awarding bonuses within their own units.

The Systems in Action

Eurocorp's formal control systems appear quite usual in many respects. Development, manufacturing, and selling tasks are distributed across units with the relevant functional expertise. All units formally document intended actions in plans and budgets. These plans and budgets are coordinated at the corporate center through an iterative process. Objectives are established. Performance against objectives is reviewed each quarter.

Commenting on the purposes of the planning system, a central-planning manager at the corporate center observed:

Planning provides a context for managers in the various units to share their ideas. This clarifies the way forward so that all the company's activities are focused on priority markets. . . . We try to ensure that all units' activities are consistent with each other and support the corporate direction.

Similar views were expressed within the units. A development-unit controller commented:

The most important role I see for planning is to ensure that all parties to a set of actions and programs hook in, that they are in fact really committed to it. It's no good having a promotion for a product in quarter one, with sales putting in the field effort in quarter two and without the manufacturing commitment. I try to extract commitment, making sure plans are "back to back."

A sales-unit planner echoed his views:

Yes, I'm dependent on them [the development units] to introduce the products I need. You could almost say I act on their behalf. We develop plans in conjunction.

These statements suggest a fairly mechanistic control procedure whereby activities are coordinated *ex ante* through the planning process. Many managers expressed reservations, like the following one from a development-unit manager, about the effectiveness of this procedure:

Planning is a good discipline . . . but it is so difficult to predict the future. My plan does not really mean anything. In 1981, IBM entered the PC market. For the first twelve months they fell flat on their nose. Between 1983 and 1985 they became the world leader in business personal computers. What are they going to be doing between 1986 and 1990? And what about the rest of the competition?

In the early days [of the PC development program], I did a three-year plan. But I tore it up every three months and went back to the corporate center with another one.

A sales manager also expressed reservations:

What we have to do is to take a view of the market situation, how we rate against our competitors, the capability of our people. . . . We will make a judgment about the information given to us by development units. . . . We can be too optimistic about product release dates.

While planning is considered useful in establishing strategic direction, operational detail is more problematic. The market makes sales quite difficult to predict; new opportunities appear, and competitors enter with new products and services. Moreover, the nonroutine nature of the product development process leads to uncertainty on product release dates. Intentions can be overtaken by events. One development-unit manager reflected on his experiences:

In theory, it should be that you establish a joint commitment at the planning stage, and you see it through. But things don't always work out that way.

In fact, managers themselves perceive a more fluid process, relying on spontaneous interaction as circumstances unfold. As one sales manager said:

I might ring someone up in the development unit, or he might ring me up. An awful lot is just the old pals act, I guess.

These spontaneous interactions are quite extensive. People in the company spend a lot of their time managing interdependencies as issues arise. Printers whirr in offices with messages from remote locations. Telephones ring. Managers visit other units to discuss opportunities and resolve problems. A development manager described his activities thus:

I get involved with manufacturing, trying to sort out supply problems, and prototyping and testing. Also with sales people in the field. They take the view either I'm a good guy who helps them solve their problems, or I'm a jerk who doesn't. The people in the field very quickly sort you out. And I believe that's the way it ought to be.

Similarly, a sales manager observed:

When development gets to the point where they decide to go for a new product, quite what the shape of that product will be is very much an interaction between senior people in the field and in the development unit. We have a very major influence.

The planning process gives an impression of preplanned and ordered activity in the bureaucratic tradition, but this understates the complexity of organized activity in the company. While planning creates a sense of corporate direction, ongoing activities appear to be largely coordinated through informal communications among interdependent units.

This use of informal communications might be expected in smaller organizations. But given the scale of operations of Eurocorp, it seems surprising. The company is relatively large. Sales, manufacturing, and development units are geographically dispersed, and they are separate management entities, each dedicated to specific tasks. There are few routine, formal, lateral linkages outside the planning and review procedures.

The unusual design of the company's responsibility structure is important to understanding this interaction. Ordinarily one might expect responsibilities to reflect task specialization. Manufacturing units would be accountable for manufacturing costs, development units for development costs, and sales regions for profit contribution (that is, revenues less controllable selling costs). Such an approach would be consistent with the controllability principle: hold managers accountable for activities within their formal authority.

In Eurocorp the controllability principle is rarely applied. Manufacturing plants are cost centers, as the principle predicts, but both development and sales units are also accountable for profit. They are not treated as profit centers in the conventional sense of buying and selling to each other; rather they are jointly accountable for the total corporate profit through the cube. Profit is sliced up along regional and product dimensions, rather than by function. Development units are accountable for profit by product, sales territories for profit by region.

Explaining the motivation for this practice, a central-planning executive observed:

We want the units to think of themselves as running businesses. Each of the development units is a worldwide product business. They sell through the sales operation, but they are accountable for the overall business results their products produce. At the same time each of the sales territories is a regionally defined business. They sell development's products, but they have responsibility for managing the overall profitability of their region.

Overlapping accountabilities are pervasive. A development manager's profit measurement will reflect, in part, the performance of manufacturing and selling units. Similarly, a sales manager's profit will reflect the performance of development and manufacturing units. This unusual practice promotes a sense of mutual dependence. Sales need marketable products designed and made to make a profit, and development units need to have their products made and sold. This should encourage cooperation, for it is in both functions' interest to bring their activities into alignment. Equally, it should create reciprocal pressures for efficiency in task performance, for inefficiencies in one function will decrease the profit of another.

Reflecting on the implications of these responsibilities, sales managers commented on their development colleagues:

Development units' accountability creates pressures to make sure products are properly priced, timely, meet specs, are highly competitive, and will sell in sufficient volumes to justify the investment.

There are few brick walls. We have a desire to share problems.

Similarly, two development managers observed:

You have to integrate across the four functions: design and development, marketing, sales, and manufacturing. A large part of my job is driving other parts of the organization. I have to make sure manufacturing and sales buy into my ideas.

I spent April traveling around the sales territories explaining my product and selling its potential.

The practice of overlapping responsibilities does not extend to manufacturing. Manufacturing is a cost center, accountable for unit costs. In part, this may be attributable to the more routine nature of the manufacturing task. By consent, however, manufacturing is subservient to development and sales activities. Only hardware products are manufactured, of course. And these are made to development's designs, in volumes jointly determined by sales and development units. In any event, the profit accountability of development and sales units leads them to apply pressure on the manufacturing plants to be efficient and responsive.

Financial performance is measured through the cube so that profit can be extracted in different ways. No transfer pricing is employed. Rather, the system relies on cost allocations. Sales and support costs incurred in the regions are apportioned to development units in the measurement of product profit. Development costs are apportioned to sales regions in the measurement of territory profit. In principle, the bases of allocation are relatively simple. Costs incurred in each sales territory are distributed across products according to an estimate of the amount of time the sales force spends selling each product. Costs incurred in each development unit are distributed across sales territories in proportion to each territory's sales of the development unit's product.

Explaining the rationale behind the system, a finance officer observed:

It encourages dialogue. Development units want to know what the territories are spending their money on. Sales territories want to know what development units are spending their money on. It creates reciprocal pressure.

The cube generates mixed feelings among managers that at times almost amounts to schizophrenia. For example, a development controller observed:

Accounting for the matrix is difficult. But I don't think it matters that much. As long as you're consistent through time you can see if you're making progress . . .

The difficulty is that it's often unclear what is factual and what is guesswork in the apportionments. Sales people don't earn money for filling in forms, so they're not always worried what they put down. If the results don't suit you, you will tend to argue more on the apportionments. That dilutes your direction. You have a partial excuse.

More emotionally, a development manager said:

Sometimes it's frustrating that my profit includes other people's costs. In fact, I get mad. . . . But I think it's right that performance is measured on an end-to-end basis, taking into account costs incurred in all the functions.

Nevertheless, positive consequences follow. As if to bear out the view from finance, the same development manager went on:

I go round the territories to count the guys I'm paying for. In one territory, I thought I was allocated too much for product support. So I did a deal. I take a reduced allocation, and I do it myself. We both gain.

This suggests a rather cozy picture of cooperation and collaboration. In fact, such a picture is only partly accurate. Managers find their responsibilities quite stressful. They are dependent on others to perform tasks on their behalf, and not having formal authority, they must rely on persuasion. Further, the large number of units interacting with each other means that the creation of interlocking agreements is extremely complex.

There is competition among units because individual managers face a wide array of options. No unit has unlimited resources; expert staff are in short supply. For the selling operations a decision to market a product (either hardware or software) in a territory is significant. It involves training and consequential support costs extending into the future. Sales managers look at products from all the development units and decide which to market in their territories. Development managers have to compete with one another for the attention of the sales teams. But at the same time, development managers also make choices; while sales managers want customized products for their territories, development managers want products with market potential across all territories. Thus, the sales territories compete for the attention of development units. Reflecting on this competition, a sales territory-controller described his predicament:

Development units complain we never put enough field resources behind their products. To some extent this reflects our lack of faith in their ability to keep their promises. But it also reflects our circumspection, in that if we tried to meet the demands of all the development units then we would overspend our cost budgets.

The competition takes place in the context of an ever-changing situation: market conditions can alter quite rapidly; lead times on product development can be short or long and are often unpredictable; competitors may introduce upgraded products; and commitments entered into at one time may cease to be advantageous. All of this leads to fluidity and impermanence, and agreements are constantly renegotiated.

Someone from development described the experience:

I think we have gone through a learning proccess. First we assumed that things happened if you put a product out. Then we assumed that if you had the commitment of people at the top of the sales organizations, things would happen.

They may not happen. The reason is that field resources are controlled at lower levels than we thought. You have to get down below the territory level. Individual sales offices have sales and profit objectives. To an extent, how they achieve those objectives is up to them. That part you thought was yours could be traded off for something else.

Now we have the names of managers handling individual customer accounts. We go straight to them. It is more effective for us.

In summary, at a superficial level, Eurocorp's control system appears to be designed according to traditional principles. Planning procedures exist, creating an initial impression of order. Formal planning is not, however, a continuous activity. In the specific market and technological circumstances of the organization, operational detail quickly becomes obsolete. Planning creates corporate direction. But in practice, ongoing coordination is achieved through a complex pattern of spontaneous interaction.

The responsibility structure is significant in supporting this interaction. Responsibility exceeds authority; managers depend on others to achieve their performance objectives, and spend much of their time coaxing other units to act on their behalf. This creates tensions in the organization, encouraging managers to think beyond their functional tasks and to manage laterally. The atmosphere is competitive, but the structure of accountability fosters an interest in bringing diverse activities into alignment.

DISCUSSION

Eurocorp has some features of formal bureaucratic organization. Simultaneously, organized action emerges through organic interaction and negotiations. The resultant picture is one of fluidity and impermanence that may seem inefficient and even chaotic.

Recall the context of the organization. The company sells products in seventy countries around the world. Products are designed and developed in upwards of twenty development centers and manufactured in several plants. The scale of task interdependence is appreciable. At the same time, the organization operates in an uncertain technological and market environment. Life cycles are short, and products are continally being developed or modified. Lead times are often difficult to predict. The marketplace is dominated by a very few suppliers; for the remainder, it is highly volatile and competitive. Eurocorp must respond to continually changing circumstances.

Furthermore, the company operates in a knowledge-intensive industry. It depends on specialists, each with detailed appreciation of the potential of individual product technologies and markets, who are typically positioned some distance down the organizational hierarchy. Knowledge is decentralized. This knowledge needs to be drawn together if an optimal set of actions is to emerge for the organization as a whole. And new knowledge needs to be incorporated as conditions warrant it.

The task of adaptation is significant. When this task is overlaid on the geographical dispersion of the units in the company, it becomes potentially enormous. Knowledge needs to be accessed, actions orchestrated, and coordination managed in such a way that the organization preserves sufficient flexibility to be responsive to changes in markets and technology.

Chandler's (1962) historical study suggests that organizations tend to respond to size, dispersion, and complexity through divisionalization. The division of an organization into self-contained units, each with its own manufacturing, development, and selling operations, reduces the scale of complexity for any one unit to more manageable proportions; this facilitates prompt adaptation by each unit to its environment. There are reasons why this does not occur in general in the computer industry. One reason concerns the economies of scale available in nearly all functions; the creation of self-contained units would likely be uneconomic. Another reason is product interdependence. Typically, business customers require "solutions": hardware and software products working together in specialized configurations. Product compatability is perceived to be competitively important, and divisionalization could lead to disparate product technologies.

Thus Eurocorp is an integrated company operating in a changing technological and market context. The only point at which activities come together in a formal sense is at the corporate center. Yet knowledge about individual markets, customers' information-processing needs, and emerging technologies is dispersed and fragmented.

Galbraith (1973) analyzed various ways in which organizations attempt to manage this situation. As alternatives to divisionalization (structuring self-containment), Galbraith suggested three possibilities. The first one uses hierarchical information-transmission processes, so that knowledge reaches the corporate center. The center then uses this knowledge to prescribe appropriate actions for each unit. This centralized approach relies on communication channels that match the vertical chain of command. Information is drawn up this chain, integrated at the center, and disseminated back down. The second possibility relies on lateral flows of information, so that tasks are coordinated through direct communications between interdependent units. Formal procedures for facilitating this include the appointment of liaison officers, or task forces and committees, and/or the institutionalization of matrix ("two-hat") responsibilities. The third possibility partially uncouples tasks through the creation of slack resources. Planned allowances for unforeseen circumstances reduce the degree of task interdependence, and hence, the requirement for ongoing coordination and communication.

All these responses can be observed in Eurocorp. Central review procedures correspond to hierarchical information transmission. Opportunities and intentions are documented in plans that are forwarded to the corporate center. Performance is reviewed at the center. This permits a degree of central coordination. Formal lateral information transmission occurs through the circulation of plans and through standing committees. In addition, task forces are often assembled around specific issues with cross-functional implications (such as product introductions). Further, managers make allowances for unforeseen circumstances—for example, in scheduling product developments and forecasting production requirements.

None of these responses appears to be sufficient to match the organization's situation. Slack resources still leave appreciable task interdependence. The formal planning system is useful for clarifying objectives and priorities, but the rate of change in markets and the nonroutine nature of development activities causes operational detail to become outdated. Task forces and standing committees facilitate (formal) lateral communications, but the requisite number of contact points within the organization is enormous; it is seldom that all those affected are involved.

In the absence of adequate formalized procedures, the organization relies extensively on informal communications to achieve ongoing coordination. People with an interest in specific outcomes contact each other spontaneously as circumstances evolve. To a large extent the informal interactions reflect senior management intentions. When issues get escalated to the corporate center, there is a noticeable tendency to push them back down for direct bilateral resolution.

This process *is* quite inefficient. It consumes a lot of management time and energy. Managers themselves feel that this time is often not spent as productively as it might be. It also introduces stress. Without formal authority over other units, managers have to persuade. Sometimes managers are suspicious that agreements may not be implemented. Frictions emerge. It is not obvious, however, that the alternatives would be any less inefficient. The uncoupling of interdependent tasks through the creation of increased slack would have adverse profit implications. The planning system is already quite rigorous in Eurocorp. These procedures are costly to operate. Increased reliance on these procedures would necessitate continual replanning to avoid decay. This could be prohibitively expensive. And the scale of interdependencies indicates that the structuring of all embracing lateral relationships in a formal matrix design would be difficult to manage.

These alternatives might not only be less efficient, but also less effective. A huge amount of qualitative information is transmitted through Eurocorp's informal interactions. Managers communicate uncertainties. They sense each other's depth of knowledge and confidence through interpersonal contact. Increased reliance on formal channels of communication could reduce the effectiveness of decisions and actions. Information flowing through formal channels typically deteriorates because of filtering, bias, transmission delay, and random errors. Subjective inferences are drawn from ambiguous evidence; formal systems transform these inferences into organizational "facts"; these "facts" often shape organizational choices with little recognition of the underlying equivocalities. Hierarchical planning procedures that consolidate information into increasing levels of generality are particularly prone to this effect. Moreover, formalized decision processes cannot be instantaneous; and given the distribution of knowledge in Eurocorp, iterations would be inevitable. Actions might be based on outdated and incomplete assumptions.

It is possible, then, that Eurocorp's curious mixture of formal procedures and informal spontaneous interaction is appropriate to its organization context. The formal planning process clarifies broad intentions. Thereafter, spontaneous interactions facilitate prompt responses to emerging conditions. Since these interactions involve people who are close to the knowledge base, the quality of decisions and actions is likely to be high, and responses immediate. The use of informal communications may seem to be at odds with the prevailing bureaucratic wisdom, but it is at least consistent with the findings of Grinyer and Norburn (1975) and Burns and Stalker (1961) noted earlier.

In the light of management practice at Eurocorp, the structuring of responsibilities is particularly interesting. The principle of controllability underlies almost all conventional prescriptions for performance measurement. Arguably, controllability is inappropriate in Eurocorp's context. Conventional performance measurements could foster insularity and a preoccupation with the efficiency of local functional tasks to the exclusion of their implications for other units' activities. Applying the controllability principle to development units, for example, would make them accountable for the costs of product development per se. This could concentrate managers' attentions on the efficiency of their development activities. But it is less than clear that they would be encouraged to respond to emerging market requirements. Product modifications are costly. Quite conceivably there would be incentives to continue with planned activities, although these might have ceased to be appropriate. Application of the controllability principle across the organization could foster disintegration and inhibit adaptation as each unit sought to enhance the efficiency of its own activities in isolation.

In fact, it may be that the controllability principle is only appropriate to centralized management practice. For it necessarily absolves unit managers of the responsibility for adapting to changed external circumstances. It implicitly throws this responsibility up to the center.

Eurocorp decentralizes the responsibility for ongoing adaptation and integration. Management accountabilities support this decentralization. Sales and development managers' responsibilities extend beyond the efficiency of functional tasks to reflect the organization's success in engineering responses to emerging market requirements. Since no unit can effect these responses completely, the organic interaction on which the organization depends is promoted.

Within the organization, opinions are divided on the desirability of Eurocorp's management practice. At the corporate center there are pressures from some quarters for more order and a greater reliance on formal planning procedures. Some feel that the potential of the formal systems is not fully realized. These feelings are shared by others in the units. The perpetual uncertainty surrounding tasks and markets is clearly disconcerting for people in the organization. Planning is seen as a way of reducing this uncertainty and as a means to stabilize the future. Moreover, concerns are expressed over the ambiguity of managerial responsibilities. When performance differs from expectations, responsibility is typically spread across various units. Some staff at the corporate center find this ambiguity frustrating. Pinpointing accountability is difficult. Equally, staff in the units sometimes feel they do not get the cooperation they need from other units and express irritation that their performance measures reflect activities beyond their formal control.

Others in the organization acknowledge these concerns but argue that existing arrangements confer positive benefits. The context of the organization is intrinsically changeful. Existing arrangements draw these changes into the organization and promote responses. Fluidity and impermanence is disconcerting, but inevitable. The design of the formal control systems creates tensions, but this motivates managers to look for solutions. While the process through which activity emerges may appear chaotic, it is in fact quite controlled. The planning process produces clear financial and nonfinancial objectives for each unit. The assignment of responsibilities leads to predictable patterns of behavior as managers attempt to achieve these objectives. To succeed in entrepreneurial ventures, managers need to enlist the support of other units. Checks and balances exist. But the system permits a degree of autonomy. In a sense, the formal control systems are structured so that integration and adaptation become systemic, rather than being imposed. This makes managerial responsibilities onerous and stressful, but not dysfunctional in this company's context.

CONCLUSION

Contemporary literature suggests two different principles for the design of formal control systems in complex organizations. Extant wisdom relies on bureaucratic traditions. An alternative wisdom places emphasis on the activation of dynamics for change. This chapter reports a study undertaken to explore the way in which tension between these principles is resolved in practice.

The findings of the study point to a dialectic between the two principles. Formal bureaucratic practices are in evidence in the company studied. But these practices appear to be insufficient in the specific market and technological circumstances of the organization. Ongoing coordination and adaptation is achieved through informal interaction. The design of the company's control systems promotes this interaction for it creates dynamic pressures within the organization. The resulting impression is one of impermanence and fluidity.

The extent to which this pattern is to be found in other organizations must be the subject of further investigation. A priori, it seems reasonable to suggest that the efficiency of this management style is likely to be dependent on context. In more stable environments with more routine tasks, bureaucratic practices may be more effective.

Among computer companies, however, Eurocorp's practices are apparently not unique. Following this study, specific inquiries were made to five other companies involved either centrally or peripherally in the computing industry. Respondents indicated that all these companies have predominantly functional organization structures. All claimed to have rigorous planning procedures, but all articulated the need for responsiveness and initiative outside these formal procedures. Each of these companies holds development units accountable for profit (sometimes in conjunction with manufacturing). This probably reflects the importance of development activities in this industry. But in two companies, executives described overlapping profit accountabilities of the type found in Eurocorp. Detailed studies are necessary in each case to uncover the effect of these practices on managerial actions and organizational process. But this does suggest that in this industry control-systems design differs from that prescribed by convention.

Raising general implications on the basis of the evidence presented in this paper is inevitably problematic, for the data relates to only one organization. The evidence, however, points to the empirical validity of the alternative principle for systems design, at least in specific circumstances. The prescriptive content of mainstream theory in control-systems design is premised on an assumption that order and coherence are desirable attributes of organizational activities. This chapter traces the functionality of confusion and ambiguity as well. This more processual perspective on control-systems design can usefully enter into the mainstream research agenda.

NOTES

1. In this connection, it is noteworthy that the pioneering contingency studies of organizations' structures by Burns and Stalker (1961) and Lawrence and Lorsch (1967) both display a high processual content. It is also pertinent that a major theme for contemporary research in social theory concerns the role of process in the creation and recreation of structures (Giddens 1979).

2. The company's name has been disguised.

REFERENCES

Abdel-Khalik, A. R., and Ajinka, B. B. 1979. *Empirical Research in Accounting*, American Accounting Association.

———. 1983. "An Evaluation of 'The Everyday Accountant and Researching his Reality.'" *Accounting, Organizations and Society* 8: 375–84.

Ansari, S. 1977. "An Integrated Approach to Control Systems Design." *Accounting, Organizations and Society* 2: 101–12.

———1979. "Towards an Open Systems Approach to Budgeting." *Accounting, Organizations and Society* 4: 149–162.

Anthony, R. N. 1965. *Planning and Control Systems: A Framework for Analysis*. Boston: Division of Research, Harvard Business School.

Brunsson, N. 1985. *The Irrational Organization*. New York: Wiley.

Burns, T., and Stalker, G. M. 1961. *The Management of Innovation*. London: Tavistock.

Burns, T. 1966. Preface to Burns, T., and Stalker, G. M. *The Management of Innovation*. 2d ed. London: Tavistock.

Burrell, G., and Morgan, G. 1979. *Sociological Paradigms & Organizational Analysis*. London: Heinemann.

Chandler, A. D., Jr. 1966. *Strategy and Structure*. Cambridge, MA: MIT Press.

Child, J. 1972. "Organizational Structure, Environment & Performance: The Role of Strategic Choice." *Sociology* 6: 2–22.

Crozier, M. 1964. *The Bureaucratic Phenomenon*. Chicago: University of Chicago Press.

Dent, J. F. 1986. "Organizational Research in Accounting: Perspectives, Issues and a Commentary." In *Research & Current Issues in Management Accounting*, edited by M. Bromwich and A. G. Hopwood. London: Pitman.

Dunbar, R. L. M. 1981. "Designs for Organizational Control." In *Handbook of Organizational Design*. Vol. 2. Edited by P. C. Nystrom and W. H. Starbuck. New York: Oxford University Press.

Galbraith, J. R. 1973. *Designing Complex Organizations*. Reading, MA: Addison-Wesley.

Geertz, C. 1973. *The Interpretation of Cultures*. New York: Basic Books.

Giddens, A. 1979. *Central Problems in Social Theory*. New York: Macmillan.

Ginzberg, M. J. 1980. "An Organizational Contingencies View of Accounting and Information Systems Implementation." *Accounting, Organizations and Society* 5: 369–82.

Grinyer, P. H., and Norburn, D. 1975. "Planning for Existing Markets: Perceptions of Executives & Financial Performance." *Journal of the Royal Statistical Society*, Series A, 138: 70–97.

Haka, S. F.; Gordon, L. A.; and Pinches, G. E. 1985. "Sophisticated Capital Budgeting Techniques & Firm Performance." *Accounting Review* 60: 651–69.

Hedberg, B., and Jonsson, S. 1978. "Designing Semi-confusing Information Systems for Organizations in Changing Environments." *Accounting, Organizations and Society* 3: 47–65.

Hedberg, B.; Nystrom, P. C.; and Starbuck, W. H. 1976. "Camping on Seesaws: Prescriptions for a Self-designing Organization." *Administrative Science Quarterly* 21: 41–65.

Hickson, D. J.; Hinings, C. R.; Lee, C. A.; Schneck, R. E.; and Pennings, J. M. 1969. "A 'Strategic Contingencies' Theory of IntraOrganizational Power." *Administrative Science Quarterly* 16: 216–29.

Jonsson, S., and Lundin, R. A. 1977. "Myths & Wishful Thinking as Management Tools." In *Prescriptive Models of Organization* edited by P. C. Nystrom and W. H. Starbuck. Amsterdam: North-Holland.

Katz, D., and Kahn, R. L. 1978. *The Social Psychology of Organizations.* 2d ed. New York: Wiley-Interscience.

Kimberly, J. R. 1981. "Appraising Organization Design Theories." In *Perspectives on Organization Designs & Behaviour* edited by A. H. Van der Ven and W. F. Joyce. New York: Wiley-Interscience.

Lawrence, P. R., and Lorsch, J. W. 1967. *Organization and Environment: Managing Differentiation and Integration.* Boston: Division of Research, Harvard Business School.

Lowe, E. A., and McInnes, J. M. 1971. "Control in Socio-Economic Organizations: A Rationale for the Design of Management Control Systems." *Journal of Management Studies* 8: 213–27.

March, J. G. 1976. "The Technology of Foolishness." In *Ambiguity & Choice in Organization* edited by J. G. March and J. P. Olson. Bergen: Universitet forlaget.

Miles, R. E., and Snow, C. C. 1978. *Organizational Strategy, Structure & Process.* New York: McGraw-Hill.

Mintzberg, H. 1979. *The Structuring of Organizations.* Englewood Cliffs, NJ: Prentice-Hall.

Mohr, L. B. 1982. *Explaining Organizational Behaviour.* San Francisco: Jossey Bass.

Pugh, D. S.; Hickson, D. J.; Hinings, C. R.; and Turner, C. 1969. "The Context of Organization Structures." *Administrative Science Quarterly* 14: 91–114.

Pugh, D. S. 1981. "The Aston Program of Research: Retrospect & Prospect." In *Perspectives on Organization Design & Behaviour* edited by A. H. Van der Ven and W. F. Joyce. New York: Wiley-Interscience.

Starbuck, W. H. 1981. "A Trip to View the Elephants & Rattlesnakes in the Garden of Aston." In *Perspectives on Organization Design & Behaviour* edited by A. H. Van der Ven and W. F. Joyce. New York: Wiley-Interscience.

———. 1982. "Congealing Oil: Inventing Ideologies to Justify Acting Ideologies Out." *Journal of Management Studies* 19: 3–27.

Thompson, J. D. 1962. *Organizations in Action.* New York: McGraw-Hill.

Tomkins, C., and Groves, R. 1983. "The Everyday Accountant & Researching his Reality." *Accounting, Organizations and Society* 8: 407–15.

Vancil, R. F. 1979. *Decentralization: Managerial Ambiguity by Design.* Homewood, IL: Irwin.

Waterhouse, J. H., and Tiessen, P. 1978. "A Contingency Framework for Management Accounting Systems Research." *Accounting, Organizations and Society* 3: 65–76.

Weber, M. 1947. *The Theory of Social & Economic Organization.* New York: Collier-Macmillan.

CHAPTER 6

Organization, Information, and People:
A Participant Observation
of a MIS-Carriage

Hein Schreuder

THIS chapter reports on a research project that was initially conceived as a case study of the design and implementation of a management information system (MIS) in an automobile company. During the period of investigation, however, two attempts of the firm to start up the MIS-design phase failed. The author has been a participant-observer of this process. Consequently, the project turned into a case study of the factors surrounding and potentially explaining this particular MIS-carriage.

The research strategy resembles the recommendations given by Mintzberg (1979a) for "direct research." It has been "as purely descriptive as we have been able to make it" and "has relied on simple—in a sense, inelegant—methodologies" (Mintzberg 1979a, 583). These methods are more appropriate to "generate theories, ideas, and hypotheses rather than test them" (Weick 1984, 112). This chapter therefore aims at providing a rich description of the case and at elaborating some ideas that may be taken up in further research.

The paper is organized as follows. First, some background information and a general introduction to the case are given. Then, the

The author thanks Bas Koene for his research assistance and Volvo Car B.V. for its willing cooperation in this project.

research theme and the organizational setting are presented in more detail. Next is a chronicle of the events studied and documentation of the research activities. The concluding sections explore the factors potentially involved in explaining the failed attempts at designing an MIS, my MIS-beliefs specifically emanating from this project, and some potential implications of a more general character that may lend themselves to future research.

BACKGROUND AND GENERAL INTRODUCTION

Volvo Car B.V. is the Dutch manufacturer of the "small Volvo": the 300-series (not available in the United States). As described in the next section, it has gone through a period of turbulent change. For a long time, it has felt that its management accounting system (MAS) is inadequate. The system generates financial accounting information that is used for both internal and external reporting purposes. The system is generally felt to have a too narrow (financial) focus, to be too labor intensive, and to operate with long cycles and time lags.

Volvo Car has successively contracted with several consulting firms to propose a plan for developing a new management information system (MIS). The first firm produced a report in October 1984. Subsequently, nothing happened. The second firm produced its preliminary plan in June 1985. After quite fierce resistance to this second plan from various parts of the organization, it was shelved in August, and work on an MIS-project was temporarily postponed. An evaluation of the Control Department and of the MAS was produced by a third agency in December 1985. A fourth consulting agency was engaged in early 1986. It is at work now, and one of its tasks is to replace the MAS. The task, however, is now much less ambitiously defined: the anticipated system is more appropriately characterized as a financial accounting system than as an MIS.

I witnessed this process from October 1984 to April 1986. During that period, I had the opportunity to be a participant-observer in the main meetings concerning the *second* report, to analyze relevant documents, and to conduct extensive and repeated interviews with the main actors involved.

THE RESEARCH THEME

Initially, my research aim was to observe a process of designing and implementing an MIS. Given the course of affairs described above, the study has instead turned on the factors involved in explaining the failure of the MIS-project to materialize. This shift of focus occurred in two stages, gradually. The gradual shift came about by observing the tensions surfacing in the discussions of the second report and by noting the divergent views of a number of the key interviewees. This evolution increased my awareness of the "nontechnical" factors underlying the divergent views on the optimal MIS. It also affected my view of this organization as an "arena" rather than a "system" (Lammers 1985). Nevertheless, when the board eventually decided not to pursue, or even amend, the recommendation of the second report, my view of the situation suddenly changed. I no longer perceived the case as a study of a search for an optimal MIS but rather as an inquiry into the reasons why this organization was not "ready" for a new MIS.

The literature on the interface of organizations and information systems/technology (IS/T) is growing, albeit slowly: "As our knowledge about information technology has improved, corresponding knowledge about its impact on people, organizations, and society has accreted at a much slower rate" (Mason 1984, 107). Reviews of the literature show that prior research has been almost exclusively concerned with the impact of IS/T on people and on organizations. Most studies have focused on the nature of such impacts as a function of the design and implementation process and/or the nature of the organization (Mohrman & Lawler 1984)—as I originally intended to do. Through the change of course described above, I stumbled into an area on which the literature is virtually silent: organizational resistance to MIS and the reasons for *failed* attempts at design and implementation.[1]

I came to this field of research with no strong preconceptions, as far as I am aware, with one important exception: my belief that there are hardly any *organizational* issues that are purely "technical." Such issues cannot be reduced to a narrow problem definition to which standard calculative analysis can be applied. Organizational issues tend to involve a mix of economic, ethical, legal, psychological, political, social, technical (and possibly other) factors. Hence, in organizational research, I do not expect "to see rationality everywhere," as Weick (1985, 112) imputes to MIS-researchers. Viewing the design of an MIS as an organizational issue, I expect to see a quite complex phenomenon with many, perhaps conflicting, aspects. From the beginning, I have therefore tried to remain as open-minded and alert as possible to detect *any* factor that might be relevant.[2] This attitude was reinforced by the following three circumstances: (1) the change of course of this case study, which took me by surprise; (2) my unfamiliarity with any previous findings in this area; and (3) my inexperience with MIS-research, which precluded my having any help or hindrance from prior experience.

THE ORGANIZATIONAL SETTING : VOLVO CAR B.V.

The history of the company dates back to 1927, when Hub van Doorne founded a machine manufacturing company. In the thirties, the company reoriented its production toward the construction of trailers, and in the fifties the first trucks and cars were produced. The name of the company was changed to Van Doorne's Automobiel Fabriek and the cars were known as DAFs. A special feature of the DAF passenger cars was their automatic transmission, the "Variomatic," designed by Hub van Doorne.

In the seventies, DAF encountered financial trouble. The Dutch chemical company DSM took a minority share in the company, while DAF also actively sought partners for its truck and car divisions. International Harvester participated in the former, Volvo in the latter (1972). The intention was to raise production levels to 300,000 (from the 82,500 cars produced in 1975).

In 1974, another financial crisis occurred, which in 1975 led to the Swedish Volvo Car Corporation (VCC) taking a majority share (75 percent) in the Car Division, DAF Car B.V. The name was changed to Volvo Car B.V. In 1976, the remaining minority link to DAF Holding was severed. The introduction in 1976 of the new model Volvo 343 was problematic, and VCC attempted to sell its majority share in Volvo Car to the Dutch government, which declined the offer.

Over the years, however, the Dutch government has provided a large amount of financial aid to DAF/Volvo Car. In 1977, it provided *another* Dfl. 100 million, and in 1978 it added Dfl. 237 million. The cumulative governmental involvement in Volvo Car had then reached the level of Dfl. 600 million (at the current exchange rate of about US$ 1 = Dfl. 2.50, about US$ 240 million).

In spite of this aid, Volvo Car remained a troubled company in the late 1970s. VCC attempted to integrate Volvo Car into the Swedish organization, which caused a lot of tensions. In 1981, another round of financial aid was necessary. This time the Dutch government indirectly took over VCC's majority share.[3] A "final" financial arrangement was made that increased the governmental involvement to a potential Dfl. 1,100–1,400 million (US$ 440–560 million). The lower numbers indicate the amount of direct financial aid, the higher numbers include governmental guarantees on company loans. VCC has invested about Dfl. 600 million (US$ 240 million) in Volvo Car over the years and still holds a 30 percent share in the company.

From 1974 to 1982, DAF/Volvo Car generated losses. In the early 1980s, this brought the company to the brink of collapse. Under the leadership of its new chairman, Mr. Deleye (1980), it resorted to "war management," which included a drastic centralization of the company and much direct personal supervision by top management of the execution of projects and operations. In 1983, profitability returned, and in 1984, a decentralization was initiated. Volvo Car now consists of three divisions, of which the Car Division is by far the largest. In 1984, the company employed about 6,300 people, produced 106,000 cars, and generated net sales of Dfl. 1,800 million, a cash flow of Dfl. 119 million, and an after-tax profit of Dfl. 18 million.

As a final note, it should be mentioned that Volvo Car is a pioneer in the Netherlands in introducing the system of "Management and Labor New Style." The system is based on the ideas of the U.S. statistician Professor Deming, which have been widely implemented in Japan. The system aims at greater cooperation between employees and departments in achieving higher quality and greater flexibility at lower costs, and propagates the use of statistical tools to diagnose problem situations. In 1982, the project "Volvo Car New Style" was started to introduce and implement these ideas in the company. The project still continues.

A CHRONICLE OF MIS-DIRECTED EFFORTS

Historically, the DAF/Volvo Car organization has been characterized by decentralized information systems. One dominant philosophy was: "Managers build their own systems." As a consequence, a number of "information islands" existed within the organization. The connections among these islands proved to be problematic.

The main part of the corporate information system consisted of the management accounting system (MAS) aimed at financial information and control. The system dates back to the DAF period. It has the following characteristics:

- a nearly exclusive focus on financial data;
- an attempt to satisfy simultaneously the information needs for management control as well as financial reporting;
- a reporting period of 6–8 weeks with information generated after a 4–5 week time lag;
- a highly labor-intensive process (for instance, part of the system—the assets administration—is still a manual operation, operating batchwise with punch cards); and
- a high degree of integration or "tight coupling" of subsystems (hardly any part of the MAS can be operated as an independent subsystem).

There has long been a consensus within the firm that the MAS should be updated; the information generated should be expanded (especially for operational control, but also for strategic purposes); the information should become available with higher frequency and with shorter time lags; and the internal consistency of the system should be improved.

A chronicle of the activities and events aimed at improving the Volvo Car information system is summarized below.

1983: Two departments, Organization and Efficiency and Systems and Automation, draw up a plan of activities for 1984, in which an exploratory study of the information problems is incorporated.

May 1984–October 1984: The exploratory study is carried out by a consulting agency. It reports its preliminary findings in July and September and produces a final report in October. It identifies major gaps in the information structure and recommends that a second phase of the project be initiated to produce a global description of the operational and management processes, adequate reporting schemata, and functional control specifications. The start of the second phase is set for January 1, 1985.

<u>Summer–October 1984:</u> Volvo Car decentralizes and reshuffles its staff departments. A new department, Information Systems and Automation (ISA), is created by joining the Systems and Automation department with the "Efficiency" part of the Organization and Efficiency department. New board members responsible for control enter the organization: Mr. Oomen (at the corporate level) and Mr. Bollen (at the Car Division level). The latter is responsible for the ISA department, the Personnel and Organization department, and the Division Control department.

<u>February 1985:</u> Mr. Bollen proposes to the board of the Car Division to start up the development of a new management information system. The project is to be carried out by a project group with the help of another consulting agency. Within half a year they are to come up with a design and implementation proposal, including a pilot study. The project is to be supervised by a steering committee, with the division controller, Mr. Rijkers, as project leader, and Mr. Bollen as chairman of the committee.

<u>March 1985:</u> Mr. Schimmel, the board member responsible for project management in the Car Division, sends Mr. Bollen a memo in which he protests against the project setup. In particular, he opposes the global, centralized approach and the influence of the Control Department. He favors a focus on financial information and a definition of the project that limits it to replacing the MAS.

<u>June 26, 1985:</u> The project group presents a preliminary report to the steering committee and some other Volvo Car representatives. The consultants have attempted to describe the thirteen main processes in the Volvo Car organization by dividing them into

- primary processes
- management and control processes
- input processes
- support processes

Management information is defined as concerning (1) goal formulation, (2) strategy formulation, (3) policy choice, and (4) control. It is proposed to start up the design of the information system with an "umbrella" encompassing a (I) values model, (II) process model, (III) organization model, and (IV) data model. Together these models should guarantee the internal consistency of the information system. The discussions have a critical flavor.

June 28, 1985: The steering committee meets to discuss the report. The main points of discussion and critique are

- the authority of the steering committee (advisory or final authority)
- the integral approach
- the fear that the system will not generate adequate "steering" information, especially for operational management
- the function of the Control Department and the meaning of the term "control"
- a top-down approach (proposed) versus a bottom-up approach
- the claim of the project upon the organizational resources
- the failure of the pilot project to demonstrate that the approach is operational

The committee decides to conduct a second pilot study and to meet again in August.

July 2, 1985: The conclusions of the steering committee are reported to the board of the Car Division. The board decides to expand the original pilot study, further detail the planning and the resource requirements, and prepare to start up the project after the summer. The board is to make a final decision in August.

August 1985: In two subsequent meetings, the board of the Car Division decides *not* to continue the project. The primary, official reason is that the project requires too many resources at a time when more important projects like new model introductions demand all the attention the company can generate. In addition, the financial situation demands attention. The projections show that the company needs to expend a lot of effort to remain in the black for 1985. Cost-reduction programs as well as personnel and expense freezes are initiated. Finally, the project has pointed toward a number of other problems in the organizational structure that in the board's view should be addressed first. A reevaluation is planned for early 1986.

Autumn 1985–spring 1986: A third consulting agency produces two preliminary reports, entitled "Replacement of MAS" and "Improving the Effectiveness of Divisional Control," in December 1985. In early 1986, a fourth agency is contracted to actually work out an MAS replacement and to evaluate the company's information systems generally.

THE RESEARCH ACTIVITIES

My research consisted of document analysis, interviews, and participant observation:

Document Analysis

Several documents were made available to me, including the reports of the consulting agencies and internal memos of Volvo Car.

Interviews

Interviews were conducted from October 1984 to April 1986.

Preliminary interviews. From October 1984 to early 1985, preliminary interviews were held to obtain information on the company in general and on the problems with its information systems. These interviews were partly an extension of earlier case study work within Volvo Car B.V. (Kunst, Schreuder, and Soeters 1986).

Main interviews. From early 1985 to September 1985, the interviews focused on Volvo Car's attempts to start up the design of an MIS with the help of the second consulting agency. All members of the project group and most members of the steering committee were interviewed at least once. Multiple interviews were conducted with the project leader, Mr. Rijkers, and the chairman of the steering committee, Mr. Bollen. An interview was held in September 1985 with the chairman of the corporate board, Mr. Deleye, shortly after the Car Division board's decision not to continue this project. All but one of the interviews were held at the Volvo Car headquarters and production facilities. In the crucial period of July 1985, the project leader came to my university for a consultation.

Evaluative interviews. After I had produced an interim report of this case study in January 1986, it was discussed in February–April 1986 with Mr. Rijkers, Mr. Bollen, and Mr. Deleye. Besides obtaining their views on my preliminary findings, these interviews served to delve deeper into some specific issues and to update my knowledge of subsequent developments at Volvo Car.[4]

Participant Observation

I was appointed as a member of the steering committee supervising the work on the second report. As such, I participated in the meetings of this committee as well as in their evaluation by the project group and Mr. Bollen.

At nearly all interviews and meetings, I was accompanied by a research assistant who made independent observations and notes. Most interviews were taped; the discussions and process characteristics of the meetings were recorded manually by the research assistant.

Finally, it is important to stress that I was already acquainted with Volvo Car from prior research. A general familiarity with the company is in my view essential to get a feel for the organizational setting in which an information systems project develops.

POTENTIAL FACTORS INVOLVED IN THE MIS-FIRING

A list of factors that may explain the failed attempt(s) at designing an MIS for Volvo Car B.V. are presented below. The aim is to provide a rich description of such factors and to provide some illustrative examples. Most factors were mentioned in my interim report and were extensively discussed again in the final evaluative interviews of early 1986. I have classified the factors as organizational, processual, substantive, and personal.

1. Organizational factors.

A common denominator for a number of the following factors is the existence of *organizational uncertainty or ambiguity.*

a.) One aspect of this ambiguity concerns the *centralization/decentralization dimension.* Volvo Car B.V. has gone through a number of swings along this dimension in recent years. The decentralization (and divisionalization) of the summer of 1984 had not (yet) produced a completely new "organizational picture" when the MIS-project was undertaken.

There is a widespread consensus in the company that the lines of responsibility, authority, and accountability are insufficiently clear. This may already be true at top management levels, in part because the corporate and divisional boards are partially composed of the same persons (three out of five), in part because of lingering effects of the highly centralized turnaround phase, in which board members exerted close personal supervision on the projects and operations. At lower levels, managers complain that the decentralization has "stopped at the divisional board level." Functional authority has not been relocated at lower levels. Consequently, the managers below the top level feel an incongruence between their responsibilities (which should have increased with decentralization) and their authority. Top management, on the other hand, perceives a lack of clear accountabilities at lower management levels.

b.) Another, albeit related, aspect concerns the *matrix organization* of the Car Division. There are vertical lines of authority and responsibility for functional areas and departments. These intersect with horizontal lines of authority and responsibility for specific projects. In addition, there is an overall responsibility for project management at the board level. The lines of demarcation are not always clear.

Chairman Deleye perceives cycles (of about five years) in which project management and functional management alternate in relative importance. In the current years, project management is relatively important given the introduction of two completely new models. Once these have been successfully introduced, functional management will again become relatively more important. How to design an organizational structure and corresponding information systems that can accommodate such cycles?

c.) Even more fundamental to the existence of ambiguity is the basic view one has of an automobile company in general and Volvo Car in particular. Is an automobile company like Volvo Car still basically *a production company* or is it gradually evolving into an *assembly company*? The latter is characterized by an increasing amount of "buy decisions" instead of "make decisions"; by externalization of all but the core functions; by the creation of a peripheral network of "preferred suppliers" who deliver their products "just in time" and follow quality procedures specified by the buyer; and by the increasing temporary use of outside specialists for special projects. Views on these developments differ within, and outside, the company.

For example, how risky is just-in-time delivery by outside suppliers who operate in an industry or a region in which strikes are known to occur every now and then?

What do these developments imply for the internal organization of the company? Is it turning into a kind of *federation* of loosely coupled departments, separated by quasi markets? To what extent can "markets" substitute for "hierarchy" *within* organizations (cf., Williamson 1975, 1985)? And how do these alternative forms affect information systems?

A final basic difference of view concerns the state of health of Volvo Car. Some interviewees saw the company in a situation of structural, financial deterioration—and possibly at the brink of collapse. Some perceived the organization to be in a crucial time period in which government cushioning against market forces was coming to an end. And some expressed the view that Volvo Car had already successfully completed a turnaround and was now in the difficult but manageable phase of introducing its new models and returning to a relatively stable situation.

d.) A more specific point can be raised: What is the *function of the Control Department?* Is it only monitoring and reporting? Or should the controllers also have a policing function? If the latter, does that include the authority to halt operations whose budgets are overrun? Do controllers work primarily or exclusively for top management, or do they also have a supporting role toward lower management? If both, how can the potential role conflict be best resolved?

e.) A specific factor is the *technical culture* of an automotive company. People talk in technical terms about Volvo Car, often neglecting social factors. This may increase the potential threats emanating from a new MIS (see the section below on personal factors). One informant described the organization as a "motor" exhibiting a lot of "friction losses." The neglect of social factors was also noted in an evaluation of the "New Style" project. In some programs this had led to the gains in technical efficiency being offset by losses in the social sphere (e.g., rising levels of absenteeism). One top manager interpreted this neglect mainly as a fear of explicitly discussing potentially unfavorable personal effects of decisions, leading at best to sub-optimal decisions and at worst to paralysis.

f.) The second attempt to design an MIS emanated from Mr. Bollen, the new board member responsible for the Personnel and Organization, Information Systems and Automation, and Division Control departments. The ISA department had been bypassed in selecting the consulting agency and in staffing the project group. Instead, the interim head of the Personnel and Organization department, which was being reorganized, was a member of that team. This may not only have caused resentment, but also fostered the impression of a *reorganization project* masquerading as an information systems project (see the summary discussion later in the chapter).

2. Processual factors.

There are two well-known interrelated options in MIS-design: an integral "grand design" approach versus a partial, sequential approach; and a top-down versus a bottom-up approach.

In the case of Volvo Car B.V. these two options were of special concern in view of the organizational ambiguity along the centralization/decentralization dimension. The consultants opted for a top-down, grand design approach, but it did not accord well with the decentralization effort of 1984. In addition, it did not harmonize with the "New Style" philosophy (which emphasizes employee participation in problem diagnosis and solution search). The consultants' report was perceived by those who had not participated in its composition as being abstract and insufficiently oriented toward practical problems.

3. Substantive factors.

Within Volvo Car the following types of information are distinguished: steering information, control information, and accounting information. These distinctions are discussed below in general terms in order to make some points relevant to the present case. The attempt is to distill the essential elements from rather divergent views on the substance of this classification, which is generally employed in the company.

Steering information. This is necessary to guide decisions at all management levels. It should result from the long-term planning of the firm and should indicate organizational targets and agreements (e.g., between departments). Substantively, it varies with the management level and the functional area, and includes, for example, financial data, technical specifications, and project milestones.

Control information. The monitoring of target realization and compliance with agreements falls within this category. Observed deviations may feed back into steering information. Opinions differ on the extent to which control is (1) more than only financially oriented and (2) proactive as well as retrospective.

Accounting information. This is oriented toward the external reporting requirements; it is purely financial, perceived as providing a representation of reality in "annual report terms." As such, it is mainly useful for top management and is not regarded as very useful for steering and controlling at lower management levels.

With these general distinctions in mind the following interrelated points can be identified as underlying the substantive discussions on the MIS.

a.) To what extent should these types of information be included in one information system? One aspect, of course, is their diversity. From my interviews, it appeared that a financial orientation was relatively pronounced at the higher management levels, while a more technical orientation became stronger at lower management levels, especially in the Production Department and related areas. How can an information system accommodate such changes in perspective and provide useful information to all management levels? Another aspect is the degree to which accounting information dominated steering information and control information. External reporting regulations have also had an *internal* impact on the information gathering and processing. In competition for scarce resources, accounting data have often gained priority over steering data and control data. Is it desirable to integrate the accounting system with the management information and control system? Or should one strive for two different (but where necessary consistent) "representations of reality," one externally oriented via the annual report and one for internal management purposes?

In an interview with the division controller we discussed the relationships between financial and technical information and the differences between accounting information and steering and control information. He searched in his monthly data file and came up with a "squalid sheet" with technical data:

"Apparently, the production manager works with this, but I don't regard it as, ah, particularly instructive."

b.) To what extent should the MIS be a totally integrated system of these three types of information for lower to top management levels? Would it not suffice to concentrate on a few "critical success factors" per responsibility area (cf., Simon 1973; Rockart 1979)? Wouldn't a totally integrated data base of all information in its finest detail take away lower management discretion and "privacy" (Markus 1983).

c.) To what extent can all steering information and control information be translated in financial terms?

One extreme view brought up at a meeting ran as follows: "Control is concerned with all financial matters. Everything in this organization has its price. Therefore, everything can be translated in financial terms and controlled." From the reactions of the other participants it was clear that they would not enjoy such a definition of control.

3. Personal factors.

In this case a number of *specific* personal factors can be identified that may have contributed to the outcome. These include the backgrounds and personalities of the main actors involved. I shall not elaborate on this point, apart from the observation that such personal factors seem underexplored in the literature.

A more general point is that people may perceive the implementation of an MIS as a very *threatening event*. At one point in the steering committee meeting of June 28, 1985, the production manager openly expressed his fears of an integral information system: "Not all responsibilities and tasks are formal; one cannot record everything; I become frightened of this." Probably this statement revealed the tip of a mountain of emotions surrounding this project.

Finally, it may be that the people who are crucial for effecting a turnaround in a crisis situation lack equivalent skills in building systems for post-crisis management.

A SUMMARY OF SPECIFIC MIS-BELIEFS

After having been as descriptive as possible in the previous section, it is probably useful to summarize the main elements of this specific case study before drawing out some implications of a potentially more general character. A broad-brush summary includes the following observations:

1. Volvo Car B.V. has operated for quite a number of years with a system that generates insufficient information, especially for controlling and steering purposes.

2. Two attempts at designing a new MIS failed at the proposal stage, despite a general consensus that "something" should be done and despite the services of consulting agencies.

3. A major reason for these failures appears to have been organizational ambiguity. The first proposal fell flat in a period of reorganization and restaffing; the second proposal "absorbed" this ambiguity, as I explain below.

4. Among the organizational problems encountered by the project group and the consultants were three areas of ambiguity: the extent of decentralization, the delineation of responsibilities in the matrix organization, and the functions of the Control Department. Possibly there was also confusion about the primary processes of the company and their future development as well as basic uncertainties concerning the future viability of the organization. Since the consultants attempted to describe the main structural characteristrics of Volvo Car in the exploratory phase, they had to either include this ambiguity or resolve it (albeit often implicitly or even as disguised as possible).[5]

5. Because of the remaining ambiguity, people read divergent organizational pictures in the proposal. Some defended the proposal as aiding the drive for decentralization, others interpreted it as a (re)centralization effort.

6. As a result of the (quasi) resolutions of the organizational ambiguity, people came to see the project less as purely MIS-oriented and more as a reorganization project.[6]

7. Points 5 and 6 help explain why this project became threatening to organization members.

8. A further explanation is provided by the proposed integral, top-down approach. The integration of control information and steering information (on an information-sharing basis) is threatening because of the confounding of top management control with operational control. The top-down approach did not har-

monize with the recent decentralization philosophy. Both elements threatened managerial discretion at lower levels.

9. The ambition of the project group to integrate the accounting, control, and steering information in one MIS led people to fear that control information would dominate steering information, and that accounting information would perhaps continue to dominate both.

10. The official reasons to postpone the MIS-project were no doubt valid. Volvo Car B.V. has announced a substantially lower profit level for 1985 (Dfl. 1 million); it has postponed the introduction of its main new model, and the MIS-project would have consumed too many resources in this situation. These official factors, however, do not explain the resistance the MIS-project met virtually from the start or the substance of the arguments against it.

CONCLUSION

This case study has not been undertaken with the sole purpose of getting to know Volvo Car B.V. and its specific MIS-happenings better. Given the knowledge concerning factors explaining success or failure in MIS-design and MIS-implementation, it was undertaken with an exploratory aim: to investigate the nature, importance, and interplay of factors involved in the interface between organizations and information systems. Paraphrasing the anthropologist Geertz (1973, 22), the object is not to study organizations, but to study *in* organizations. What insights drawn from this study may have a potentially wider relevance and may be taken up, for instance, in further research or in experiments in practice? I see four themes emerging.

The first is the concept of *ambiguity*. Many of the organizational factors involved were subsumed under this umbrella term. This concept has been introduced earlier in the organization literature, most notably by March and his collaborators (e.g., Cohen and March 1974; Cohen, March, and Olsen 1972). In Cohen and March (1974, ch. 9) four fundamental ambiguities are recognized in their research setting (universities): ambiguities of purpose, power, experience, and success. These ambiguities collectively go far in denoting the phenomena I have attempted to describe. It may be, however, a matter of interpretation whether they jointly convey the essential feature I want to bring out. As I have used the term, it refers not only to *the rules of the game* in an organization, but also to *the nature of the game* itself. The participants in this case study differed widely in their definitions of the situation (see "Potential Factors Involved in the MIS-firing"). I have used the word ambiguity as an umbrella covering widely divergent world views. A theme emerging from this research is the interrelationships that exist between information systems and different levels of ambiguity (along several dimensions) in organizations. A hypothesis emanating from this case study is that high levels of ambiguity preclude the successful introduction of new management information systems.

A second, related insight is that information systems should be designed and implemented so as to *fit* with the other relevant characteristics of the organization. These characteristics, which include the strategic, structural, and cultural properties of the firms, are not always readily observable (Mintzberg 1979; Miller 1986; Hofstede 1980). There are a number of options in designing and implementing an MIS. The choice among them should be guided by a thorough knowledge of the company and, ideally, by a clear and shared vision of its future development. These conditions circumscribe, for instance, the extent to which outsiders, such as consultants, can do a good job in the time normally allotted to them. And the fit between the MIS-characteristics and the organizational characteristics may also indicate when and where to expect resistance to MIS-projects (Markus 1983). Underlying this resistance will often be a competition (or a power struggle) concerning organizational issues rather than MIS-issues per se.

A third, and again related, insight is that MIS-design is indeed a complex phenomenon. Here I have classified the aspects involved into organizational, processual, substantive, and personal factors. All of these categories are multifaceted. Had the MIS-project developed further, then surely technical factors would have come into play as well. MIS-designers are well advised to maintain a broad awareness of all such factors. A narrowing of the design focus to only the technical parameters will tend to exacerbate any problems located in the other categories. In a sense, then, the MIS should not only fit the organization, it should also exhibit an internal fit with these factors. Only if an MIS fits, will it not be a MIS-fit.

Finally, a more specific issue in the accounting and control area surfaced in this case. A major issue in the discussion of the MIS-project was the extent to which information for both internal and external purposes could be combined in one information system. A distinct feeling among most managers was that externally oriented accounting did not match their internal information needs. While they recognized the need for following accounting conventions that are externally acceptable, most managers maintained that they needed other information for their own "steering and control" purposes. Their information requirements included much more nonfinancial data (increasingly so at lower management levels located in or near production). Conventional accounting budgets were seen as the imposition of the external accounting representation of reality upon a particular part of the firm. This representation was difficult to reconcile with their own view of relevant factors. Thus, the point discussed here is not only that the local managers seem to want more (and other) information than the accounting system generates, but also that they operate on the basis of a view of reality that they find hard to reconcile with the accounting model imposed on them. In this sense, and if I am allowed a last play on words, the accounting model-in-use is locally perceived as an MIS-representation of their reality. It will be a challenging research task to investigate in what circumstances such divergencies are perceived to exist and how the resulting differences in information needs can be simultaneously satisfied.

NOTES

1. One of the best exceptions was brought to my attention after the HBS colloquium in June 1986; see Markus (1983), "Power, Politics and MIS Implementation." Other exceptions include Kling (1980), Markus and Pfeffer (1983), and Weick (1985).

2. This raises an interesting methodological point. Weick (1985, 112) argues that MIS-researchers tend to see rationality everywhere, "partly because their prior beliefs assume rationality, partly because the methods they use preserve their prior beliefs." To what extent have I seen a complex phenomenon, partly because I have assumed complexity, partly because my research methods preserved this prior belief?

3. It used three intermediary organizations: the National Investment Bank acquired 49 percent of Volvo Car; two other intermediaries gained 3 percent and 18 percent each. As a consequence, Volvo Car became 70 percent Dutch-owned.

4. Mainly concerning the distinctions between accounting, control, and steering information discussed later (see the chapter discussion of "Substantive factors").

5. One example was the attempt to avoid the term "control" and use "administration of the division" instead. This was induced by pressures not to let the MIS-project become a "controller's project." Exactly the opposite effect, however, occurred. People read an expansion of the Control Department's responsibilities into the new term.

6. In response to this point, the project leader stated to me that for him the major lesson had indeed been that an MIS-project had developed into an organization-development project. The intraorganizational power dimensions of this perceived reorganization crystallized in the discussions on the functions of the Control Department.

REFERENCES

Geertz, Clifford. 1973. *The Interpretation of Cultures*. New York: Basic Books.

Hofstede, G. 1980. *Culture's Consequences: International Differences in Work-Related Values*. London: Sage.

Kling, Rob. 1980. "Social Analyses of Computing: Theoretical Perspectives in Recent Empirical Research." *Computing Surveys* 12: 61–110.

Kunst, Paul; Schreuder, Hein; and Soeters, Sjo. "De ontwikkeling van DAF/Volvo Car: een beschrijvende case study." University of Limburg, Working Paper 86-004.

Lammers, Cornelis. 1985. *Organisaties Vergelijkenderwijs*. Utrecht: Het Spectrum.

Markus, M. Lynne. 1983. "Power, Politics, and MIS Implementation." *Communications of the ACM*, (June) 430–44.

Markus, M. Lynne, and Pfeffer, Jeffrey. 1983. "Power and the Design and Implementation of Accounting and Control Systems." *Accounting, Organizations and Society* 205–18.

Mason, Richard O. 1985. Introduction to *The Information Systems Research Challenge*, edited by F. Warren McFarlan. Boston: Harvard Business School Press.

Miller, D. 1986. "Configurations of Strategy and Structure: Toward a Synthesis." *Strategic Management Journal* 233–49.

Mintzberg, Henry. 1979a. "An Emerging Strategy of Direct Research." *Administrative Science Quarterly*, (December), 582–89.

———. 1979b. *The Structuring of Organizations*. Englewood Cliffs, NJ: Prentice-Hall.

Mohrman, Allan M. Jr., and Lawler, Edward E. III. 1985. "A Review of Theory and Research." In *The Information Systems Research Challenge*, edited by F. Warren McFarlan. Boston: Harvard Business School Press.

Rockart, John F. 1979. "Chief executives define their own data needs." *Harvard Business Review* (March–April) 81–93.

Simon, Herbert A. 1973. "Applying Information Technology to Organization Design." *Public Administration Review* 33: 268–78.

Weick, Karl E. 1985. "Theoretical Assumptions and Research Methodology Selection." In *The Information Systems Research Challenge*, edited by F. Warren McFarlan. Boston: Harvard Business School Press.

Williamson, Oliver E. 1975. *Markets and Hierarchies: Analysis and Antitrust Implications*. New York: The Free Press.

———. 1985. *The Economic Institutions of Capitalism*. New York: The Free Press.

PART III

*New Directions for Cost
Management Systems*

Accounting for Labor Productivity in Manufacturing Operations: An Application

Rajiv D. Banker and Srikant M. Datar

INTRODUCTION

REDUCING manufacturing costs and improving productivity by controlling manufacturing operations has become a key competitive dimension for U.S. industry. In a recent article in *Fortune* (McComas 1986), 78 percent of chief executive officers of *Fortune 500* companies cited cost containment and productivity improvement as the most important issues requiring their attention.[1] Productivity improvement is of particular importance for manufacturing operations characterized by stable and standardized technologies and mature products. In these industries competitive advantages and profit increases arise largely from following a low-cost strategy that emphasizes productivity improvements. Furthermore, in recent years, U.S. corporations have found themselves at a competitive disadvantage relative to low-cost foreign producers. These factors have resulted in a revival of and increased focus on productivity improvement programs.

A necessary condition for the implementation of successful productivity improvement programs is a measurement system that measures and evaluates productivity-enhancing efforts.[2] Such a measurement system enables an evaluation of the costs and benefits associated with various productivity improvement programs and provides a

169

mechanism to monitor and control these programs. The manufacturing accounting system can thus serve an important function by measuring productivity gains from one period to the next. Accounting textbooks and the academic literature in accounting have, however, largely ignored the issue of productivity measurement.[3]

When productivity improvement and cost control are key determinants of a corporation's profitability, productivity measurement should be integrated into the manufacturing accounting and control system. As Kaplan (1983) argues, however, most accounting systems have paid little attention to measuring and monitoring productivity. He asserts that manufacturing accounting systems continue to emphasize a financial accounting mission and focus narrowly on adequately valuing inventories for financial reporting purposes.

Several factors influence the productivity and efficiency of manufacturing operations. To control their manufacturing operations and costs, manufacturing managers focus on such diverse factors as scrap and defect rates, absenteeism, capacity utilization, machine downtime, and setup time. Thus the manufacturing accounting system should attempt to quantify, in financial terms, the cost impact of variation in these factors. Isolating the effects of such factors is of considerable value in improving operating performance and in making decisions that involve trade-offs across these factors. Research in management accounting has only recently begun to address these issues. In order to capture the richness and complexity of the real-world settings in which these problems most frequently occur, these models need to be developed in stochastic, multiproduct environments.[4]

We study the various issues discussed above, particularly those pertaining to labor productivity measurement, in the context of the manufacturing accounting and reporting system within a manufacturing plant. We did not consider an exhaustive list of potential sites. Instead, we found a site with the following characteristics:

1. Cost containment and productivity improvement are key dimensions of the competitive strategy of the business.

2. The company has a reputation for leadership and innovation in productivity measurement.

3. Corporate, divisional, and plant-level managers exhibit active interest, cooperation, and involvement in the productivity study.

The particular site chosen was a large division of a highly diversified *Fortune 500* company. Our objective was to identify their best practices in productivity measurement. In the past eight years, the corporation has recognized and stressed productivity improvement and cost control as important components of its competitive strategy. Productivity gains were also emphasized by the chairman in his reports to stockholders. A major corporate-level effort was under way to establish productivity measurement systems. Indeed, a separate corporate department for productivity measurement and cost control was established to develop and maintain productivity and cost statistics. The company is recognized as a leader in the implementation of productivity-based systems for manufacturing and cost control. It is also active in promoting the discussion and development of these ideas in trade association meetings and other public forums.

The division we studied has adopted productivity improvement as a key strategic dimension. The division manufactures two mature products using a stable and standardized technology. The critical success variable is the division's ability to deliver a quality product at the lowest cost. Customers impose strict quality standards so that cost reduction cannot be achieved by compromising quality. Instead, the division seeks to control cost by improving productivity and by an ongoing scrutiny of manufacturing operations. The division also seeks to reduce cost by obtaining price concessions in negotiated annual agreements with suppliers of input materials. The improvements in productivity, however, are expected to provide the division with sustained long-run cost advantages since lower input prices are generally available to competitors as well. An important objective of the manufacturing accounting system is to quantify, in physical and financial terms, the effects of various productivity improvement programs. The specific site for our study is a manufacturing plant, with a labor-intensive production technology, that had recently instituted a labor productivity improvement program.

In this chapter, we examine and evaluate the manufacturing accounting and reporting system at both the plant and division levels. We describe the basic information captured at the plant level and the manner in which it is aggregated for divisional reporting purposes. In the section that follows, we argue that even though productivity enhancement is an important objective at both the plant and divisional levels, this objective has not been integrated into the manufacturing accounting system for planning and control purposes. The accounting system does not focus attention on isolating the costs and benefits associated with various productivity improvement programs such as reduced setup times and machine downtimes. Consequently, the accounting system does not adequately monitor the productivity enhancement effort. Instead, we observe that the manufacturing accounting system has a strong financial accounting orientation, emphasizing inventory valuation and preparation of the income statement.

Our second objective is to describe and evaluate the *gain-sharing* program that had been implemented at the plant in order to motivate workers and improve labor productivity by sharing productivity improvement gains with workers. Direct and indirect labor constitute approximately 50 percent of total cost at the plant.

Labor productivity is the ratio of the quantity of physical outputs produced in a period to the physical labor hours employed to produce those outputs. By focusing on physical measures, fluctuations in the prices of input resources consumed or outputs produced do not influence the incentive compensation paid to workers. Successful implementation of a productivity improvement program critically depends on the ability of the manufacturing accounting system to quantify the gains in productivity attributable to labor since this system constitutes the basis of the workers' incentive payments.

The cost accounting and management accounting literature provides little guidance for designing accounting systems to quantify labor productivity gains. A measurement system designed by a consulting firm for our study company was approved by the labor union and implemented by management. Over a fifteen-month period after the implementation of the program, the system recorded significant gains in productivity that resulted in substantial gain-sharing payments to workers. Plant management was concerned, however, that these payments were made despite increases in unfavorable direct labor variances reported by the accounting system in some months. Perhaps workers were being rewarded for productivity gains according to the agreed-upon formula when in effect no *real* productivity gains had been realized. We explore these issues in detail in our discussion of the gain-sharing program and identify the conceptual problems that arose once the system actually had been implemented.

We found three principal problems with the gain-sharing agreement.[5] First, the gain-sharing formula assumes that total labor hours changes proportionately with production volume. If the actual total labor hours increases less than proportionately with production volume (as we anticipate they will), the gain-sharing formula will, for higher (lower) volumes, predict a much higher (lower) benchmark for total labor hours than is warranted by the anticipated behavior of total labor hours with production volume. This will distort computations of *real* productivity gains. In our analysis and interpretation of the data, we propose a modification of the gain-sharing agreement as a way to separate volume effects from productivity gains at a given volume of production.

Second, changes in product mix are reflected as productivity gains or declines in the gain-sharing formula. This problem indicates the need for considering multiple products in management accounting research. The product-mix problem arises because the factors that cause indirect labor to vary are not identified. Cooper and Kaplan (1987) refer to such factors as cost drivers. The gain-sharing formula assumes that the variable component of indirect labor hours varies proportionately with direct labor hours. We show that if this relationship does not in fact hold, a change in product mix per se will signal a productivity gain. It is important to emphasize that whereas the volume effect identified earlier arises due to the *fixed* component of indirect labor costs (relative to production volume) the product mix effect arises due to the *variable* component of indirect labor not varying in proportion to the direct labor requirements of individual products. Our modification of the gain-sharing formula evaluates productivity improvements after controlling for both volume and product-mix effects.

The third problem arises from the method used to compute productivity. The gain-sharing formula computes productivity gains by measuring the ratios of actual labor inputs to standard direct labor hours in both the base period and in the period under evaluation.[6] Rather than comparing input-output ratios in the two periods, we propose a method that computes a *benchmark* for labor hours, given the volume and mix of outputs produced. Our proposed productivity ratio is the ratio of the benchmark labor hours over the actual hours. The proposed measure is free of the problems of volume and mix noted earlier. It differs from the gain-sharing formula because it compares benchmark inputs with actual inputs rather than input-output ratios over two periods. Also, the benchmark may be estimated more tightly to reflect the *minimum* (rather than the average) quantity of labor required to produce any volume or mix of products.

PLANT AND DIVISION
MANUFACTURING ACCOUNTING
SYSTEMS

In this section we report on the manufacturing accounting systems at both the plant and divisional levels. Each month the man-

Exhibit 7-1 Manufacturing Profit and Loss Statement

Division: *ABC*	Plant: *XYZ*		Month: *January 1986*
		Product A	Product B	Total

	Product A	Product B	Total
Gross Sales			
Less: Returns			
Net Sales - Customer			
- Intercompany			
Standard Cost of Net Sales			
Materials			
Direct Labor			
Manufacturing Expense			
Total Standard Cost			
Gross Profit at Standard			
Percent of Sales			
Variances			
Materials			
Direct Labor			
Mfg. Exp. - Variable			
Mfg. Exp. - Fixed			
Scrap			
Freight			
Supplies			
Inventory Adjustment			
Other _____			
Total Variances:			
Gross Profit at Actual			
Percent of Sales			
Operating Expenses			
Administrative-Works			
Administrative-Staff			
Selling			
Product Development			
Other Income and Expense			
Total Operating Expenses			
Profit Before Tax and Allocations			
Less: Divisional Allocations			
Less: Corporate Allocations			
Profit Before Tax and Interest			
Percent of Sales			
Less: Allocated Interest Expense			
Profit Before Tax			

ufacturing system matches expenses with sales to compute plant-level profits. The principal report at the plant level for evaluating manufacturing performance is the monthly manufacturing profit and loss (MP&L) statement shown in Exhibit 7–1. The reported numbers are all driven by sales. The manufacturing costs are the costs associated by the accounting system with the goods sold during the month. The MP&L statements for individual plants are aggregated to give the divisional P&L statement. Each quarter, this statement (together with other statements on divisional assets and liabilities) is discussed in a meeting with plant managers, plant controllers, the divisional controller, and the divisional manager.

The income or profit orientation of the MP&L statement obscures the evaluation of manufacturing performance in the period. A key question of interest in evaluating manufacturing performance in a particular period is the efficiency with which input resources such as materials, labor, and capital are converted into outputs. The MP&L statement, however, emphasizes the cost of sales (which may depend on manufacturing performance efficiency in some prior period). The reporting system does not provide the cost of materials or cost of labor associated with the outputs *produced* in a given period. Thus, the MP&L makes it difficult to obtain any trends in productivity or cost efficiency. Information on productivity and cost efficiency is available elsewhere, in the less formal plant records, but this information is not displayed in the principal divisional reports.

At the end of each period, work-in-process (WIP) inventory and finished-goods (FG) inventory are valued at standard costs. Variances are computed as the difference between actual costs and the standard costs of goods sold (CGS), WIP inventory, and FG inventory. Calculating variances in this way causes the computed variances to correspond to manufacturing performance in the period. We illustrate this via a simple numerical example.

We consider a simple two-period example in which the standard (variable) cost is $4 per unit. The actual cost per unit produced at standard input prices is $4.27 in Period 1 and $4.33 in Period 2. In each period 100 units of the product are produced. Sales in Period 1 are 90 units, and Period 2 sales are 110 units. The actual cost of manufacturing 100 units of the product in Period 1 is $427, and the standard cost is $400; the standard CGS is $360 at the end of the period, and FG inventory is $40; this generates an unfavorable variance of $27, which exactly corresponds to the manufacturing inefficiency in Period 1. In Period 2 the beginning inventory is valued at a standard cost of $40. The actual manufacturing cost for 100 units is $433. The standard CGS is $440 (110 units at $4 each), yielding an unfavorable variance of $33. Once again this unfavorable variance accurately reflects manufacturing inefficiency.

Although the absolute magnitudes of the variance computations accurately mirror the underlying manufacturing performance, the sales focus of the MP&L clouds the magnitude of the variances relative to total manufacturing costs. To see this more vividly we return to our simple example. It is evident from the example that manufacturing performance in Period 2 is worse than the manufacturing performance in Period 1. (The actual cost of manufacturing 100 units is $427 in Period 1, $433 in Period 2.) The unfavorable (usage) variance of $27 in Period 1 is less than the $33 unfavorable variance in Period 2, both relative to $400 of standard manufacturing costs in each period. The MP&L statement will show the standard CGS as $360 ($4 × 90 units) in Period 1 and $440 ($4 × 110 units) in Period 2. The variance as a percentage of cost of goods sold is

$$\text{Period 1} \frac{27}{360} \times 100 = 7.5\% \quad \text{Period 2} \frac{33}{440} \times 100 = 7.5\%$$

indicating no difference in these ratios over the two periods and concealing the inferior manufacturing performance in Period 2. Consequently, the ratios derived from the MP&L statement are not very useful in analyzing trends in manufacturing performance and productivity.[7]

For accounting systems that value inventory at actual, rather than at standard, costs, the inefficiencies in manufacturing in a particular period will not necessarily appear as costs in that period. For instance, continuing our example, the actual CGS in Period 1 equals $384.30 ($4.27 × 90 units), compared to the standard (expected) cost of $360, resulting in an inefficiency of $24.30. However, the actual inefficiency in the production of 100 units is $27 ($427-$400). The problem here is that the inefficiency of $2.70, attributable to 10 units of the product, is *inventoried* at the end of Period 1 and becomes part of CGS only in Period 2.

Our discussions with plant and divisional management strongly suggested that cost control and productivity improvement are important objectives at the plant and divisional level. We did not, however, observe the manufacturing accounting system providing the necessary information to control these costs. Although information on non-financial measures such as scrap and defect rates, absenteeism, setup time, and machine downtime is collected informally at the plant on a regular basis, these measures (with the exception of scrap) are not integrated into the manufacturing accounting system. Even scrap variances are computed as the difference between the cost of materials and labor (up to the point the product is scrapped) and salvage value. They do not include the additional relevant costs of confusion, congestion, and queuing delays—discussed, for instance, by Banker,

Datar, and Kekre (1987)—that are caused by reprocessing the scrap or initiating new production to complete the order.

The plant manager believes that controlling these nonfinancial factors is essential for achieving his financial goals. The manufacturing accounting system, however, does not quantify, in financial terms, the impact of nonfinancial factors that affect manufacturing performance. The manager frequently has to make trade-offs among nonfinancial objectives. For example, tighter controls for reducing scrap may increase machine downtime for setup if scrap reduction requires that setups be made with greater precision. Similarly, employing inexperienced or temporary labor may reduce the labor rate, but it may also produce higher absenteeism, scrap, defects, and downtime. Evaluating these trade-offs requires a financial analysis of the impact of variations among these nonfinancial factors.

Our discussions with divisional management revealed that nonfinancial measures of plant performance are not reported to the divisional level. Divisional management indicated that although such information is not reported, the information, if desired, is easily obtained from individual plant managers or plant controllers. This explanation, of course, does not address the question of the benefit from a manufacturing control standpoint of a summary nonfinancial indicator of aggregate plant performance such as overall plant productivity. Indeed, we find the manufacturing accounting system focuses largely on computing a measure of plant *profitability* (with an emphasis on matching revenues with costs) for aggregation into divisional *profit* measures, rather than on production performance (to emphasize input-output relationships and their financial consequences). This is consistent with the observation by Kaplan (1983) that management accounting systems have a strong income statement orientation; consequently, manufacturing-performance evaluation requirements are often not adequately addressed by such systems.

GAIN-SHARING PROGRAM

In the previous section we evaluated the manufacturing accounting and reporting system's role in facilitating decision making and management control. We indicated that an important function for manufacturing accounting systems is to quantify the effects of various nonfinancial factors such as productivity.

Productivity improvements were considered by managers at the corporate, divisional, and plant levels to be essential to the success of the division. The plant produces two very mature and standardized products—Product A and Product B—in a highly stable technological environment. The critical success variable is the ability to produce high-quality products at minimum cost. The division expends effort to obtain the input resources at minimum prices, but these benefits are generally available to competitors as well. Sustained competitive cost advantages come from improvements in the physical use of resources; that is, from producing more outputs with fewer inputs. Among these resources, labor productivity is particularly important since labor represents about 50 percent of total cost. Improving labor productivity represents an important component of the cost-control program at the plant.

A gain-sharing agreement with the labor union had been instituted to reward workers for their productivity.[8] The goal, much in the spirit of responsibility accounting, was to evaluate labor costs after controlling for output and labor rates.

Although the concept of the gain-sharing arrangement is clear, the difficulties in implementation are considerable. (This problem is compounded by the lack of insights in the management accounting literature into productivity measurement and the computation of productivity gains.) The gain-sharing program is the outcome of a cooperative effort over several months between a consulting firm, the divisional controller's office, and the plant's industrial engineering department. The gain-sharing agreement applies to the entire labor force: direct labor, indirect plant labor, and salaried staff. Direct labor includes direct productive labor and inspection labor. Indirect plant labor includes repairs and maintenance labor, toolroom labor, setup labor, and general indirect labor. Salaried staff includes administrative, accounting, and personnel employees at the plant level, but not the plant manager.

The basic steps in the gain-sharing computation are described below. A particular base period is first identified as a benchmark against which labor productivity gains are measured. The standard direct labor hours per unit for each product (based on industrial engineering estimates and obtained from the standard cost accounting system) are multiplied by the quantity of each product produced in the base period to give the *standard* direct labor hours (s_b) in the base period. Standard direct labor hours represent the direct labor content of production in the base period. The *actual* total labor hours (both direct and indirect—the latter including indirect plant labor and sal-

aried staff), is also computed for the base period: this is denoted by
a_b. The ratio of the actual direct and indirect labor hours to standard
direct labor hours in the base period determines a *base ratio*, denoted
by r_b $(= a_b/s_b)$. In each subsequent month (t), the actual total labor
hours (a_t) and the standard direct labor hours (s_t), based on the direct
labor content of products produced in period t, are obtained, and the
ratio $r_t = a_t/s_t$ computed. The gain-sharing fraction (g_t) for a period t
is calculated as

$$\frac{r_b}{r_t} = \frac{a_b/s_b}{a_t/s_t}.$$

Values of g_t greater than one indicate a productivity gain whereas values of g_t less than one indicate a productivity decline. If g_t in period t
is less than one, workers are paid wages at the base-period wage rates.
In a sense, workers are ensured against productivity declines. If g_t is
greater than one, however, half of the productivity gains are paid as
bonus to labor. For example if g_t is 1.10, which corresponds to a 10
percent increase in productivity under the gain-sharing plan, all
workers are paid a bonus of 5 percent of their base wage or salary.
    An interesting and novel feature of the gain-sharing arrangement
is the inclusion of indirect plant labor and salaried staff. They are
included for two reasons. First, indirect labor (including salaried staff)
constitutes a significant component (approximately 60 percent) of total
labor costs; consequently, any attempts to control labor costs must
necessarily consider indirect labor costs. Second, their inclusion explicitly recognizes the potential for productivity gains from greater
efficiency in the use of indirect labor (both plant and administrative).
Including indirect labor and salaried staff as part of the gain-sharing
agreement also facilitates union negotiations, since all labor is included in the new arrangement.
    The gain-sharing agreement discusses in considerable detail the
necessary adjustments to the gain-sharing formula resulting from the
introduction of productive capital inputs. This, however, is not relevant for the period of our study since no new capital investments were
made during this period. Another issue of interest is whether the
gain-sharing agreement creates an incentive for labor to produce more
units of poorer quality. Fortunately, this is not a major concern since
strict quality standards are imposed by customers. This, in turn, has
led to the adoption of detailed quality control and inspection procedures within the plant. Furthermore, any customer returns in a sub-

sequent month are treated as a reduction in the production volume. Indeed, scrap and returns as a percentage of production show little change in the months preceding and succeeding the gain-sharing agreement.

The gain-sharing formula implicitly assumes that the total quantity of labor employed changes proportionately with the standard direct labor hours for the products produced in a period. The gain-sharing formula may erroneously show productivity changes as a result of changes in production volume and product mix, even though at a given volume for a given mix no productivity changes have occurred.

The volume effect arises if actual total labor hours increases less than proportionately with standard direct labor hours (or production volume). The intuitive argument is best illustrated in Exhibit 7-2 and is also discussed in Banker (1985). Exhibit 7-2 plots actual total labor hours versus standard direct labor hours. It indicates that actual labor hours bear an approximately linear relationship to standard direct labor hours with a *positive* intercept. The reasons for the positive intercept are intuitive. Whereas we might expect actual direct labor hours (production and inspection labor hours) to increase proportionately with standard direct labor hours, an examination of the various components of indirect labor (such as maintenance labor, toolroom labor, setup labor, accounting and personnel staff) suggests that it consists of a fixed and a variable component. Thus, indirect labor hours will increase less than proportionately with production volume (standard direct labor hours).

The gain-sharing formula, however, computes a base period ratio as

$$\frac{\text{Average total labor hours in base period}}{\text{Average standard direct labor hours in base period}} = \frac{a_b}{s_b}.$$

This point is represented by the point A. The line OA represents the predicted actual labor hours for various quantities of standard direct labor hours according to the gain-sharing agreement. That is, the gain-sharing formula assumes that actual hours increase or decrease proportionately with standard direct labor hours so that the projected total labor hours in period t are given by

$$\frac{a_b}{s_b} \times s_t.$$

Exhibit 7-2 Plot of Actual Total Labor Hours versus Standard Direct Labor Hours: Gain-Sharing and Regression Estimates

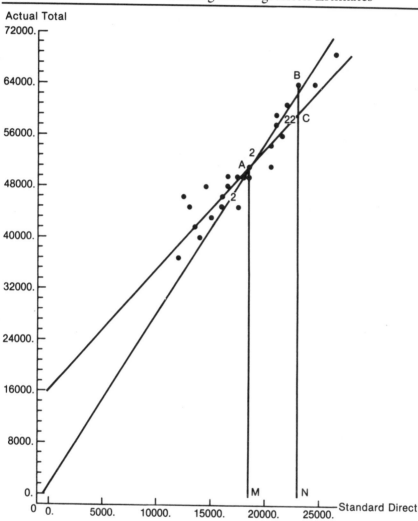

NB = Total Labor Hours Estimated by Gain-Sharing Formula
NC = Total Labor Hours Estimated by Regression Equation

Table 1. Standard Direct and Indirect Labor Hours per Unit of Products A and B.

	Direct Labor Hours per Unit	Indirect Labor Hours Per Unit
Product A	3	1
Product B	2	1

For a period t in which standard direct labor hours (say ON) are greater than the average standard direct labor hours in the base period, the gain-sharing formula will compare the actual total labor hours incurred (say CN), with the projected labor hours BN and signal a productivity gain. In effect the gain-sharing ratio

$$g_t = \frac{AM/OM}{CN/ON} = \frac{BN/ON}{CN/ON} = \frac{BN}{CN} > 1.$$

Based on the actual relation between actual labor hours and standard direct labor hours, the actual labor hours consumed in period t exactly equals estimated labor hours and no gain or loss in productivity results. In fact, observations in the range BC, which are evidently less productive (since actual labor hours exceed labor hours estimated on the basis of the underlying relation), will have gain-sharing ratios greater than one (resulting in a productivity gain under the gain-sharing formula). That is, when standard direct labor hours exceed the average base-period standard direct labor hours, productivity declines may be overshadowed by the favorable volume effects inherent in the gain-sharing formula. In analogous fashion, when standard direct labor hours are less than average, volume effects will be unfavorable and *real* gains in productivity may be reflected as productivity declines by the gain-sharing formula.

Changes in the product mix relative to the average product mix in the base period may also confound the productivity gain computations in the gain-sharing formula. This effect can be illustrated with a simple numerical example in which changes in product mix occur over two periods without any *real* productivity gains being realized. In order to distinguish product-mix effects from volume effects, we assume that the variable component of indirect labor hours varies proportionately with the number of units of Products A and B produced.[9] The standard direct and indirect labor hours per unit of Products A and B are described in Table 1.

We further assume that in Period 1, 100 units each of Product A and Product B are produced and that in Period 2, 200 units of Product

A and 50 units of Product B are produced. In order to highlight the impact of mix changes on productivity calculations, we assume that there are no labor usage variances. That is, the actual labor hours in each of the two years will exactly equal the standard direct and indirect labor hours for the number of units of Products A and B produced. Thus, actual labor hours in Period 1 equal $100 (3 + 1) + 100 (2 + 1) = 700$ and in Period 2, $200 (3 + 1) + 50 (2 + 1) = 950$. By construction, there is no change in the labor productivity of manufacturing operations over the two periods. As described below, however, the gain-sharing formula indicates a productivity gain in Period 2 relative to Period 1. The ratios of actual labor hours to standard direct labor hours in Periods 1 and 2 are given by

$$\frac{\text{Actual labor hours in Period 1}}{\text{Standard direct labor hours in Period 1}} =$$
$$\frac{100(3 + 1) + 100(2 + 1)}{100(3) + 100(2)} = \frac{700}{500} = 1.4$$

$$\frac{\text{Actual labor hours in Period 2}}{\text{Standard direct labor hours in Period 2}} =$$
$$\frac{200(3 + 1) + 50(2 + 1)}{200(3) + 50(2)} = \frac{950}{700} = 1.357$$

The gain-sharing ratio for Period 2 is computed as $\frac{1.4}{1.357} = 1.032$, which corresponds to a 3.2 percent gain in productivity. According to the gain-sharing agreement, half the gain will be paid to workers as a bonus. Therefore, each worker will receive 1.6 percent of his wages as a productivity bonus in the second period, even though, in fact, no productivity gains have occurred. Product-mix changes are reflected as productivity gains because the proportion of actual labor hours (direct plus indirect) to standard direct labor hours differs for the two products. In Period 2, more of Product A is produced, and the product has a lower ratio of actual hours to standard direct labor hours. This causes the total ratio of actual labor hours in Period 2 to standard direct labor hours in Period 2 to decline relative to Period 1. This decrease is reflected as a productivity gain in the gain-sharing formula. The problem occurs because the productivity computations do not distinguish between the varying relationship of total labor hours (including indirect labor hours) to standard direct labor hours for the two Products A and B.

Perhaps the distortive volume and mix effects documented above were intentionally written into the gain-sharing agreement. For instance, if increases in volume are interpreted as productivity gains, labor has incentives to produce more, thereby decreasing the average costs of the products produced. In our many meetings with plant and divisional managers, we explored this and other potential explanations for rewarding manufacturing labor on the basis of changes in volume and mix of products produced. Our discussions revealed that the division sells all of its products to other manufacturers. Thus, increases in volume and changes in mix are dictated by customers' demands for various products rather than the plant's ability to produce a higher volume or a more favorable mix. Production responds to customer orders and the plant can do little to influence the demand for its products. Manufacturing labor, therefore, should not be rewarded for higher volumes or favorable changes in mix, nor should it be penalized for unfavorable changes in volume and mix. Since changes in volume and mix are exogenous to the productivity of plant labor, labor compensation should be based on productivity improvements at a given level of activity and mix of products.[10] In the next section, we outline an approach for addressing these issues.

ANALYSIS AND INTERPRETATION

In this section we use actual data prior to and subsequent to the gain-sharing agreement to examine the two effects discussed at the end of the previous section.[11] We suggest simple modifications in the formula as a means to control for changes in the volume and mix. In our initial analysis we maintain certain basic assumptions about the production technology, such as the nonsubstitutability of capital and material for labor over the period of our analysis and the linearity and separability of the relation of Products A and B with direct or indirect labor consumption. In the next section we suggest generalized methods of measuring productivity if the specific features about the production technology maintained in our analysis do not hold.

The linearity and separability assumptions discussed above are precisely the assumptions that are necessary to justify the usual variance analysis in management accounting. Even under these assumptions, however, the gain-sharing formula cannot be interpreted in terms of simply a labor usage variance. The latter concept applies exclusively to direct labor whereas the gain-sharing concept extends to both direct and indirect labor. Furthermore, when the specific assumptions about the production technology are relaxed (as in the data envelopment analysis formulation that we discuss in the next section), the notion of labor productivity does not correspond to a labor usage variance.

Monthly data on actual direct and indirect labor hours and standard direct labor hours were obtained for 48 months. The gain-sharing agreement took effect in month 34. It was based on labor performance in the preceding 33 months. We shall refer to the first 33-month period as the *base period*. The particular base period was chosen because divisional management believes that the technology employed and the operating conditions in the plant prior to and subsequent to the gain-sharing agreement are largely identical. Recall that the gain-sharing agreement compares the ratio of average actual direct and indirect labor hours to average standard direct labor hours in the base period with the same ratio computed for each month after month 34. If the ratio for a particular month is greater than the base ratio, then a productivity gain is indicated; if it is less, then a productivity decline is signaled.

The data collected by us suggest that significant changes in volume and mix occurred over the 48-month period that we analyze. This will cause the gain-sharing productivity calculations to be confounded by volume and mix changes. We first model and estimate the relationship between actual labor hours and standard direct labor hours. This provides us with some insight as to whether actual labor hours increase proportionately with standard direct labor hours (or production volume).

Direct labor comprises productive labor and inspection labor. Indirect plant labor consists of repairs and maintenance labor, toolroom labor, equipment-handling labor, setup labor, and labor for inspection of setups. Salaried employees are administrative, personnel, and accounting staff at the plant. This suggests that labor hours associated with each labor category will vary differently with changes in volume. We expect actual direct labor hours to vary proportionately with standard direct labor hours whereas we anticipate indirect labor hours to vary less than proportionately with volume. The traditional management accounting model suggests that indirect labor consists of a fixed component that does not vary with volume and a variable component that varies proportionately with standard direct labor hours.[12] Finally, it is expected that salary hours are relatively independent of variation in production volume in the relevant range. Our analysis of the behavior of direct and indirect labor with changes in volume indicates that actual total labor hours varies linearly with standard direct labor hours with a positive intercept.

We estimate a linear relationship between total actual labor hours (as the dependent variable) and standard direct labor hours (as the independent variable) using the monthly data for months 1 through 33.[13] The estimated regression equation is presented as Equation 1 in Exhibit 7-3.[14] The coefficient of the intercept term is 15.537 with a t-ratio of 6.32.[15] The highly significant intercept term indicates that actual labor hours increase less than proportionately with increases in standard direct labor hours. The coefficient of 1.94 for standard direct labor hours is greater than one since total labor hours includes both actual direct labor hours and the variable component of actual indirect labor hours.

The regression equation provides a reasonable benchmark for predicting average total actual labor hours at various levels of activity defined in terms of standard direct labor hours.[16] We use the regression equation to propose a different measure of productivity. Our measure of productivity—d_t (for each month t following the gain-sharing agreement)—is computed by dividing the *predicted* labor hours based on Equation 1 by the actual labor hours in month t. Values of d_t greater than one indicate an increase in productivity relative to the average productivity in the base period. The measure evaluates the percentage savings in labor hours relative to a *standard*. Values of d_t less than one indicate productivity declines relative to average productivity in the base period. Instead of comparing input/output ratios in the two periods, our proposed productivity measure compares *predicted* labor hours with actual labor hours within a period. The productivity measure evaluates productivity gains at the actual volume for the period; that is, it controls for volume effects.

Exhibit 7-4 summarizes the productivity calculations under the gain-sharing formula (g_t) and our proposed measure (d_t) based on the estimated relation between actual total labor hours and standard direct labor hours for each of the 15 months following the gain-sharing agreement. Recall that if g_t is greater than one, half the gains are paid as bonus to workers. For values of g_t less than one, workers are paid their base wages. The Bonus column indicates the bonus percentage paid to workers each month. The next column evaluates the difference in the two productivity measures ($d_t - g_t$). Negative values indicate that the gain-sharing measure exceeds the regression-based productivity measure whereas positive values indicate the reverse. The

Exhibit 7-3 Regression Equations Estimating Direct, Indirect, and Total Labor Hours as Functions of Standard Hours or Product Units.

Equation 1:
TOT ACT = 15,537* + 1.94* STD DIR
           (6.32)   (14.91)
   ADJ R² = 0.874
      DW = 2.17

Equation 2:
ACT DIR = 612 + 1.15* STD DIR
           (0.92) (32.69)
   ADJ R = 0.971
      DW = 1.56

Equation 3:
ACT IND = 14,925* + 0.792* STD DIR
           (6.72)   (6.74)
   ADJ R² = 0.581
      DW = 2.47

Equation 4:
TOT ACT = 13,598* + 32.60* PROD A + 9.52* PROD B
           (5.87)   (14.84)   (8.09)
   ADJ R² = 0.897
      DW = 2.15

Equation 5:
ACT DIR = 740 + 18.92* PROD A + 4.78* PROD B
           (0.58) (15.58)   (7.34)
   ADJ R² = 0.901
      DW = 2.32

Equation 6:
ACT IND = 12,858* + 13.68* PROD A + 4.74* PROD B
           (6.42)   (7.21)   (4.67)
   ADJ R² = 0.688
      DW = 2.38

Equation 7:
STD DIR = 217 + 16.23* PROD A + 4.24* PROD B
           (0.21) (16.60)   (8.10)
   ADJ R² = 0.913
      DW = 2.13

Notes: TOT ACT = Actual Total Labor Hours
        STD DIR = Standard Direct Labor Hours
        ACT DIR = Actual Direct Labor Hours
        ACT IND = Actual Indirect Labor Hours
        PROD A = Number of Units of Product A
        PROD B = Number of Units of Product B
The t-statistics are indicated in parentheses in each equation
DW indicates the Durbin-Watson statistic in each equation
* indicates the coefficients are significant at the 1 percent level

Exhibit 7-4   Gain-sharing Formula and Regression-based
Productivity Measures Using Standard Direct Labor Hours

Month	Actual Total Labor to Standard Direct Labor Ratio (r_t)	Gain-sharing Formula Productivity (g_t)	Bonus Percent Paid $100(g_t - 1)$	Regression-based Productivity Measure (d_t)	Difference in the Two Productivity Measures $(d_t - g_t)$	Standard Direct Labor Hours Relative to Base Period (s_t/s_b)
34	2.567	1.082	4.122	1.005	−0.078	1.312
35	2.740	1.014	0.695	1.085	0.071	0.812
36	3.062	0.907	0.000	0.990	0.083	0.768
37	2.698	1.030	1.479	0.974	−0.055	1.217
38	2.625	1.058	2.923	1.061	0.003	0.992
39	2.456	1.131	6.561	1.104	−0.027	1.085
40	2.474	1.123	6.149	1.061	−0.062	1.223
41	2.593	1.071	3.574	1.081	0.010	0.970
42	2.644	1.051	2.542	1.033	−0.018	1.060
43	3.250	0.855	0.000	0.918	0.063	0.803
44	2.878	0.965	0.000	0.970	0.005	0.983
45	2.443	1.137	6.872	1.082	−0.055	1.193
46	2.516	1.104	5.216	0.989	−0.115	1.531
47	2.636	1.054	2.711	1.034	−0.021	1.069
48	2.651	1.048	2.407	1.088	0.040	0.887

last column (s_t/s_b) is the ratio of standard direct labor hours in period t to the average standard direct labor hours in the base period. Values greater than one correspond to larger production volumes in period t relative to the average production volume in the base period. Values less than one correspond to smaller production volumes relative to the base-period average.

We can use the data in Exhibit 7-4 to address plant management's concern that during some of the months in the postagreement period, workers were being rewarded for productivity gains according to the formula when in effect no *real* productivity gains were realized. Our analysis suggests that increases in volume are being shown as productivity gains according to the gain-sharing formula. This is evident by comparing columns $(d_t - g_t)$ and (s_t/s_b) in Exhibit 7-4. In months 34, 37, 40, 45, and 46, higher values of standard direct labor hours relative to the average standard direct labor hours (in the base period) correspond to higher values of productivity according to the gain-sharing formula compared to the regression-based productivity measure. Conversely, when production volume is low, as in months 35, 36, 43, and 48, the gain-sharing productivity measure with its adverse volume effects is smaller than the regression-based productivity measure. Recall that the regression-based productivity measure controls for volume effects. Thus, the differences in productivity measures based on the two methods are attributable to volume effects.

Equations 2 and 3 in Exhibit 7-3 provide the estimated linear relationship between actual direct labor hours and standard direct labor hours and actual indirect labor hours and standard direct labor hours. Estimating these relationships separately determines individual benchmarks for controlling each component of labor. We use the estimated relationships to verify our hypotheses about the behavior of direct and indirect labor hours in relation to production volume.

We first consider Equation 2 and verify that actual direct labor hours increase proportionately with standard direct labor hours. We cannot reject the null hypothesis that the intercept is equal to zero at 5 percent level of significance ($t = 0.92$). The coefficient on standard direct labor hours is 1.15. The null hypothesis that this coefficient is equal to one is rejected at 1 percent level of significance. This indicates that direct labor standards are set rather tight with average direct labor usage being about 15 percent more than the standard requirement.

We next consider Equation 3 and reject the null hypothesis that the intercept term is equal to zero at 1 percent level of significance. This implies that indirect labor hours vary disproportionately with standard direct labor hours. Furthermore, the coefficient on standard direct labor hours differs significantly from zero indicating that indirect labor hours increase, as postulated, with production volume.

An assumption maintained throughout our analysis thus far and implicit in the gain-sharing formula is that the product mix does not change during the period of our analysis. In our study of the gain-sharing program, we indicate how changes in the product mix may be reflected as productivity gains or losses in the gain-sharing formula. We next outline an approach to control for both volume and mix effects in calculating labor productivity. We continue to assume that Products A and B affect direct labor consumption and indirect labor consumption in a linear and separable manner.

Our earlier analysis assumes that actual labor hours vary linearly with total production volume. The objective here is to identify the factors that cause actual labor hours to vary. Our goal is to identify the various drivers of direct and indirect labor (Cooper and Kaplan 1987) which together constitute total labor.

We start by considering direct labor hours. Direct labor requirements for each of the Products A and B are clearly specified in production-specification and routing records. We expect actual direct labor hours to be closely related to and determined by the quantities of Products A and B produced.

Identifying factors that cause indirect labor hours to vary is considerably more difficult. Of the total indirect *manufacturing* labor hours, about 75 percent consists of machine-related labor hours for maintenance, repairs, setups, toolroom work, inspection of setups, and other tasks, while 10 percent consists of product-related labor hours, such as warehouse labor, and 15 percent consists of general supervisory labor. This suggests that a major factor behind variations in indirect labor hours is machine hours. Unfortunately, machine-hour data are not available for the entire period of our analysis. Our discussions with production planning suggested that machine hours bears a close relationship to the quantities of Products A and B produced. Machine hours also varies with the mix of Products A and B produced. The other component of indirect labor, contributed by administrative, accounting, and personnel staff, was relatively stable over the period of our study. Thus, key determinants of variations in actual labor hours are quantities of Products A and B produced.

We model actual total labor hours as a linear function of the products produced and do not restrict the intercept term to be zero. This formulation obviously controls for volume effects since actual labor hours are not assumed to increase proportionately with the quantities of Products A and B. Moreover, since the impact of each product on actual labor hours is separately considered, the effect of changes in product mix on indirect labor hours is explicitly modeled and estimated.

The regression equation is estimated using data from months 1 through 33. The estimated ordinary least squares regression equation and the corresponding t-values are given in Equation 4 of Exhibit 7-3. The significantly positive intercept indicates a fixed component of labor hours; that is, even after controlling for product mix, actual labor hours increase disproportionately with increases in volume. The coefficients of both the independent variables are also significant, implying that the quantities of Products A and B are both important determinants of total labor hours. The adjusted R^2 of 89.7 percent shows that most of the variation in actual labor hours is explained by variation in the quantities of Products A and B produced.

The regression equation provides a reasonable benchmark for predicting average actual labor hours at specified volumes and mix of

Exhibit 7-5 Comparison of Two Regression-Based Productivity Measures

Month	Based on Products A and B (p_t)	Based on Standard Direct Labor Hours (d_t)	Difference in the Two Measures ($p_t - d_t$)	Product-Mix Ratio (x^B_t / x^A_t)
34	1.055	1.005	0.050	2.519
35	1.095	1.085	0.010	1.229
36	1.000	0.990	0.010	1.215
37	0.993	0.974	0.019	1.405
38	1.085	1.061	0.024	1.348
39	1.137	1.104	0.033	1.503
40	1.094	1.061	0.033	1.645
41	1.096	1.081	0.014	1.592
42	1.039	1.033	0.006	1.522
43	0.920	0.918	0.002	1.282
44	0.982	0.970	0.011	1.353
45	1.115	1.082	0.033	1.352
46	1.022	0.989	0.033	2.287
47	1.055	1.034	0.022	2.234
48	1.116	1.088	0.027	2.406

Products A and B. Analogous to the productivity measure proposed earlier, the productivity p_t (in each month t following the gain-sharing agreement) can be computed by dividing the predicted labor hours based on Equation 4 in Exhibit 7-3 by the actual labor hours in month t. By construction, the productivity measure (p_t) evaluates productivity after controlling for both volume and mix effects. As before, values of p_t greater (less) than one indicate increases (decreases) in productivity relative to the average productivity in the base period.

Exhibit 7-5 summarizes the productivity computations (d_t) based on standard direct labor hours and the productivity computations (p_t) we propose based on the individual products A and B for each of the 15 months following the gain-sharing agreement. The column ($p_t - d_t$) evaluates the difference in the two productivity measures. This difference is positive for all 15 months indicating that the productivity measure based on individual Products A and B is greater than the productivity measure based on standard direct labor hours. This suggests that the benchmark for actual labor hours is higher when the regression equation is estimated using Products A and B than when the estimates are based on standard direct labor hours.

The last column, (x_t^B / x_t^A) in Exhibit 7-5 shows the ratio of the number of units of Product B produced relative to the number of units of Product A produced in month t. The ratios for each of the 15 months in the postagreement period indicate that the mix of outputs in the postagreement period shifted to a higher proportion of Product B.[17] This shift in product mix in the postagreement period provides an explanation for why the productivity measure p_t is higher than the productivity measure d_t, based on standard direct labor hours. First, we examine the estimated relationship between standard direct labor hours and the individual products A and B as shown in Equation 7 of Exhibit 7-3. The intercept term is not significantly different from zero whereas the coefficients on Product A and Product B are significantly positive. The ratio of the coefficient on Product B to the coefficient on Product A in Equation 4, which estimates total labor hours, is $9.518/32.599 = 0.292$. The ratio of the coefficient on Product B to the coefficient on Product A in Equation 7, which estimates standard direct labor hours, is $4.241/16.2295 = 0.261$. As the volume of Product B increases relative to Product A, standard direct labor hours will increase disproportionately to labor hours. If standard direct labor hours are used to estimate a benchmark for comparing against actual total labor hours, then the lower standard direct labor hours will yield a lower benchmark than the benchmark based directly on the two products A and B. Because of the lower benchmark based on standard direct labor hours, the productivity measure d_t will be smaller than the productivity measure p_t based on the two products A and B.

DATA ENVELOPMENT ANALYSIS

We now relax the underlying assumptions of the gain-sharing agreement. The agreement assumes that the quantities of Products A and B affect total labor hours in a linear and separable manner. These assumptions were maintained by us to facilitate a comparison of our targets and benchmarks with the targets based on the gain-sharing formula. Next, we indicate methods to measure productivity if the assumptions of linearity and separability do not hold. In essence, we specify a more general method for estimating the productive relationship between inputs and outputs.

The ordinary least squares regression estimates the average total labor hours as a function of standard direct labor hours (Equations 1,

2, and 3 of Exhibit 7-3), and the individual products A and B (Equations 4, 5, and 6 of Exhibit 7-3). The benchmark obtained from the regression compares actual total labor hours in a particular month with the *average* total labor hours predicted, based on performance in the estimation period. For incentives purposes, however, it may be necessary to set tighter benchmarks or targets; for instance, the benchmark may be set to reflect the minimum (rather than the average) quantity of labor required to produce specified quantities of Products A and B.

An added motivation for estimating the minimum rather than average labor hours necessary to produce a given set of outputs is that the microeconomic theory of the firm defines a production function as an extremal relationship. We use data envelopment analysis (DEA) to identify the production frontier estimating the minimum labor hours necessary to produce a given mix of Products A and B.[18] Introduced by Charnes, Cooper, and Rhodes (1978), DEA provides a new nonparametric method for evaluating the relative productivity of decision-making units in the manufacturing, service, other commercial, and not-for-profit sectors. Banker, Charnes, and Cooper (1984) show its flexibility in modeling complex production operations in multiple output environments. DEA technique has been employed in a wide variety of empirical settings. For instance, Charnes, Cooper, and Rhodes (1981) describe applications for program evaluation; Bessent, Bessent, Kennington, and Reagan (1983) evaluate school district efficiencies; Lewin and Morey (1982) measure efficiencies of courts; Banker, Conrad, and Strauss (1986) estimate hospital production functions; and Banker (1985) and Banker and Maindiratta (1986) consider productivity measurement for manufacturing operations. Other settings in which DEA models have been employed include fast-food restaurants (Banker and Morey 1986b), pharmacy stores (Banker and Morey 1986a), coal mines (Byrnes, Fare, and Grosskopf 1984), and steam-electric power generation (Banker 1984).

We continue to assume that the consumption of individual inputs (such as materials, direct labor, indirect labor, and capital) does not depend on the extent of other inputs used but only on the quantities of Products A and B produced. In other words, inputs are assumed to be separable or nonsubstitutable.[19] We relax the assumption of linearity, however; that is, we allow the marginal input requirement per unit of output (say Product A) to depend on the quantity of Product A produced. In other words, input consumption is allowed to be a nonlinear function of the output produced. Furthermore, we permit

cross effects of joint production so that the marginal input requirement per unit of Product A may depend not only on the quantity of
Product A but also on the quantity produced of Product B. We model
a general production relation between actual total labor hours and the
two products as follows:

$$\text{Actual total labor hours} = h(x^A, x^B)$$

where

$$x^A = \text{Product A quantities produced}$$
$$x^B = \text{Product B quantities produced}$$

The input-output relation modeled above may be estimated by
assuming some *parametric* form for the function $h(\cdot)$ that allows for
nonlinearities and cross-effects (such as a translog function). A theoretical basis for the structure imposed, however, is difficult to justify,
and consequently the estimates and hypothesis tests based on the
model are difficult to interpret since such tests and estimates are *conditional* on the parametric specification of the model correctly reflecting the underlying production relation.[20] Instead, we employ the nonparametric DEA technique that does not impose any particular
functional form. The method postulates certain regularity properties
for the production function, such as monotonicity and convexity of
the input-output function and, based on past data observations, provides a maximum likelihood estimate of the production frontier that
determines the minimum amount of total labor hours required to produce given quantities of Products A and B.

We first illustrate the DEA technique for the one input-one output case. Exhibit 7-6 plots actual total labor hours versus standard
direct labor hours for the first 33 months. The DEA technique uses
the 33 observations to determine a frontier given by the line segments
joining the points A, B, C, and D. (The actual frontier is obtained by
solving a linear programming problem.) The frontier represents the
minimum quantity of actual total labor hours for any given level of
standard direct labor hours. We use this estimated frontier to compute
the actual total labor productivity for each month subsequent to the
gain-sharing agreement. Exhibit 7-7 gives a graphical illustration of
the labor productivity calculation. The productivity for each month
is computed as the ratio of the minimum quantity of total labor
hours—shown as PQ in Exhibit 7-7—to the actual quantity of total
labor hours—QR in Exhibit 7-7. Thus, labor productivity would be
measured by QP/QR. The column titled (e_t) in Exhibit 7-8 contains

Exhibit 7-6   Plot of Actual Total Labor Hours versus Standard
Direct Labor Hours: Frontier Estimated by Data Envelopment
Analysis

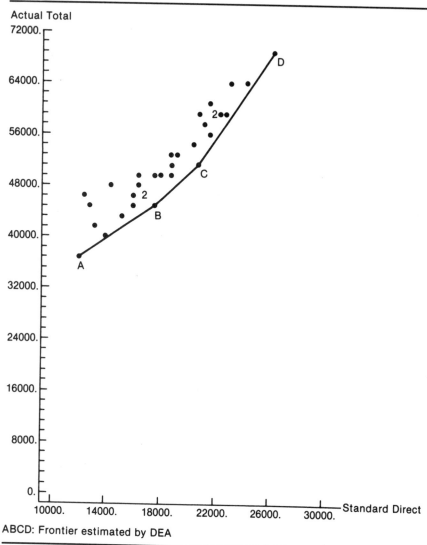

ABCD: Frontier estimated by DEA

Exhibit 7-7 Plot of Actual Total Labor Hours versus Standard
Direct Labor Hours: Frontier Estimated by Data Envelopment
Analysis

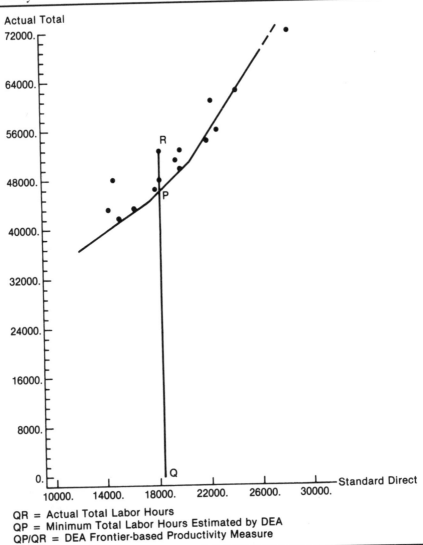

QR = Actual Total Labor Hours
QP = Minimum Total Labor Hours Estimated by DEA
QP/QR = DEA Frontier-based Productivity Measure

Exhibit 7-8 Comparison of Different Productivity Measures

	DEA Frontier		Regression		
Month	Based on Products A and B (f_t)	Based on Standard Labor Hours (e_t)	Based on Products A and B (p_t)	Based on Standard Labor Hours (d_t)	Gain-Sharing Based on Formula (g_t)
34	1.000	0.984	1.055	1.005	1.082
35	1.020	0.997	1.095	1.085	1.014
36	0.936	0.916	1.000	0.990	0.907
37	0.969	0.920	0.993	0.974	1.030
38	1.001	0.957	1.085	1.061	1.058
39	1.065	0.998	1.137	1.104	1.131
40	1.084	1.005	1.094	1.061	1.123
41	1.006	0.977	1.096	1.081	1.071
42	0.959	0.933	1.039	1.033	1.051
43	0.859	0.846	0.920	0.918	0.855
44	0.905	0.875	0.982	0.970	0.965
45	1.084	1.012	1.115	1.082	1.137
46	1.000	1.000	1.022	0.989	1.104
47	1.053	0.934	1.055	1.034	1.054
48	1.068	0.990	1.116	1.088	1.048

labor productivity measures for months 34 through 48 based on standard direct labor hours. Productivity values greater than one (in months 40 and 45) indicate productivity improvements over *best practice* in the preagreement period. In contrast, the linear regression identifies seven months (35, 38, 39, 40, 41, 45, and 48), in which the performance was at least 6 percent better than average. DEA productivity values less than one (particularly in months 36, 37, 42, 43, 44, and 47) indicate productivity declines in the postagreement period relative to the best practice in the base period. This latter identification is in general agreement with the regression results.

We next estimate the production relation when actual total labor hours is modeled as a general monotonic and convex function of the Products A and B. The production frontier determines the minimum quantity of total labor hours required to produce given levels of Products A and B. For the actual mixes of Products A and B in the postagreement period, actual labor productivity is computed as the ratio of the minimum labor required (as determined by the frontier) to the actual labor consumed. The labor productivities for months 34 through 48, when actual labor hours are estimated as a function of the Products A and B produced, is given in the column titled (f_i) of Exhibit 7-8. Note that the DEA productivities f_i are always greater than the corresponding numbers e_i. Although not true in general, this reflects the additional flexibility from using two independent variables (instead of just one) to determine actual total labor consumption.

A comparison of the productivity measures shown in Exhibit 7-8 indicates that the computations using the frontier are always lower than the productivity numbers based on the regression estimates. This follows since the frontier reflects best practice (the minimum amount of labor required to produce given outputs). The regression equation on the other hand estimates the average quantity of labor required to produce given outputs. We can also obtain estimates between the average and frontier estimates by using quantile regressions (Koenker and Bassett 1978), maximum likelihood parametric and non-parametric estimation (Banker, Datar and Rajan 1987), or stochastic data envelopment analysis (Banker 1987a).

The DEA technique also allows for substitutable inputs. This is the case, for instance, when the production technology is such that capital can be substituted for labor. The aggregate productivity can be disaggregated into a technical efficiency and an allocative efficiency.[21] Technical efficiency measures the efficiency with which a given mix of inputs has been used to produce outputs. It is a physical measure of efficiency relating the physical inputs consumed to the physical outputs produced. Allocative efficiency measures the extent to which the mix of inputs used deviates from the cost-minimizing (or profit-maximizing) mix of inputs. Aggregate productivity is the product of technical efficiency and allocative efficiency. We elaborate on the application of data envelopment analysis to productivity measurement in these general settings in Banker and Datar (1987a, 1987b).

CONCLUSION

Accounting textbooks have discussed the role of management accounting systems in controlling manufacturing operations. Kaplan (1983) has, however, argued that existing systems have not quantified the impact of various factors important for manufacturing control. Here we studied the manufacturing accounting and reporting system in a division of a large diversified corporation, emphasizing productivity improvements in its strategic considerations. We find that the manufacturing accounting system is focused largely on the income statement rather than on quantifying key factors influencing plant performance.

To enhance labor productivity in a plant, the division had implemented a new gain-sharing program that rewarded workers on the basis of productivity gains realized relative to a base-period average. We studied this gain-sharing program by interviewing the managers and other workers involved in its design and implementation, examining related documents, and analyzing cost and production data. We employed statistical tests to draw inferences about the behavior of various management accounting measures useful for productivity analysis and to assess the performance of the gain-sharing formula adopted by the plant to reward its workers.

We found some fundamental conceptual problems inherent in the productivity measure employed to assess labor performance. In particular, we have documented the distortive effect of changes in the volume and mix of products on the computed productivity measure and provided modifications that control for these effects and yield conceptually sound management accounting procedures for monitoring labor productivity. It was interesting that some of these problems were indeed suspected by management, although the existing accounting system did not provide the evidence to verify them. Our empirical analysis served to identify and highlight these conceptual problems.

An interesting possibility for future empirical research in management accounting is to identify and measure whether productivity improvement plans have a positive, negative, or neutral impact on plant performance. Essential to such a study is a careful examination of the conceptual management accounting issues in modeling productive relationships to ensure proper measurement of productivity. The approach developed in this chapter provides a basis for addressing these issues.

NOTES

1. McComas (1986) states: "Gone are the days when rapid inflation allowed companies to raise prices automatically, thereby covering up a host of problems on the cost side."

2. As Lord Kelvin so aptly put it, "When you can measure what you are speaking about and express it in numbers, you know something about it; but when you cannot measure it . . . your knowledge is of a meager and unsatisfactory kind." See Hayes (1982).

3. An oft-mentioned rationalization for this is the belief that the usual usage variances provide the necessary information about the productivity and efficiency of the enterprise. That this is not the case is discussed more fully in Banker, Datar, and Kaplan (1987) and Banker and Datar (1987a).

4. In a recent paper, Banker, Datar, and Kekre (1987) quantify the impact of increased capacity utilization and setup time in a stochastic, multiproduct environment. The impact of the resulting shop floor congestion and confusion is quantified for management control purposes in terms of longer inventory queues and corresponding holding costs.

5. Although the gain-sharing agreement explicitly allows for the impact of the introduction of new capital on actual labor usage, it presumes that on a short-term (temporary) basis substitutions between labor and capital will not occur. Throughout our analysis, we maintain this basic assumption about the production process. In the "Analysis and Interpretation" section, we indicate possible extensions of the measure we propose.

6. The standard direct labor hours serve as a measure of the direct labor content of the outputs.

7. Kaplan (1974) reports on similar problems in using accounting data to evaluate hospital performance. The relationship between hospital costs and service provided (that is, a matching of inputs with outputs) is best examined and understood using detailed records of individual departments.

8. This plan has also been implemented at other companies by the consulting firm from which it was purchased.

9. This is not a restrictive assumption since indirect labor hours bear a linear relationship to the quantities of Products A and B produced. In this example, we focus only on the variable component of indirect labor.

10. Other nonfinancial measures, such as percentage of on-time deliveries, may also be required to motivate the workers to meet daily production targets.

11. All actual data have been multiplied by a constant to maintain confidentiality.

12. In a later part of the chapter we focus on the specific factors that cause indirect labor to vary. This results in a more refined method of estimating indirect costs.

13. We verified the stability of the parameters of the estimated production technologies considered in this section by testing for possible differences between the first 16 and the next 17 months. Also, note that this specification of the relation does not restrict the intercept term of the regression equation to be zero.

14. For each regression equation that we estimate, we test for serial correlation (using Durbin-Watson statistics) and heteroscedasticity (using the Goldfeld-Quandt test). There was no evidence rejecting any of the usual OLS assumptions for all the regressions specified in Exhibit 7-3.

15. The magnitude of the estimated intercept term in this model may be influenced by changes in the product mix. Later in this section, however, we show that the intercept term is significant even after controlling for product mix.

16. The explanatory ability of the estimated regression equations can be further enhanced by including a dummy variable for the month of July when production lines are shut down and more maintenance activities occur. The basic insights of our analysis, however, do not change.

17. Welch's (1937) two-means test indicates that the mean of the ratio of Product B volume (units) to Product A volume (units) which is 1.407 in the preagreement period is significantly different at 12 percent level from the mean of the same ratio (equal to 1.659) in the postagreement period. The nonparametric Mann-Whitney (1947) test indicates that the median ratios are different at 6 percent level of significance.

18. Banker (1987b) shows that DEA provides maximum likelihood estimates for *all* probability density functions decreasing in the inefficiency term, including half-normal (truncated), exponential, and rectangular distributions.

19. This assumption is for simplicity in presentation. The case of substitutable inputs can be easily addressed in a manner analogous to the joint outputs situation considered in the text.

20. See, for instance, Hildenbrand (1981), Varian (1984), and Caves and Christensen (1980).

21. Rigorous development of these measures in the context of production economics theory is provided in Banker and Maindiratta (1987).

REFERENCES

Banker, R. D. 1980. "A Game Theoretic Approach to Measuring Efficiency. *European Journal of Operational Research* (October): 262–66.

———. 1984. "Estimating Most Productive Scale Size Using Data Envelopment Analysis." *European Journal of Operational Research* (July): 35–44.

———. 1985. "Productivity Measurement and Management Control." In *The Management of Productivity and Technology in Manufacturing*, edited by P. Kleindorfer. New York: Plenum.

———. 1987a. "Stochastic Data Envelopment Analysis." *Management Science*. Forthcoming.

———. 1987b. "Maximum Likelihood, Consistency and Data Envelopment Analysis." Carnegie-Mellon University. Mimeo.

Banker, R. D.; Charnes, A; and Cooper, W. W. 1984. "Models for the Estimation of Technical and Scale Inefficiencies in Data Envelopment Analysis." *Management Science* (September): 1078–92.

Banker, R. D.; Charnes, A; Cooper, W. W.; and Maindiratta, A. 1987. "A Comparison of DEA and Translog Estimates of Production Functions Using Simulated Data from a Known Technology." In *Studies in Productivity Analysis*, edited by A. Dogramarci and R. Fare. Boston: Kluwer Academic Press.

Banker, R. D.; Charnes, A.; Cooper, W. W.; and Schinnar, A. 1981. "A Bi-Extremal Principle for Frontier Estimation and Efficiency Evaluation." *Management Science* (December): 1370–82.

Banker, R. D.; Conrad, R. F.; and Strauss, R. P. 1986. "A Comparative Application of DEA and Translog Methods: An Illustrative Study of Hospital Production." *Management Science* (January): 30–44.

Banker, R. D., and Datar, S. M. 1987a. "Productivity Accounting and Variance Analysis." Carnegie-Mellon University. Mimeo.

———. 1987b. *Productivity Accounting for Manufacturing Operations*. Research monograph commissioned by the American Accounting Association, in progress.

Banker, R. D.; Datar, S. M.; and Kaplan, R. S. 1987. "Productivity Measurement and Management Accounting." Carnegie-Mellon University. Mimeo.

Banker, R. D.; Datar, S. M.; and Kekre, S. 1987. "Relevant Costs, Congestion and Stochasticity in Production Environments." *Journal of Accounting and Economics.* Forthcoming.

Banker, R. D.; Datar, S. M.; and Rajan, M. V. 1987. "Measurement of Productivity Improvements: An Empirical Analysis." *Journal of Accounting, Auditing, and Finance.* Forthcoming.

Banker, R. D., and Maindiratta, A. 1987. "Nonparametric Analysis of Technical and Allocative Efficiencies in Production." *Econometrica.* Forthcoming.

———. 1986. "Piecewise Loglinear Estimation of Efficient Production Surfaces." *Management Science* (January): 126–35.

Banker, R. D., and Morey, R. C. 1986a. "Efficiency Analysis for Exogenously Fixed Inputs and Outputs." *Operations Research* (July/August): 513–21.

———. 1986b. "Data Envelopment Analysis with Categorical Inputs and Outputs." *Management Science* (December): 1613–27.

Bassett, G., and Koenker, R. 1978. "Asymptotic Theory of Least Absolute Error Regression." *Journal of the American Statistical Association* (September): 618–22.

Bessent, A.; Bessent, W.; Kennington, J.; and Reagan, B. 1982. "An Application of Mathematical Programming to Assess Productivity in the Houston Independent School District." *Management Science* (December): 1355–67.

Byrnes, P.; Fare, R.; and Grosskopf, S. 1984. "Measuring Productive Efficiency: An Application to Illinois Strip Mines." *Management Science* (June): 671–81.

Caves, D. W., and Christensen, L. R. 1980. "Global Properties of Flexible Functional Forms." *American Economic Review* (June): 422–32.

Charnes, A.; Cooper, W. W.; and Rhodes, E. 1978. "Measuring the Efficiency of Decision-Making Units." *European Journal of Operational Research* 2 No. 6: 429–44.

———. 1981. "Evaluating Program and Managerial Efficiency." *Management Science* (June): 668–97.

Cooper, R., and Kaplan, R. S. 1987. "How Cost Accounting Systematically Distorts Products Costs." Ch. 8 of this volume.

Farrell, M. J. 1957. "The Measurement of Productive Efficiency." *Journal of the Royal Statistical Society,* Series A, 253–90.

Hayes, R. H. 1982. "A Note on Productivity Accounting." Boston: Harvard Business School, 9-682-084.

Hayes, R. H., and Clark, K. B. 1985. "Exploring the Sources of Productivity Differences at the Factory Level." In *The Uneasy Alliance: Managing the Productivity-Technology Dilemma*, edited by K. Clark, R. Hayes, and C. Lorenz. Boston: Harvard Business School Press.

Hildenbrand, W. 1981. "Short-run Production Functions Based on Micro-data." *Econometrica* (September): 1095–1125.

Kaplan, R. S. 1983. "Measuring Manufacturing Performance: A New Challenge for Managerial Accounting Research." *The Accounting Review* (October): 686–705.

———. 1974. "Management Accounting in Hospitals: A Case Study." In *Accounting for Social Goals*, edited by J. L. Livingstone and S. C. Gunn. New York: Harper & Row.

Koenker, R., and Bassett, G. 1978. "Regression Quantiles." *Econometrica* (January): 33–50.

Lewin, A. Y.; Morey, R. C.; and Cook, T. J. 1982. "Evaluating the Administrative Efficiency of Courts." *Omega 10 No. 4:* 401–11.

Mann, H. B., and Whitney, D. R. 1947. "On a Test of Whether One of Two Random Variables is Stochastically Larger than the Other." *The Annals of Mathematical Statistics* (March): 50–60.

McComas, M. 1986. "Atop the Fortune 500: A Survey of the C.E.O.s." *Fortune*, 28 April.

Varian, H. 1984. "The Nonparametric Approach to Production Analysis." *Econometrica* (May): 579–97.

Welch, B. L. 1937. "The Significance of the Difference Between Two Means When the Population Variances are Unequal." *Biometrika* (June): 350–62.

CHAPTER 8

How Cost Accounting Systematically Distorts Product Costs

Robin Cooper and Robert S. Kaplan

INTRODUCTION

IN order to make sensible decisions concerning the products they market, managers need to know what their products cost. Product design and new product-introduction decisions will be influenced by the anticipated cost and profitability of the product. Similarly, the amount of effort expended on trying to market a given product or product line will depend upon its apparent profitability; the higher the return, the larger the effort. Conversely, if product profitability drops, the question of discontinuance will be raised. In some environments, product costs play an important role in setting prices. This is particularly true for customized products with low sales volumes and without readily available market prices.

The cumulative effect of decisions on product design, introduction, support, discontinuance, and pricing helps define the strategy that the firm is enacting. If the product cost information is biased, there is no guarantee that the firm will enact an appropriate strategy. For example, the low-cost producer often achieves competitive advan-

We gratefully acknowledge the helpful comments made by Professors Michael Jensen and Ronald Hilton on a previous draft.

tage by servicing a broad range of customers. This strategy will be successful if the economies of scale exceed the additional costs caused by producing and servicing a more diverse product line. These additional costs, which represent diseconomies of scope, can become significant. If the cost system does not correctly attribute the additional costs to the products that cause them, then the firm might end up competing in a segment where the scope-related costs exceed the benefits from larger scale production. Similarly, a differentiated producer achieves competitive advantage by servicing those markets where the costs of differentiation are smaller than the additional prices charged for special features and services. If the cost system fails to measure differentiation costs properly, then the firm might choose to compete in a segment where these costs are too high.[1]

Despite the importance of cost information, there is still disagreement as to whether product costs should be measured by full or by variable cost.[2] In a full-cost system, fixed production costs are allocated to products. Reported product costs are meant to reflect the *total* cost of manufacture. In a variable-cost system, the fixed costs are not allocated; reported product costs are meant to reflect the *marginal* cost of manufacturing.

Academic accountants, supported by economists, have argued strongly that variable costs are the relevant ones for product decisions. They have demonstrated, using increasingly complex models, that setting marginal revenues equal to marginal costs will produce the highest profit. In contrast, accountants in practice continue to report full costs in their cost accounting systems.

Another major difference between the two approaches is the time frame over which the product decisions are made. The definition of variable cost that academic accountants use assumes that product decisions have a short time horizon, typically a month or a quarter. Costs are variable if, and only if, they vary directly with monthly or quarterly changes in production volume. Such a definition is appropriate if the volume of production of all products can be changed at will and there is no way to change simultaneously the level of fixed costs.

In practice, managers reject this short-term perspective. In their eyes, the decision to manufacture a product creates a long-term commitment to manufacture, market, and support that product. Given this perspective, short-term variable cost is an insufficient measure of product cost. Indeed, a long-term measure is required.

While full cost is meant to be a surrogate for long-run manufacturing costs, in nearly all of the companies we visited, management was not convinced that their full-cost systems were adequate for product-related decisions. In particular, management did not believe that their systems accurately reflected the costs of resources consumed to manufacture products. But they were also unwilling to adopt a variable-cost approach. The goal of this study, therefore, was to determine a relevant measure of product costs that would facilitate product decisions.

SITE SELECTION

The initial objective of the research was to document how firms determined the cost of their products. Sites were selected because they were either introducing or had introduced innovative product-costing systems, or because the existing cost systems were known to report erroneous product costs. The innovative firms were identified in two ways. Some self-selected; that is, they contacted the researchers and suggested that their new cost systems were worth studying. The rest were identified by reputation. Numerous managers and consultants mentioned certain firms as innovative. The researchers contacted these firms and asked if they were willing to participate.

The firms with poorly designed cost systems were identified in three ways. Again, some self-selected; they were aware that their cost systems were failing to report accurate product costs and contacted the researchers for advice. Some of them agreed to participate in the research. Some were contacted through personal friends of the researchers; if the firms had interesting cost systems or cost-system problems, and they agreed to participate, they were visited. The rest were contacted directly by the researchers because they were in industries that the researchers thought might pose interesting product-costing problems.

The site-selection process was not random. It purposely selected both innovative and troubled firms and included many self-selected firms. While this could have biased the research findings, there is substantial anecdotal evidence to suggest that this is not case. First, the managers at the research sites had often been previously employed by other companies. Typically, they viewed the failing of cost systems as a common phenomenon. Second, the consultants, other managers, and academics who have reviewed the research findings have generally agreed that they are representative of their own experiences. Finally, the research supports a theory that suggests when conventional cost systems will report distorted product costs. This theory is grounded in the mathematics of cost accounting; it is not an artifact of site selection.

Detailed records on such matters as how many firms were contacted and how many refused to participate were not kept. In all, about twenty-five firms were approached. Of these, around twenty agreed to site visits. (In one case, the firm made a presentation to the researchers.) To date, the cost systems of ten firms have been documented in depth.[3]

As more firms were visited and documented, a pattern of systematically distorted product costs began to emerge. Three firms were particularly important in providing useful insights. These companies had several significant common characteristics. They all produced a large number of distinct products in a single facility. The products formed several distinct product lines and were sold through diverse marketing channels. The range in demand volume for products within a product line was high, with sales of high-volume products frequently exceeding 1,000 times the sales of the lowest-volume products. As a consequence, products were manufactured and shipped in highly varied lot sizes.

While our findings are based upon these three companies, the same effects (though often to a lesser extent) were observed at the other sites.

THE COMPANIES

Mayers Tap

A privately owned machine-tool manufacturer, the company produces a full line of taps, drills, and reamers.[4] The firm's catalogs contain over 5,000 distinct items; about 3,000 distinct items are produced annually. Certain products are manufactured each year while others are manufactured on an as-needed basis.

Two factories, one designed for high-volume and the other for low-volume production, produce Mayers's output. Management believes that it is not possible to manufacture efficiently the high- and low-volume products under the same roof. The actual product mix being manufactured, at any one time, in either facility, varies widely.

Mayers Tap competes with a number of much larger firms and numerous smaller- and similar-sized firms. To offset the disadvantage of its relatively small size, the company differentiates itself by providing a very high-quality product with guaranteed availability. Management believes that its two-factory approach provides unmatched delivery times on both high- and low-volume items.

Schrader Bellows

This firm is the largest producer of pneumatic products in the world, although it does not have the largest market share in any of its individual product markets.[5] Schrader has several U.S. and overseas factories. The U.S. facilities each produce a limited number of product lines, but the production processes in each plant are similar. The company is one of six divisions of a conglomerate company that has recently been taken private via a leveraged buyout.

The facility we visited produces about 2,500 unique products, primarily valves and preparators assembled from approximately 20,000 different components.[6] The firm's product catalog contains considerably more items than are actually manufactured in a given year. The same manufacturing processes are used for the high- and low-volume items though some of the machinery is dedicated. Producing products with highly different volumes in the same facility apparently causes considerable manufacturing inefficiencies. High-volume runs are often interrupted to accommodate a low-volume run. The high-volume run is restarted when the low-volume item is completed.

Schrader Bellows is a full-line producer both in the pneumatic market and in the preparator and valve segment, where it is positioned as a high-quality, high-cost producer. This position reflects the firm's relatively high manufacturing costs and the competitive niche it has carved out for itself. Schrader has achieved virtual domination of the mill supply house distribution channel because of its willingness to handle low-volume orders.

Rockford

A division of a medium-sized industrial products conglomerate, Rockford produces bearings in several U.S.-based manufacturing facilities. With the exception of the main manufacturing plant, each facility produces a relatively narrow range of products. The company has recently opened a number of new facilities that are specifically designed to produce either high- or low-volume-run products. The trend toward focused factories is expected to continue.

The facility we visited produces four distinct product lines that together contain about 5,000 distinct items, of which 3,500 are manufactured in a typical year. These products vary from high-volume items to relatively special items with quite low-production volumes. The management of the plant is actively considering opening a new facility for the low-volume items.

In summary, all three firms are full-line producers. The management of each company stated that providing a single source for all of its customers' needs is a major competitive advantage. Management clearly believes that customers are willing to pay a premium for this service, though all acknowledge that a focused competitor, offering substantial discounts, could cause customers to split their orders.

The majority of products offered by these full-line producers are variants of other products and by themselves have relatively small sales volumes. These producers are therefore selling a portfolio of products in which a few products have very high sales volumes while most other products have quite low sales volumes. The firms are well characterized by the "80/20 rule"; 80 percent of the company's sales are generated by 20 percent of the products.

With their large product portfolios, the three firms were faced with continual decisions on product introductions. In most cases the products being introduced were designed for the specialized needs of a particular customer. The frequency of product-introduction decisions, and their limited importance, had led senior management in all three firms to delegate such decisions to relatively low levels of the organization.

Discontinuance decisions were much rarer; products tended to stay in the line even when no orders had been received for several years. Managers identified several reasons why it was harder to discontinue products than it was to introduce them. The most important reason was the desire to maintain a reputation for reliability of supply. This required keeping very low-volume items in the product line so that customers who needed them could still obtain them. The policy was even more evident for spare parts, which were stocked for many years after an item had been withdrawn. A second reason for keeping products was their ability to generate some contribution and "help pay for the overhead." Several managers voiced concern that dropping low-volume products would produce unabsorbed overhead. Personal reasons also affected product-retention decisions. In one company, the president had introduced a new product line while he had been the marketing manager, and no one was willing to discontinue the line even though it was performing poorly.

The net effect of making it easy to introduce but hard to discontinue products was a gradual, steady increase in their number and diversity. In retrospect, the introduction of new products was definitely a long-term decision; but ideally, the decision should have been made by recognizing the long-term costs of proliferating the product line.

THE IMPORTANCE OF PRODUCT COSTS

In all three companies, product costs played an important role in the decisions that surrounded the introduction, pricing, and discontinuance of products. While less obvious, reported product costs also appeared to play a significant role in the determination of how much effort should be assigned to selling products.

Typically, the individual responsible for introducing new products was also responsible for setting prices. Cost-plus pricing to achieve a desired level of gross margin was predominantly used for the special products, though substantial modifications to the resulting estimated prices occurred when direct competition existed. Such competition usually occurred for high-volume products but rarely occurred for the low-volume items. Frequently, there was no obvious market for low-volume products since they had been designed to meet a particular customer's needs.

In Schrader Bellows, the same margin was set for all products; the standard production cost was simply marked up by the desired margin. The majority of this firm's low-volume products showed a relatively stable 40 percent gross margin.

In Rockford, the desired margin was a function of the volume of production. If the product's production volume was low, then the desired margin was three times the margin expected of a high-volume product. The higher margin policy for low-volume products had only recently been introduced. (Previously, the same target margin had been used for all products.) In some cases, the higher margins were being achieved, but in others, the customer had refused to pay the increased prices and the firm had backed off.

In Mayers Tap, the targeted gross margin was a function of the product line; each product line had a specific gross margin target and new products were expected to at least meet this requirement. The cost accounting system played a significant role in setting the lower boundary of product prices.

Thus, in all three companies, product costs that included arbitrary allocations of fixed costs played an important role in determining price. This finding contrasts with some economics and accounting literature where there has been considerable debate about the validity (and existence) of cost-plus pricing. Our observations suggest that, for low-volume products, the cost of determining market prices outweighed the benefits. Pricing routines for high-volume products, in contrast, were typically based upon market considerations. As the economic penalty for being wrong increased, the firms expended more energy to determine appropriate prices for these products. Also, there likely were more market transactions for the higher-volume products so that market prices were easier to observe. Management argued that the dual approach to pricing was valid because their customers adopted a similar perspective. They were willing to pay any reasonable price for low-volume items but would shop around for the best price for high-volume ones.

ACCURACY OF PRODUCT COSTS

Managers in all three firms expressed serious concerns about the accuracy of their product-costing systems. These concerns were demonstrated in several ways.

Rockford explained its much higher margins for low-volume products as an ad hoc adjustment, based on its belief that the cost system was grossly underestimating the cost for these products. But management was not able to justify its decisions on cutoff points to identify low-volume products or the magnitude of many increases. Further, Rockford's management believed that a faulty cost system explained the ability of small firms to compete effectively against it for high-volume business. These small firms, with no apparent economic or technological advantage, were winning high-volume business with prices that were at or below Rockford's reported costs. And the firms seemed to be prospering at these prices.

In Schrader Bellows, production managers believed that certain products were not earning their keep because they were so difficult to produce. But the cost system reported that they were some of the most profitable products in the line. The managers were also convinced that they could make certain products as efficiently as anybody else. Yet competitors were consistently pricing comparable products considerably lower. Management suspected that the cost system was in some way responsible for the problem.

In Mayers Tap, the financial accounting profits were always much lower than those predicted by the cost system but no one could explain the discrepancy. The senior managers were also concerned by their failure to predict which bids they would win or lose. They often won bids they had overpriced because they did not really want the business and lost bids they had deliberately underpriced in order to get the business.

EXISTING COST SYSTEMS

As we examined the cost systems of the three firms, we discovered many common characteristics. Most important was the use of a two-stage cost allocation system: in the first stage, costs were assigned to cost pools (often called cost centers), and in the second stage, costs were allocated from the cost pools to the products.

The companies used many different allocation bases in the first stage to allocate costs from plant overhead accounts to cost centers. Rockford had thought seriously about each overhead account and had attempted to devise an allocation base that best represented the use of this overhead resource by the cost centers. Schrader Bellows used significantly fewer allocation bases, and direct labor hours played a major role in the allocation of plant overhead to the cost centers. Mayers Tap had only one cost center for its two plants and used direct labor hours to allocate all overhead.

Despite the variation in allocation bases in the first stage, all companies used direct labor hours in the second stage to allocate overhead from the cost pools to the products. Direct labor hours was used in the second allocation stage even when the production process was highly automated so that burden rates exceeded 1,000 percent. Exhibit 8-1 illustrates a typical two-stage allocation process.

Of the three research sites, only one had a cost accounting system capable of reporting variable product costs. Variable cost was

Exhibit 8-1 The Two-Stage Progress Using Direct Labor Hours

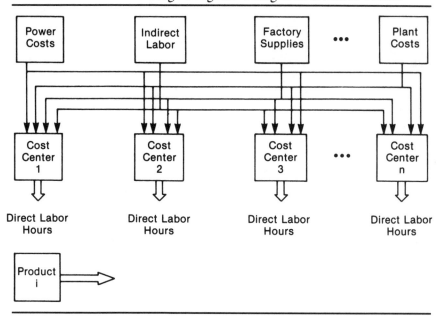

identified at the budgeting stage in one other site, but this information was not subsequently used for product costing. The inability of the cost system to report variable cost was a common feature of many of the systems we observed. Reporting variable product costs was the exception, not the rule.[7]

There was only one cost system in use at each firm even though costs were collected and allocated for several purposes, including product costing, process control, and inventory valuation. The cost systems seemed to be designed primarily to perform the inventory valuation function for financial reporting since they had serious deficiencies for process control (too delayed and too aggregate) and for product costing (too aggregate).

THE FAILURE OF MARGINAL COSTING

The extensive use of fixed-cost allocations in all the companies we investigated contrasts sharply with the advocacy by academics, for the past sixty-five years, to use marginal costs for product decisions. If the marginal-cost concept had been adopted by companies' management, then we would have expected to see product-costing systems that explicitly reported variable-cost information. Instead, in only a minority of research sites, did we observe cost systems that reported variable as well as full costs.

Product discontinuance was the only example of marginal costing, or incremental analysis, that we observed. Managers were reluctant to drop products because of their concern with unabsorbed overhead and, hence, decreased profits. In Mayers Tap, this perspective led the president to allow orders to be accepted, without review, even when the price quoted was as low as 60 percent of full cost. The president explained that variable cost was about 60 percent of total cost and his actions stopped the firm from selling below marginal cost.[8] Thus, the absence of a cost system capable of reporting variable product costs is not evidence that marginal costing, in some form, is not being used. But all of the managers we talked to were committed to using full cost for the majority of their product decisions.

We were able to identify two major reasons for managers' reliance upon full-cost information for product decisions. First, the relative ease of introducing products versus discontinuing them meant that the decision to introduce a product had long-term implications.[9] The managers felt that pricing was similarly long term in its orientation and had to be handled very carefully with the future in mind. They believed that it was easier to drop prices than to raise them. If market conditions mandated lower prices, this was usually accomplished by introducing or raising discounts off list price rather than by actually reducing list prices. Also, it was believed that salespersons would be tempted to shave prices closer to variable cost if they had this cost information. Using full cost reduced this temptation and apparently provided a degree of protection against underpricing.

Second, managers felt that variable costs did not adequately reflect the demands different products placed on their fixed or capacity resources. In their minds, full costs better reflected the consumption of these resources. This perspective is reasonable, given the context of the thousands of different products being produced by these firms and the varying demands by each product.

In summary, the traditional academic recommendation for marginal costing may have made sense when variable costs (labor, material, and some overhead) were a relatively high proportion of total manufactured cost and when product diversity was sufficiently small that there was not wide variation in the demands made by different products on the firm's production and marketing resources. But these conditions are no longer typical of many of today's organizations. Increasingly, overhead (most of it considered "fixed") is becoming a larger share of total manufacturing costs. In addition, the plants we examined are being asked to produce an increasing variety of products that make quite different demands on equipment and support departments. Thus, even if direct or marginal costing were once a useful recommendation to management, it is likely that direct costing, *even if correctly implemented*, is not a solution—and is perhaps a major problem—for product costing in the contemporary manufacturing environment.

THE FAILURE OF FIXED-COST ALLOCATIONS

While we consistently observed managers avoiding the use of variable or marginal costs for their product-related decisions, we also observed, as noted earlier, their discomfort with the full-cost allocations produced by their existing cost systems. We believe that we have identified the two major sources for the discomfort. Both reasons, which need to be understood in the context of the two-stage allocation process used by all the firms we studied, indicate serious inadequacies in the product-costing systems used by virtually all multiproduct organizations—not just the manufacturing firms described in this study or manufacturing firms in general; most service organizations have precisely the same failure in their product-costing systems.

The first problem arises from the use of direct labor hours in the second allocation stage to assign costs from cost centers to products. This procedure may have been adequate many decades ago when direct labor was the principal value-adding activity in the material conversion process. But as firms introduce more automated machinery, direct labor is increasingly engaged in setup and supervisory functions (rather than actually performing the work on the product) and no longer represents a reasonable surrogate for resource demands by products. In many of the plants we visited, labor's main tasks are to load the machines and to act as troubleshooters. Labor frequently works on several different products at the same time so that it becomes impossible to assign labor hours intelligently to products.

Some of the companies we visited had responded to this situation by beginning experiments using machine hours instead of labor hours to allocate costs from cost pools to products (for the second stage of the allocation process).[10] Other companies, particularly those adopting just-in-time or continuous-flow production processes, were moving to material dollars as the basis for distributing costs from pools to products.[11] Material dollars provide a less expensive method for cost allocation than machine hours because, as with labor hours, material dollars are collected by the existing cost system. A move to a machine-hour basis would require the collection of new data for many of these companies.

Shifting from labor hours to machine hours or material dollars provides some relief from the problem of using unrealistic bases for attributing costs to products. In fact, some companies have been experimenting with using all three allocation bases simultaneously: labor hours for those costs that vary with the number of labor hours worked (e.g., supervision—if the amount of labor in a product is high, the amount of supervision related to that product is also likely to be high), machine hours for those costs that vary with the number of hours the machine is running (e.g., power—the longer the machine is running the more power that is consumed by that product), and material dollars for those costs that vary with the value of material in the product (e.g., material handling—the higher the value of the material in the product, the greater the material-handling costs associated with those products are likely to be).

Using multiple allocation bases allows a finer attribution of costs to the products responsible for the incurrence of those costs. In particular, it allows for product diversity where the direct labor, machine hours, and material dollars consumed in the manufacture of different products are not directly proportional to each other.[12] For reported product costs to be correct, however, the allocation bases used must be capable of accounting for all aspects of product diversity. This is not always possible, even using the three volume-related allocation bases described above. As the number of product items manufactured increases, so does the number of direct labor hours, machine hours, and material dollars consumed. The designer of the cost system, in adopting these bases, assumed that all allocated costs have the same behavior; namely, that they increase in direct relationship to the volume of product items manufactured. But there are many costs that do not behave in the above manner. They are driven by diversity and complexity, not by volume.

The Cost of Complexity

The complexity costs of a full-line producer can be illustrated with a simple example. Consider two identical plants. One plant produces 1,000,000 units of product A. The second plant produces 100,000 units of product A and 900,000 units of 199 similar products. (The similar products have sales volumes that vary from 100 to 100,000 units.)

The first plant has a simple production environment and requires limited manufacturing-support facilities; there are minimal set-ups, and this reduces inventory movements and scheduling activities. The other plant presents a much more complex production-management environment. Its 200 products have to be scheduled through the plant, and this requires frequent setups, inventory movements, purchase receipts, and inspections. To handle this complexity, the support departments must be larger and more sophisticated.

The traditional cost accounting system plays an important role in obfuscating the underlying relationship between the range of products produced and the size of the support departments. First, the costs of most support departments are classified as *fixed*, making it difficult to realize that these costs are systematically varying. Second, the use of *volume-related* allocation bases makes it difficult to recognize the way in which these support-department costs vary.

Support-department costs must vary with something since they have been among the fastest growing in the overall cost structure of manufactured products.[13] As the simple example demonstrates, support-department costs vary not with the *volume* of product items manufactured, rather they vary with the *range* of items produced (i.e., the complexity of the production process). The traditional definition of variable cost adopts a monthly perspective and this effectively means volume related. Under most circumstances, complexity-related costs will not vary significantly in such a short time frame. Consequently, the costs of complexity are traditionally called fixed. Across an extended period of time, however, the increasing complexity of the production process places additional demands on support departments, and their costs eventually rise.

The output of a support department consists of the activities its personnel perform. These include such activities as setups, inspections, material handling, and scheduling. The output of the departments can be represented by the number of distinct activities that are performed. These activities typically generate paperwork, so the output of the departments can also be represented by the number of transactions handled. But since most of the output of these departments consists of human activities, output can increase quite significantly before an immediate deterioration in the quality of service is detected. Eventually, the maximum output of the department is reached and additional personnel are requested. The request typically comes some time after the initial increase in diversity and output. Thus, support departments, while varying with the demanded output, grow intermittently. The practice of annually budgeting the size of the departments further hides the underlying relationship between the mix and volume of demand and the size of the department. The support departments are often constrained to grow only when *budgeted* to do so.

These costs are perhaps best described as "discretionary" since the level of support-department cost is budgeted and authorized each year. The questions we must address are as follows: What determines the quantity of these discretionary fixed costs? Why, if these costs are not affected by the quantity of production, are there eight people in a support department and not one? What is generating the work, if not physical quantities of inputs or outputs, that requires large support-department staffs? We believe the key to understanding what causes discretionary overhead costs (i.e., what drives these costs) is to analyze the transactions generated by the production complexity of full-product-line producers.

TRANSACTION COSTING

Relying solely upon volume-related bases to allocate from cost centers to products produces a systematic bias in reported product costs. Low-volume products create more transactions per unit manufactured than their high-volume counterparts. The per unit share of these costs should therefore be higher for the low-volume products. But when volume-related bases are used to allocate support-department costs, high-volume and low-volume products are not treated differently because each individual unit produced represents the same volume of production.[14] Thus, when only volume-related bases are used for second-stage allocations, high-volume products receive an excessively high fraction of support-department costs and, therefore, subsidize the low-volume products.

As the range between low-volume and high-volume products increases, the degree of cross-subsidization rises. Support departments expand to cope with the additional complexity of more products, leading to increased overhead charges. The reported product cost of *all* products consequently increases. The high-volume products appear more expensive to produce than previously, even though they are not responsible for the additional costs. The costs triggered by the introduction of new, low-volume products are systematically shifted to high-volume products that may be placing relatively few demands on the plant's support departments.

Most of the transactions that generate work for support departments can be proxied by the number of setups. For example, the movement of material in the plant is often related to the commencement or completion of a production run. Similarly, the majority of the time spent on parts inspection occurs just after setup. Thus, while the support departments are engaged in a broad array of activities, it is possible to attribute a considerable portion of their costs to the number of setups associated with each product. Adopting this approach makes the cost associated with each setup relatively high, and hence, in the transaction-based cost system, the reported product costs of the low-production-volume items becomes much higher than in the direct-labor-based system.

Not all of the support-department costs are related (or relatable) to the number of setups. The cost of the setup personnel relates more to the quantity of setup hours than to the actual number of setups. Other overhead costs relate to the number of shipments received and still others to the number of shipments dispatched. For example, the number of inspections of incoming material is often directly related to the number of receipts, as is the time spent on moving the received material into inventory. The number of outgoing shipments is often a major factor in the activity level of the finished-goods and shipping departments. The assignment of these costs using a transaction-based approach reinforces the effect of the setup-related costs because the low-sales-volume items tend to trigger proportionally more small incoming and outgoing shipments.

Schrader Bellows had recently performed a "strategic cost analysis" that significantly increased the number of bases used to allocate costs to the products;[15] many second-stage allocations now used the number of transactions to assign support-department costs to products, and in particular, the *number* of setups was used to allocate a sizeable percentage of the support-department costs to products.

The effect of changing these second-stage allocations from a direct labor to a transaction basis was dramatic. While the support-department costs accounted for about 50 percent of overhead (or about 25 percent of total costs), the change in the reported product costs ranged from about minus 10 percent to plus 1,000 percent.[16] The significant change in the reported product costs for the low-volume items was due to the substantial cost of the support departments and the high variation in the lot sizes.

The magnitude of the shift in reported product costs can be seen in Exhibit 8-2.[17] It shows the costs for seven representative products as reported both by the firm's conventional cost system and by its new transaction-based system. The existing cost system reported gross margins that varied from 26 percent to 47 percent, while the strategic analysis showed gross margins that ranged from minus 258 percent to plus 46 percent. The trends in the two sets of reported product profitabilities were clear (though in neither case were they followed perfectly): the existing direct-labor-based system had identified the low-volume products as the most profitable, while the strategic cost analysis indicated exactly the reverse.

There are three important messages in the exhibit and in the company's findings in general. First, traditional systems that assign costs to products using a single volume-related base materially misreport product costs. Second, this misreporting is systematically biased. The low-volume products are consistently undercosted, and the high-volume products are consistently overcosted. Third, accurate product costs cannot be achieved by cost systems that rely only on volume-related bases (even multiple bases such as machine hours and material quantities) for second-stage allocation. A different type of allocation base is required since some overhead costs vary with the complexity of production. These bases must be transaction related to reflect the number of transactions performed, as opposed to the volume of product produced.

The shift to transaction-related allocation bases is a more fundamental change to the philosophy of cost-systems design than is at first realized. In a traditional cost system that uses volume-related bases, the costing element is always the product. It is the product that consumes direct labor hours, machine hours, or material dollars. Therefore, it is the product that gets costed. In a transaction-related system, the costing element is that which consumes the activity that caused the transaction to be originated. For example, if the transaction is a setup, then the costing element will be the production lot because each production lot requires a *single* setup. The same is true

Exhibit 8-2 Comparison of Reported Product Costs Using Existing and Transaction-Based Cost Systems at Schrader Bellows

Product	Sales Volume	Existing Cost System		Transaction-Based System		Percent of Change	
		Unit Cost[a]	Unit Gross Margin	Unit Cost[a]	Unit Gross Margin	Unit Cost	Unit Gross Margin
1	43,562	7.85	5.51	7.17	6.19	(8.7)	12.3
2	500	8.74	3.76	15.45	(2.95)	76.8	(178.5)
3	53	12.15	10.89	82.49	(59.45)	578.9	(645.9)
4	2,079	13.63	4.91	24.51	(5.97)	79.8	(221.6)
5	5,670	12.40	7.95	19.99	0.36	61.3	(93.4)
6	11.169	8.04	5.49	7.96	5.57	(1.0)	1.5
7	423	8.47	3.74	6.93	5.28	(18.2)	41.2

[a] The sum of total cost (sales volume × unit cost) for all seven products is different under the two systems because the seven products only represent a small fraction of total production.

for purchasing activities, inspections, scheduling, and material movements. The costing element is no longer the product but those elements the transaction affects. In the transaction-related costing system, the unit cost of a product is determined by dividing the cost of a transaction by the number of units in the costing element. For example, when the costing element is a production lot, the unit cost of a product is determined by dividing the production-lot cost by the number of units in the production lot.

This change in the costing element is not trivial. In the Schrader Bellows strategic cost analysis (see Exhibit 8-2), product 7 appears to violate the strong inverse relationship between profits and production-lot size for the other six products. A more detailed analysis of the seven products, however, showed that product 7 was assembled with components also used to produce two high-volume products, (numbers 1 and 6) and that it was the production-lot size of the components that was the dominant cost driver, not the assembly-lot size, or the shipping-lot size.

In a traditional cost system, the value of commonality of parts is hidden. Low-volume components appear to cost only slightly more than their high-volume counterparts. There is no incentive to design products with common parts. The shift to transaction-based costing identifies the much lower costs that derive from designing products with common (or fewer) parts and the much higher costs generated when large numbers of unique parts are specified for low-volume products. In recognition of this phenomenon, some companies are experimenting with assigning material-related overhead on the basis of the total number of different parts used, and not on the physical or dollar volume of materials used.

LONG-TERM VARIABLE COST

The nonvolume-related support-department costs, unlike traditional variable costs, do not vary with short-term changes in activity levels. Traditional variable costs vary in the short run with production fluctuations because they represent cost elements that require no managerial actions to change the level of expenditure.[18] In contrast, any decrement in overhead costs associated with reducing diversity and complexity in the factory will take many months to realize and will require specific managerial actions. The number of personnel in support departments will have to be reduced, machines may have to be sold off, and some supervisors will become redundant. Actions to accomplish these overhead cost reductions will lag, by months, the complexity-reducing actions in the product line and in the process technology. But this long-term cost response mirrors the way overhead costs were first built up in the factory; as more products with specialized designs were added to the product line, the organization simply muddled through with existing personnel. It was only over time that overworked support departments requested and received additional personnel to handle the increased number of transactions that had been thrust upon them.

The personnel in the support departments are often highly skilled and possess a high degree of firm-specific knowledge. Management is loathe to lay them off when changes in market conditions temporarily reduce the level of production complexity. Consequently, when the workload of these departments drops, surplus capacity is allowed to develop.

The long-term perspective of management toward its products often made it difficult to utilize the surplus capacity. We did not observe or hear about a situation in which this capacity was used to introduce a product that had only a short life expectancy. Some companies justified the acceptance of special orders or incremental business because they "knew" that the income from this business more than covered their variable or incremental costs. They failed to realize that the long-term consequence from accepting such incremental business was a steady rise in the costs of their support departments.

THE SIGNIFICANCE OF NOT KNOWING
PRODUCT COSTS

The magnitude of the errors in reported product costs and the nature of their bias make it difficult for full-line producers to enact sensible strategies. The existing cost systems clearly identify the low-volume products as the most profitable and the high-volume ones as the least profitable. Focused competitors, on the other hand, will not suffer from the same handicap. Their cost systems, while equally poorly designed, will report more accurate product costs because they are not distorted as much by lot-size diversity.

With access to more accurate product-cost data, a focused competitor can sell the high-volume products at a lower price. The full-line producer is then apparently faced with very low margins on these products and is naturally tempted to de-emphasize this business and concentrate on apparently higher-profit, low-volume specialty business. This shift from high-volume to low-volume products, however, does not produce the anticipated higher profitability. The firm, believing in its cost system, chases illusory profits.

The firm is victimized by diseconomies of scope. In trying to obtain the benefits of economy of scale by expanding its product offerings to better utilize its fixed or capacity resources, the firm does not see the high diseconomies it has introduced by creating a far more complex production environment. The cost accounting system fails to reveal this diseconomy of scope. Schrader Bellows is a good example of this phenomenon. It was misled by its cost system. At the time of our visit, over 70 percent of its products were being sold below the sum of short-term and long-term variable cost. The owners, believing there was little they could do to turn the division around, eventually sold it to a competitor that was in a better position to rationalize its product offering.

In the other companies, it is more difficult to determine the severity of the cross-subsidization. The companies all manufacture products with a wide range of production-lot sizes, and therefore their volume-based cost systems very likely misreport product costs. Without a transaction-based cost system, however, it is impossible to measure accurately the magnitude of this misreporting. In Rockford, management requires higher margins for small-volume products because they believe these products are more expensive to manufacture than their cost system reports. The magnitude of the cost distortions shown by Schrader Bellows suggests that while Rockford is correct in increasing the desired margin for its low-volume products, it almost certainly underestimates the adjustment required for many of these products.[19]

SUMMARY

One message comes through overwhelmingly in our experiences with the three firms, and with the many others with whom we talked and worked. Almost all product-related decisions—introduction, pricing, and discontinuance—are long-term decisions.

Management accounting thinking (and teaching) during the past half-century has concentrated on information for making short-run incremental decisions based on variable, incremental, or relevant costs (all terms commonly found in cost and management accounting textbooks); it has missed the most important aspect of product decisions. Invariably, the time period for measuring "variable," "incremental," or "relevant" costs has been about a month; that is, the time period corresponding to the cycle of the firm's internal financial reporting system. While any discussion of costs, in textbooks or in classes, opens with the admonition that notions of fixed and variable are meaningful only with respect to a particular time period, instructors immediately discard this warning and teach the rest of the course from the perspective of one-month decision horizons.[20]

This short-term focus for product costing has led to the situation we found in all the companies we visited. A large and growing proportion of total manufacturing costs is considered "fixed." This paradox—that what we call "fixed" costs are, in fact, the most variable and most rapidly increasing costs—seemingly has eluded most accounting practitioners and scholars. The key for unlocking the paradox arises from introducing two fundamental changes in our thinking about cost behavior.

First, the allocation of costs from the cost pools to the products should be achieved using bases that reflect cost drivers. Since many overhead costs are driven by the complexity of production, not the volume of production, nonvolume-related bases are required. Second, many of these costs are somewhat discretionary, and while they vary with changes in the complexity of the production process, these changes are intermittent. A traditional cost system that defines variable costs as varying in the short term with production volume will misclassify them as fixed costs.

The misclassification arises from an inadequate understanding of the actual cost drivers for most overhead costs. Our investigations and those of Miller and Vollmann reveal that many overhead costs vary with transactions: transactions to order, schedule, receive, inspect, and pay for shipments; to move, track, and count inventory; to schedule production work; to set up machines; to perform quality assurance; to implement engineering change orders; and to expedite and ship orders.[21] The cost of these transactions is largely independent of the size of the order being handled; the cost does not vary with the amount of inputs or outputs. It does vary, however, with the need for the transaction itself; if the firm introduces more products, if it needs to expedite more orders, or if it needs to inspect more components, then it will need larger overhead departments to perform these additional transactions.

Product costs are almost all variable costs. Some of the sources of variability relate to physical volume of items produced. These costs will vary with units produced, or in a varied, multiproduct environment, with surrogate measures such as labor hours, machine hours, material dollars and quantities, or elapsed time of production. Other costs, however, particularly those arising from overhead support and marketing departments, vary with the diversity and complexity in the product line.[22] The variability of these costs is best explained by the incidence of transactions to initiate the next stage in the production, logistics, or distribution process.

A comprehensive product-cost system, incorporating the long-term variable costs of manufacturing and marketing each product or product line, should provide a much better basis for managerial decisions on pricing, introducing, discontinuing, and reengineering product lines. The cost system may even become strategically important for running the business and creating sustainable competitive advantages for the firm.

NOTES

1. Porter (1985) develops the concepts behind the two generic strategies of low cost and differentiation. He also emphasizes the important role for cost systems if either strategy is to be successfully executed.

2. Fixed costs are those costs not expected to be affected by variations in production activity during a period; variable costs are those costs expected to vary, usually proportionately, with the level of outputs produced or inputs consumed during a period. Here, the terms marginal and variable cost are used interchangeably. Marginal cost is the term more commonly used in microeconomics, and variable cost is more commonly used in accounting.

3. Some of these field trips have also been documented in a number of Harvard Business School teaching cases. These cases have been disguised (where requested) and so written that they can be taught in eighty-minute segments. When read in conjunction with the teaching notes, these cases provide an in-depth description of the cost systems encountered by the researchers.

4. See Harvard Business School, Case Series 9-185-111, for a more detailed description of the company, its product line, production process, and accounting system.

5. See Harvard Business School, Case Series 9-186-272, for a more detailed description of the company, its product line, production process, and accounting system.

6. Valves control the flow of gases through a system; preparators control the quality of the gas by removing impurities such as oil, dust, and water vapor.

7. One of the most popular cost accounting software packages had to be specially modified (by the user!) to report both variable and fixed overhead.

8. A subsequent redesign of the cost system showed that, for the entire firm, variable cost amounted to 74 percent of total cost.

9. Only if the product was a real disaster was it likely to be quickly discontinued.

10. This has been discussed in the literature for several years but rarely implemented. See Fisher Technologies, Harvard Business School, Case 9-186-188. A major commercially available cost accounting system has only recently introduced a machine-hour version.

11. See The Ingersoll Milling Machine Company, Harvard Business School, Case 9-186-189 and "Direct Labor Costs Not Always Relevant at H-P," *Management Accounting* (February 1985), p. 10.

12. Products are said to be diverse when the patterns of resources they consume are different.

13. J. G. Miller and T. E. Vollmann, "The hidden factory," *Harvard Business Review* (September–October 1985): 142–50; in particular, see Exhibit I, p. 143.

14. For example, returning to our two-plant example of the preceding section, a product with an annual output of 800 units in the second plant will be allocated about .08 percent of the overhead costs by any volume-related measure—whether direct labor, machine hours, or material dollars. Product A, on the other hand, with annual demand of 100,000 units, will be allocated about 10 percent of factory overhead by any volume-related measure.

15. This work was undertaken by William F. Boone, vice president of planning at Schrader Bellows's parent company.

16. Some products had reported product costs that increased several thousand percent. These were extremely low-volume items, however, and should be considered anomalous.

17. This exhibit is taken from the teaching case on the company. The numbers reported in this exhibit, while disguised, are representative of the company's findings.

18. This is definitely true of cost elements such as material and power. It is not as true for direct labor. The modern labor force is often better represented as a traditional fixed cost, or more accurately, in our terms, a long-term variable cost.

19. Rockford tripled its desired margin. This has the same effect as maintaining the original margin but finding out that the product is twice as expensive to manufacture.

20. All fixed in the very short run; all variable in the long run.

21. "The hidden factory."

22. The attribution of marketing costs to products is also highly important, but it is rarely performed by existing cost systems. We considered this topic to be beyond our scope here, but the relevant issues are described in the "Winchell Lighting" case series. Harvard Business School, Case Series 9-187-073, 9-187-074, and 9-187-075.

CHAPTER 9

Adapting a Cost Accounting System to Just-in-Time Manufacturing: The Hewlett-Packard Personal Office Computer Division

James M. Patell

INTRODUCTION

Say, Jim, the manufacturing group converted the Touchscreen assembly line to just-in-time over the weekend, and I just wanted to make sure that it wouldn't accidentally raise any red flags over here in accounting. "No sweat, Bill. I'll bet that Debbie can reprogram a few lines of code and you'll never know the difference."

The above exchange between two pivotal characters in this study is intended both to introduce the central issue of the case and to impart a sense of the personalities involved. As the dialogue suggests, the case focuses on the changes that were induced in an established and elaborate cost accounting system by the introduction and evolution of just-in-time manufacturing for the assembly and test of microcomputers.

This chapter attempts to provide a comprehensive and detailed picture of a particular situation in the hope of stimulating hypotheses for further study; it is intended to do more problem finding than

Many people at the Hewlett-Packard Personal Office Computer Division have been both generous and patient in explaining their operation; I am especially grateful to James Luttenbacher and Debbie Wirsing for the knowledge and time that they have contributed to this study. Professor J. Michael Harrison's advice also is much appreciated. Helpful comments were received from M. Edgar Barrett, Alison Kirby, Katherine Schipper, G. Peter Wilson, and Mark Wolfson.

problem solving. Yin (1984) defines a case study as "an empirical inquiry that investigates a contemporary phenomenon within its real-
life context when the boundaries between phenomenon and context
are not clearly evident and in which multiple sources of evidence are
used."[1] My study's initial purpose was to detect whether Hewlett-
Packard's just-in-time manufacturing experience had spawned fundamentally new approaches to cost accounting or had uncovered fundamental weaknesses in traditional procedures. Perhaps the most
interesting questions and insights to emerge, however, concern the
boundaries between cost accounting and production in both the design and the operational phases.

The opening dialogue is facetious in one regard; one does not "go
just-in-time" overnight. The study site uses modern manufacturing
processes to produce complex high-technology products, and both the
products and the processes have undergone a series of frequent and
sometimes drastic changes over a three-year production history.
Moreover, evolutionary development seems to be an integral feature
of just-in-time manufacturing, in which the reduction of buffer stocks
and a careful attention to quality control are intended to uncover hidden flaws in the production process. Finally, as the information system is reconfigured to represent adequately the continually evolving
production process, changes in the cost accounting systems necessarily lag changes on the shop floor.

On the other hand, the opening dialogue accurately portrays the
interpersonal dynamics and organizational behavior of the main actors; the Hewlett-Packard (HP) personnel who participated in this
study are energetic and resourceful, and they seem genuinely eager
to meet the challenge of adapting to just-in-time manufacturing. For
example, although one might be skeptical when members of an accounting department make such remarks as, "We need to turn off the
paperwork," or, "Reduce the infrastructure," it is easier to envision a
group working to reduce its own size in a firm that maintains a reputation for keeping its personnel gainfully employed in the face of
severe business fluctuations.

Many of the specific changes described here also have been instituted at other firms and other HP divisions, and what emerges is a
portfolio of procedures assembled to fit the situation at hand rather
than a single brilliant stroke. The HP atmosphere is one of intelligent
people doing reasonable things in a fast-changing and very cost-
conscious environment. Thus, while a theorist probably cannot ap-
peal to the invisible hand of market efficiency to sift out optimal ad-

aptations within a single firm, there do not seem to be any artificial or "cultural" constraints on the innovations that can be tried or the established procedures that can be discarded.

The next two sections of the chapter describe the manufacturing environment. The fourth section examines the cost accounting systems in detail, including three sets of changes that accompanied the introduction of just-in-time manufacturing. The fifth section devotes special attention to the measurement of quality in the production process, and the sixth section describes the final accounting report package. Four potential areas for further inquiry are discussed in the seventh section, and conclusions appear in the last section.

THE SITE

The study was conducted from May 1985 through June 1986 at the Hewlett-Packard Personal Office Computer Division (POD) located in Sunnyvale, California. In November 1982, HP combined two divisions to form POD; in the beginning, it produced and marketed terminals and printed circuit boards, with terminals representing two-thirds of total sales. In March 1983, HP decided to focus on a newly designed personal computer as its high-volume entry into the microcomputer market. POD was reconfigured to concentrate on this product line and it now has worldwide responsibility for the research, development, and manufacturing of personal computers.

The product line includes two personal computers: the HP150 Touchscreen and the HP Vectra. Introduced in October 1983, the Touchscreen is an MS-DOS personal computer featuring an innovative touch-screen monitor that uses a matrix of light beams embedded along the sides of the display. The Vectra, which uses the Intel 80286 microprocessor, is a somewhat larger personal computer that is compatible with and a competitor to the IBM PC/AT; it was introduced in October 1985.

During its 1985 fiscal year, the Hewlett-Packard Company employed 84,000 persons worldwide and earned net income of $489 million on revenues of $6.5 billion. HP operates 23 U.S. and 14 international manufacturing facilities. It maintains sales and support offices in 100 cities in the United States and 275 other locations in 75 countries. As part of HP's measurement, design, information, and manufacturing equipment and systems product group, POD has

Exhibit 9-1 Personal Office Computer Division (POD)

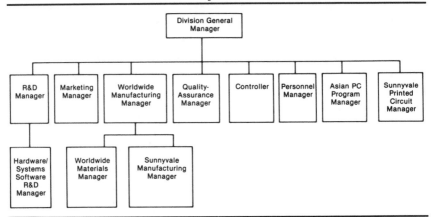

worldwide responsibility for the Touchscreen/Vectra product line. HP's Grenoble (France) division manufactures these two microcomputers for the European market. Both the Sunnyvale and Grenoble sites produce only the system processing units: keyboards are manufactured by the HP Singapore Division; other accessories are produced in Puerto Rico.

Essentially all of POD's output is delivered to the Personal Computer Distribution Center (PCDC) located in San Jose, about five miles away. While the PCDC division is responsible for domestic distribution of POD's microcomputers and fifteen other product lines, POD makes its own market forecasts and sets its own production schedules.

Approximately 1,025 employees work at the POD's one-building facility. Exhibit 9-1 shows the internal organization of POD, and Exhibit 9-2 depicts the details of the accounting function within the finance department.

JUST-IN-TIME MANUFACTURING AT
THE HP PERSONAL OFFICE
COMPUTER DIVISION (POD)

During the ten months preceding the Touchscreen decision (November 1982–August 1983), POD made fifty types of circuit boards and twelve kinds of terminals.[2] Production was organized as a pure batch process in which specific work orders were generated to

Exhibit 9-2   Personal Office Computer Division Finance Unit

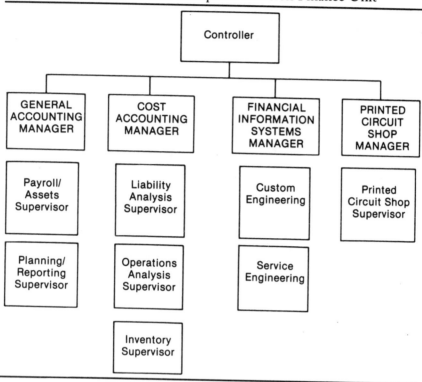

meet customer orders or to replenish inventory; the number of units produced per work order varied widely. Carts containing the necessary parts for the order originated from raw material stores and were routed through a series of work stations where subassemblies were completed and integrated into the final product. From work order issuance to completion, a typical batch spent about six weeks in production, with costs being accumulated on the work order in a more or less textbook job-order costing fashion. Raw materials were stored on the factory floor and, together with the work-in-process inventories at the various work centers, occupied approximately 50 percent of the factory floor space. Finished goods were transferred to a nearby warehouse. As a rough measure of manufacturing-process quality, management estimated that approximately 10 percent (dollar value) of all purchased material ultimately was lost as scrap.

Design of the HP150 Touchscreen began early in 1983, and in

March HP decided to position the product as a major new entry in the personal computer market. Because the Touchscreen's estimated sales volume would be ten times greater than a typical data terminal product, three major decisions were made:

1. Production of other terminal products would be transferred to other divisions or to subcontractors. (Over the next three years, several of these products were discontinued entirely.) POD also would subcontract fabrication of the keyboards to the HP Singapore Division, and one major circuit board with high-labor content would be subcontracted to an outside vendor.

2. Production would be scheduled to maintain level production rates. Only the main system processing unit (SPU) would be made at POD; these units would be produced to stock and shipped immediately to PCDC where they would be combined with keyboards, printers, and other items for final distribution.

3. The manufacturing process would employ just-in-time (JIT) techniques. At first, two elements were stressed. First, raw material and work-in-process inventories were strictly limited so that parts would be provided to the next production stage only as needed. Second, production along the entire assembly line would be stopped if parts were missing at any stage.

In part, these changes were adopted simply to meet the impending jump in scheduled production volume and to provide space for the production lines and associated inventories of parts and subassemblies. About this time, however, published descriptions of JIT manufacturing at firms like Toyota (and at least two other HP divisions) began to document substantial improvements in quality attributed to two features of JIT.[3] First, defective parts or subassemblies are caught quickly, before they are built into a large number of buffered subassemblies; and second, workers become more involved in quality because a defect at any station can shut down the whole line. HP had just begun to emphasize quality assurance at POD, so many causally separate quality-control improvements developed in parallel with JIT. Nevertheless, the quality-control aspects of JIT did contribute substantially to the decision to convert to JIT methods.

The production process at POD consists of two main sections that operate in series: printed circuit board assembly (PCA) and final assembly and test (FA&T). The PCA lines produce circuit boards used in the Touchscreen and Vectra computers. The first version of the Touchscreen contained seven circuit boards, six of which were assembled from component parts at POD. The major steps in the PCA process are as follows:

1. Automatic insertion of components onto boards, using sophisticated loading equipment—about 50 percent of the components are inserted in this way
2. Hand insertion of parts that require special preparation
3. Wave soldering of components to boards
4. Backloading—hand attachment of components that cannot withstand wave soldering
5. Final testing (other inspection processes occur at earlier stations)

The Touchscreen and Vectra have separate final assembly and test lines, although the following generic process describes both products.

1. Unpacking and initial test of chassis assemblies that are delivered directly to the FA&T line
2. Hand attachment of boards and other major subassemblies to the chassis
3. A turn-on test, with the possibility of moving units that fail to a rework station
4. A power-cycle (burn-in) test lasting approximately three hours, during which the units reside on a slow-moving conveyor belt
5. Button up—adding plastic trim and closing the housing
6. Final test
7. Packaging for delivery to PCDC

The Touchscreen system processing unit is entirely standardized, while five different models of the Vectra are produced on the same line. The models differ primarily in their combinations of random access memory (RAM) and disc drive. The daily production schedule specifies the mix of Vectra model types.

JIT procedures were introduced first in FA&T, where they now have evolved to include card techniques, which HP refers to as *Kanban*. (This term covers a wide variety of inventory-control techniques at different companies.)[4] Each day, an external supplier delivers chassis assemblies directly to the FA&T lines in boxes that carry *Kanban* cards. The cards are pulled from the boxes as the chassis assemblies are needed, accumulated at the delivery point, logged, and returned to the driver or material handler to initiate the next day's delivery. It appears that about one-and-a-half day's usage also is held at POD as a safety stock.

The finished circuit boards produced in PCA are placed in a buffer at the head of each FA&T assembly line; different boards are used in the Touchscreen and Vectra. Set points (i.e., minimum allowable levels) in each buffer regulate production in PCA, and a materials handler reloads each buffer several times daily with transfers from the PCA line.

Under the JIT implementation rules, only two units plus the unit in process at the station can be held between work stations on the FA&T lines (except, of course, on the conveyor holding the burn-in test). If a defect is discovered, investigative action is taken immediately, which can result in shutting down the line. The overall cycle time on FA&T is about five hours for the Touchscreen, including a total of approximately three-and-a-half hours of testing.

The PCA line converted to JIT somewhat later, and the JIT procedures have undergone more modification there. The PCA raw-material-stores inventory on the plant floor now contains about seven days' worth of parts, stored in standard-size boxes in racks. The standard quantity in a box varies by part number, with many in the range of 800 to 1,000 parts.

Originally, a *Kanban*-like system was installed with a separate card for each individual box. This proved unwieldy, however, as too many cards were being handled and misplaced in the stores area. Now, as a box of parts is pulled from stores by a line operator, a data entry ("cashing") transaction is made directly into the computerized inventory-tracking system. As the board is assembled, a maximum of three units is allowed to accumulate between work stations prior to the wave-soldering operation; downstream from wave soldering, the allowable buffer is ten units. At the end of the PCA line, boards are transferred to the buffers in FA&T.

Although this description may give the impression of an initial changeover to JIT manufacturing followed by a series of small refinements, in practice many of the subsequent changes have been relatively drastic. Moreover, other significant changes occurred in both the product and the manufacturing process. For example, the Touch-screen computer underwent sequential design changes that were, for the most part, transparent to the user but that had significant effects

Table 1 POD Product Life Spans

Model	Dates
150A	10/1/83 to 8/31/84
150B	9/1/84 to 4/30/85
150C	5/1/85 to present
Vectra	10/1/85 to present

Table 2 Inventory Reductions and Material-Handling Statistics

	11/83	10/84	11/85	04/86
Inventories (% of 11/83 amounts)				
Raw Material	100%	56%	39%	28%
Work-in-Process	100%	24%	27%	11%
Persons Handling HP150 Parts				
Before Production Line	90	28	33	20

on the assembly of the product. Three separate models have been produced, and it is important to note that the first and second models had life spans of only eleven and eight months, respectively; the HP150C has just passed the one-year mark. (See Table 1.)

A major Touchscreen redesign effort was made to reduce the number of separate parts, especially the handloaded ones. The HP150A and HP150B models each had over 500 part numbers, while the HP150C parts list contains approximately 150 part numbers. The main technical feature of the new Touchscreen design was the reduction from seven printed circuit boards to one (actually two, one of which is a small board attached to the rear of the monitor assembly). Material costs were cut by 50 percent, and the board reduction together with other process changes reduced assembly time by over two-thirds (from 4.22 to 1.32 hours, not counting burn-in testing), with a corresponding drop in direct labor cost.

The physical layout of the plant and the assembly procedures underwent major modifications both to accommodate the product-design changes and to effect other improvements in the production process. Over the 29-month period from October 1983 through February 1986, the shop floor was reconfigured at least four times. In addition to identifying changes in assembly procedures to reduce work-in-process inventories and improve quality, POD made changes in material handling prior to production, with concomitant reductions in indirect labor charges. Table 2 displays the reductions in raw material and work-in-process inventories that were achieved (using the end-of-year-one values of the 150A as a basis of comparison).

COST ACCOUNTING AT POD

Overview of the Systems

POD maintains a complex system of computer software modules to manage information flows. The overall system configuration appears in Exhibit 9-3. (Many of the main elements reside on separate computers.) The system itself, like its graphical representation, can be somewhat overpowering, and the impetus to reduce the infrastructure at POD includes efforts to simplify the software network and, in some instances, to eliminate the need for automated data processing.

The cost accounting segment includes the sales and cost of sales system (SACS) and the set of modules known as COSACS2. Originally designed as a "work order tracking" tool, SACS tracks all sales of products, parts, and accessories from the division. It also reconciles shipments to the general ledger to ensure product-shipment accuracy. SACS includes consignment, which records the sales of products on consignment. The COSACS2 components are clustered in the lower central portion of Exhibit 9-3, and the module names are self-explanatory: physical inventory, work order, material, labor, standard cost, standard revision, and variance. These programs are used widely throughout HP, but as POD moves away from a true work order environment, the need for adaptation or replacement of COSACS2 has become apparent.

Three other systems interact frequently with COSACS2:

1. INVENTORY CONTROL SYSTEM (ICS). This is both a material-tracking/stores-control module and a production/procurement-order maintenance program. It maintains the balance of parts in stores, holds purchase orders open, processes dock receipts, records pulls of PCA raw materials, maintains the backorder file, transmits material-movement and material-accumulation charges to COSACS2, and performs a host of other functions.

2. ORBIT. A perpetual finished-goods inventory system that receives and acknowledges order requirements from the sales office and processes shipment data.

Exhibit 9-3 POD: Management Information System FY 85

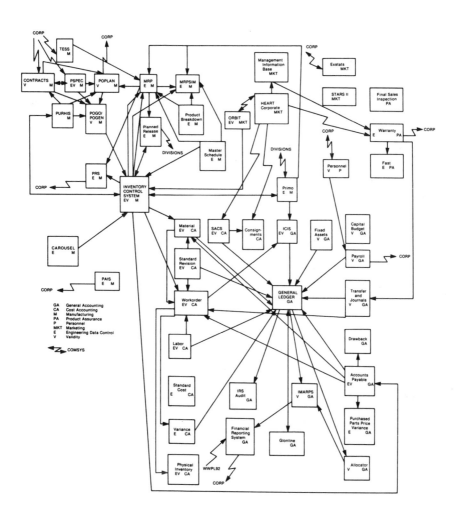

3. HEART. The sales order system at corporate headquarters that receives daily orders from sales offices and transmits them to the supplying divisions.

Budgets and Standard Setting

Much of the accounting activity at POD, for both planning and product costing, is organized within the two six-month cycles comprising the October 31 fiscal year. POD uses a standard cost system together with other target items to formulate a six-month operating budget; the six-month target production volume implies a total standard production cost that, when combined with period cost targets, yields a semiannual net income goal. Monthly production plans provide intermediate targets from which monthly variance reports are generated.

The standard costs per unit are revised every six months, and the standards are set to be achievable by the end of the six-month period, so they implicitly involve learning and other process improvements. Therefore, the monthly variances are expected to be unfavorable at the beginning of each semiannual period, with gradual reduction and perhaps reversal by the end. The standards are reviewed monthly for the first three months of the period to see if they are grossly inappropriate; a revision is possible at the discretion of the divisional controller, although such revisions are extremely rare events.

Preparation of the next period's standards begins at about the three-month point and is estimated to consume the equivalent of one full-time person for two-and-a-half months. Material cost estimates are supplied by the division's buyers; the production line supervisors supply direct labor estimates in the form of production rates, standard times per operation, and wage rates. Targets for indirect labor are supplied from production, procurement, and support, and these are allocated through the overhead procedure described below. Finally, an internally generated market forecast drives the production plan, which implies a denominator volume for the various application rates.

Exhibit 9-4 contains the "POD Cost by Process" diagram that lays out labor, overhead, subcontracting, and administrative targets for the fiscal year. Although the version shown in Exhibit 9-4 contains only percentage data in some of the fields, this planning and control document has become a standard communication format within POD; it displays target and actual dollar expenditures for each cate-

Exhibit 9-4   POD Cost by Process Diagram
Labor, Overhead, Subcontract, & Administrative Targets, FY 1985

```
                    System Processing Unit
                        x.x% POD Cost

              MFG ENGINEERING            QA
                  x.x%                 x.x%
                         SPU PRODUCTION
 V    F            INT DISTR    PCA     150B/C    x.x%      P    z
 E    R   PRO-       x.x%      x.x%     VECTRA            C    %
 N    E   CURE                                           D    R
 D    I   x.x%                                           C    e
 O    G                                   FA&T                v
 R    H                                                       e
 S    T                                                       n
      x.x%                                                    u
                                                             e
              INFO SUPPORT            MFG MGMT
                  x.x%                 x.x%
              COST ACCOUNTING       ACCTS PAYABLE
                  x.x%                 x.x%


                 System Accessories and Support
                        y.y% POD Cost

              MFG ENGINEERING        ORDER PROCESSING
                  y.y%                   y.y%
 V    F          SC SCHEDULE      SC        DISTRI-         C    z
 E    R               &         DIRECT      BUTION         U    %
 N    E          PROCUREMENT    COSTS        y.y%          S    R
 D    I                                                    T    e
 O    G             y.y%         y.y%                      O    v
 R    H                                                    M    e
 S    T                                                    E    n
      y.y%                                                 R    u
                                                           S    e
              INFO SUPPORT            PLANNING
                  y.y%                 y.y%
              COST ACCOUNTING       ACCTS PAYABLE
                  y.y%                 y.y%
```

gory. Its intent is to heighten awareness of and assign responsibility for factory overhead, and it serves as a plan of attack for cost reduction. Although the document is labeled "Targets for the Fiscal Year," the cost accounting group continually updates the actual "year to date" displays, and the diagram is used to discuss changes in targets, the likely effects of process changes, and so forth. In interpreting Exhibit 9-4, note that system accessories and support refers to the supply of parts that POD maintains to service demands for repairs or accessories over the life cycle of the products it has produced. This often means holding supplies up to ten years.

To facilitate continual design work on product enhancement and process improvement, the accounting group has access to a computer program called COSTIT, which enables it to generate quickly (from within minutes to, at most, two hours) a response to the question, "What would the product cost if certain specific design changes were made?" COSTIT accesses the various modules of the engineering data control (EDC—see the legend in Exhibit 9-3) and COSACS2 data base systems that contain current standard-part lists for each subassembly and complete product, standard costs by part number, standard direct labor times at the subassembly and complete product levels, standard direct labor wage rates, and current overhead application rates for both material (at the part level) and labor (as it appears). When queried, the program rolls up the standard cost of a product by retrieving and aggregating the data in a dual-field display. The standard field rolls up the product cost according to current design specifications. The current field allows the user to turn on or turn off any part or assembly, in order to estimate total production cost per unit (at current application rates) for a wide variety of design modifications. The accounting group estimates that COSTIT is accessed an average of 100 times each month.

Overhead Allocation

The overhead allocation and application procedures underwent major revisions during the time of this study. In February 1983, as design changes and subcontracting arrangements were reducing the direct labor content of many of HP's products, a task force was established at the corporate finance level to analyze HP's use of direct labor as the basis for allocating manufacturing overhead costs to parts and products. The resulting new system, which came on line at POD in August 1985, uses two application rates, a labor-based rate for production overhead and a material-based rate for procurement. A schematic representation appears in Exhibit 9-5.

The allocation process involves three overhead accumulation accounts or "buckets."

1. Support-manufacturing overhead expenses support the overall manufacturing process, both production and procurement, without a specific causal relation to any direct manufacturing ele-

Exhibit 9-5 Dual Application Rate for Manufacturing Overhead

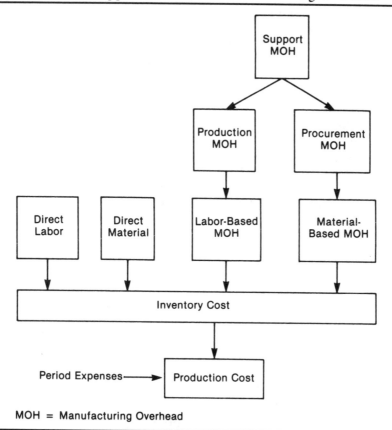

MOH = Manufacturing Overhead

ment. These expenditures include manufacturing engineering, quality assurance, manufacturing management, and central electronic data processing (EDP) support (including allocations from administration). Various bases are used to allocate support overhead between production and procurement, including estimated percentages of time devoted to the two areas and the relative personnel counts of the production and procurement groups.

2. Production-manufacturing overhead expenditures include direct labor benefits, direct labor supervision, indirect labor, supplies, depreciation, and other operating expenses (excluding allocated EDP) related to the production, assembly, test, and shipping functions.

3. Procurement-manufacturing overhead expenditures include purchasing, receiving, incoming inspection, stockrooms, material
handling, production planning and control, freight-in expense,
manufacturing specification costs, materials engineering, subcontracting, and corporate materials charges (excluding allocated
EDP).

The same overhead rates are applied to both the Touchscreen and
Vectra products, and to both the PCA and FA&T lines. At various
times preceding the two-basis system, overhead application rates at
POD had ranged from 600 percent to 1,600 percent of the direct labor
cost, and different rates had existed for different models of the
Touchscreen. Even with the dual application system in place, the labor-based application rate has exceeded 500 percent in some periods,
while the material-based rate usually falls in the 10 percent to 30 percent range. Note, however, that the direct material costs per unit of
the Touchscreen and Vectra greatly exceed the direct labor costs per
unit, which tends to counterbalance the application rates so that comparable dollar amounts of overhead are applied to the products
through labor and through materials. Nevertheless, the sensitivity to
variation in the basis remains much higher for the labor-based manufacturing overhead.

Three Adaptations to Just-in-Time (JIT)

Before the introduction of JIT, all products were produced in and
accounted for as batch jobs, with costs accumulating on the work
orders as the batches passed through work centers. As JIT gradually
transforms the production process into one more closely resembling
the continuous flow of undifferentiated units, the cost accounting system might be expected to evolve toward process costing. This section
describes three discrete sets of changes that roughly conform to this
hypothesis: perpetual work orders, passive labor vouchering, and
streamlined relations with suppliers.

1. Perpetual Work Orders. As indicated in Exhibit 9-3, all of the computer-based inventory tracking systems are perpetual: ICS for stores
and work-in-process (WIP) and ORBIT for finished-goods inventory
(FGI). Because finished computers are shipped to PCDC daily, and
ORBIT is relieved at each shipment, little change in the finished-

Exhibit 9-6   Multi-Bucket Work in Process

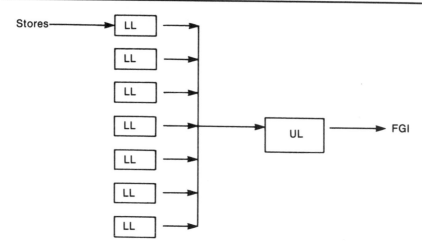

Solid Line = ICS Transaction

LL: Lower-level Printed Circuit Board Assembly Lines
UL: Upper-level Fabrication and Test Lines
FGI: Finished-goods Inventory

goods accounting system has been necessary. Significant adaptations, however, have occurred in the WIP procedures. When Touchscreen production began, the WIP data flows naturally were modeled after the actual material flows in the production process. As Exhibit 9-6 indicates, a Multi-Bucket WIP system designated each of the seven printed circuit board assembly lines as a "Lower-level" (LL) WIP station, within which standard and actual quantities and times were recorded daily. Unit transfers to the fabrication and test lines (which were designated "Upper-level" [UL] WIP stations) were recorded as they occurred, and ORBIT would track units from WIP to FGI on a daily basis. COSACS2 then integrated dollar amounts with the unit data in a batch computer job each night.

The first change occurred when the number of boards in the HP150C was reduced to only one (excluding the small monitor board). The production process was represented as a Double-Bucket WIP system in which the entire lower-level PCA area and the entire upper-level FA&T area each became a single WIP accumulation point. This system is currently in place and is shown in Exhibit 9-7. The reader should bear in mind that the single PCA line now pro-

Exhibit 9-7   Double-Bucket Work in Process

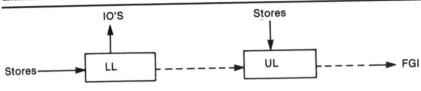

Solid Line = ICS Transaction
Dotted Line = Journal Entry

LL: Lower-level Printed Circuit Board Assembly Lines
UL: Upper-level Fabrication and Test Lines
FGI: Finished-goods Inventory
IO: Internal Order

duces different boards for Touchscreen and Vectra, which in turn are assembled on two separate FA&T lines.

Second, perpetual work orders were introduced. In the perpetual work order system, ICS continues to track units and accumulate costs internally on a work order basis, but it is "tricked" into using a single work order that remains open for the full six-month accounting period. At the end of the period, the work order is closed on COSACS2 through a manual journal entry that triggers "post-deduct" or "back-flush" calculations. That is, the operator instructs the system to total the actual number of finished units transferred to ORBIT during the period and to aggregate all standard and actual costs associated with those units. Variances are calculated (see the section on cost accounting controls later in the chapter), and the operator manually closes them to the general ledger, thus zeroing out the work order. A second manual journal entry then reopens a new six-month work order on COSACS including the current WIP balance.

Ultimately, POD plans to move to the Single-Bucket WIP system shown in Exhibit 9-8, unless other changes in the accounting software (e.g., complete replacement of the ICS and COSACS2 modules) intervene. A pure process costing system will be achieved when (1) the entire production process is treated as a single WIP accumulator, and (2) the close of the accounting period, not the completion of a batch, becomes the event to trigger the "post-deduct" averaging of costs over production.

2. Passive Labor Vouchering. A recent article describing JIT manufacturing and accounting at an HP printed circuit fabrication facility in

Exhibit 9-8   Single-Bucket Work in Process

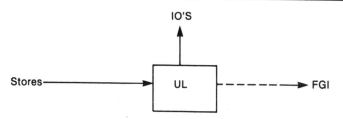

Solid Line = ICS Transaction
Dotted Line = Journal Entry
UL: Upper-level Fabrication and Test Lines
FGI: Finished-goods Inventory
IO: Internal Order

the Disc Memory Division proposes a system where "direct labor is no longer accounted for as a separate cost."[5] In the proposed system, direct labor becomes part of manufacturing overhead (which in turn is treated as an expense charged directly to cost of goods sold). Overhead charges associated with the remaining WIP and finished-goods balances are maintained with end-of-period adjusting entries.

POD uses a system that it calls "passive labor vouchering," in which direct labor still is accounted for as a separate cost, and a direct labor efficiency variance is calculated. Considerable simplification, however, has been effected, which seems justified when direct labor accounts for less than 5 percent of the direct costs incurred at POD in assembling the Touchscreen and Vectra products. The accounting group estimates that the passive labor vouchering system has reduced the administrative costs of tracking labor by 15 percent.

To provide the data necessary for passive labor vouchering, employees fill out time-cards of actual hours worked, paid time off, sick days, and holidays. POD has a flexible arrival and departure time policy, although there is little variation in arrival times for the direct labor employees. Actual labor costs are calculated by multiplying recorded employee hours by wage rates. Supervisors are responsible for keeping a log of downtime, direct labor hours on special work performed for other divisions, and any other unusual circumstances that arise on the production line during the month. Rework supervisors record the number of personnel per month devoted to rework tasks.

ICS computes a monthly "system" (i.e., within ICS's internal

Table 3 Three-Step Procedure for Accounting for Direct Labor Costs.

1. Labor is applied to work-in-process and finished goods at standard cost:
   Ending WIP   [Physical count × standard labor rate]
   + Stockflows to FGI [Units shipped × standard labor rate]
   − Beginning WIP   [Physical count × standard labor rate]
   = Direct labor applied to production

2. A labor efficiency variance is computed. Although the actual steps are somewhat more involved, the computation can be reduced to:

$$\text{Direct labor efficiency variance} = [\text{Target production for month} - \text{Actual production for month}] \times \text{Standard labor rate per unit}$$

   The direct labor efficiency variance is booked to the General Ledger as a period expense.

3. Any difference between actual direct labor purchases and the direct labor applied in step 1 that is not explained by paid absences, rework, billings to other divisions, or the efficiency variance computed in step 2, is treated as manufacturing overhead:

   Actual direct labor-part-time   [Wages paid or payable]
   - PTO, Sick, Holiday, etc.   [Recorded]
   = Available direct labor
   - Direct labor applied to production   [From step 1]
   - Direct labor applied to rework   [Recorded]
   - Billings to other divisions   [Recorded]
   - Direct Labor Efficiency Variance   [From step 2]
   = Overhead   [Residual]

data base) WIP inventory figure that is verified by and adjusted to a physical count of WIP inventory taken at the end of each month (see the section below on cost accounting controls). At this time, direct labor costs are accounted for in a three-step procedure. (See Table 3.)

As a final "reasonableness" check, the computed labor efficiency variance is compared to the downtime and training hours recorded by the supervisors.

3. Streamlined Relations with Suppliers. Most discussions of JIT manufacturing emphasize the need to improve the quality of the firm's relations with its suppliers, with respect to both the reliability of the parts delivered and the dependability of delivery schedules. Typically, the firm must have its own JIT program well under way before pushing the concept upstream to suppliers, and this phase seems to be a particularly slow process.

POD has modified four aspects of its supplier relations:

1. Reduction of the number of suppliers. From October 1983 to May 1986, the number of different suppliers for the Touchscreen was reduced from approximately 125 to 39; 85 percent of the Vectra's parts are supplied by these same vendors. (HP divisions supply only about 15 percent of POD's material purchases.)

2. Improved quality of delivered parts. Ideally, parts should be delivered directly to the assembly line with little or no incoming inspection. At present, this occurs only on the upper-level FA&T lines, for the large chassis/monitor assembly, and the plastic housing and trim.

3. JIT delivery. As of April 1986, eight vendors delivered on a daily JIT basis to POD.

4. Reduction of the paperwork associated with delivery. Two aspects are included here. First, as the frequency of deliveries increases, the volume of invoices to be processed explodes unless the process is simplified. Second, as quality of parts delivered increases and the need for returns (and eventually the need for inspection) falls, the paperwork associated with the return process should fall.

To implement item four, POD has instituted a "no invoice" receiving and accounts payable procedure. This process is intended to capture both parts of item four; i.e., reduced paperwork for both the receipt of good parts and the return of defective parts. Note, however, that JIT delivery can precede the introduction of a no invoice procedure, and as of May 1986, the no invoice process was used with only one of POD's eight JIT suppliers, although it was used with all six of the JIT suppliers at PRCD.

Exhibit 9-9 contains a flowchart description of the no invoice procedure. To interpret the chart, note that

1. The term "contact" usually means a telephone conversation with no mandatory immediate, or follow-up, written communication

2. A "transaction" is a computer entry into the ICS system

3. Receiving documents are accumulated for one week and physically delivered to accounts payable on Tuesdays; accounts pay-

Exhibit 9-9 "No Invoice/Debit Memo" Procedure

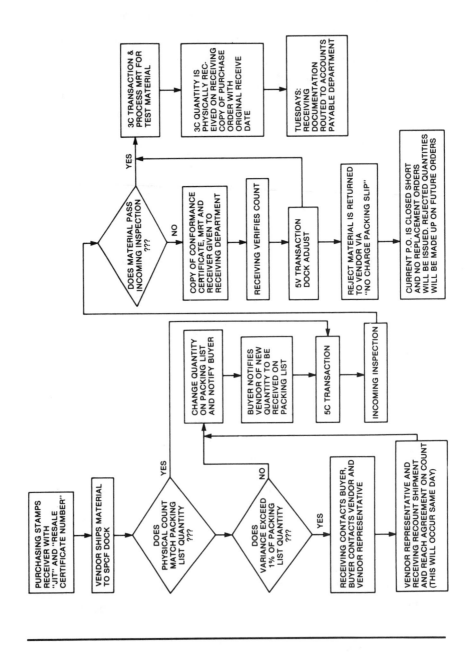

able inputs them on Tuesday afternoon or Wednesday morning at the latest, and the software does most of the "matching" to internally stored purchase order numbers.

Cost Accounting Controls

In monitoring the accuracy of the cost accounting data, POD's goals are system simplification, process visibility, and quick response to problems. Although for product-costing purposes the perpetual work order is closed only at six-month intervals, ICS is recording physical flows on a daily basis. This "system count" is built up from data entries occurring as materials enter either the lower-level PCA line or the upper-level FA&T lines.

As described in the earlier secion on JIT manufacturing, lower-level stores consists of uniform boxes of parts stored on racks; about seven days' worth of parts are held. HP has designed a Barcoding Inventory Control System (BICS) that produces a barcode descriptor for each part type, containing such information as stores location, part number, quantity, and purchase order information. Rather than using a *Kanban* card system, a single barcoded card exists for each part type, and as a box of parts is withdrawn from stores, the card is "cashed." Cashing is a computer transaction that relieves the stores on hand balance and places the materials into ICS's lower-level WIP bucket.

On the upper level, the bulky chassis/monitor assembly is delivered directly to the FA&T assembly line, using a full *Kanban* card system. *Kanban* cards are pulled from the boxes as needed, logged, and accumulated for daily collection and return. At night, a single computer run enters these flows into ICS. To avoid extensive reprogramming, the items are entered in a transaction as though they went through the typical delivery and inspection phase that ICS originally was designed to model, although this physically no longer occurs.

All work-in-process inventory is counted physically every month; this manual process requires a two-hour halt of the lines. The physical count is compared to the ICS "system count," and variance reports are created that show, by part number within WIP location, actual versus system quantities and dollars. These reports are distributed to the various WIP locations on the same day, and production personnel check the discrepancies. After traceable errors are corrected, the final material-quantity variance is booked into the general ledger, and the system count is updated to actual. Portions of the lower-level stores inventory are counted continually on a scheduled cycle, and the entire stores inventory is counted manually every six months.

As a less formal element of process control and understanding, cost accounting personnel make several visits each day downstairs to observe the status of the lines and to talk with the supervisors and operators in the production and materials areas. The accounting group feels that the visits promote a proactive, consultative role for their group.

THE MEASUREMENT OF QUALITY

Most discussions of JIT manufacturing emphasize the issue of improved quality because JIT procedures detect failures quickly, and, with little or no buffer stock between operators, defective parts will have been built into only a few units before they are detected downstream. Production along the whole assembly line, however, can be interrupted until the problem is identified and corrected, so if one is to achieve reasonable flow rates with JIT, failures must be reduced.

Note also that one can embark on a total quality mission without necessarily adopting JIT manufacturing. HP's top management decided to strive for a total quality process late in 1980, well before either the merging of divisions that produced POD or the later introduction of JIT. Even after 1983, many important aspects of POD's quality-assurance program developed independently from, but in parallel with, JIT, although the evolutions of the two endeavors certainly were symbiotic and eventually became inextricably intertwined.

A one-person "failure-analysis laboratory" was set up in 1981, staffed by a reliability engineer who had worked previously in another HP laboratory facility. This unit was and still is part of quality assurance, which reports directly to the division manager rather than to manufacturing. The lab was given a blank check to improve quality, and its occupant embarked on a self-education program in quality measurement and control. The quest for quality began in circuit board assembly, the main focus in the pre-Touchscreen period. As a result, new quality-assurance procedures tended to be introduced first to the PCA lines, from which they spread to final assembly.

Some initial data on quality existed in the form of reports from a board replacement program which focused on repairing products that had failed in the field. HP also maintained yield data (i.e., per-

Table 4 Defect-Analysis Matrix (by week)

Part No.	Number of Failures		
	Before Turn-on	After Turn-on	Field
x			
y z			

centage of boards that passed test procedures) in the plant, and POD was aware that it was achieving only 40-percent to 50-percent yields while some competitors in Japan were reporting 95-percent yield rates for comparable boards. The first systematic measurement project was a one-and-a-half year data-collection and correlation study that assembled and analyzed a data base portrayed in Table 4.

After it became apparent that field data often took six months to be routed back to POD and that report accuracy was uneven, attention shifted inward. The first attack was focused on pre-turn-on testing, where conventional wisdom within POD held that its low yields (sometimes only 40 percent before turn-on alone) were due to poor quality components from suppliers. Pre-turn-on testing was done with a "bed-of-nails" apparatus—a mechanism from which multiple probes extended to make contact with and test many individual components simultaneously. Components that failed were replaced at a rework station, and most failed parts were dumped into bags to await gold-reclamation processing.

The first change in measurement procedures was to require board repair operators to place every removed part into an envelope and code it with part number, date, symptom, and process point at which failure was detected. At the same time, the failure analysis lab developed the "failure-analysis shopfloor tracking" system (FAST— shown on the software schematic in Exhibit 9-3) to maintain the data base. Detailed laboratory analysis of the failed parts themselves, in conjunction with interpretation of the data base, produced three insights:

1. The false negative error rate in the bed-of-nails test procedure was high, and the assumption that vendors delivered many defective parts was largely incorrect. Many of the parts that were removed were not, in fact, defective. Both design problems and poor maintenance of the test mechanisms appeared to be at fault.

2. A significant portion of the true negatives (boards that were in some way defective) were due not to defective components but rather to faulty interconnects between the components, and the test procedures were not designed to detect this situation.

3. A few vendors actually were delivering components with high defect rates, and some others occasionally would drift in and out of this condition.

Steps were taken to remedy each of these problems:

1. The bed-of-nails testers were replaced with electronic tool (ET) testers that test the whole board and not just its component parts for functionality. At later dates and at higher-level assemblies (up through the complete product), this approach evolved into product designs that built in self-test procedures.

2. The layouts of the printed circuit boards were changed to reduce the number of inadvertent solder bridges and other interconnect defects.

3. Certain vendors were dropped; others received help to correct their own manufacturing problems.

These changes eventually led to a 10-to-1 improvement in quality: in 1980, it was not uncommon to replace 11,000 parts per month before turn-on; in 1985, only 1,000 parts per month were usually replaced (both before and after turn-on) at roughly comparable volume levels. Moreover, the quality-assurance group believes that another 5-to-1 reduction may be achieved by changes that have been or will be induced by their tracking procedures.

The advent of computerized wand reading of barcodes printed on adhesive strips or serial number faceplates in 1983 coincided with the redesign of the POD production lines to produce the Touchscreen. This new data-collection technology helped the quality-assurance group to extend its focus further downstream in the lower-level printed circuit board assembly line and eventually to the upper-level final assembly line. FAST was rewritten to utilize barcode information, and barcode strips were printed and attached to all boards as they entered the PCA line, as well as to assemblies entering the FA&T line.

Thus began a second round of data collection, analysis, and corrective action. Using the barcode information read in at the rework stations, FAST accumulated a board repair data base for approximately one year. Again, an important insight emerged: between 30 percent and 40 percent of the rework was devoted to boards that had already been reworked at least once. It became clear that the component-replacement process (particularly the dissipation of heat) damaged previously perfect components or interconnects. Operations responded with a simple decision: if (after any rework) a board fails a second time, discard the entire board. An ancillary lesson arose from increased awareness of the importance of avoiding false negatives in any test process—reworking a perfect board often wrecked it.

Both cycles of measurement, analysis, and response described here recount the successes achieved by a dedicated "quality guru" who earned respect and credibility by individual hard work. They are not the result of the cooperative efforts of the entire production force typically ascribed to a JIT program. As JIT took hold at POD, however, quality assurance again extended its measurement program in a way that both spread its influence more evenly throughout the entire assembly process and dovetailed more closely with the JIT approach.

The focus of the quality-assurance program was broadened to encompass the production process qua process as well as the product. This theme was captured succinctly in the statement that, "A cycle time that is more than two sigma away from the mean is just as much a defect as a computer that doesn't work." Up to this point, FAST data entry had occurred only at the rework stations. To monitor the production process itself, FAST barcode-reading equipment was installed at strategic points along the assembly lines, and measures of both the level and the variability of the production rate were compiled. For example, the variability of the production rate is measured by its "linearity," defined as one minus the coefficient of variation of the hourly production rate; that is,

$$\text{linearity} = 1.0 - \frac{[\text{standard deviation (hourly build rate)}]}{[\text{mean (hourly build rate)}]}$$

In addition, the FAST barcode system is not the only source of information on quality. As each Touchscreen chassis reaches the turn-on test station, a process sheet is attached that carries the unit's serial number and its sequence number on the line (see Exhibit 9-10). As the unit passes down the line, the operators enter the time and various codes taken from either the external test equipment or the built-in test readouts.

Exhibit 9-10 HP150C Process Sheet

Serial #	**Sequence #**

(1) *Turn-On Test:* Pass   Emp. # .... Date ___/___/___
                   Fail

    1st Fail Code........................... Date ___/___/___
    2nd Fail Code........................... Date ___/___/___

(2) *Power Cycle:*   In Time___:___   Date ___/___/___
    High POT   ☐ Yes Emp. # ....
    Test   ☐ No

    1st Fail Code .... Date ___/___/___ Time___:___
                (2nd)   In Time ___:___   Date ___/___/___
    2nd Fail Code .... Date ___/___/___ Time___:___
                (3rd)   In Time ___:___   Date ___/___/___
    3rd Fail Code .... Date ___/___/___ Time___:___

(3) *OC Test:*   Passed   Date ___/___/___ Time___:___
                           Passed   Date ___/___/___ Time___:___
    1st Fail Code .... Date ___/___/___ Time___:___
    2nd Fail Code .... Date ___/___/___ Time___:___
    3rd Fail Code .... Date ___/___/___ Time___:___

(4) *Final OC:*
    Rejected   Passed Emp. # .... Date ___/___/___
    Fail Code/Descrip. ....
    High POT Test Verified ☐ Yes
                           ☐ No
(5) *Rework Station:*
    1st Repair .... Date ___/___/___ Time___:___
    2nd Repair .... Date ___/___/___ Time___:___
    3rd Repair .... Date ___/___/___ Time___:___

The assembly lines also operate under strict JIT rules regarding the procedures to be followed when a defect is discovered; Exhibit 9-11 summarizes the system response. Note that a lot size here refers to a set of units to be inspected when a defect is discovered. As Exhibit 9-11 indicates, if a second defect is found in the specially monitored group of twenty, the line is shut down until the cause is located and corrected.

A shutdown of the line triggers a Cause and Effect Diagram with the Addition of Cards (CEDAC); in this group problem-solving ap-

Exhibit 9-11   Quality-Control Process Flow Chart

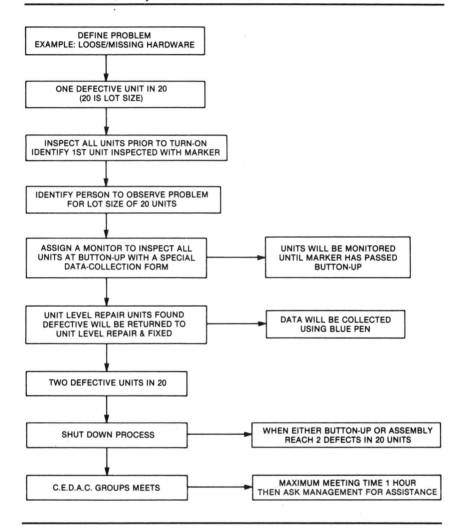

proach, the production line operators brainstorm to list potential causes of the shutdown, each is written on a separate card, and the group, together with the supervisor, defines performance measures that indicate the actual cause of failure. Operators use sheets of paper containing four ruled grids to construct bar-charts of the frequency of the potential causes or error types that occur at their stations. These data are shared among the group, and the supervisor writes up

Exhibit 9-12   Production Operations Report

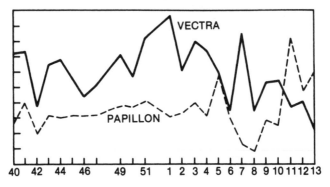

HOURS OF DOWNTIME
Sum of cycle times greater than 10 min

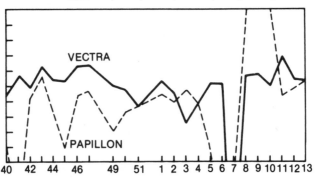

LINEARITY
1—std___dev (hourly build)/mean (hourly build)

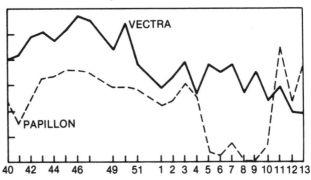

PRODUCTION RATE
As Measured by the Number of Labels Printed

Exhibit 9-12   (*Continued*)

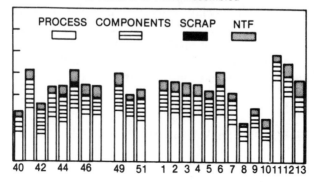

DEFECT PPM AT BD REPAIR
Per Number of Parts Assembled

PROCESS   COMPONENTS   SCRAP   NTF

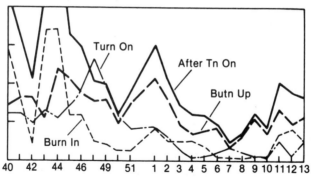

VECTRA FA&T DEFECT RATES
Normalized by the Number of Units Boxed

Turn On
After Tn On
Butn Up
Burn In

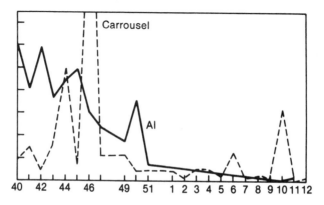

GROSS $ — CYCLE COUNT ADJ

Carrousel

Al

the experience including proposed corrective changes (and, later, the extent to which the change helped). Supervisors also can extract data from FAST for use by their production group. These records are shared more widely in weekly "quality council meetings" attended by the engineering and manufacturing managers. Eventually, data from all of these sources are compiled and summarized in weekly production operations reports like the one shown in Exhibit 9-12, and these are circulated to the accounting department and other areas of responsibility.

THE MONTHLY REPORT PACKAGE

The monthly cost accounting report is distributed to the division general manager, the manufacturing manager, the controller, the manager of the information systems department, and corporate headquarters. It contains fifteen to twenty pages of tables and graphs that can be categorized under four main headings.

Financial Measures:
- POD facility overall manufacturing- and production-cost analysis
- The split of manufacturing and production costs between system processing units and the system accessories and support segments
- Labor and overhead per dollar of material assembled and per parts assembled
- Major operating expenses and variances
- Actual cost versus standard cost for the Touchscreen and Vectra

Quality Data:
- Moving 15-month total of defects per million parts assembled, including causes and steps taken to remedy
- Burn-in test results
- Monthly average linearity

Inventory Data:
- Worldwide inventory (consolidated, factory, and distribution centers)
- Worldwide days' worth of supply
- POD Sunnyvale inventory (total, days' worth of supply, and split between system processing units and the system accessories and support)

- Inventory transactions (number of ICS cashing transactions)
- Inventory integrity (adjustments made to reconcile monthly physical WIP inventory count and stores-cycle adjustments)

Other:
- Purchasing metrics (number of vendors, number of part numbers)
- Safety metrics

ISSUES FOR FURTHER CONSIDERATION

The Relations Between Cost Accounting and Quality Assurance

Except for providing accounting with the report shown in Exhibit 9-12, the quality-assurance group sees itself as functionally separate from cost accounting and as having a fundamentally different mission. Several persons in accounting, on the other hand, mentioned that they admire the gains that have been achieved by the quality-assurance personnel, that the quality measurements are important, and that it would not be surprising if they were to develop closer ties with the quality-assurance group—"to have one of us sitting down there." The current functional separation, however, is a long way from the textbook scenario in which cost accounting measurements are the primary source of data on whether the production process is "in or out of control."

Moreover (and perhaps more interesting from a systems-design viewpoint), I see two divergent trends with respect to level of detail. In the JIT environment, cost accounting is systematically withdrawing from the precise identification of individual units or batches; it is reducing the fineness of its information structure. Unit products or batches no longer bear job cards or work orders on which specific work times and material usage are recorded. Rather, a much less finely detailed procedure measures costs by the *ex post* averaging of accumulated expenditures over produced units.

At the same time, the quality-assurance information systems are reaching for ever-increasing fineness of detail through the FAST bar-code-reading system, which explicitly identifies and tracks individual units and even individual subassemblies within units. It is almost as if the quality-assurance personnel are attaching their barcode strips

Exhibit 9-13 Use of Manufacturing and Cost Accounting Data

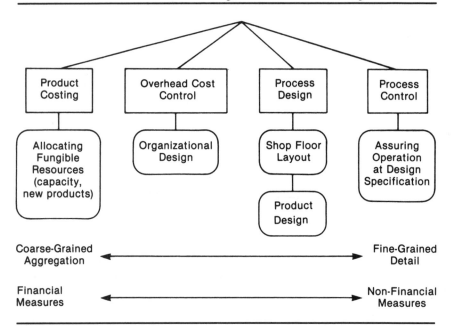

and process test sheets in the space formerly occupied by the account-ant's job card. Similarly, while the accounting group at POD still computes a labor efficiency variance (although the cost accountants at some other HP divisions have abandoned the practice), the compu-tation compares the actual total *monthly* production to the target total for the month. Quality assurance, on the other hand, computes a line-arity statistic at the hourly level, to ask essentially the same question (although with more explicit recognition of the stochastic nature of the underlying process): To what extent did the actual production rate deviate from standard?

These differences in fineness of detail also correspond to the use of financial versus nonfinancial measures, and they suggest the spec-trum of decisions sketched in Exhibit 9-13. At one pole we find the cost accounting group supplying product-cost data in aggregate, fi-nancial terms. This procedure seems appropriate for decisions involv-ing the allocation of capital (a fungible, financial resource) in capacity decisions, product entry or exit decisions, make-or-buy decisions, and pricing strategies. At the other end, we have the quality-assurance group monitoring the production process to assure operation at design specification. Their measurements naturally involve detailed, physical (nonfinancial parameters) such as flow rates and defect descriptions.

There are two intermediate points involving the transformation of financial budgets into manufacturing reality: the design of the manufacturing process (including the product itself) and the design of an organization to support that process, both physically (e.g., material handing and maintenance) and administratively. At POD, these nodes are revisited often, as both process control and product-costing data indicate potential improvements in the process, the product, or the organization; the virtually constant accessing of the COSTIT system is a prime example. Both the interplay between financial and physical measures, and the iterative nature of the design process make these two functions interesting candidates for future modeling and empirical investigation.

The Distinction Between Fixed and Variable Costs

In the various discussions with the cost accounting staff, the terms "fixed cost" and "variable cost" seldom were used; the relevant distinction at HP seems to be "controllable versus noncontrollable" costs. Two caveats deserve immediate mention. First, I do not mean to imply that JIT has changed the underlying cost structure into a predominantly fixed or a predominantly variable one. It is true that direct labor expenditures have become less variable in the traditional sense of a strict proportionality with output, but they also have become small in relation to material costs, and these material costs have become even more strictly proportional as quality-assurance procedures reduce scrap and rework. Nor has the distinction between fixed and variable costs become so hidden in the labor- and material-based overhead application rates that people are being fooled when COSTIT appears to offer a large overhead saving from designing parts or labor out of a product. On the contrary, cost accounting staff seem to understand clearly how to interpret COSTIT's output, and they feel that the design engineers also fully appreciate that overhead application rates will change as the bill of materials does.

What may be changing are the relevant *action set* and *time frame* within which costs can be controlled, regardless of whether they are fixed or variable. Because quality improvements have significantly reduced material losses on the line and because HP maintains a stable labor force, relatively little more can be done to control variable costs on a day-by-day basis. On the other hand, fixed costs are no longer regarded as monolithic items that can be affected only by massive, "once-a-decade" changes in the physical plant. The relevance of the distinction between fixed and variable costs may have diminished because now both are controlled by making incremental improvements in the product or the process—improvements that can occur over a three- to nine-month period. For example, design changes to reduce the parts number count from 550 to 150 can be conceived and implemented in less than a year, causing significant reductions in *both* variable manufacturing costs and the fixed overhead required to inspect, store, and transport those parts. Continual quality-control efforts can identify potential fixed and variable cost savings that require a change in the assembly process. Such changes, including rearranging the layout of the physical plant, can be accomplished several times a year. Thus, the six-month planning and control period is one in which both fixed and variable costs can be reduced, and often both are reduced by the same process or product improvement.

JIT and Fluctuating Demand

When Hewlett-Packard embarked on JIT production of the Touchscreen, it abandoned its "pure job shop, make-to-specific-customer-order" practices to pursue a "level production, make-to-stock-if-necessary" strategy. And POD did encounter periods, at least at the outset, in which large inventories of finished goods accumulated at PCDC. On one occasion the excess had to be stored in vans in a parking lot. This awkward event made everyone aware that while JIT methods greatly reduce raw-materials and work-in-process inventories, the pursuit of "linearity" (a constant production rate) implies that fluctuations in customer demand must be absorbed either by finished-goods inventories or by marketing responses (e.g., pricing or promotions to move excess inventories, and placation of customers whose orders are backlogged). Large finished-goods inventories do not necessarily conflict with JIT's emphasis on quality so long as no degradation can occur once the product has been sealed in its shipping container.

The ultimate questions, of course, are who bears the costs of variability in demand, how those costs can be reduced, and how the variability itself is affected both by production performance and by marketing policy. POD now freezes its production schedule four weeks in advance on the basis of its own demand forecasts. Under the passive labor vouchering system, those deviations of the build rate from schedule that are caused by changed market forecasts (rather than production problems) are classified as labor efficiency variances. The underlying cause can be identified correctly in the monthly cost accounting report. It seems likely that JIT should increase both the value of accurate market forecasts over the three- to six-month horizon in which corrective capacity decisions can be implemented and the value of marketing techniques that smooth customer demand.

External Accounting Issues

Hewlett-Packard's internal auditors typically spend a total of three to four weeks annually at POD, and the external audit team from Price Waterhouse makes a shorter annual inspection. As one might expect, the reduced inventories have facilitated certain tasks in both the internal and external audits.

Because Hewlett-Packard uses FIFO for financial reporting, the tax effects of inventory reduction probably are not severe. For a LIFO firm, however, that has built up many layers of inventory through a long inflationary period, a JIT-induced drastic inventory reduction will liquidate many LIFO layers and result in high taxable profits and correspondingly large tax liabilities. Three possible responses come to mind. First, if the typical JIT inventory reduction is accomplished over a two- to three-year period, the firm may be better off filing with the IRS for a ten-year amortization period for the recapture payment after a switch back to FIFO, and accepting the one-time liability for all previously avoided tax even though the bottom-most layers would not be liquidated. Extending the payment period might counterbalance a smaller liability recognized over a much shorter horizon. A second approach would time the JIT reductions to occur in periods of lower tax rates—from either firm-specific tax conditions (e.g., investment tax credits, loss carryback or carryforward) or overall changes in the tax codes. Third, on a larger political scale, LIFO firms converting to JIT might lobby for special tax treatment of the liquidation tax.

CONCLUSION

The cost accounting procedures at POD have changed; they have been simplified and streamlined as the system evolved from job order to process costing. One can sense a critical and continual evaluation of the costs and benefits of various levels of data aggregation. Similarly, more effort is being directed to understanding the causal structure of indirect manufacturing costs. The most promising research opportunities to emerge from this study, however, lie at the interfaces between cost accounting, process control, and product design. While most cost accounting texts warn that traditional product-costing reports are not the sole source of useful measurements and that inventory costing and income determination are not the sole uses for these data, little research has occurred to flesh out our understanding of the alternatives. Detailed observation of actual manufacturing installations may help to inform models of the quality-assurance and product/process-design functions. One can envision analyses that run the gamut from the abstract information structures of Hurwicz or Demski to the introspective protocol analyses that recount individuals' conscious information-processing methods.[7] The challenge lies in capturing the special characteristics of these engineering functions while retaining a level of generality that will encompass a wide variety of manufacturing environments.

NOTES

1. Robert K. Yin, *Case Study Research: Design and Methods* (Beverly Hills, CA: Sage Publications, 1984).

2. Several portions of this section are condensed from the case entitled "Hewlett-Packard Personal Office Computer Division," written by Macon Finley and J. Michael Harrison.

3. See, for example, Richard J. Schonberger, *World Class Manufacturing* (New York: The Free Press, 1986).

4. See, for example, Bruce R. Neumann and Pauline R. Jaouen, "KANBAN, ZIPS and Cost Accounting: A Case Study," *Journal of Accountancy* (August 1986): 132–41.

5. Rick Hunt, Linda Garrett, and C. Mike Merz, "Direct Labor Cost Not Always Relevant at H-P," *Management Accounting* (February 1985): 58–62.

6. Note that incoming chassis assemblies already embody significant subcontractor labor in their material costs.

7. For examples of information-system analyses, see Leonid Hurwicz, "On In-

formationally Decentralized Systems." In *Decision and Organization*, ed. C. B. Mc-Quire and R. Radner (Amsterdam: North-Holland Publishing Co., 1972) 297–336; or Joel S. Demski, *Information Analysis*, 2d ed. (Reading, MA: Addison-Wesley, 1980). For a discussion of protocol analysis and related issues, see "Studies on Human Information Processing in Accounting," *Journal of Accounting Research*, supplement to volume 14 (1976).

CHAPTER 10

Accounting, Incentives, and the Lot-Sizing Decision: A Field Study

Jerold L. Zimmerman

INTRODUCTION

Most job shop manufacturing processes involve repetitive production of parts in batches. For example, manufacturing typewriters requires either purchase or production of numerous parts in batches of predetermined and usually fixed sizes. This is followed by an assembly process of the parts and subassemblies into the final product. Such job shop batch manufacturing requires a determination of the lot sizes for each individual part (the number of units comprising a batch). Parts manufacturing requires numerous machining steps on each part. Each machining operation can require several hours to set up and test the machine. The longer the machine run for a given part, the fewer setups, but the larger the inventory of work-in-process of each part.

Queuing delays are often an important aspect of batch-type production processes. Parts wait for other parts in the same batch to finish a machining operation. Batches wait for processing until other batches finish. These queuing delays and their attendant costs can be

The research assistance of Victoria Posner and useful comments from Uday Karmarkar, Ray Ball, and Robert Kaplan are gratefully acknowledged.

substantial. It has been estimated that a single part spends only 5 percent of its time on machine tools and the remaining 95 percent of the time is spent moving between machining operations or waiting for the next machining operation (Schaffer 1981, 153; Banker et al. 1985, 4).

Standard operations research models (e.g., economic order quantity [EOQ] models) are often used to set batch sizes. These models trade inventory holding costs off against production efficiencies from producing in large lots, thereby reducing nonproductive setup between consecutive jobs. These simple EOQ models, however, fail to take account of the externalities created by large batch sizes in a "complex" job shop. A complex job shop is one in which multiple products are produced on many different machines. Each part often requires time on several machines, and many types of parts (each requiring a machine setup) compete for the same machining resources.

The *queuing externality* results when a particular job in the queue causes other jobs in the queue to wait until that job is finished and the machine is free. Waiting times increase not only owing to the added processing times of the preceding jobs, but also from disruption, congestion, confusion, and expediting that result from the number and different types of jobs in the shop. EOQ models only consider the inventory holding cost of the batch under consideration when computing "optimum" lot sizes. But large lot sizes increase the waiting time of all the batches behind the lot currently using the particular machine. These additional holding costs are either ignored or subsumed into other variables in standard EOQ models.

Varying lot sizes across items causes processing demands to become less uniform (Karmarkar, Kekre, and Kekre 1985). Uniform production (in terms of equalizing the amount of time a job spends on a machine across all jobs) creates a more balanced flow of work in the shop; it reduces the time jobs wait for a particular machine, thereby reducing queues and inventory holding costs.

If the number of products and parts being manufactured in a plant increases over time, the manufacturing process becomes more "complex," thereby exacerbating the queuing externality. Simple EOQ models' failure to take account of the inventory holding costs of jobs being delayed while the current job is being processed produce "optimum" batch sizes that are too large (see Karmarkar 1983; Zipkin 1983).

When the queuing externality is small and it is costly to estimate the cost of the delayed jobs, it is convenient to ignore this cost in deriving optimum batch sizes. But when the queuing externality becomes a larger fraction of manufacturing cost either because real interest rates rise or production queues lengthen, ignoring this externality produces suboptimal lot sizes.

Incentive systems both measure and reward managerial performance. The cost accounting system is an integral part of the incentive system because it is one of several bases for measuring performance. Queuing externalities (inventory holding costs of delayed jobs) are ignored in traditional cost accounting systems. Even when top management desires smaller batch sizes, unless the cost accounting system is modified to measure the inventory holding costs, middle managers will not be rewarded for reducing lot sizes, and they will be reluctant to attempt to do so. If the cost accounting system measures, and the incentive system rewards, efforts to reduce direct manufacturing costs (ignoring inventory holding costs), managers have less incentive to take account of the queuing externality in their lot-sizing decisions. A successful performance measurement system will reward parts manufacturing managers for delivering the right parts at the right time at an acceptable level of quality and at minimum total cost (which includes the cost of queuing externalities).

Over time, successful manufacturing firms tend to develop optimal rules of thumb and incentive systems. Changes in technology, competition, or relative prices make old rules of thumb and incentive schemes nonoptimal. In particular, in noncomplex job shops, the queuing externality is relatively unimportant. Hence, ignoring the effects of queuing delays does not cause actual batch sizes to depart from optimum batch sizes. Incentive schemes will be devised that emphasize large batch sizes. As manufacturing complexity or inventory holding costs rise, optimal batch sizes become smaller. But unless the incentive schemes are revised, including the internal accounting system, actual batch sizes are unlikely to fall because managers and workers are likely to continue using the old (now suboptimal) rules of thumb.

This chapter describes a field study of a job shop manufacturing firm. Interviews were conducted with managers from various levels of the firm. I found that the internal accounting system reinforced other incentives to produce in large lot sizes. Even though senior managers emphasized the overall benefits of producing in smaller lot sizes, production managers were reluctant to follow the new guidelines because they were penalized for not delivering parts on schedule. This led parts manufacturing managers to produce "safety stocks" (and hence larger lot sizes) to cover unanticipated manufacturing delays. Reinforcing these incentives were cost accounting and performance systems that did not reward managers for reducing inventory holding costs.

My principal objective is to describe the existing cost accounting and incentive systems in the context of the lot-sizing decision. Considerable interest and analysis exists in the operations management literature regarding the lot-sizing question (e.g., Karmarkar et al. 1985). As a secondary objective, the chapter provides some observations on the field study methodology. Individuals are assumed to be motivated by self-interest (individuals are resourceful, evaluative, and maximizing). Furthermore, incentive systems such as the performance measurement and reward/punishment systems (including accounting systems) affect individuals' behavior. Given these assumptions, I seek to understand how the extant accounting and incentives systems affect the lot-sizing decision.

The remainder of the chapter is organized as follows. The next section describes the firm in the field study. The third section describes the research process, including the interview process. The fourth and fifth sections describe the accounting and incentive systems used in the manufacturing process. The sixth section analyzes the lot-sizing decision. The last section offers observations from the study. One set of observations involves the effects of the accounting and incentive systems on the lot-sizing decision; another set of observations involves the field study method used in this research.

THE FIRM

The firm selected was accessible, and some of its managers indicated concern that lot sizes were "too big" because of incentives induced by the accounting systems. The research site was not chosen in a random fashion and caution will be exercised in generalizing the conclusions.

The firm in the study is a large, diversified, high-technology *Fortune* 500 company. The firm is organized as three major divisions: marketing, manufacturing, and research and development. The manufacturing division consists of numerous parts manufacturing departments and assembly departments; it produces roughly 2,000 products, involving 25,000 part numbers, and is treated as a cost center.

During the course of my study, management announced a major

firmwide reorganization. The functional organization was replaced with a product-line organization. Numerous Lines of Business (LOB) were created and given bottom-line profit responsibilities. The LOB are responsible for the design, manufacturing, and marketing of products. Manufacturing assembly line departments are now formally part of their LOB. The parts manufacturing departments are not in any LOB because they produce parts for several LOB. The parts manufacturing departments remain a core organization, and the costs of parts produced are transferred to the assembly departments and incorporated into the LOB product costs.

Also during the study, the manufacturing division's internal accounting system was being modified. The controller's office described the changes as "separating manufacturing costs from LOB costs and giving better visibility of those costs to manufacturing managers." This reorganization and accounting system conversion is an interesting study in its own right. But the resources needed to analyze such a large reorganization were not available to me. The accounting system I describe is the one used under the previous functional organization. The parts manufacturing costs of products are, however, being transferred to and hence are being used in evaluating the performance of the LOB.

One parts manufacturing department is analyzed. This department manufactures parts for an office product. The manufacturing process includes sheet metal stamping, welding, grinding, and numerous high-precision tooling operations. The department has numerically controlled machines and some robots. It employs several hundred workers. The department's output is transferred to one assembly department. Parts produced by the parts manufacturing department, purchased parts, and subassemblies are assembled into the final product. Marketing determines assembly and manufacturing schedules up to one year in advance. The schedules are revised, often quarterly.

THE RESEARCH PROCESS

The manufacturing division controller indicated that the department in this study is reasonably representative of other parts manufacturing departments within the manufacturing division. There are great differences, however, among the various parts manufacturing departments in terms of number of employees, manufacturing technologies, and complexity of operations.

The research process started with an interview of the controller and his immediate staff. All interviews were conducted jointly with a doctoral student. Interview notes were later transcribed for a permanent record. Follow-up questions were answered in telephone interviews. We interviewed four levels in the controller's office; the fourth and lowest level was the cost accounting analyst in the parts manufacturing department. Then the manager in charge of the parts manufacturing department was interviewed. Several other managers in the manufacturing department were questioned. The manager of the parts manufacturing department described his organization, how he uses the accounting system reports, how he is evaluated, how his workers are evaluated and compensated, and how he perceives the lot-sizing decision. Finally, I circulated an earlier draft of this chapter within the controller's office and its corrections and comments were incorporated.

As a condition for participating in this study (and consistent with its policy), the firm did not make operating data available to the research team. This severely limited the scope of the analysis.

THE ACCOUNTING SYSTEM

The internal accounting system is based on a job order cost system. The complexity of the manufacturing process and its scale of operations, however, makes the accounting system very complicated. This section first provides an overview of the accounting system and then describes the two major accounting reports.

Overview of the Accounting System

Exhibit 10-1 is a diagram of the cost accounting system; several subsystems, such as labor distribution and accounts payable, provide the input for the cost collector. The cost collector then provides input for reporting systems such as the general ledger. Two important output subsystems are the product bill and the parts/product cost systems. The product bill system costs each finished product, and the parts/product cost system reports the unit manufacturing cost of each product and part. The product bill then is sent to the corporate office for product-line profitability studies and pricing decisions.

Exhibit 10-1 Cost Accounting Systems, Data Collection, Time and Attendance Payroll

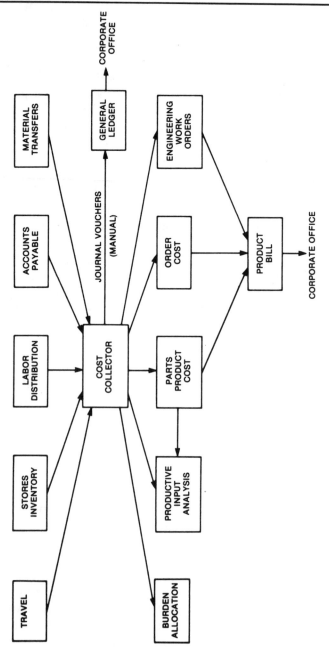

The accounting system uses standard costs. Standard costs are set at the time the part cost is first estimated. When a part number is new, or changes owing to a redesign, the industrial engineer rebids or reestimates the standard cost of the product. An important component of the standard cost is the amount of labor required for the part. For each manufacturing process required by a part, the standard number of good units produced in a normal eight-hour day is estimated by the industrial engineer. These standards are then used in setting workers' incentives.

The parts manufacturing department uses two main accounting reports. These are used by management on a monthly basis and are described next.

Direct Labor and Indirect Expense Report

Exhibit 10-2 is a facsimile of a direct labor and indirect expense report. It gives fictitious numbers for one parts manufacturing department. At the beginning of the year, forecasts are constructed for direct labor, indirect labor, other indirect costs, and various uncontrollable costs. These estimates are reported in the column labeled "Forecast/Month." For example, direct labor is forecasted to be $240 per month. These forecasts are made once the annual production plan is set at the beginning of the year. Forecasted uncontrollable costs are per dollar of direct labor. For example, "Employee Benefits" are forecasted to be $0.51 for every direct labor dollar.

Each month, actual direct labor, controllable, and uncontrollable dollars are reported in the rows labeled "Actual." Actual direct labor expense for each month to date is reported in the first row. The "Budget" rows are the forecasted dollars in the cost category times the ratio of actual to forecast direct labor. If actual direct labor is 20 percent greater than forecast, the indirect budgeted amount is 20 percent larger than the forecast. For example, "budgeted" indirect labor in month 1 is less than the forecast because actual direct labor is below forecasted direct labor ($150 = 180 \times 200/240$). The monthly actual amount is deducted from budget to derive a variance.

In this system, a "flexible budgeting system" for indirect cost items is used. Each cost item, however, is treated as either entirely fixed or variable, but not both. In the reports examined, all of the forecasted controllable costs were treated as variable, and none of the

Exhibit 10-2   Direct Labor and Indirect Expense Report

	Forecast/ Month[a]	Month 1	Month 2	Year to Date
DIRECT LABOR	$240	$200	$215	$415
CONTROLLABLE COSTS				
Indirect Labor	$180			
Budget[b]		$150	$157	$307
Actual		$161	$164	$325
Variance		($11)	($7)	($18)
Other Indirect costs	$100			
Budget[b]		$83	$88	$171
Actual		$85	$87	$172
Variance		($2)	$1	($1)
TOTAL CONTROLLABLE				
Budget[b]	$280	$233	$245	$478
Actual		$246	$251	$497
Variance		($13)	($6)	($19)
UNCONTROLLABLE COSTS				
Employee Benefits	$0.51			
Actual dollars		$104	$106	$210
Actual rate[c]		0.52	0.49	0.51
Rate variance		($0.01)	$0.02	$0.00
Depreciation & utilities	$0.30			
Actual dollars		$64	$65	$129
Actual rate[c]		0.32	0.30	0.31
Rate variance		($0.02)	$0.00	($0.01)
Division Overhead	$0.35			
Actual dollars		$62	$78	$140
Actual rate[c]		0.31	0.36	0.34
Rate variance		0.04	−0.01	0.01
Total Rates*	$2.33			
Actual rate[c]		$2.38	$2.33	$2.35
Rate variance		($0.05)	$0.00	($0.03)

a. forecast is the expected amount determined at the beginning of the year.
b. budget = forecasted dollars × (actual dir. lab./forecast dir. lab.).
c. actual rate = actual dollars/actual direct labor.
* includes controllable costs.

forecasted cost items was considered fixed. Treating forecasted costs, which contain in reality both fixed and variable components, as being entirely variable causes larger favorable variances when volume exceeds forecasts and larger unfavorable variances when volume is less than forecasted. Hence, by assuming that all indirect expenses are purely variable, the budgets create incentives for managers to produce more than forecasted and hence to "overproduce" or build inventories.

Treating all costs as being variable further reinforces parts managers' incentives to underforecast direct and indirect costs. Underforecasts produce larger favorable variances and smaller unfavorable variances when all costs are treated as variable than when costs are treated as containing both fixed and variable components.

While these accounting procedures produce incentives to expand inventories, there are important constraints that limit managers' discretion to do so. The parts manufacturing managers must have customers. The production control system issues release orders for raw materials into the shop. These work orders authorize parts managers to produce a maximum number of parts for delivery to assembly at a future date and thus act as upper bounds on the amount of inventories managers can build.

The empirical importance of excluding fixed costs in the flexible budgets cannot be assessed without further study and access to manufacturing cost and production data. The incentives created by excluding fixed cost components may, in fact, be trivial and overwhelmed by other incentives. For example, in this manufacturing organization, parts manufacturing managers have incentive to reduce parts quality, thereby generating rework. Rework increases the manager's direct labor budget, thereby increasing budgeted indirect costs.

In the portion of the report labeled "Uncontrollable Costs," actual dollars are converted to a rate by dividing actual dollars by forecasted direct labor. For example, actual employee benefits were $104 in month 1. This represents $0.52 per direct labor dollar ($.52 = 104/200). The actual rate is then deducted from the forecasted rate in the first column to derive a rate variance.

The last rows, "Total Rates," are the sum of the uncontrollable and total controllable costs. For example, in month 1, $2.38 of (hypothetical) indirect expenses were incurred for every dollar of direct labor in this parts manufacturing department. This rate was five cents above the forecasted indirect expense rate.

Exhibit 10-3   Part/Product Cost System

Part Description	STD Quantities @ STD Cost	Unit $ Repair	Unit $ In-Process Scrap	Unit $ Assembly Scrap	Unit Cost This Period
Spring Drive	0.023	0.004	0.013	0.008	0.048
Lever	0.034	0.000	−0.001	0.001	0.034
Strap	0.018	0.000	0.003	0.001	0.022
Arm	0.033	0.003	−0.011	0.004	0.029
Total	0.108	0.007	0.004	0.014	0.133

Note: STD Quantities @ STD Cost
  first time labor, burden, and material at std.
Unit $ Repair
  unitized, secondary operations for a part (rework).
Unit $ In-Process Scrap
  unitized, in-process scrap for a part (includes first time variances from std).
Unit $ Assembly Scrap
  unitized assembly scrap for a part (assembly scrap occurs during assembly).
Unit Cost This Period
  sum of first four columns.

Part/Product Cost Report

Exhibit 10-3 presents a typical report from the part/product cost (PPC) system, again with fictitious numbers. The report gives detailed cost calculations for each part comprising the finished product or subassembly.

The first column contains the part description (part numbers have been deleted). The next column, "Std Quantities @ Std Cost," is the labor, overhead, and material for a part at standard cost. Labor rate, material price, and overhead variances are not included in the part costs reported in PPC. Standard material prices and labor rates are set one year in advance. The column entitled "Unit $ Repair" gives the per unit cost of any secondary rework operation on the part. "Unit $ In-Process Scrap" is the per unit cost of scrap. It also contains any first time variances from labor and material standards. "Unit $ Assembly Scrap" is the per unit cost of any parts scrapped during the assembly process. "Unit Cost This Period" is the sum of the preceding four columns.

The part/product cost report is designed to report on the production efficiency of the parts manufacturing operation. Material price, labor rate, and overhead variances are not included in the report. Instead, the report focuses on material quantity variances, scrap and rework variances, and labor efficiency variances. These variances are not shown separately but rather are included in columns 3-5 in the repair and scrap variances. Part/product costs are the basis for the transfer price of the completed manufactured goods transferred to the line of business responsible for selling the product. Overabsorbed and underabsorbed variances and material price and labor rate variances are not in the part/product cost but are charged to the lines of business directly.

The parts manufacturing manager offered several comments on the accounting system in general and on the preceding two reports in particular. He said the system is probably fine for external reporting and taxes. It is inadequate, however, for managing his manufacturing process. Reports, and in particular, the variances are not timely. Unit costs this period are not equal to total cost/unit.

While the part/product cost report is prepared monthly, the reported unit costs in Exhibit 10-3 do not represent the previous month's manufacturing costs. The reported numbers in this report are a weighted average of all parts not shipped as completed products to distribution. That is, as long as a part is still in the manufacturing process, its cost is still in the average. When completed products are shipped to distribution, the cost of the parts in the product are removed from the average at the average part cost. Current manufacturing costs are added to the numerator and completed product parts are deducted from the numerator at average cost. Current manufacturing costs, if different from the average, affect the average only by the ratio of the current costs to total dollars invested in work-in-process inventory. If parts inventory costs are large relative to current period production costs, current costs will have a small impact on reported average cost in the part/product cost report. This progressive averaging of unit costs causes current actions to be diluted with old costs. If inventories are large relative to current production, it can take several months for significant cost savings to appear in the part/product cost report.

Currently management is attempting to reduce inventories. As work-in-process inventories are reduced, weighted average costs will more closely reflect current period costs. The weighted average accounting system provides some incentive for parts manufacturing managers to reduce inventories because with falling costs, smaller inventories allow current period cost reductions to appear more quickly in the reported weighted average costs. But again, the importance of such incentives is impossible to assess without access to the data.

Also, the manufacturing manager said the reporting system is "too gross." It reports on the entire department. Individual cells or sections of his department are not disaggregated along the lines his department is organized on. He would like reports on each of his section managers.

The parts manufacturing manager mentioned that the accounting system does not directly measure his overall performance correctly. If he institutes major labor savings by substituting indirect labor and capital for direct labor to reduce total cost, the accounting reports do not reflect the savings. The indirect expense report (Exhibit 10-2) will show his indirect expense budget being reduced because less direct labor is used (budgeted indirect expense = ratio of actual to forecast direct labor × indirect expense forecast), but actual indirect expenses are higher. Thus, large unfavorable variances are reported. The problem arises because forecasted costs only are revised annually; forecasts are not revised immediately after labor savings are instituted. The manager is evaluated against both parts/product cost and the indirect expense report. He feels these two reports are important, but he would like a single report that measures his total costs. While he has been able to reduce direct labor input, the indirect expense report shows him as being over budget.

The controller's office pointed out that department heads who supervise the parts manufacturing managers should be aware of significant improvements in productivity resulting from new technology or process-engineering efforts and the impact of these activities on direct labor. These labor reductions "should be forecast during the budgeting process."

Several interviewees said that many of the indirect cost numbers in Exhibit 10-2 were easily manipulated to show the supervisors in the best light. Various maintenance accounts were used to "bank" dollars in the event that cost overruns were incurred in other areas. Such manipulations reduce the ability of the accounting system to report managerially relevant data. By reporting biased forecasts of indirect expenses, the operating managers contribute to reducing the utility of the accounting numbers for decision making. The accounting system is being used to control operating managers, to measure their performance, and to provide managerially relevant data, in addition to satisfying tax and external reporting requirements.

If the operating manager is well versed in the accounting system, the two reports (part/product cost and indirect expense report) give all the data necessary for the manager to assess operations. Problems arise if operating managers do not use the accounting system frequently enough to learn and retain the high level of understanding necessary to interpret the data in managerially relevant ways. Using the accounting reports only once a month is too infrequent. Manufacturing managers cannot acquire and retain the specialized knowledge of the accounting procedures to use the accounting information for routine operating decisions. The controller's office currently is developing accounting-based tools to be used by manufacturing managers on a weekly basis.

INCENTIVE SYSTEMS

Worker Incentive System

A formal incentive system is used to motivate factory workers. To make the bonus, 600 minutes of output must be achieved each day. "Minutes of output" is measured as good units produced times standard labor minutes per unit. Standard minutes per machine setup are counted toward the 600-minute target. Parts inspection usually occurs following production. In some departments the worker incentive system is a group system. Unless the entire group as a whole achieves the 600-minute standard based on total labor input, no one in the group receives a bonus. Group sizes range from about 8 to 200 people depending on the department. On most days the workers in the parts manufacturing departments receive the maximum bonus. One interviewee reported that about 75 percent of the time workers receive the maximum bonus. The bonus amounts to 15 percent of the production worker's base salary.

The worker incentive system requires a large industrial engineering staff to maintain the standards underlying the bonus system. Each manufacturing process for each part and every setup requires a standard number of minutes to be stated. Every time the production process changes, the standards should be revised; but that is not always done. One manager stated that many standards are "way off the mark." The current incentive system was installed about twenty years ago. There are currently about thirty different versions of the plan in use. Several interviewees believed the system is now obsolete. "They are a nonfactor, at least in most parts manufacturing departments. The engineers have not maintained what a standard minute is for every operation. People don't pay attention to these standards, and the incentive system has no effect on worker productivity."

Another manager said there is no incentive to produce more than 600 minutes of output per day. The 600-minute standard tends to work as a cap. If workers find an efficient production technique and achieve the 600-minute standard, they reduce output for the rest of the day.

Large group-size dilutes the incentive of individual workers. One worker in a group of one hundred only impacts a hundredth of the group's output; but one worker in a group of two impacts one-half of the group's output. Hence, large group-size reduces the effectiveness of the incentive system.

These and other problems in the worker incentive system have caused management to review all such systems and in many cases eliminate them. The controller's office reported, "Performance measures are currently being devised to 'weight heavily' the quality of parts produced." (Note: after the study was completed, the worker incentive system was abolished.)

Management Incentives

There is no formal bonus system linking the compensation of parts department managers to their output. Rather, annual merit pay increases are based on the manager's performance in attaining multiple objectives. These objectives include meeting the production schedule, the indirect expense budget, parts/product cost, and production quality improvement targets. Schedule goals are defined as the delivery of minimum and maximum inventory of parts at a scheduled time. These multiple objectives force managers to make trade-offs among the often conflicting and ill-defined goals. For example, one manager stated that his performance objective depends on the time of the year. At the beginning of the year it is the expense budget; then it becomes meeting scheduled delivery dates. At other times of the year it is first-time labor costs. Until recently, parts costs were not stressed; "They didn't even matter."

The controller's office responded to the existence of multiple and often conflicting objectives.

Conflicting signals from management and the stress they produce are inherently a part of the transition phase of any major shift in management's objectives, such as our shift to profit/loss responsibility for LOB managers. As we proceed through this transitional phase, the signals from management should become clear and more consistent.

Parts manufacturing managers who consistently are unable to produce parts in a timely manner for assembly do not advance in the organization and do not receive above-average merit pay increases. Meeting delivery schedules is very important and difficult. One senior executive offered the opinion that up to 30 percent of the scheduled delivery dates are not met. He claimed that the strictures that arise from missing delivery dates encourage parts manufacturing managers to build longer lead times into production schedules and to build safety stocks against part shortages.

Some parts manufacturing managers object to smaller lot sizes because they lead to more machine setups. More setups reduce the available machine hours for producing parts, thereby increasing the chances of parts stock outs. Thus, operating managers seeking to reduce stock outs resist reducing batch sizes.

An important factor in reducing batch sizes, inventories, and cost is reducing setup times. Faster setups increase throughput, reduce queuing externalities, and allow smaller lot sizes. Faster setups are usually accomplished through new technologies, such as flexible manufacturing systems, by redesigning existing processes, and in some cases by redesigning parts.

Managers are also evaluated on meeting unit cost targets. Until recently, there was very little emphasis on parts cost as a performance measure. There was greater emphasis placed on meeting direct labor and indirect expense targets.

Several individuals stressed that meeting delivery schedules was *the* critical performance criterion for parts production managers. Meeting the expense budget was less important; rework gave them more direct labor dollars and larger expense budgets. Some emphasis is now placed on unit costs and quality improvement, but the dominant factor still remains producing parts in a timely fashion.

INCENTIVES, ACCOUNTING, AND THE DECISION-MAKING PROCESS

Each parts manufacturing department has some discretion in setting lot sizes. A parts manufacturing manager described the lot-sizing process as follows:

Originally, the manufacturing division used computer models for setting lot sizes. But now, we consider how many parts we can physically handle in the available space. This provides an upper bound on the lot size. Many parts should be produced in variable lot sizes due to space considerations. For example, if we start with a piece of sheet metal, a large number of sheets can be stacked in a relatively small space. But as it is formed into say a box, it takes up more space, and hence the lot size should be decreased. One problem with cutting lot sizes is that workers do not like doing setups; they prefer larger lots. If the predominant problem with large lots is physical space, we can usually get the lot sizes down. Otherwise, the lot sizes are large because of worker preferences. In some cases, pressure from senior management to decrease lot size was resisted. In other cases, lot sizes were reduced to prevent flooding the shop floor with inventory and to monitor worker quality. That is, lot sizes were constrained to the amount produced during one shift. This allowed us to evaluate each worker's productivity and the quality of the parts produced during his shift. When lot sizes were reduced, unit costs rose because setup costs were spread over fewer units. We got killed [on part/product costs] in some cases.

In this firm, lot sizes are not set by EOQ models. The computer system sets initial lot sizes, but the computer program was written over twenty years ago and has been modified since then. No one interviewed knew with much confidence exactly what the computer program did. But several managers stated that the computer-generated lot sizes were adjusted manually for various reasons.

The production system within departments is characterized by fairly large lot sizes for "normal" production and numerous smaller lot sizes for "expedited" jobs. A dispatching system released work orders and materials into the parts shops based on future production of final products and normal lead times for the parts for these products. Jobs initiated in this way are for "normal" production. They are usually started several months before final product assembly. And, since these jobs tend to produce all the parts needed by assembly for several weeks (or even months), their lot sizes tend to be large. "Expedited" jobs are those that produce parts to meet short-term emergency requirements. If an assembly line expects a parts shortage in a few days or discovers an existing part requiring rework prior to assembly, then an expedited job is placed in the parts department to produce the necessary parts. Getting these parts quickly to assembly generates jobs with small lot sizes.

As discussed in Karmarkar, Kekre, and Kekre (1985), mixing large- and small-lot-size jobs causes nonuniform processing demands. Within the shop, some machines are running large batch sizes and some are running very small batch sizes. Such unbalanced production increases congestion, queues, and waiting times for all jobs because the small-batch-size jobs wait for the larger-lot-size jobs to finish. Ideally, all machine-processing times are perfectly synchronized, with parts flowing from one process to another at the same time. While this ideal is never realized, job shops with both large and small batch sizes exacerbate the queuing externality.

In several discussions, managers stressed that informal worker incentives kept lot sizes large. They mentioned that doing machine setups is harder than running parts production. "Workers like to come to work each day and have the machine ready to go with their setup on it from the day before." "It is difficult to explain to workers the importance of cost reduction and working efficiently when they are spending much of their time doing setups." The workers see the direct materials, labor, and indirect cost of the parts. The reduction in inventory holding cost via reductions in queues and the queuing externality is much more difficult to explain to operators, especially since it is not being measured and reported.

The accounting system tends to reinforce the incentive to produce parts in large lot sizes. It does not measure inventory holding costs, thus there is little incentive for the parts manufacturing department manager to reduce lot sizes since reported costs of parts will be higher. As described earlier, the variances reported in the direct and indirect expense report create further incentives to expand production. Favorable variances are larger and unfavorable variances are smaller when output is higher.

At the outset of my study, management's main concern was to attempt to reduce lot sizes. But with the reorganization and the resulting profit incentives created for the LOB managers, attention shifted to the make-or-buy decision as lower-cost, externally produced parts were substituted for higher-cost internally produced parts. Until recently, almost all parts had been made internally if capacity was available. Parts were purchased externally if there was a clear cost advantage and management was satisfied the supplier could meet delivery schedules and quality standards.

Manufacturing engineers in the manufacturing assembly organization had been responsible for the make-or-buy decision. Manufacturing was treated as a cost center and product-line profitability was judged at the corporate level. Under the decentralization plan, the functional organization was replaced with a product-line organization. The manufacturing engineer, who is still in the manufacturing assembly organization, continues to make the make-or-buy decision, but that individual's incentive has changed because the assembly department is part of the LOB, which has profit responsibilities. The manufacturing engineer had always been assigned the task of comparing the external price to the out-of-pocket costs of making the part and holding quality and delivery times constant. But because LOB managers are now concerned with product profits, the external price will likely be compared to the internal product bill cost as reported by the accounting system. The product bill cost is higher than out-of-pocket costs because it contains overhead and indirect labor allocations. Also, any inefficiency in parts production will be passed through to the line of business if unfavorable manufacturing variances are passed through to the LOB. Since the LOB managers have the discretion to purchase parts externally and since they have profit responsibilities, it is likely the fraction of parts produced internally will fall.

The controller's office commented, "It is not necessarily bad that some parts, which were traditionally manufactured 'in-house,' will be purchased in the future. . . . We must consider where we want to use our resources and our long-term ability to compete, using delivery, cost, and quality as performance measures."

While LOB managers have profit incentive to purchase parts externally, the accounting system biases the make-or-buy decision toward making the parts internally. Only direct, indirect, and overhead costs are included in the parts cost. Capital costs on raw materials and work-in-process are not included in total parts cost. Nor are confusion, congestion, and the opportunity costs of delaying other parts included in total parts cost. Capital costs on internally produced parts can be a substantial portion of total parts cost because throughput time, from raw material purchase to final assembly, can be three to nine months in some cases. Survival of external parts suppliers presumably will cause them to price their parts to return their capital costs. Hence, the internally produced parts will have a lower (accounting-based transfer) price than externally purchased parts. The empirical magnitude of this bias depends on the length of time the part remains in inventory. If it only takes three weeks from the time the raw material is purchased until the part is delivered to assembly, and if inventory holding costs are relatively small (less than 30 percent of average total costs), then the bias is less than 2 percent of average total costs.

The controller's office agreed that it is "theoretically correct to include them [inventory holding costs]" in parts costs, but they argue, "It would be somewhat cost prohibitive to implement: after developing a distribution rate, a mechanism would have to be developed to apply this rate to thousands of parts and to remove these same costs for financial reporting purposes."

CONCLUSIONS

This exploratory study sought to describe one firm's accounting and incentive systems and how they affect the lot-sizing decision; as expected, it found that the accounting and incentive systems reinforced the tendency to maintain large lot sizes. The next step requires access to detailed data on costs, quantities, and production schedules to estimate the magnitude of the various effects. The remainder of this section offers some observations on the research site and then comments on the field study research process.

The Research Site

Incorporating the parts manufacturing divisions along with the assembly lines into the product lines of business will overcome some of the dysfunctional incentives that exist in the current separate organizations. The LOB is responsible for return on investment. Grouping the parts manufacturing and assembly departments into one unit causes the externalities to be internalized, at least at the LOB level. For example, if a parts department fails to meet a delivery schedule, it imposes a cost on the assembly department within the LOB; unless the incentive scheme of the parts manager is set to capture correctly the cost imposed on assembly of failing to meet delivery schedules, then the parts manager makes the wrong trade-off between incurring additional parts manufacturing costs and the costs of failing to meet the production schedule. If the parts and assembly departments are in one organization, the LOB manager will control both parts manufacturing and assembly and can compare the additional parts manufacturing costs incurred to meet assembly schedules to the cost of missing the schedule and delaying assembly. Under the current separate organizations, if the costs of delaying assembly vary over time, the parts manufacturing managers' incentives also have to vary, or else the parts manager has an incentive to make the wrong decision.

Incorporating parts manufacturing into the LOB eliminates the need to compute a transfer price, thus eliminating the dysfunctional incentives of interdepartmental transfer pricing. Eliminating internal transfer prices will increase the frequency of "correct" make-or-buy decisions. A "correct" decision maximizes firm value, which is not necessarily the same as maximizing accounting profit or minimizing reported accounting cost.

There is another advantage of grouping parts and assembly under the LOB. If the LOB is evaluated on return on assets, the opportunity cost of holding inventories is automatically charged to the LOB. The LOB manager, through direct reports, is responsible for and has control over, inventory levels within the LOB organization; currently, the LOB is not charged for inventory holding costs on parts in production or awaiting assembly.

The disadvantage of incorporating the parts departments into the LOB is the loss of synergy from grouping similar functional processes. For example, having all the punch presses in one department facilitates technological innovation and efficiency transfers resulting from experimentation. Economies of scale are larger when similar machine processes are grouped together. If a punch press breaks down, other presses in the press department can meet the work demands.

The Field Study Process

Field research can prove enormously useful in furthering our understanding of management accounting. In fact, it is often the only way to gather observations and data to generate new insights. All empirical research is "field research," and like other forms of empirical research, a field study is subject to various methodological problems. These methodological problems do not necessarily invalidate the study. Often new theories, insights, and hypotheses are suggested from a few limited observations. The scientific standards applied to more mature areas of inquiry should not be applied to early exploratory studies seeking to generate insights. On the other hand, readers ought to be aware of the difficulties and problems associated with a given field study.

Comments are offered regarding three aspects of this particular field study: 1) potential sources of bias, 2) the importance of data to assess empirical magnitudes, and 3) the partial nature of the analysis.

My field study involved extensive use of interviews. Field interviews raise two potential biases. One is interviewee response bias; that is, did the interviewees accurately describe the systems, or did they describe what the system ought to be? Or did they describe what they thought we or their superiors wanted to hear (Cook and Campbell 1979, 67)?

The second source of bias is researcher bias. The researcher has a preconceived model of the process under investigation and is prone to hear more readily those comments that fit this model. The researcher is not deliberately slanting the study to prove a hypothesis but *tends* to absorb and retain those observations that are understood and not pursue those comments not understood. Often questions are phrased in such a way as to elicit answers that are consistent with the "theory" being tested. That is, instead of gathering data and trying to refute a null hypothesis (the usual scientific approach), lines of questioning that support the implicit theory are pursued. Therefore, results are shaded or slanted in certain subtle ways by the investigator (Iannii and Orr 1979, 96–97).

Biases in field studies raise the question as to whether the results can be replicated (Smith 1982, 606). Would another researcher, using the same or an otherwise equivalent organization, make different observations? In fact, the same researcher might come to different conclusions if different people were interviewed or if the same people were interviewed at a different time. Lacking the historical knowledge of the organization, it was very difficult to ask meaningful questions. In most of the discussions, individuals had "hidden agendas." The topics under investigation were important to the interviewees. Our not knowing how their welfare depended on the systems being investigated made it very difficult to conduct the interviews to generate responses that helped illuminate how the various systems interacted.

Only one parts manufacturing department was analyzed. There is a serious question as to the extent the observations from this one department apply to other departments within the manufacturing division. Many responses from interviewees were fairly general in that they applied to various systems in other departments and not just the department under investigation. Interviewees were asked to focus on the one department, but fairly generic comments were forthcoming. The organizationwide nature of the information perhaps increases our ability to generalize the results to include the whole organization; but it also makes it more difficult to assess the impact of the accounting and incentive systems on the lot-sizing decision within the department under study.

All empirical studies are subject to various forms of biases; field research is not unique in this regard. But in field research the magnitude of the bias is potentially larger, and in many cases the direction of the bias is unknown. Often, field study researchers, even those conducting "descriptive" studies, fail to state explicitly the underlying theory directing their data gathering.* This makes it difficult to assess the direction and magnitude of researcher bias. Biases of empirical studies that use publicly available data sets (e.g., CRSP and COMPUSTAT) are easier to assess. Other studies often raise and investigate the bias (e.g., the survivorship bias in COMPUSTAT but not CRSP). Studies using public data sets can be replicated to test for various biases. Field studies also can be replicated, but the organization and the original participants have likely changed. In most cases, the original study has been read by the managers, and this is likely to affect their responses to the replication.

A second limitation of this study relates to the lack of data to assess empirical magnitudes. Managers are (rightly) reluctant to disclose cost data. But without such data, it is easy for the investigator to fail to appreciate the relevant trade-offs. For example, the chapter emphasizes the importance of inventory holding costs and that by excluding these costs the current accounting system is inducing dysfunctional incentives. Omitted inventory holding cost, however, might be insignificant relative to direct and indirect cost differences between the firm and its competitors. Management is correct to ignore inventory holding cost if the magnitudes are small relative to the competitive pressures on prime costs.

A third problem with the field study approach is its tendency toward *partial analysis*. I analyzed the current accounting and incentive systems, but such systems are not static; they evolve as continual modifications are made to solve defects and to adapt to new circumstances. In all systems there are both costs and benefits of the extant procedures. It is much easier for the researcher to document the dysfunctional aspects of the current system than the problems the current system has overcome via the numerous modifications made to previous systems. Thus, the researcher does a *partial analysis* of the existing system and documents all the warts. The investigator cannot reconstruct all the trade-offs previously considered in earlier versions of the system. Often the existing management cannot reconstruct such a history because it was not present when the decisions were made. It is tempting to be overly critical of existing management systems and to conclude that they are far inferior to some unidentified, and usually

---

*Not all data and facts can be collected and reported—the world and field sites are too complex. Some theory, underlying model, or framework always directs the researcher to those facts considered interesting or important to collect and report.

costless to implement, alternative. ". . .[A] deduced discrepancy between ideal and the real is sufficient to call forth perfection by incantation, that is, by committing the grass is always greener fallacy. This usually is accomplished by invoking an unexamined alternative" (Demsetz 1969, 3).

These three limitations not only restrict the generalizability of the study's findings but also limit the usefulness of the study to the management of the organization under study. After reading an earlier draft of this chapter, management offered the following general comment:

It is my impression that the author has fallen into the same trap as other academicians who try to point out how accounting systems and practices lead manufacturing managers to the wrong decisions. While they point out many valid concerns over current practices, they fail to give us any viable alternative approaches. He has failed to give us any advice other than incorporating the manufacturing operations into the LOB organizational structure. This, however, does not address the underlying issues, which, he feels, are leading us to the wrong decisions.

Clearly, to participate in such field studies, management wants prescriptive solutions. Before such normative suggestions can be offered, however, the researcher must identify the key underlying forces (i.e., develop an accurate positive model of the extant systems). Understanding the organization and identifying such forces often requires access to sensitive corporate data to assess empirical magnitudes and refute alternative hypotheses. Such analyses are very costly and time consuming. There is a real concern as to whether academic research operating within the usual constraints of limited research resources can produce the underlying causal factors and derive prescriptive solutions in a timely fashion to justify management's cooperation.

REFERENCES

Banker, R. D.; Datar, S. M.; and Kekre, S. 1987. "Relevant Costs, Congestion and Stochasticity in Production Environments." Carnegie-Mellon University. Working paper.

Campbell, D. T. 1979. "Degrees of Freedom and the Case Study." In *Qualitative and Quantitative Methods in Evaluation Research*, edited by C. S. Reichardt and T. D. Cook, 49–67. Beverly Hills, CA: Sage Publications.

Demsetz, H. 1969. "Information and Efficiency: Another Viewpoint." *Journal of Law and Economics* 12 (April): 1–22.

Iannii, F. A., and Orr, M. T. 1979. "Toward a Reapproachment of Quantitative and Qualitative Methodologies." In *Qualitative and Quantitative Methods in Evaluation Research*, edited by S. S. Reichardt and T. D. Cook, 87–97. Beverly Hills, CA: Sage Publications.

Karmarkar, U. S. 1987. "Lot Sizes, Lead Times and In-Process Inventories." *Management Science* 33 (March): 409–18.

Karmarkar, U. S.; Kekre, S.; and Kekre, S. 1985. "Lot-Sizing in Multi-Item Multi-Machine Job Shops." *IIE Transactions* 17 (September): 290–98.

———. 1983. "Multi-item Lot-Sizing and Manufacturing Lead Times." University of Rochester. Working paper No. QM8325.

Karmarkar, U. S.; Kekre, S.; Kekre, S.; and Freeman, S. 1985. "Lot-Sizing and Leadtime Performance in a Manufacturing Cell." *Interfaces* (March–April): 1–9.

Schaffer, G. H. 1981. "Implementing CIM." *American Machinist Special Report 736*.

Smith, H. W. 1982. "Improving the Quality of Field Research Training." 35 *Human Relations* (July): 605–19.

Zipkin, P. H. 1983. "Models for Design and Control of Stochastic, Multi-Item Batch Production Systems." Columbia University, Columbia Business School. Research Working paper No. 496A.

PART IV

Measuring Management Performance

The Use of Relative Performance
Evaluation in Organizations

Michael W. Maher

INTRODUCTION

ALTHOUGH a major use of accounting in organizations is to set performance standards and monitor employees' performance, little is known about the actual process by which that is accomplished or about the causes of the great variety of practices among firms. A major issue in evaluating divisional performance is the separation of performance results that are controllable by division managers from the effect of environmental factors outside of their control. For instance, division managers can be held accountable for achieving a fixed target independent of the performance among peers (e.g., other divisions operating in similar product markets), or their performance can be evaluated relative to the performance of other divisions. The latter approach, known as relative performance evaluation (RPE), is analo-

I appreciate the excellent cooperation by numerous people at Honeywell and the other companies that were studied. I am particularly grateful to Lynn Timgren, at Honeywell, who coordinated the interviews there and provided helpful information. I am also grateful to the following people for helpful comments and discussions: Rick Antle, Stan Baiman, Paul Beck, Steve Butler, Ron Dye, Kirsten Ely, Tom Frecka, Bob Kaplan, Bob Magee, Mark Penno, Abbie Smith, Ira Solomon, Bot Swieringa, and participants in the Roedger Lecture colloqium at the University of Illinois.

gous to "grading on the curve" in which sources of uncertainty common to all division managers in the peer group are removed. Using RPE, the evaluation of a manager or division performance is conditional on how well the peers are doing; a division earning a 10 percent profit margin would be evaluated more favorably if the peers averaged 5 percent than if the peers averaged 20 percent.

The purpose of this research was to investigate whether and how companies use RPE to appraise divisional performance. According to economic theory, the use of RPE can increase the efficiency of contracting between a principal (e.g., top management) and an agent i (e.g., a division manager) by taking into account the performance of other agents who face a similar environment. If measures of the other agents' performance are informative about the state faced by agent i, then the efficiency of contracting can be improved because agent i's risk is reduced without a reduction in incentives.[1] Hence, the theory implies that RPE will be used when an agent's output (not input) performance is contracted upon, and other agents face a similar environment.

Antle and Smith (1986) empirically investigated whether the top three executives of firms were compensated *as if* their firm's performance was evaluated relative to the performance of other firms in the same industry. Their study of thirty-nine firms for the period 1947–1977 had mixed results; top executives were compensated *as if* firm performance was evaluated relative to industry performance in sixteen firms, but not in the other twenty-three firms. Although economic theory and the Antle and Smith research helped motivate and guide my inquiry, they leave several questions unanswered. First, Antle and Smith's results imply that executives are compensated *as if* RPE is used in some of the firms studied; but the research is not designed to indicate how companies make *explicit* use of RPE. If RPE is used explicitly, how is the set of firms facing a common environment determined? For example, Antle and Smith included ten firms in the aerospace industry, but some are prime contractors (e.g., Boeing) and others are secondary contractors (e.g., Bendix).[2] Do these two firms face a common environment or are they in two (or more) separate industries for RPE purposes? Knowledge of how firms, themselves, determine the set of their competitors can be useful for firm-industry matchings in future empirical research.

A second question involves Antle and Smith's finding that compensation is associated with RPE in some firms, but not in others: What characteristics of firms and contracts give rise to RPE in some cases, but not in others? Third, Antle and Smith's investigation was restricted in scope: It was limited to the use of RPE in top management compensation, and did not study divisional performance evaluation.[3]

The purpose of this study is to address these questions by using the results of field studies in several firms. The description of corporate practice presented here is intended to help develop hypotheses about the use of RPE in incentive contracting: For example, under what conditions will RPE be used? Will it only be used in firms in which there is considerable information asymmetry between top and division managers? What accounting choices are made in selecting the RPE measures? How is the peer group determined?[4]

Although the motivation and primary focus of the research are on the use of RPE, the research also initiates some unexpected inquiries into strategic planning and the trade-offs among variables in the corporate objective function that I discuss later. The major conclusions of the study are (1) that interfirm divisional RPE is used primarily in setting divisional performance targets and not in *ex post* adjustments based on events occurring during the performance period, and (2) that both the amount of risk faced by division managers and the information asymmetry between top and division managers are variables to consider in determining conditions under which interfirm RPE will be used in divisional performance evaluation.

The rest of the chapter is organized as follows. The next section summarizes the key issues and discusses the research approach. It describes the rationale for the decisions I made in conducting the inquiry and considers both positive and negative consequences of those decisions. The third section outlines the findings from Phase I—a study of five firms to collect data on the characteristics of firms that use RPE. The fourth section discusses findings from Phase II—an extensive study of the use of RPE in Honeywell, Inc. The last section presents conclusions and implications of the study.

RESEARCH ISSUES AND METHODS

Holmstrom (1982) shows that RPE is valuable in contracting between principals and agents if agents face some common uncertainties and if one agent's output provides information about another agent's state uncertainty.[5] This proposition provided the motivation for my study. I expected to find RPE used when agents faced common uncertainties and when information about other agents' performance was informative about the performance of the contracting agents. The key is "informativeness," not controllability; that is, there are informative variables available for use in performance evaluation whether or not those variables are under the contracting agent's control.[6]

Based on the theory, I expected to find the performance of division managers evaluated relative to the performance of managers in the same markets, even if those markets are not faced by other divisions in the firm. If division managers in a particular firm operated in different industries, then I expected divisional performance to be evaluated relative to other firms, and/or to divisions in other firms, in the same industry. What remained to be learned, however, were the conditions under which each of these approaches were informative in contracting, and the methods used by firms in implementing them. Given these issues and my particular interest in studying interfirm RPE, I selected research sites in which division managers faced an environment not faced by other division managers in the same firm.

Research Methods

In general, my approach followed that suggested by Kaplan (1986, 446–7):

Initially, one would study a few organizations in considerable detail to learn, not just whether or not, but why they did (or did not) adopt . . . performance evaluation schemes. From this initial set of studies, the researcher may formulate hypotheses on where the schemes would be expected to be adopted and where not. These hypotheses would then serve both to guide the sample selection for the next set of companies and to be the targets for the testing/disconfirmation procedures. When examining the management control procedures for the new set of companies, the researcher would be interested both in prediction (whether adoption . . . of relative performance evaluation occurred where expected and whether [it] did not occur where [it was] not expected) and also in whether the *reasons* for adoption and non-adoption were consistent with the reasons given in the researcher's hypotheses. In other words, field studies in a theory testing mode can serve not only to document the existence or non-existence of practices but also to confirm *how* and *why* certain practices have, or have not, been implemented.

My first, and perhaps most important decision, was to choose between describing a major part of the management control process, such as the budget process, or investigating a more narrow topic that has been implied by economic theory. I opted for the latter for three reasons: (1) starting with theory helps focus and structure the inquiry; (2) there are greater opportunities for generalizing the findings if they can be related to theory; and (3) starting with theory potentially contributes toward improving models and refining empirical tests.

Research Sites

The choice of research sites was primarily determined by the research questions. First, I selected a group of five firms ranging from a diverse conglomerate where divisions are investment centers to an integrated, centralized firm operating in only one two-digit SIC industry whose divisions are cost centers. My purpose in choosing this set was to include two types of firms. First, I included firms with divisions in different industries facing different environments, such that intrafirm RPE comparisons would presumably be less informative than interfirm comparisons.[7] This would enable me to study whether and how interfirm comparisons are made. Second, I wanted to include one firm in which all of the division managers faced essentially a common environment so that (presumably) intrafirm comparisons would be more informative than interfirm comparisons.

Phase II studies RPE in greater depth for a particular company. The findings in Phase I imply that interfirm divisional RPE is more likely to be used in evaluating divisional performance if firms have divisions operating in diverse industries. Consequently, for Phase II, I decided to study divisional performance evaluation at Honeywell, Inc., a company with divisions in several industries. My plan for Phase II was to obtain data about performance evaluation from top management down through the division level to supervisors and project managers. I hoped to gain a good understanding of how and why (or why not) a significant part of the organization uses (or does not use) RPE by talking to people "out on the floor," not just to those in corporate planning offices who develop these schemes.

FINDINGS FROM PHASE I

In this section, I discuss the findings from my research in five firms to ascertain the characteristics of firms using RPE. I picked these firms for study of divisional performance incentives because they share certain common characteristics: they are relatively large (between $3 billion and $14 billion in sales), publicly traded, manufacturing-dominated firms. An important difference is their diversity of operations. I had no knowledge about their use of RPE, in particular, or about their divisional performance evaluation practices, in general, before the research started.[8]

"Conglomerate"

The first two companies are excellent contrasts. The first company, which I call Conglomerate, is a classic conglomerate with multiple product lines in diverse industries (e.g., insurance, telecommunications equipment, automobile components). It operates in twenty-four different two-digit SIC industries and has the most diverse product lines of all the companies studied. With this diversity, there is little correlation among divisional outputs.

Top management of Conglomerate has historically focused on earnings growth as the measure of corporate performance. This is conveyed to division managers through explicit financial performance targets: namely, meeting divisional return on investment and profit objectives. Meeting these performance targets explicitly determines a division manager's bonus, and failure to meet the targets for two years in a row frequently results in dismissal. Each year is "a new game" for division managers. They have incentives to be short-run oriented and to focus on financial targets. In short, this company is an excellent example of "managing the company by the numbers." In fact, several business units have been acquired in the past because they provided stable earnings or had the potential to reduce variance in earnings, not because the products fit into corporate product-line strategy.[9]

Conglomerate is not timid about buying and selling companies to achieve financial targets. (Since 1984, it has sold businesses that had provided more than 30 percent of its annual revenues to help achieve corporate financial goals.) It is presently divesting some of its diverse product lines to put more resources into product lines that it (and its financial analysts) believe have more profit potential. The plan to reduce diversity has not, however, affected the divisional performance evaluation and incentive system, which still focuses on explicit short-term financial performance measures.

Accounting measures of division performance. As might be expected, with this much emphasis on financial measures of division performance, Conglomerate has carefully specified the accounting procedures to be followed by divisions. There is a short list of external financial statement items that are excluded from divisional profit computations, such as the effects of natural disasters and labor strikes, and changes in the statutory tax rate. Little else is modified, however. Corporate headquarters costs are allocated to divisions, as are imputed interest, foreign currency adjustments, and income taxes. The accounting divisional performance measures used are divisional profit and return on total capital. Current year actual amounts are compared to current year budgets and to last year's actuals in assessing division performance.

Although decision making is decentralized, the internal financial reporting system is as centralized as feasible, given the diversity of operations. Division controllers have a solid-line reporting responsibility to the corporate controller's office. Division managers have little opportunity to manipulate accounting numbers.

Use of relative performance evaluation. The company has explicit short-term financial performance targets for top management, as well as for division management. For top management performance, there is no explicit comparison of the total firm's performance with that of competitors. There is an implicit comparison with the economy as a whole, however, and with the company's own past performance.

RPE is used to set the performance targets for division managers. Division managers have strong incentives to bring to the budget negotiations information about competition and industry performance that will help them make their case when setting performance targets. Conglomerate rarely changes these targets after they are agreed to by division and corporate management. There is no application of flexible budgeting or *ex post* budgeting to adjust targets, except for very unusual items such as natural disasters.

Absolute versus relative performance evaluation. A potential disadvantage of RPE is that it can reduce managers' incentives to make strategic moves into new industries. By filtering industry risk, it may be in a manager's interest to continue operating in a poorly performing industry in which the manager's division performs well compared to the competition instead of moving into a more profitable industry in which the manager's division would be a better performer using *absolute* measures of performance but a worse performer relative to the competition. Both top and division managers at Conglomerate are expected to behave opportunistically, seeking new profit opportunities. At the division level, this expectation is incorporated into division financial performance budgets; managers of divisions that are performing poorly on an absolute basis are expected to find new profit opportunities to achieve division and corporate financial goals. The emphasis on seeking new profit opportunities is a function of the company's overall performance—divisions are expected to place greater emphasis on seeking new profit opportunities when overall company performance is below goals.

"Heavy Equipment" Company

In contrast to Conglomerate, which operates in twenty-four, two-digit SIC code industries, Heavy Equipment Company operates in a single two-digit SIC industry even though it has sales exceeding $7 billion. It is the most centralized of all the firms I studied. Divisions are comprised of plants, which are cost centers. The company's production is integrated, requiring considerable coordination of plant operations by corporate headquarters.[10] Plant (division) managers carry out the production orders specified by corporate headquarters.

Heavy Equipment has been a leader in manufacturing high-quality construction equipment, farm equipment, and engines. The corporate strategy historically has been to produce "high-quality products that sell at premium prices and let the product sell itself." Cost control was not believed to be as important as product quality and volume of output. In recent years, decline in market demand and competition from lower-cost foreign competitors have resulted in consecutive loss or near-loss years. (See Exhibit 11-1.) So in the face of stiff competition in recent years, they have emphasized cost control in plants. Furthermore, they have closed many U.S. plants in favor of Oriental sources of materials and labor.

Unlike Conglomerate, this company does not buy and sell businesses to manage its portfolio or earnings. Top management is committed to its current products, and it expects to take whatever steps are necessary to ride out the current downturn in the market for the company's products.

Use of financial performance measures. Of all the companies studied, this company relies the least on financial performance measures in incentive contracting. Contracts between plant managers and top

Exhibit 11-1 Comparison of Top Executive Compensation and
Company Performance:
Heavy Equipment Company
(amounts rounded)

	1978	1979	1980	1981	1982	1983	1984
Profit amount (million)[a]	$600	$500	$600	$600	−$200	−$300	−$200
Profit margin[a]	8%	7%	7%	6%	—	—	—
Return on equity[a]	21%	16%	17%	15%	—	—	—
Top three executives total compensation (thousands)[b]	$800	$1,100	$1,000	$1,300	$1,400	$1,300	$1,400

[a]Source: Financial statements.
[b]Source: Proxy statements.

management are based on meeting explicit production requirements. Meeting cost targets has also become important in recent years because the company has attempted to become more cost competitive. Plant managers are evaluated on the basis of numerous performance measures, including meeting cost standards, but also meeting volume, quality, efficiency, and other standards. In contrast to Conglomerate, top management relies on its knowledge of the product, the tasks division managers are expected to implement, and observation of division managers' actions.

Relative performance evaluation. The company does not compare a division's financial performance with its industry competitors outside of the firm. Division managers within the company are compared to each other, but the comparisons are based on how well a division implements top management orders, meets production schedules, and achieves cost and efficiency standards. Top management's subjective evaluation of personnel is an important variable in division manager performance evaluation. Because production is so highly integrated, it is important that division managers meet production schedules regardless of environmental factors; consequently, environmental factors typically are not considered in determining whether division managers meet the production schedules. (A major event like a strike would be taken into account, of course.)

For the entire firm, I could not find evidence of explicit interfirm financial comparisons, but the plight of the industry has been considered in evaluating top management's performance. Further, as shown in Exhibit 11-1, the trend in top management compensation did not change appreciably between the profit and loss years. (There was no top management turnover during this period.) Despite the company's recent financial performance, it remains a leader in the industry in the United States.

"Tire/Diverse" Company

I selected the name Tire/Diverse for the third company because it has evolved from a company with a single product line (tires) into several diverse business segments such as aerospace, defense, and broadcasting. It operates in nine two-digit SIC industries. The company has been managed by members of the founder's family since it began in the nineteenth century. The family currently owns more than 10 percent of the company's stock.[11]

Use of relative performance evaluation. Like Conglomerate, there is no explicit comparison with other firms' performance in evaluating top management performance. Comparisons with industry performance are used explicitly in setting profit and return on investment divisional performance targets (much like Conglomerate). This company does not manage-by-the-numbers as strictly as Conglomerate does, but it evaluates divisions on the basis of profit (return on asset and return on equity), and it compares division performance with competitors' in the industry. Consequently, in 1984 division managers in the tire division, which earned about 4 percent return on assets that year, were not penalized, unlike managers in other divisions, such as plastics and industrial products, which earned 25 percent return on assets in 1984.

The company attempts to reward division managers for good performance regardless of how the rest of the company is doing. Top management's philosophy is that if four out of five divisions are performing poorly compared to their industry, it is important to reward the one division that is performing well. Otherwise, they believe "there will be five divisions performing poorly instead of just four."

"Food Products" Company

This company has a core business of consumer food products and agricultural products that it has been producing and selling for many years. Members of top management have considerable experience with their business and believe they are effective managers. In this respect, the company is similar to Heavy Equipment Company, although less centralized.

Historically, the company, located in the Midwest near its "roots" in agricultural products, was product oriented. The company was managed by its founding family until the late 1960s. By that time, it was clear that growth and profit possibilities in its product lines were limited. The industry was mature, and there were (and still are) many well-established competitors. Consequently, the company began investing in the restaurant business by purchasing fast-food restaurants.

The diversification created problems because management's expertise in food processing and agribusiness was not particularly applicable to the restaurant business.[12] This is an important problem because the corporate strategy is to invest more in restaurants, which presently contribute 51 percent of operating profits on 42 percent of company sales. Top management is presently uncertain about appropriate performance criteria for its restaurant business.

This firm is more explicit and public about its financial targets than any other firm studied. Its annual report lists objectives for pretax and aftertax returns on equity (25 percent and 18 percent, respectively) and annual percent earnings per share growth (6–10 percent on a real basis). Divisional targets are a function of these published, firmwide targets.

Use of relative performance evaluation. RPE is part of the performance evaluation criteria used to judge top management and firm performance. The company compares itself with fourteen competitors in the consumer food products industry, primarily through return on asset comparisons. (Its rank is in about the middle of the set.) Top management's compensation is related to the firm's overall RPE by the board of directors. RPE is used *ex post* to take into account the actual performance of competitors during the performance period.

Interfirm RPE has not yet been used as a gauge for divisional performance, but is expected to be implemented soon. Until the acquisition of the fast-food restaurants, top management did not see incremental benefits from using RPE to evaluate division performance; division performance was evaluated intrafirm and within divisions over time. Top management knew the company's basic product line well enough to understand what constituted good or bad performance without explicit interfirm financial RPE. After acquiring the fast-food restaurant business, top management decided to start using explicit, interfirm, divisional financial-performance evaluation for that business because top management has little knowledge of what is "reasonable performance to expect" for the new business. The lack of information about division performance is the motivation for implementing RPE.

"Health Care," Inc.

This company makes health care products, including pharmaceuticals, over-the-counter drugs and toiletries, and products for hospital and other professional medical use (e.g., dressings, diagnostic equipment). It operates in three two-digit SIC industries, all in health care businesses. Nearly one-half of the voting stock is under the control of the firm's founding family and foundations established by the family. (The company went public in the 1940s.) The company is decentralized, comprised of a large number of divisions that are essentially stand-alone operating companies making several, related products.

Relative performance evaluation. Unlike Conglomerate, which manages divisions according to short-term accounting targets, top management of Health Care has a long-term strategy for new product development and corporate image. Short-run high divisional ROI and profit performance do not indicate good performance if they come at the expense of corporate image and new product development. (In this industry there are opportunities for substantial profits if new products are successful and for substantial losses if products are marketed before they are adequately tested.)

The company uses a "council of peer companies" against which it evaluates firm performance and division performance. Identifying industry competitors for divisions is generally not difficult, although some divisions produce unique products for which there are no direct competitors. Unlike the other companies studied, Health Care's top management compares not only short-run financial performance (ROI and division profit), but also new product development because top management believes new product development is an important part of its corporate strategy.

PHASE II: USE OF RELATIVE PERFORMANCE EVALUATION AT HONEYWELL

The findings from Phase I imply that RPE is more likely to be used in companies operating in diverse industries or in companies with new acquisitions. Four of the five Phase I companies used explicit financial RPE to evaluate divisional peformance. The one company that did not was centralized and operated in only one industry.

The use of divisional RPE appeared to be inversely related to top management's knowledge about divisional activities. Based on these findings, I expected RPE to be used in companies with decentralized, diverse operations. Honeywell is such a company. It is a diverse, decentralized company operating in fourteen different two-digit SIC industries. My Phase II research intended to go into much more detail about how and why RPE is used than Phase I did, so I concentrated on one of four businesses (i.e., groups of divisions): the Aerospace and Defense Business (A & D).

Research Methods

In this phase, my objective was to understand why RPE was or was not used at the division level (and below), to learn about the choice of accounting variables in divisional RPE, and to understand the process of implementing RPE. My findings for Honeywell are based on reviews of documents and interviews with twenty-six managers and staff members, ranging from the vice president and chief financial and administrative officer to project managers. These interviews were conducted at three organizational levels. First, my interviews with top corporate and A & D management and staff provided an understanding of Honeywell's corporate culture. Most of my information about the use of RPE was obtained from A & D management in corporate planning and finance. Second, I interviewed operating and financial managers in five divisions making different products in the A & D group of divisions to verify what I had learned about Honeywell's corporate culture at the A & D group level and to see how these divisions implemented RPE themselves. Third, I interviewed eight operating managers who were between the supervisory and profit center levels to verify what I had learned at the higher levels of the organization. Although most of the research was conducted in the A & D group, I also interviewed other division-level people in other parts of the company to compare my A & D findings with practices in other groups of divisions.

RPE is currently being implemented at Honeywell. RPE is not used explicitly in managerial incentive contracts at this time; whether a division manager keeps his division in line with top competitors, however, is a factor in performance evaluation. More use is expected after the company learns more from its present experiments with RPE. At this time, RPE is primarily being used for strategic purposes and to initiate change in the company. This section starts with a description of the Honeywell company culture, which turns out to be important for understanding how and why RPE is used at Honeywell.

Institutional Context

Honeywell has almost one hundred divisions organized into the following four businesses:

1. Aerospace and Defense (A & D). A & D's products include guidance systems and controls for military and commercial aircraft, spacecraft, missiles, and other military vehicles and naval vessels. It sells both to the U.S. government and to such commerical companies as Boeing.

2. Control Products. Control Products produces electronic control products, switches, thermostats, and sensor products for residential, industrial, and commercial markets.

3. Control Systems. Control Systems produces fire and burglary alarm systems, energy management systems, and related services.

4. Information Systems. Information Systems produces computers, data processing systems, and related services (e.g., maintenance services).

Segment financial data are presented in Exhibit 11-2.

Honeywell is a technology-oriented company, particularly in the Aerospace and Defense Business. Most of the top managers have engineering backgrounds. Honeywell's first product was a furnace thermostat. From this, it expanded into other types of control products and systems. What is now the Aerospace and Defense Business started during World War II. Expanding into computers and com-

Exhibit 11-2 Financial Data by Segment, 1984
(excludes corporate assets and expenses)

	Profit Margin	Percent of Total Company Revenue	Return on Segment Assets	Revenue Growth
Aerospace & Defense	7.2%	26%	14.5%	4.4%
Control Products	13.8%	17%	21.0%	15.2%
Control Systems	8.4%	27%	12.7%	2.9%
Information Systems	9.9%	30%	13.7%	9.5%
		100%		

puter services was natural because of the computer's importance in its control products and systems area.

Historically, the company has not been "run by the financial numbers" exclusively. In A & D, given a choice between one project that is very profitable, but not technically challenging, and another that is less profitable, but has greater technical interest, the company will usually choose the latter. As an example, they showed me data for three mutually exclusive capital investment projects that met minimum discounted cash flow requirements; the most profitable one had little technical interest and the most technically challenging one showed the least promise for short-term profits. They expected to choose the latter project.

The company does not abandon contracts that have turned out to be unprofitable. A few of these "leakers," as they are called in A & D, have had a large negative impact on division and group ROI, but the company's concern about its image and long-term relationship with customers has kept it from cutting its losses on these contracts. Although division financial numbers are obviously important in evaluating division managers' performance, they do not dominate division incentive contracts as they do at Conglomerate. My interviews with managers and financial people at all levels in A & D lead me to believe that managers have historically not had strong incentives to maximize reported financial performance. Instead, the emphasis has been on growth, customer satisfaction, and new product development.

Greater Emphasis on Financial Performance

Several years ago, the company began shifting attention to financial measures of performance. Incentive contracts for top management and division managers were changed to emphasize return on investment. A & D, in particular, has been going through a "peer company analysis" to reassess the status quo. A common response to my questions to managers and financial people throughout A & D was a concern that A & D and the entire company were too complacent about financial performance. A & D prided itself on good products and strong customer relations, but these have not necessarily been translated into good financial performance.

The A & D strategic-planning group that performed the peer group analysis first identified twenty-two competitors in aerospace and defense. Of these competitors, nine are prime contractors (e.g., Boeing and Lockheed) that, although they are in aerospace and defense, do not face the same market environment. Of the remaining thirteen competitors, public data have not been available for two competitors: Hughes and Ford Aerospace. This leaves eleven competitors that A & D believe face the same market environment.[13]

A & D found considerable variance when it made financial comparisons on one year's data, so it used a five-year average of return on assets, operating profit margin, and revenue growth for the comparable segments. Based on these comparisons, A & D ranked near the bottom of the third quartile. Given this finding, A & D then examined the characteristics of competitors to see what its higher ranked competitors were doing that A & D was not. By examining what has made competitors successful, A & D hoped to learn how to improve its financial performance.

Competitive Analysis for Strategic Purposes

In comparing its position with competitors, A & D discovered that some of the high-ranking competitors' business practices were not consistent with Honeywell's culture (tastes); these included selling products to certain Middle Eastern countries, walking away from contracts that are "leakers," and drastically reducing the number of employees to cut costs when the volume of business declines. Nevertheless, the analysis has led to a change in the way A & D does business. Many A & D managers had operated on the basis that obtaining contracts was the key variable for success; more volume meant more size, which in turn implied more profit dollars. Also, obtaining more contracts resulted in more funding of research and development, which led to new ideas and products. Cost control has now become more important because fewer contracts are cost reimbursed. Peer company analysis has been used to emphasize the importance of return on investment and cost control.

Honeywell's use of peer company analysis is designed more to provide information about how to improve future performance than to evaluate managers' past performances. One reason for the comparison is to develop strategies for moving into new product lines. It is used in strategic planning at functional levels in the organization to reassess financial measures compared to competitors. This is consistent with top management's incentive compensation, which now relies more on corporate return on investment than it has in the past. Although the company examines the reasonableness of its overall ROI performance by computing a composite ROI from industry data in the Forbes Index, RPE is not used explicitly in top management incentive contracts.

CONCLUSIONS AND IMPLICATIONS

The object of my research was to obtain a better understanding of the use of accounting numbers in divisional performance measurement and in division managers' incentive contracts. I expected to find division managers of diverse, decentralized companies being evaluated relative to industry peers because information within the firm between top and division managers is asymmetric; I expected less emphasis on interfirm RPE in relatively centralized, less diverse companies. My findings generally support this idea, with certain qualifications. I was surprised to find divisional RPE just being implemented at Honeywell, despite its considerable diversity in divisional operations and markets. Honeywell's current work with peer company analysis is primarily designed for strategic purposes and to give managers incentives to compare themselves with competitors, not to filter risk.

Why had Honeywell not implemented RPE before? According to the theory, improved efficiency in contracts occurs because of the opportunity to reduce risk without reducing incentives. Honeywell's A & D managers face less personal risk than managers at a company like Conglomerate, where a substantial portion of division managers' compensation and employment opportunities depends on meeting explicit financial performance targets. If meeting financial targets becomes more important at Honeywell, risks to division managers will increase. We expect to see an increased use of RPE in division performance measurement. Another possible explanation for the failure to use RPE was the cost of using it. I rule this out as an important explanation at Honeywell because the cost for A & D appeared to be less than about two-person months per year. In summary, the degree of information asymmetry and the amount of division manager risk appear to be factors affecting the choice of RPE in divisional performance evaluation.

RPE Used in Setting Performance Targets

Where it was used, RPE was used primarily in setting division performance targets, not in *ex post* performance evaluation. This allows division managers to be "ensured" against industry factors that are considered when budget contracts are prepared, but not those that occur during the period, except for extraordinary events like natural disasters. If division managers face loss of pay and employment prospects from failure to achieve performance targets, as at Conglomerate, then we expect them to negotiate slack into performance targets. (There was evidence that this is common at Conglomerate.)

Absolute versus Relative Performance Evaluation

Antle and Smith (1986) suggest that it may not be in the shareholders' best interest to filter industry risk for top management who are responsible for selecting the firm's industry. I found some evidence that RPE is not used for top management in cases where the company regularly buys and sells businesses in various industries. Of the six firms studied, two (Conglomerate and Tire/Diverse) regularly buy and sell business in various industries. These companies do not use RPE at the top management level. Top management does considerable buying and selling to achieve predictable annual earnings increases. In both companies, RPE is used in evaluating division managers who do not have the same opportunities or responsibilities to move into and out of industries.

Further, companies that do not operate in conglomerate mode tend to use RPE for top management. The two companies where I found explicit RPE (Food Products and Health Care) typically grow from within.[14] Food Products has been investing in restaurants in recent years, but top management does not operate in conglomerate mode. Although I found no evidence of *explicit* relative performance comparisons for a third company (Heavy Equipment), the plight of the industry has been considered in compensating top management. Future studies of top management RPE may benefit from separate analyses of top managers who are expected to select profitable industries and those who are expected to stay within their industries.

Why Not Use RPE?

I conclude that there are at least two cases where interfirm financial RPE will *not* be used in division incentive contracts: (1) if division managers face low risks, as at Honeywell, then the risk-filtering benefits of RPE do not warrant its use; (2) if division managers operate in a centralized, integrated firm like Heavy Equipment, then interfirm financial comparisons are likely to be replaced with input monitoring and intrafirm evaluations.

NOTES

1. See Holmstrom (1982) for a discussion of the theory, and Kunkel and Magee (1983) and Antle and Smith (1986) for empirical studies of RPE in top management incentive contracting. Also see Wolfson (1985) for an application of RPE to shared equity real estate contracts and Kinney (1969) for an early venture into this field.

2. This heterogeneity within industry does not necessarily pose a problem for Antle and Smith's tests because they construct an "industry index" that assigns higher weights to firms whose financial measures are more highly correlated with the sample firm.

3. Although evidence about the use of RPE to evaluate division managers is sparse, Eccles (1985, 162) reports on a company that uses it to evalute a division manager's performance: "Performance was evaluated against objectives described as 'achievable but tough' and against the performance of the top one-third of the companies competing against the division."

4. The focus of this research is on performance evaluation, so I investigate the use of RPE in *performance evaluation*, not *compensation*.

5. Holmstrom's (1982) Theorem 8 provides two particular output structures in which

$$\text{I: } x_i(a_i, \theta_i) = a_i + \eta + \varepsilon_i, i = 1, \ldots, n$$
$$\text{II: } x_i(a_i, \theta_i) = a_i(\eta + \varepsilon_i), i \ldots, n$$

where X_i and a_i are output and agent i's action, respectively; $\theta_i = (\eta, \varepsilon_i)$, η is a common uncertainty parameter, but ε_i's are independent, idiosyncratic risks. It is assumed that η and ε_i are independent and normally distributed. The efficiency of contracts can be improved by "ensuring" an agent against the common uncertainty parameter.

6. For an elaboration of the "controllability" concept, see ch. 12 of this volume.

7. Both inter- and intrafirm comparisons could simultaneously improve the efficiency of contracting, of course.

8. More extensive discussion of these firms' divisional performance incentive plans and performance is presented in Butler and Maher (1986). I am grateful to Steve Butler for his contribution to our research in these five companies.

9. One company in the food industry was purchased because, according to the CEO, "even in bad times, people have to eat."

10. Applying Ouchi's (1979) framework, this is an excellent example of using a bureaucratic control mechanism, instead of a market control mechanism. All of the other companies I studied relied more on the market to control division managers' actions.

11. This company and the next two I discuss have concentrations of stock in the founding family, which still has some managerial involvement in the firm. I could find no evidence that this type of ownership affected the use of relative performance evaluation.

12. They presently operate in three two-digit SIC code industries.

13. These eleven are divisions of Sperry, TRW, Harris, Litton, Texas Instruments, Emerson, Singer, Gould, Aerojet of Gencorp, Raytheon, and AVCO.

14. By "explicit" I mean RPE is included in presentations to the compensation committee of the board of directors; RPE was not written into compensation plans in Proxies.

REFERENCES

Antle, R., and Smith, S. 1986. "An Empirical Investigation of the Relative Performance Evaluation of Corporate Executives." *Journal of Accounting Research* (Spring): 1–39.

Butler, S., and Maher, M. 1986. "Management Incentive Compensation Plans." University of Michigan. Working paper.

Eccles, R. G. 1985. "Transfer Pricing as a Problem of Agency." In *Principals and Agents: The Structure of Business*, edited by J. W. Pratt and R. J. Zeckhauser. Boston: Harvard Business School Press, 151–186.

Holmstrom, B. 1982. "Moral Hazard in Teams." *The Bell Journal of Economics* (Autumn): 324–40.

Holmstrom, B., and Milgrom, P. 1986. "Aggregate and Linearity in the Provision of Intertemporal Incentives." Yale University. Working paper.

Kaplan, R. S. 1985. "The Role for Empirical Research in Management Accounting." Unpublished working paper, Harvard Business School.

Kinney, W. 1969. "An Environmental Model for Performance Measurement in Multi-outlet Businesses." *Journal of Accounting Research* 7 (Spring): 44–52.

amination of Theory and Some Empirical Results." Northwestern University. Working paper.

Merchant, K. 1987. Ch. 12 of this book.

Ouchi, W. 1979. "A Conceptual Framework for the Design of Organizational Control Mechanisms." *Management Science* (September): 833–48.

Wolfson, M. 1985. "Tax, Incentive, and Risk-Sharing Issues in the Allocation of Property Rights: The Generalized Lease-or-Buy Problem." *Journal of Business* (April): 159–72.

CHAPTER 12

How and Why Firms Disregard the Controllability Principle

Kenneth A. Merchant

INTRODUCTION

ONE of the most commonly cited principles of control is that individuals should be held accountable only for results they can control. Here is a representative expression of the controllability principle:

It is almost a self-evident proposition that, in appraising the performance of divisional management, no account should be taken of matters outside the division's control.[1]

In practice, however, the controllability principle seems often to be ignored; it is common, even typical, for managers to be held accountable for areas over which they have little, or even no, control. For example, Harold Geneen, the former long-time chief executive of ITT believes:

Managing means that once you set your business plan and budget for the year, you must achieve the sales, the market share, the earnings, and whatever to which you committed yourself. . . . An experienced chief ex-

---

This paper has been abridged considerably for publication. For a more complete discussion, see Kenneth A. Merchant, "An Investigation into the Reasons for Firms' Selective Disregard of the Controllability Principle: A Field Study." Harvard Business School Working Paper, #9-787-010.

ecutive can choose from among a thousand good plausible explanations for a no-fault rationale of why the company failed to achieve the results he had promised at the beginning of the year. . . . However, if you believe that *management must manage*, then all those perfectly logical explanations do not count. The only thing that counts is that the desired results were achieved or that they were not achieved.[2]

Here, as an important step toward developing a theory of practice in the area, I report the findings of a field study designed to explore managers' thinking about the controllability issue. The following research questions were explored:

1. Do firms hold their profit center managers accountable for results and events over which they do not have complete control? If so, when and why? Can firms be ordered along a continuum according to the extent to which they implement the controllability principle?
2. What are the consequences, both favorable and unfavorable, of holding managers accountable for uncontrollables?
3. If firms differ in their implementation of the controllability principle, what causes the difference?

The field study was conducted in three corporations chosen from different industries. The findings suggest that firms do indeed differ markedly in the extent to which their managers are held accountable for uncontrollable events. Comparisons and contrasts made among firms' managerial-evaluation practices provide a basis for a tentative refinement and elaboration of the controllability principle.

LITERATURE SEARCH

Before starting the field portion of the study, I reviewed the literature related to the controllability issue. The rationale for the controllability principle, which is discussed in many works, including Magee (1986, 268–69), Merchant (1985, 21–24), and Maciariello (1984, 135–36) is: first, if performance indicators are influenced by uncontrollable events, the indicators become less informative about the desirability of the actions the individual has taken; and second, holding individuals accountable for uncontrollable events can lead to dysfunctional behavior. If individuals feel their evaluations are not fair—for example, if they are being evaluated poorly when they feel their personal performance has been good—the consequences may include game playing, loss of motivation, and employee turnover.

Some research has presented plausible reasons for not implementing the controllability principle. It has used both deductive and inductive reasoning.

The deductive work, based on economic theory, has presented three arguments as to why principals (e.g., upper-level managers) should hold agents (e.g., lower-level managers) accountable for outcomes over which they do not have complete control. One argument shows that holding agents accountable for the effects of random and uncontrollable phenomena (e.g., changes in product demand) and the effects of actions of other managers (i.e., those effects caused by organizational interdependency) will cause agents' decisions to reflect "a [proper] degree of risk aversion, and the combined risk-bearing abilities of the owner and manager will exceed that of either alone" (Demski 1976, 233). This argument introduces the desirability of having subordinates share risks with their superiors as a justification for evaluating subordinates on random outcomes.

A second reason for holding agents accountable for some categories over which they have no control is to tell them how their decisions affect areas outside their control. Baiman and Noel (1985) show that it can be useful to charge agents for the costs of capacity. Zimmerman (1979) makes a similar argument for assigning the costs of shared resources.

A third argument is that in situations with imperfect postdecision information, agents should be evaluated on their accomplishments as they compare with those of other agents who face the same environment—even though those other agents' accomplishments are clearly outside the first agent's control. This relative performance evaluation is desirable because the broader data provide information about the agent's unobservable actions (Baiman and Demski 1980; Holmstrom 1982).

These deductive works are based on some simplifying assumptions. For example, in Demski's (1976) model, simplifications include excluding the cost of evaluation and the existence of alternative risk-sharing possibilities. Demski also assumed that principal and agent were cooperative; that is, preference and belief information were assumed to be freely and completely passed among the individuals. Whether the findings are descriptive of a more realistic setting remains largely untested. The single empirical study available to date provided only partial support for the relative performance evaluation argument (Antle and Smith 1986; but see Maher 1987).

Inductive researchers have not discussed the controllability principle by name, but they have provided some limited evidence about managers' lack of complete implementation of the controllability principle and some plausible reasons for the managers' actions. Hofstede (1967, 32) observed several cases where the accounting system did not coincide with the responsibility structure of the organization, "mostly because the rather static reporting system had not followed recent changes in the responsibility organization."

Vancil (1979) collected data from 291 firms and found that profit-center managers almost never have control over all the items for which they are held responsible. He concluded that assigning largely uncontrollable expenses (e.g., for administrative services) can be functional because it tells managers they should become involved in the benefit/cost trade-offs involved.

RESEARCH METHOD

With this knowledge of the literature, I conducted a field study in three firms: (1) a large distribution corporation, (2) a large chemical corporation, and (3) a medium-sized high-technology corporation. The firms were selected because they are divisionalized and arguably well run. I did not know the extent to which each of the firms implemented the controllability princple prior to the initial contact with the firm.

To limit the scope of investigation, the study focused on one important role: lower-level general managers. I made this choice because within the decentralized form of organization, which predominates among firms of any significant size (see surveys by Reece and Cool 1978; and Vancil 1979), the general manager is probably the most important position over which good control must be exercised (Solomons 1965; Vancil 1979).

To understand the extent to which each firm implemented the controllability principle at the general-manager level, I interviewed corporate staff personnel who were knowledgeable about how the firm's general managers were evaluated and rewarded. Also at this time, relevant written company documents were reviewed. Then I interviewed a small sample of general managers, their immediate superiors and, where appropriate, financial staff at either (or both) organizational levels.

All interviews were largely unstructured so as to minimize the possibility of interviewer bias and to allow the managers to describe the factors they felt were important. Two interviewers were present at most interviews.

At the corporate level, the questioning was designed to provide a basic understanding of the degree to which the company's philosophy reflects the controllability principle and how that philosophy is implemented. At the general-manager level, the emphasis was on understanding the managers' business(es), probing for recent events that affected measures of performance but were not totally controllable by the general manager, understanding the extent to which the general managers were held accountable for those events, and learning the managers' reactions to and feelings about their company's incentive systems.

The following sections provide brief descriptions of each of the companies studied and one or more examples that illustrate the extent to which the company holds its general managers accountable for events outside their control.

THE DISTRIBUTION CORPORATION

The distribution corporation has annual revenues of several billion dollars; it ranks among the *Fortune* 50 list of largest diversified service companies. Its businesses distribute a wide range of products, including paper, pharmaceuticals, office products, steel, beverages, and gifts and glassware.

The corporation consists of approximately eighty companies. The manager of a company is called a company president. The companies are organized into groups, headed by group vice presidents who report to the president of the corporation.

The corporation has grown primarily by acquiring privately held businesses. It attempts to retain the identity and management of the acquired companies.

Performance of the distribution corporation has been excellent.

In the twenty years since its founding, it has grown one hundredfold and more in both revenues and net income.

Management Bonus Plan

The distribution corporation uses a management bonus plan to give substantial extra compensation to managers, at the level of company president and higher, who achieve certain predetermined performance objectives. Company presidents can earn up to 50 percent of base salary as compensation under the plan.

Performance of each company is judged in terms of two components:

1. The *income component* is defined as either profit before tax or gross profit, depending on the business. This income number excludes (in addition to taxes) allocated corporate expenses, gains or losses on investment transactions, interest expense or income, and gains or losses from foreign currency translation.

2. The *key objectives component* is usually comprised of one or more of the following: selling, general and administrative expenses as a percent of gross profit, days' sales outstanding, inventory turns, return on capital employed, and/or return on investment.

The income component is included in all company plans and is weighted very heavily (60–80 percent). Furthermore, if a minimum level of performance on the income component is not reached, no bonus is paid, regardless of how good performance is in other areas. The elements of the key objectives component are chosen in advance, based on a judgment of what is important to the business and, very often, where performance is judged to need improvement.

For bonus calculation purposes, adjustments are made for unanticipated, nonrecurring gains or losses during the year. The corporate manager in charge of monitoring the plan acknowledged some ambiguity in it. He observed that "it is difficult to legislate when you make exceptions and when you don't." The following examples show some adjustments made and not made.

Example #1: Adjustments for Uncontrollables

In 1985, circumstances arose that had significant effects on the performance of a liquor distribution company. During the 1985 annual planning process, group and company management were aware of several factors

- a federal excise (FET) tax increase scheduled for October 1, 1985
- possible consolidation of the operations of the company with those of a company operating in an adjacent territory
- the expiration of the Teamster labor contract at the rectifying plant where a major private brand is produced

The impact of each of these items caused management to consider performance adjustments with bonus implications.

The *FET increase* was planned for and an increase in sales was forecasted owing to expectations that customers would try to "beat the tax increase." Results around the nation were mixed, but in this company's territory, sales were up significantly and operating profits for the year were well above plan. This performance, while extraordinary, was thought to have occurred, to some degree, because of the efforts of management. Consequently, the increases in sales and profits were accepted for bonus award; no adjustments were made.

Some time after the 1985 bonus parameters had been established, group management decided to *consolidate* the company's operations with those of an adjacent company to make the physical distribution system more efficient. The work, which took place in November and December 1985, caused some unusual expenses. These expenses were deducted from the 1985 operating results, but the practical effect was nil since the company's actual operating-profit performance already exceeded the bonus program maximum. If this had not been the case, an adjustment to the actual results would have been made; the expenses would have been removed.

With the pending *expiration of the labor contract* at the production facility, group management decided to require each distributor location to increase private-brand inventory by the equivalent of one month's sales as protection against the possibility of a work stoppage. The president of the company had a key performance objective based on inventory turns' performance, so at the close of the fiscal year, it became necessary to adjust the actual inventory turns' number by an estimate of the impact of the centralized decision. Without the adjustment, the inventory turns' number would have been 12.0, below the allowable minimum; with the adjustment, it became 13.0. The adjustment increased the company president's bonus by just over $1,000 (2 percent of salary).

Example #2: An Adjustment Not Made

In another liquor distributorship, a decision was made not to adjust for an event that cost the manager all of his 1986 bonus. His company faced a major price war which broke out in February 1986. The war caused the margins on a case of product (spirits, wines, water) to decline from a normal level of $6–7 per case to $1.50. (Distribution costs were approximately $4.20 per case.) It was decided early in 1986 to make no adjustment for the effects of the price war.

When the plan for 1986 was being prepared, the company president knew of the possible price war; he saw a nonfull-service wholesaler making market share gains at the expense of a full-service company. But he noted that

There is no way to include such things in the forecast. Such "blips" occur on the upside as well as on the downside. For example, we have experienced tremendous sales growth of wine coolers which no one forecast.

At the time of the interview the manager felt that his chances of getting a bonus for 1986 were "nil to none." A price war is particularly costly because it affects both margins and sales volume, and it is impossible to reduce the fixed expenses to match falling revenues. He felt that he could have met his plan if the price war had not started until the second or third quarter, instead of the first. While he was not happy about the prospect of losing his 1986 bonus, he recognized that such possibilities are part of being a company president.

Hypothetical Adjustments

To enrich our understanding of the types of uncontrollables that are and are not adjusted for in calculating management bonuses, we asked managers who evaluate the performances of the company presidents how they would deal with four hypothetical events: a labor strike, a fire in a warehouse, the loss of a supplier, and a new competitor. They concluded that they would adjust for a strike and a fire; they would adjust for the loss of a supplier only if the company was highly dependent on a single source; they would not adjust for the effects of a new competitor entering the market.

Two managers also commented generally about making adjustments:

We don't want to make an adjustment for every uncontrollable event that comes along. We say that if the economy turns sour, it's too bad. If you owned your own company, who could you turn to? (Nobody was complaining last year when the economy was better than forecast.) We might, though, take personal consideration into account, such as if a manager was retiring or if we wanted to make a commitment to someone for retention purposes.

I frequently receive calls from company presidents claiming that they are suffering costs which are uncontrollable and which, therefore, should be adjusted for. I have to explain to them that while these things might be unexpected from their point of view, most of them are just part of running their business. For instance, it is common for managers to ask me for allowances toward the extra costs they have incurred to support an unexpected increase in sales volume, such as to build a new warehouse. I explain to them that the profit calculations are designed to test whether these incremental expenditures should have been made.

Discussion

These examples show that the managers in this corporation attempt to implement the controllability principle, but only partially. Their basic definition of profit excludes some potentially major expense items that are largely uncontrollable by company presidents: corporate G&A, interest expenses, exchange gains and losses, and taxes. Also, they tend to make adjustments to actual results so as not to hold managers accountable when decision-making autonomy is taken away from them or when completely uncontrollable events occur.

On the other hand, the corporation is willing to have its company presidents bear considerable business risk. If economic conditions change after the plan is finalized, the presidents are expected to adapt to the new reality. This does not seem to trouble them as many were the president of their company when it was acquired; they are used to bearing that risk. The presidents' risks have actually been lessened now that they are part of a large corporation because the risk is borne only until changing economic scenarios are incorporated in the new annual plan.

The interviews provided some indication that the adjustments tend to be somewhat one-sided; that is, adjustments are more likely to be made for uncontrollable events that hurt company presidents; they are less likely when surprises affect performance favorably.

THE CHEMICAL CORPORATION

The chemical corporation has annual revenues of several billion dollars; it is on the *Fortune* 100 list of largest industrial corporations. Many of the corporation's businesses are mature, and the corporation wants to redeploy assets toward some new faster-growing businesses.

The corporation is organized into groups that are divided into a total of twenty functionally organized divisions. The autonomy of the division managers varies considerably; some of the divisions are nearly totally self-contained, while others have to rely on extensive support from group-level functions.

The corporation has a long, successful history, but its recent performance has not been good. Sales have been flat for five years, and profitability has been only moderate (about 7 percent of sales, after tax). The year 1985 showed a large loss, however, owing to a major corporate restructuring that involved write-offs, plant closings, and layoffs.

The Definition of Net Income

The corporation regards each entity as an independent unit so it pushes as many costs as possible down to the operating-unit level. Thus, the key business-unit and manager-performance measure—net income—includes a nearly full allocation of corporate costs, interest expense, currency expense, other income (or expense), corporate headquarters expenses, and taxes.

As many elements of cost as possible are charged to business units on the basis of usage, but significant amounts of indirect expenses remain. Most indirect expenses are allocated as a percent of capital employed in the business. For most businesses, the corporate allocation is less than two percent of sales. Only a few nonoperating items, such as those caused by acquisitions and debt defeasances, are not allocated and are, therefore, excluded from the operating units' net income calculations.

Performance Incentive Plan

The chemical corporation uses a single short-term, performance-dependent incentive plan for its general managers.[3] Annual awards of cash and restricted stock are made to managers.

The calculation of awards is done in three steps. First, a total award fund is determined, depending on the corporation's net income performance compared with budget. Subjective adjustments of the award funding are permitted, but they are rarely made. Upper-level managers observed that every year some unforeseen economic factors, such as demand changes, currency devaluations, or changes in significant factor inputs (e.g., oil), affect net income performance, and these are often discussed by the compensation committee. Almost without exception, however, the committee has ignored these factors. In the words of one manager, "They don't bend very much."

In the second step, the award fund is allocated to the various operating entities by comparing net income performance to budget at the entity level. The CEO can vary the allocation of awards among the groups, but he is constrained by the total of the corporate award fund.

The third step is to determine the awards for each individual. The manager of each entity has complete discretion in recommending the amount of the award for each reporting subordinate, although the compensation committee does review the recommendations.

The intent of the system is to have the managers vary the awards according to each individual's accomplishments, with the evaluation done as an established part of the corporation's MBO system. Each year as part of the annual planning process, individuals prepare a list of the targets that are most appropriate for their position, a weighting of these targets, and a list of environmental factors that could affect performance in any or all of these areas. The document is updated during the year if necessary.

The quantitative goals are supposed to be adjusted only if actual conditions differ from those assumed when establishing the goals and only if the manager being evaluated had identified those conditions as contingencies. One manager noted, however, that the system has evolved so that most superiors were more sensitive to the actual conditions faced whether the managers identified them beforehand or not. This evolution has reduced the need for managers to change their MBO document, which some managers had been doing four or five times during the year to capture all the contingencies.

The actual implementation of the individual award assignments apparently varies considerably across the company. Some managers implement the system as designed, while others assign the same percent award to all managers.

An Example: A Subjective Award

A general manager in one of the chemical divisions described his goals for 1985 as being 30 percent quantitative and 70 percent qualitative. Quantitative targets were set for cash flow, net income, and return on capital. The weighting among these factors was not specified, but according to the manager, it was clear that cash flow was his most important goal. (His division sells products in the mature phase of the product life cycle.) The qualitative targets included a list of concerns, including accomplishment of information-system-development milestones and personnel outplacement.

The year 1985 was a very poor year for the corporation. Significant losses were incurred at the corporate level. Sales were flat, and top management took strong steps to reposition the company toward faster-growing markets. They wrote off some businesses, laid off a significant number of people, and implemented an early retirement program. According to the formula for the performance incentive plan, no bonuses should have been paid. Bonuses were paid, however, on a subjective basis, to about 25 percent of the personnel participating in the plan. These bonuses were called "special payments."

The manager of the chemical division described above was one of the individuals who received a special payment. He said he thought he received the award because it was recognized that he handled well the restructuring of his business, which included a plant closing.

Discussion

This corporation can be said to implement the controllability principle partially, but in a way that is quite different from that of the distribution corporation. Measures are purposefully designed to provide good measures of the businesses as inputs for divestment, investment, and acquisition decisions. The use of these bottom-line measures for performance evaluation purposes means that managers are held accountable for many items over which they have little or no control.

The controllability principle is implemented partially by moving away from a strict formula and allowing for subjective judgments of individual performance. There is some evidence, however, that different managers impart different degrees of subjectivity to their evaluations, so implementation of the controllability principle apparently differs throughout the corporation.

THE HIGH-TECHNOLOGY CORPORATION

The high-technology corporation has total annual revenues of several hundred million dollars. Most of the corporation's products use electronics and microprocessor-based technologies. The firm targets its products for rapid-growing niches in large markets.

Performance of the high-tech corporation has been excellent. Its ten-year compounded growth rate is 38 percent in sales, 42 percent in net income, and 23 percent in earnings per share. The corporation has grown both internally and through acquisition.

The firm has three levels of general managers. Presidents of twenty-four companies report to four group vice presidents who report to the corporate president. Each company is nearly self-contained, with its own product-development, control, administration, marketing, and sales staff. Each company writes its own checks. There is little interdependence among the companies, and no pressure is applied to the company presidents to source internally.

Incentives for Company Presidents

The high-tech corporation has an executive bonus program for company presidents.[4] The bonus, expressed as a percent of base salary, is computed according to the following formula:

$$F x \left[0.35 \times ROS + 0.15 \times ROA + 0.50 \times \frac{\Delta PBT}{0.2Sp} \right] \times 100 \times \text{size factor}$$

where

F = factor defined by level in the organization—for company presidents, F equals 1.7;

ROS = ratio of profit before tax to sales, with a maximum ratio value of 0.50;

ROA = ratio of profit before tax to average net asset base, with a maximum value of 1.00—net asset base is calculated as the average at the beginning of each of the four quarters;

ΔPBT = change in profit before tax from previous fiscal year—the ratio of $\Delta PBT/0_{,}2Sp$ has a maximum value of 1.00;

Sp = sales of prior fiscal year;

Size factor = ratio from zero to one, depending on the size of the company. (In 1986, for all companies with annual sales greater than \$3.2 million, this ratio equals 1.0.)

The payments under the bonus plan are large; the maximum bonus possible for a company president is 140 percent of salary, and 80–100 percent bonuses are typical.

Accountability for Uncontrollable Events

In the high-tech corporation, I conducted interviews in four companies with managers who gave examples of factors that affected bonuses and over which they had little or no control, such as economic conditions, interest rates, and the success of major customers. Here are two specific examples.

In one company that sells automation and video graphics products to television networks and stations, sales were virtually flat last year, and the budget was missed by a substantial margin. One major problem was that the merger and takeover activities in the communications industry had caused many potential customers to delay their capital expenditure plans. Although it was agreed that the slowdown was not the fault of the company president, no adjustment was made for purposes of assigning bonuses.

Similarly, in another company, a customer that had been expected to buy a full 15 percent of the company's total output got into financial difficulty and, in fact, later went out of business. No allowance for this sales problem was granted to the company president for bonus purposes.

Discussion

The high-tech company has implemented the philosophy espoused by Harold Geneen; the controllability principle is purposely not implemented. Managers are allocated corporate and group expenses over which they have virtually no control, and they are held accountable for changing economic conditions. The bonus formula is absolute; the

Exhibit 12-1   Implementation of the Controllability Principle

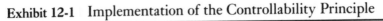

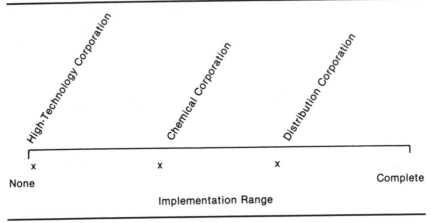

payoffs are not calibrated according to the annual budget targets, and no adjustments are made for events outside the managers' control.

SYNTHESIS AND TENTATIVE CONCLUSIONS

The discussion of the data collected from the companies is organized in terms of the research questions presented earlier.

#1: Do firms hold managers accountable for results and events over which they do not have complete control?

The simple answer to this question is yes! None of the corporations implements the controllability principle in the extreme form in which it is usually stated. In all of the situations studied, the managers are held accountable for at least some uncontrollable factors.

Exhibit 12-1 is a crude ordering of the three firms studied as to the extent to which they implement the controllability principle. Immediately apparent is the large dispersion of the firms. At one end of the range, the distribution corporation attempts to eliminate the effects of some uncontrollable factors before bonuses are assigned. At the other end of the range, the high-technology corporation subjects managers to the risks of many uncontrollables.

The discussion of the treatment of uncontrollables can be sharpened, however, by distinguishing among the firms' treatment of three types of uncontrollables: (1) uncontrollable but relevant cost and revenue factors, (2) economic and competitive conditions, and (3) acts of

Exhibit 12-2 Managerial Accountability for Uncontrollable Factors

Type of Uncontrollable					
Uncontrollable but relevant cost and revenue factors			D		C H
	None				Complete
Economic and competitive conditions			C	D	H
	None				Complete
Acts of nature		D		C	H
	None				Complete

Extent to Which Managers Are Held
Accountable for Each Factor

Key: D = Distribution Corporation
      C = Chemical Corporation
      H = High-Technology Corporation

nature. The uncontrollable but relevant cost and revenue items are those that affect the corporation's performance and that can be traced (although perhaps with some difficulty) to operating entities. Examples are taxes, interest expenses and income, exchange gains and losses, the costs of centralized administrative functions, and the effects of entity-relevant decisions for which the entity manager does not have complete autonomy. The economic and competitive conditions include such concerns as business cycles and price and product competition. These concerns are largely uncontrollable ones that most firms want managers to respond to. They can be distinguished in theory (but perhaps not at the margin) from those acts of nature that are uncontrollable: usually large, one-time events with adverse effects on performance that are beyond the ability of managers to anticipate, including disasters such as fires, earthquakes, and accidents.

Exhibit 12-2 shows a subjective ranking of the three firms in terms of the degree to which they hold managers accountable for each of these types of uncontrollables. For the first factor, the *uncontrollable but relevant cost and revenue factors*, a major difference was observed between the distribution firm and the other two firms. For bonus purposes, the high-tech and chemical corporations, in charging or allocating virtually all group- and corporate-level expenses, hold managers accountable for nearly all elements of cost. The chemical company is rated slightly lower because a few items of expense are not charged back to the operating entities (e.g., costs of litigation, gains from debt defeasance). The distribution corporation, on the other hand, evaluates managers on profit *before* taxes, interest, corporate allocations, and gains or losses on investments and foreign exchange.

All three firms hold their managers accountable for most *economic*

and competitive conditions. The high-technology corporation is an extreme example of a company that ignores the controllability principle
for economic and competitive conditions. In this company, the payout
function is not linked to the annual plan, so that bonuses are never
calibrated by economic and competitive conditions. Managers are
made to bear the same risk as the firm's shareholders; in fact, their
risk is even more because the shareholders' returns are diversified
across the twenty-four companies in the firm.

In the chemical and distribution corporations, managers bear the
risk of uncontrollable economic factors only within the planning horizon. When a plan is revised, managers can adjust their performance
targets to economic conditions. Allowing more frequent revisions is
one way to limit managers' risk. For this reason, the chemical corporation is rated lower than the distribution corporation because its subjective performance evaluations of individuals in essence allow the
evaluators to apply totally flexible performance standards.

The greatest variance among the firms is for the *acts of nature.* In
the high-tech corporation, no adjustments are allowed. In the distribution corporation, the evaluators attempt to adjust for most of the
effects of acts of nature, although they apply a materiality rule: no
adjustment unless the effect is material. In the chemical corporation,
acts of nature are discussed by the board of directors, but they rarely
influence decisions. At the level of evaluating individuals, however,
adjustments presumably are made for their effects.

*#2: What are the consequences of holding managers accountable for re-
sults and events over which they do not have complete control?*

The consequences of holding managers accountable for uncontrollables can be usefully discussed in terms of each of the three types of
uncontrollables described above. As the diversity in practice suggests,
holding managers accountable for each type of uncontrollable has advantages and disadvantages.

Uncontrollable but Relevant Cost and Revenue Factors

When managers are held accountable for uncontrollable but relevant
cost and revenue factors, they pay attention to these factors. For example, several managers in the high-tech and chemical corporations
mentioned that they consider taxes and allocated costs in making de-

cisions. Taxes and corporate expenses are outside the concern of managers in the distribution corporation, however, so upper management in this firm occasionally has to intervene and modify decisions proposed by general managers in order to incorporate these factors. This takes autonomy away from their profit-center managers.

Contrary to the prevailing textbook wisdom, some of the managers in the high-tech and chemical corporations mentioned they actually prefer to be assigned the full range of relevant costs. The assignments give them (and upper management) the feeling that they are managing a complete, presumably more autonomous, entity, and this gives them some power to influence centralized functions in ways that are beneficial to their profit centers.

In the firms I studied, managers mentioned two arguments against assigning a full set of relevant cost and revenue factors. First, it is sometimes difficult to determine what factors are relevant for the profit centers to see. The links between the cost/revenue elements and profit-center decision making become difficult to see after a point, and assignment of irrelevant costs on the basis of controllable factors changes the economics of the decisions, perhaps in dysfunctional ways.

A second, related argument against assigning full costs and revenues is that the managers sometimes feel that the assignments of uncontrollable expenses are unfair. For example, in the high-tech firm, a manager who was feeling considerable budget pressure complained about the allocations going up:

> There are certain things you can't control that other people can, such as corporate G&A. Assigning these costs can lead to bad feelings. The numbers aren't large, but it bugs me that they have gone up. We're below 20 percent profit this year, and I'm fighting for everything I can get. When corporate changes the rules, even a tenth of a percent can hurt because it can be a significant part of the margin we're trying to close.

If allowed to build and persist, feelings of unfairness may lead to decreases in managerial morale and possibly higher turnover.

Economic and Competitive Conditions

All three firms usually hold managers accountable for uncontrollable economic and competitive conditions, so it is apparent that there is a feeling that the advantages of doing so outweigh the disadvantages.

The main argument in favor of not adjusting performance for fluctuations in economic and competitive conditions is the same as that for the uncontrollable cost and revenue factors: managers will then react to these conditions, and that is clearly desirable.

Managers also argue that it is difficult to adjust objectively for uncontrollable economic factors, and they have strong feelings against subjective performance evaluations. For example, a manager in the high-technology corporation stated:

> I think having no subjectivity in the assignment of awards is good [for the corporation]. Subjective interpretations can lead to a lot of bad feelings about managers who have to work together. At [a corporation at which he used to work], subjectivity was used to limit awards, and it didn't work well. If I have a bad year, I can accept it because I understand the rules of the game. If subjectivity is allowed, I will assume my boss is supposed to forgive some of the things that went wrong. If he does not, I will feel bad, and I'll probably hold it against him.

The main argument against the firms' practices and in favor of making adjustments for changing economic and competitive conditions is that without them some evaluations are unfair. The unfairness argument is usually presented in support of managers who are perceived to be doing a good job in difficult times, not when the reverse is true. This argument is so compelling in some circumstances that such adjustments are made occasionally in both the chemical and distribution corporations.

Most of the general managers, however, either were unconcerned about, or felt that they *should be* held accountable for, economic and competitive factors. One manager in the high-tech corporation observed that "these things have a way of cancelling each other out. I don't see any problem with it." Another noted that:

> I've seen a lot of people try to blame economic conditions for their poor performance. That's a lot of [expletive]. In the technology field, you're finding opportunities; you're insulated from the market. External forces are just an excuse. When I hear a manager give those excuses, it tells me he is just a passenger, not a driver.

Most managers at all levels in the high-tech firm go one step further and argue that the bonus awards should not even be calibrated by the annual planning targets, even though this shields the company presidents from some risk. Their argument is that such shields cause the presidents to bias their plans in a conservative direction. It should be observed, though, that this type of sandbagging does not always seem to occur in other firms. In the distribution corporation, for example, top management considers most company plans to be optimistic.

Acts of Nature

Adjusting for acts of nature is easier to justify than adjusting for uncontrollable economic and competitive factors. Acts of nature tend to be large, single events, and they clearly bias the performance measures downward; yet their effects are relatively easy to calculate. Furthermore, it is usually not necessary for the manager to respond to the events except to minimize the one-time damage.

The distribution and chemical corporations tend to make, or at least consider, adjustments for these types of events. The high-tech corporation, on the other hand, is apparently unwilling to risk getting into subjective discussions of gray areas, such as whether an event is an act of nature or an economic or competitive condition, or whether the effects are large enough to warrant consideration for an adjustment, or how the effects should be calculated.

#3: What causes the differences in firms' implementation of the controllability principle?

Although it is obvious that these three firms exhibit considerable diversity in the extent to which they implement the controllability principle, explaining why these differences exist is not easy. The obvious answer is that the managers in each firm have made judgments as to the relative benefits and costs of each of the predicted consequences of holding managers in the firm accountable for each uncontrollable result or event. In the high-tech firm, top management judgments are important because a corporatewide policy has been implemented. In the other firms, some of the judgments have been delegated to group management (and even lower), and some intrafirm variance in applying the controllability principle is present.

While much more research is necessary to get a better understanding of the judgments made by the managers in each of these firms, some tentative observations can be made. It is tempting to ascribe the high-tech firm's complete disregard for the controllership principle to its history. The firm has grown by acquisition, and company presidents are often the original founder of their company.

Thus, they are used to bearing full responsibility for risk and facing the consequences of uncontrollable factors. As entrepreneurs, they perhaps even enjoy risk.

Although this explanation is probably essentially correct, it is not complete because the distribution firm, too, has grown primarily by acquiring small privately held firms, and most of its managers were also the owner of the firm at the time of its acquisition. This company, however, has chosen to shield the managers from part of the risk, perhaps because the environment is more stable, the uncontrollable shocks are therefore fewer, and their effects are easier to calculate.

The chemical corporation by itself is an interesting case. It has vacillated over the years in the extent to which it allows subjective judgments of actual performance to influence assigning bonuses. The cause of this vacillation appears to be top management style, particularly the chairman's taste for allowing subjectivity in performance evaluations.

System cost also seems to be an important concern in the chemical corporation. Its current concern is not to measure managers; it is to measure business entities so that the corporation's primary data base can be used as an input to important upper-management strategic decisions, particularly those concerning the businesses to be in. A dual emphasis—one that seeks good information about both the business entities and the controllable performance of their managers—would demand a very complex and confusing system.

Other than these few observations, little can be said about why the managers of these three firms made their choices. The differences among the corporations do not seem to be related to firm size or industry. It is certainly possible, however, that in a study of a larger number of firms, or even just a different set of firms, these variables might have useful explanatory power.

Clearly the best-supported conclusion of this study is that the absolute form of the controllability principle, as described at the start of this chapter, is incorrect. The agency-theory-modified controllability principle proposed by Baiman and Noel (1985) and Holmstrom (1982)—that managers should be evaluated using all information that gives insight into their action choices—seems to provide a better description of some of the practices used in the three firms. But that modified principle is at best incomplete because it does not explain all of the practices observed. This study has described some of the concerns that seem to affect management judgments of the costs and benefits of various alternatives, but further research is necessary before a much more definitive controllability principle, or perhaps set of principles, can be proposed.

NOTES

1. D. Solomons (1965, 83).

2. H. Geneen (1984, 106, 109). Emphasis in original.

3. The company also has a stock option plan that annually awards stock options with a ten-year horizon to general managers. I have not described that plan because the number of shares awarded is determined by grade level, not performance.

4. The high-tech corporation has recently implemented a stock option plan. The plan is not described here because company presidents reported that they are not familiar with its details and that it has not yet affected their decisions.

REFERENCES

Antle, R., and Smith, A. 1986. "An Empirical Investigation of the Relative Performance Evaluation of Corporate Executives." *Journal of Accounting Research* (Spring): 1–39.

Baiman, S., and Demski, J. S. 1980. "Economically Optimal Performance Evaluation and Control Systems." *Journal of Accounting Research*, Supplement, 184–220.

Baiman, S., and Noel, J. 1985. "Noncontrollable Costs and Responsibility Accounting." *Journal of Accounting Research* (Autumn): 486–501.

Demski, J. S. 1976. "Uncertainty and Evaluation Based on Controllable Performance." *Journal of Accounting Research* (Autumn): 230–45.

Geneen, H. 1984. *Managing.* Garden City, NY: Doubleday.

Hofstede, G. H. 1967. *The Game of Budget Control.* Assen, the Netherlands: Van Gorcum.

Holmstrom, B. 1982. "Moral Hazard in Teams." *Bell Journal of Economics* (Autumn): 74–91.

Maciariello, J. A. 1984. *Management Control Systems.* Englewood Cliffs, NJ: Prentice-Hall.

Magee, R. P. 1986. *Advanced Managerial Accounting.* New York: Harper & Row.

Maher, M. W. 1987. Ch. 11 of this volume.

Merchant, K. A. 1985. *Control in Business Organizations.* Cambridge, MA: Ballinger.

Reece, J. S., and Cool, W. R. 1978. "Measuring investment center performance." *Harvard Business Review* (May–June): 28–49.

Solomons, D. 1965. *Divisional Performance: Measurement and Control.* Homewood, IL: Dow Jones-Irwin.

Zimmerman, J. L. 1979. "The Costs and Benefits of Cost Allocations." *The Accounting Review* (July): 504–21.

CHAPTER 13

Planning, Control, and Uncertainty: A Process View

Robert Simons

INTRODUCTION

ACCOUNTING systems have traditionally played an important role in providing managers with information needed to successfully control an organization. Planning and budgeting techniques, for example, provide accounting data and estimates useful for decision making, evaluation, and control. Although these systems are widely used, little is known concerning their relevance in companies that operate in worldwide markets with sophisticated product technologies, diversified product portfolios, and greatly enhanced communication networks.

In this study, I attempted to understand how planning and control systems are used in a well-managed company that competes in multiple and uncertain environments. A model is presented to illustrate that planning and control systems may be usefully differentiated according to the degree of involvement of operating managers.

I will argue that planning and control processes may be either

For helpful suggestions and comments on an earlier draft of this paper, I thank Joseph Bower, Robert Eccles, Robert Kaplan, Kenneth Merchant, Krishna Palepu, Richard Vancil, and the colloquium participants. I am also grateful to the managers of Johnson & Johnson who, through their gracious participation, made this study possible.

programmed, with little involvement of operating managers, or *inter-active*, with considerable attention and interaction of management. This distinction helps explain the role of planning and control in various types of firms.

The chapter is organized as follows: first, I review prior published research as background; then, the methods followed in the study are described, including the selection criteria for the subject company and the procedures followed in gathering data; the last sections present the major findings of the research and describe and discuss a model to structure those findings.

BACKGROUND

The information-processing model of organizations predicts that, in an effectively functioning organization, the amount of information processed increases with increasing levels of uncertainty (Galbraith 1973; Tushman and Nadler 1978).

The major source of uncertainty for an organization is its environment (Thompson 1967; Katz and Kahn 1978; Weick 1979), comprising five external components: competitors, customers, suppliers, regulatory groups, and the technological requirements of the industry (Bourgeois 1985).[1] In addition, a firm's business strategy may also influence its actions in positioning products in certain niches or market segments of the competitive environment (Porter 1980).

Environmental uncertainty is highest for firms facing heterogeneous and dynamic environments. Environmental heterogeneity describes complexity and diversity in an organization's activities (Child 1972). Heterogeneity produces uncertainty owing to an absence of relevant information for decisions. This is illustrated in Galbraith's definition of uncertainty as "the difference between the amount of information required to perform a task and the amount of information already possesed by the organization" (Galbraith 1973, 36). To reduce this type of uncertainty, additional information may be gathered and processed to allow solution of a problem or completion of a task.

Environmental dynamism, by contrast, is the condition of instability and turbulence; i.e., changes in the environment are difficult to predict (Miles, Snow, and Pfeffer 1974; Duncan 1972). This is a different type of uncertainty and relates to the ambiguity and conflicting interpretations inherent in information (Daft and Lengel 1986; Weick

1979). With this type of uncertainty, the problem or task may be poorly understood or subject to multiple interpretations (Mintzberg, Raisinghani, and Théorêt 1976). Collecting and processing additional information may be insufficient to clarify opportunities, problems, and solutions.

The belief that the administrative structure of an organization should be aligned with its external environment (Lawrence and Lorsch 1967) is one of the central paradigms of modern organization theory. The number of studies, however, that have explored the information-processing link between environmental uncertainty and formal planning and control procedures is limited. Still unknown are conditions under which the bureaucratic organization (Weber 1947), controlled through specialization of tasks, rules and policies, and a clear hierarchy of authority, is appropriate or inappropriate to firms operating in uncertain environments.

Early empirical work, such as Burns and Stalker (1961), indicated that uncertain environments require flexible, organic forms of organization. Conversely, stable and relatively predictable environments require bureaucratic, mechanistic forms of structuring. Burns and Stalker argued that organic firms operating in uncertain environments minimize their reliance on formal controls. Similar findings were reported by Miles and Snow (1978).

Other studies, however, have concluded that environmental uncertainty in the form of intense product competition (Khandwalla 1972), product innovation (Kamm 1980), and certain types of business strategy (Simons 1987; Miller and Friesen 1982) can be associated with the increased use and perceived "tightness" of control procedures.

Most of these empirical studies have focused on an array of organizational characteristics in which formal controls represented a single variable from a larger set. The diversity of results in these studies illustrates that little attention has been given to understanding either the type of controls used by firms or the nature of the uncertainty that they face in their environments.

This study responds to the need for more firsthand knowledge of the ways in which management accounting techniques are actually used in modern business organizations (Kaplan 1984). Accordingly, this study uses interviews, observation, and the examination of relevant documentation in one well-managed company to focus on the role of control in uncertain business environments.

DESCRIPTION OF THE STUDY

The Company

Two criteria were considered critical in selecting a company for study. First, the company needed to be clearly operating in conditions that presented major and ongoing uncertainties to managers. Environments needed to be heterogeneous and dynamic. High degrees of diversification, wide product lines, notable and ongoing product innovation, diversity in geographic operations, and highly competitive markets are examples of conditions that I viewed as characteristic of environmental uncertainty. Second, since I wanted to document and abstract from the best of practice, it was essential to examine evidence from a well-managed company.[2] I wanted some assurance that the observed planning and control techniques were due to the efforts and choices of well-informed managers.

To aid in the selection, I consulted the annual surveys published by *Fortune* in which 250 top American corporations in 25 industries are rated by senior executives throughout the country. Johnson & Johnson was selected for this study since it is widely regarded, as evidenced by the *Fortune* survey, to be innovative and well managed.

Johnson & Johnson comprises 155 autonomous subsidiaries operating in three health care markets: consumer products, pharmaceutical products, and professional products. Exhibit 13-1 provides details of the business operations of the company. Johnson & Johnson operates manufacturing subsidiaries in 46 countries and employs 75,000 people worldwide. Sales in 1985 were $6.4 billion with pretax profits of $900 million.

Each operating company is structured as an independent entity with a president and a "board of directors" comprising the key functional vice presidents of the operating company. The operating company president reports to a member of the corporate Executive Committee either directly or through a Company Group Chairman. The corporate Executive Committee is chaired by the president of Johnson & Johnson who reports through the chairman and chief executive officer to the board of directors.

Sources of environmental uncertainty. The nature of the uncertainty facing business managers at Johnson & Johnson differs according to the business in which they compete. For the consumer businesses (43 percent of total sales, of which 60 percent are U.S. sales and 40 per-

Exhibit 13-1   Johnson & Johnson Major Business Segments

Consumer
- Chicopee - fabrics
- Devro - sausage casings
- J&J Baby Products - infant care
- J&J Products - wound and oral care
- McNeil - pain and cold medications
- Personal products - feminine hygiene

Pharmaceutical
- Janssen - original research drugs
- McNeil - prescription drugs
- Ortho Pharmaceutical - family-planning and dermatology products

Professional
- Codman - neurosurgical equipment and supplies
- Critikon - operating-room equipment and supplies
- Ethicon - wound-closure equipment and supplies
- Iolab - intraocular-implantation eye lenses
- J&J Cardiovascular - open-heart surgery products
- J&J Dental Products - orthodontic, preventive, and restorative products
- J&J Hospital Services - marketing services for other J&J professional companies
- J&J Ultrasound - diagnostic-imaging equipment (sold 1986)
- Ortho Diagnostic - diagnostic instruments
- Pitman-Moore - veterinarian equipment and supplies
- Surgikos - disposal products for minor surgery
- Technicare - diagnostic imaging (sold 1986)
- Vistakon - contact lenses
- Xanar - laser devices

cent are international sales), the major uncertainties relate to product innovation, competitor actions, and differing consumer tastes in a global business. All of the consumer markets in which Johnson & Johnson competes are highly competitive in terms of new products, brand advertising, and pricing. New product introductions represent a significant percentage of annual sales revenue. Advertising and promotion expenditures to meet competitive activity are high. Cost competition is intense in segments of the market, particularly where products are sold to institutional customers. In addition to international operations in Canada and Europe, Johnson & Johnson operates consumer companies in Latin America, Africa, the Middle East, Asia, and the Pacific.

In the professional businesses (34 percent of total sales—70 percent U.S. and 30 percent international), products are used by health care professionals, hospitals, diagnostic laboratories, and clinics. Product innovation to develop and support new medical procedures is important to success in this industry. Major uncertainties are present due to dramatic changes in supply and demand patterns produced by shifts in hospital reimbursement procedures, reduction in hospital admissions, and the demand from health care professionals for innovative, cost effective products. These environmental changes have increased competition in pricing and new product introduction. The Johnson & Johnson companies in the professional sector have wide product ranges; for example, one company that specializes in neuro-spinal equipment offers over 2,700 products worldwide. The development and manufacture of products in the professional category require advanced technologies from such fields as metallurgy, electronics, and optics.

The pharmaceutical segment (23 percent of total sales—54 percent U.S. and 46 percent international) consists principally of prescription drugs. Research spending for this segment exceeds 15 percent of sales. Uncertainty in the pharmaceutical businesses arises from the discovery, testing, and licensing of products for sale in the United States and abroad. The discovery process, which involves synthesizing chemicals into compounds, may have a success rate of less than one in several thousand attempts. After discovery of a new compound, clinical testing and regulatory approval in each country may take up to ten years, and the product may have to be withdrawn during this process if unexpected problems with the drug are encountered. Competition against existing products is intense as competitors introduce new products, and as generic substitutes become available.

Research procedures. The primary source of data for the study was in-depth interviews with sixteen senior managers located at six operating sites in New Jersey and Massachusetts.[3] The second source of data was direct observation of the planning and control process in action. One of the business units allowed me to sit through a series of meetings and discussions called to develop interim planning and budget projections for submission to corporate headquarters.

The final source of data was the examination of documents provided to me by company managers. These included summaries of control procedures, strategic and financial plans, and documents relating to evaluation and remuneration policies, mission statements, and other related matters.

Planning and Control at Johnson & Johnson: A Model

To describe the planning and control process at Johnson & Johnson and to abstract from the specifics of the situation, I distinguish between two types of control process. The first I term "interactive control" to describe situations in which *business managers actively use planning and control procedures to monitor and intervene in ongoing decision activities.* This is the type of control practiced by coaches of professional sports teams. Interactive control involves motivating and pushing athletes to their limit; offering advice and suggestions during and after a game; monitoring the outcome of player efforts; and providing feedback. All the factors relevant to the decision situation are examined and periodic intervention is practiced with each of the players.

By contrast, the term "programmed control" can be used to identify control processes where *business managers direct their attention primarily to ensuring that predetermined control procedures are established and maintained by designated subordinates.* For programmed control, managers intervene only if outcomes are not in accordance with predetermined standards. Programmed control is exercised by the governing body of the sport: ensuring, through subordinates, that rules exist and are enforced and that procedures exist for adjudication of disputes and for adjustment of procedures as necessary. Control procedures are codified and delegated.

Using these definitions, a control *process* is determined to be either interactive or programmed based on the extent to which *business managers use planning and control procedures to personally involve themselves in decision activities of subordinates.*

At Johnson & Johnson, certain accounting-based planning and control processes are interactive: business managers are highly involved in the control process. Others are programmed: managers are primarily concerned with establishing assurance that appropriate control procedures are in place; the monitoring and maintenance of these procedures is delegated to others. The existence of this difference in process, and an understanding of the way in which Johnson & Johnson has exploited it so successfully, is important to understanding how planning and control processes differ among classes of organizations; it provides considerable insight into these processes in uncertain environments.

Interactive control at Johnson & Johnson. In this section, I shall briefly review the procedures used at Johnson & Johnson to make two systems—long-range planning and financial planning—highly interactive.

*#1. Long-range planning system.*Long-range plans, prepared annually, are formulated by the lowest levels of the organization and are aggregated and transmitted upward through successive levels of management. There are no planning staff units at Johnson & Johnson.

The competitive environment of each operating company is constantly scanned. Information on market and competitive conditions is purchased from information services when available. In addition, operating company managers are expected to prepare estimated income statements by product line for all major competitors. These pro forma statements include sales, standard costs, gross profits, and discretionary expenses such as advertising and promotion. At the corporate level, public data are collected for prime competitors and distributed throughout Johnson & Johnson.

The long-range plan is primarily intended to reflect marketing strategies, focusing on business issues and opportunities instead of accounting numbers. Only three financial estimates are prepared: estimated sales, estimated net income, and estimated return on investment. Accompanying these numbers is a narrative description of how these targets will be achieved; it includes analyses of market shares, growth rates, and new product development.

Johnson & Johnson uses two techniques to make long-range planning interactive instead of ritualistic. First, the planning horizon is fixed so that, over time, managers are held accountable for earlier estimates and plans. Second, long-range plans are subject to intense debate and challenge. I will briefly describe each of these techniques.

To ensure that managers are committed to their long-range plan, Johnson & Johnson requires that the planning horizon remain fixed over a five-year period. Thus, in 1983, a budget and second-year forecast were prepared for 1984 and 1985, and a long-range plan was developed for the years 1990 and 1995. In each of the years 1984 through 1987, the long-range plan is redrawn only for years 1990 and 1995. Only after five years (in year 1988), will the planning horizon shift five years forward to cover years 1995 and 2000. These two years will then remain the focus of subsequent long-range plans for the succeeding four years and so on.

The procedure of freezing the planning horizon forces managers throughout Johnson & Johnson to review previous plans over the relevant ten-year period and incrementally revise the plan each year. Senior managers believe that the review and revision process has two consequences. First, the critical reevaluation of previous estimates allows learning about the nature of the business and the competitive environment. Second, changes in accounting-based sales and profit-projection estimates require an action plan to deal with the changed circumstances. As an operating company manager explained, "If your projection for 1990 is below last year's, how do you intend to make up the shortfall?" As we shall see, every perceived environmental change produces a demand that managers recommit themselves to a new course of action.

The pattern of information debate, the second interactive feature of long-range planning, occurs throughout Johnson & Johnson. Long-range plans are prepared by each operating company. The process involves estimates and competitive analysis from the major functional areas of the operating company. The board of directors of the operating company (typically the functional vice presidents within the operating company) meet to discuss the long-range plan. Assumptions and changes in unit-volume-growth projections from previous plans receive special attention at all levels of management in anticipation of careful review by the corporate headquarters Company Group Chairman and the Executive Committee.

A recurring feature of long-range planning is the recycling and reworking of estimates and plans as superiors and peers react to early drafts. After review at each level, plans are often reworked if the gap between current expectations and growth commitments from previous plans is anticipated to be troublesome to senior management. Meetings are scheduled sequentially as information on commitments and performance results flow up and down between operating companies and the Executive Committee at corporate headquarters. Membership in these meetings interlocks as managers present results, proposals, and reactions to different levels of management.

After approval by the operating company president, the tentative plan is then reviewed with the Company Group Chairman and ultimately with an Executive Committee member. Close questioning and testing of assumptions may lead to additional revisions.

The plan approved by the Group Chairman and Executive Committee member is then summarized by the operating company president in a two-page letter, sent directly to the Johnson & Johnson chairman at corporate headquarters. Each September, the corporate Executive Committee meets to review and discuss the long-range plans prepared by the operating companies. Executive Committee members present the plans for the operating companies under their responsibility. These presentations often generate serious debate concerning assumptions, arenas of operation, and suitable risk levels. Action plans and items for follow-up relating to long-range plans are published for limited circulation within the Executive Committee.

Long-range and financial planning meetings, at all levels, are uniformly described in terms such as "very frank," "extremely challenging," and "grilling." Expectations concerning communication at these meetings reflect the commitment to succeed and the depth of operating experience in the company.

Clearly, the pressure to improve and meet the expectations of superiors is common to most organizations. At Johnson & Johnson, however, the need for all managers to continually evaluate, revise, and present new commitments to action as part of the long-range and financial planning process makes these systems highly interactive.

During review meetings, the need for change and improvement is communicated clearly. Executive Committee meetings dealing with proposed plans and commitments routinely begin with a review of that business unit's operating results for the past five years. The need to outperform the trend animates the discussion. During these presentations and meetings, participants soon learn whether their proposed plans are acceptable to peers and superiors. During a research interview, I asked a senior corporate headquarters executive how senior managers ensure that targets are suitably challenging. In answering, he laughed and responded, "That reminds me of hearing, 'That's not good enough.' I've heard that so many times about the proposals coming up from the bottom. It is a way of life."

In accordance with company management style, however, only the affected operating manager decides whether a revision is necessary. The purpose of committee reviews of long-range plans, financial plans, and financial results at all levels is to challenge ideas, not to dictate or change proposals. None of the managers interviewed could recall an instance of a committee or superior unilaterally overturning a commitment or decision taken at a lower level.

As the president stated, "J&J is extremely decentralized, but that does not mean that managers are free from challenge as to what they are doing. If a manager insists on a course of action and we [the Executive Committee] have misgivings, nine times out of ten we will let him go ahead. If we say 'no' and the answer should have been 'yes,' we say [to the manager], 'Don't blame us; it was your job to sell us on the idea, and you didn't do that.'"

The culmination of the discussions is a commitment to action, based on the long-range planning process, by all managers in the company. Challenge and debate have exposed assumptions, problems, and opportunities, and the involvement of all managers in the company makes long-range planning highly interactive.

#2. Financial planning systems. The second highly interactive system is the financial planning system. All the managers I interviewed at Johnson & Johnson reported that financial planning requires a tremendous amount of time and effort; it encompasses every aspect of the business and requires managers to reassess constantly budget goals and action plans. The financial planning system comprises annual financial budgets prepared down to the expense-center level for each operating company for the upcoming operating year. A second-year forecast is also prepared in a similar, but less detailed, format.

Budget projections, like long-range plans, are prepared from the bottom up. Guidelines concerning acceptable profits, sales, or spending levels for upcoming periods are never issued by senior management in advance of budget preparation at the operating company level.

Financial budget targets are developed by reference to the long-range plans and the second-year forecast prepared the previous year. Significant changes in these documents (positive or negative) in projected sales, net income, or asset bases, due to changed environmental conditions since the last projection, require convincing explanations that all opportunities for growth and profit have been explored. In a process similar to that used for long-range planning, explanations and profit revisions are transmitted upward through sequential meetings between operating company managers, Group Chairmen, and the Executive Committee members. Budget projections may be reviewed at each succeeding level and sent back down for reconsideration and a search for additional opportunities.

After six months of preparation and review at all levels, original budgets for all operating companies for the upcoming calendar year and the second-year forecast are presented and discussed at the corporate Executive Committee meeting in November. Commitments are formalized at this session; occasionally, members undertake to reexamine their proposals to ascertain if higher levels of performance are possible.

As the budget year progresses, a series of revisions takes place that requires managers to report on their progress and recommit themselves to action for the remainder of the budget year. Sales and net income projections are revised and presented to the Executive Committee in March. A complete budget revision is prepared for the

Executive Committee's June meeting. An update is prepared for consideration at the November meeting, at which time the second-year forecast is revised to become the preliminary detailed budget for the upcoming year.

Each revision receives intense review at all levels of management. Previous commitments and environmental changes are examined and discussed. The president of one operating company said that, due to the interactive involvement of all managers in this process, corporate objectives are continuously clear to managers. As a result, it is not necessary to publish and distribute summaries of corporate goals on a periodic basis to managers.

Key financial results for each operating company are transmitted to corporate headquarters regularly. Group Chairmen at corporate headquarters receive weekly sales numbers, and each month they receive a full income statement and balance sheet from each operating company, including a commentary to explain significant variances. Currency translations are not included; foreign subsidiaries are evaluated in their own currency and compared for growth against country specific gross national product indices.

The procedures for variance analysis differ according to the size of the operating company. In smaller operating units, the monthly commentary is written by the operating company president in consultation with his immediate subordinates. At one of the company's larger operating units, division controllers discuss the reasons for variances with functional managers. The vice president of finance of the operating company then convenes a review meeting with the divisional controllers to analyze and summarize the reasons for the fluctuations. A summary analysis is then presented to the board of directors of the operating company (i.e., key functional executives) for review, discussion, and approval. Once approved, this commentary is sent to the Group Chairman at corporate headquarters.

As discussed above, budget revisions and updates are the topic of Executive Committee meetings in March, June, and November. The background for these discussions is year-to-date results. Since budget revisions are accepted only after stringent challenge and debate, the causes and remedies for unfavorable variances or the opportunities presented by favorable variances are the subject of intense interest by Executive Committee members. At Johnson & Johnson, the monitoring of results is strongly linked to the ongoing preparation of new action plans.

The involvment of all managers in this process is very high. In many settings, the intensity of the planning and control process could be expected to lead to a short-term focus in decision making. At Johnson & Johnson, however, "managing for the long term" is a key phrase that surfaced repeatedly in discussions. Managers believe that decisions must make sense in a long-term perspective. This view is reinforced by the long tenure of senior managers, a policy of promoting from within, and the structuring of all incentive plans around long-term results through stock option and deferred compensation plans. In addition, senior managers monitor "investment spending" (e.g., research and development and advertising as a percent of sales) to ensure that long-term trends are being maintained.

Because the financial planning system is interactive and commitments are altered over time, organizational rewards cannot be tied to the achievement of predetermined objectives. Thus, remuneration is subjectively determined and related to the *efforts* of the manager in the circumstances. During the interviews, numerous examples were cited of individuals rewarded for extra efforts during unforeseen economic downturns. For example, the president recounted the story of an operating company president who received financial recognition for convincing the Executive Committee of the need to close down major portions of his business. Another example provided by a senior operating company manager related to an unexpected twenty percent contraction in market demand:

We forecasted modest growth of one percent. In fact, the bottom dropped out of the market. By mid-January, we saw what was going to happen and, by the first week in February, we had a plan in place to try to keep up margins. Profits were way down, but the president and the other managers were evaluated on how well we responded, not on absolute results.

OBSERVATIONS CONCERNING INTERACTIVE CONTROL

The long-range and financial planning processes at Johnson & Johnson are interactive. There are at least six features embedded in these accounting-based procedures that lead to this assessment:

1. Staff specialists have limited roles in preparing and interpreting information;

2. The process requires frequent and regular attention from operating managers at all levels of the organization;

3. Data are interpreted and discussed in face-to-face meetings of superiors, subordinates, and peers;

4. Information generated by the process represents an important agenda to be addressed by the highest levels of management;

5. The process relies on the continual challenge and debate of underlying data, assumptions, and action plans; and

6. The process is fueled by a reward of effort rather than results.

After observing interactive control in action at Johnson & Johnson, several observations and speculations can be offered concerning situations in which interactive control is appropriate.

First, the decision activities encompassed by interactive control at Johnson & Johnson are nonroutine and unstructured (Mintzberg, Raisinghani, and Théorêt 1976). Decisions are embedded in unique settings that require analyses based on the specifics of each situation. The context of marketing, production, and financing decisions is constantly changing. The competitive environment is uncertain owing to competitor activities, new products and technologies, and sociopolitical factors inherent in a worldwide business.

Second, decision activities covered by interactive control at Johnson & Johnson tend to affect all, or a substantial portion, of organizational activity. The commitment of business managers to involve themselves in the control process—the defining characteristic of interactive control—arises from the belief by senior managers that the activities under review are important to substantial segments of the firm.

These characteristics—nonroutine tasks that impact major segments of the organization—suggest that interactive control is appropriate when organizational learning needs are high. Organizational learning describes the processes by which an organization influences the learning of its individual members and the manner in which this acquired knowledge is stored and transmitted. Organizational learning involves the cumulative activities of individuals in gathering information to adjust the organization's activities to match reality and to improve the fit with the environment (Hedberg 1981; Argyris and Schön 1978).

Organizational learning does not refer only to the learning of top management concerning activities in the organization. Organizational learning, as distinct from individual learning, acknowledges that processes in the organization can facilitate the search for information, its analysis and interpretation, and a sharing of acquired knowledge by all individuals involved in decision making.

Based on the Johnson & Johnson experience, interactive control appears to be necessary when both operating and corporate managers have a low level of understanding of the problems and opportunities that surround decision activities. Specific goals are at first unspecified. Interactive control occurs when a strong need exists for managers to invest effort in situational analysis both prior to commitment to a decision and as the outcome of that decision unfolds.

At Johnson & Johnson, learning needs are high owing to ongoing product innovation, market diversity, changes in technologies, and intense competition. Given this uncertainty, top managers require assurances that ongoing business decisions throughout their large decentralized organization are based on proper assumptions and analysis. Senior managers must be assured that subordinates are realizing their full potential for information gathering and opportunity analysis. Information must be exchanged effectively among managers at different levels of the organization and among operating units. Ongoing uncertainty requires substantially more analysis and information sharing than a less complex business environment (Galbraith 1973; Tushman and Nadler 1978).

Personalized management style is necessary for interactive control to be effectively employed. By definition, interactive control *is* management involvement in the control process. The type of involvement, however, differs fundamentally from hands-on management. Interactive control does not usurp the decision rights of subordinates; it involves senior management at critical phases in the decision process to ensure that decisions are being made within a defined framework and to obtain information necessary to manage personal commitments.

The periodic sampling of information and intervention in decision processes is similar to the annealing process described by Leifer and White (1986). Successful annealing requires individuals to heat up periodically the process and then to withdraw so that they affect outcomes without overtly intervening.

New alignments and proposals emerge from the wheelers and dealers below, with intermittent periods of "cooling" and "heating" until reasonable alternatives surface. . . . Annealing has the right imagery for our purposes. . . . It involves no *ex ante* directives, which would interfere with the perceived autonomy of the wheeling and dealing "bodies" on which it operates. Annealing is thus fully consonant with a decentralized system, where effectively exercised control is diffuse in nature.

Interactive control at Johnson & Johnson has been carefully designed to institutionalize these processes. Returning to our sports analogy, the only goal for interactive control is to succeed. The methods of achieving success, the plays used and the players put in the game, are worked out in the heat of the contest based on how the game develops. Decisions are delegated; each player assumes personal responsibility for acting during the game.

Delegation and decentralization are, however, insufficient to explain the use of interactive planning and control processes. The information needs of top managers in any decentralized formal organization can be accommodated through the upward flow of information through formalized reporting channels operated by specialized staff groups. Diversified businesses can be run "by the numbers." Interactive control occurs under conditions of high uncertainty in the business environment; not only is decision making decentralized to the players, but the playing field itself is turbulent and changing (Emery and Trist 1965).

Accounting data can be used to interpret and create a shared reality from past and present environmental cues (Hopwood 1986). Bourgeois (1985) has shown that the performance of a firm is related to the congruence between senior managers' perceptions of environmental uncertainty and the objective reality of the environment. The defining characteristic of interactive control is the involvement of managers in the control process. Interactive control fosters learning to produce a deeper understanding of the decision context, the business environment, and the capabilities and efforts of individual managers.

This knowledge also makes it both possible and desirable to reward managers for actions and efforts rather than for desired outcomes. Since goals cannot be effectively established in advance, and commitments are changed over the course of time, Johnson & Johnson bases performance rewards on effort levels. Compensation bonuses throughout the company are subjectively determined and are not a function of meeting targets.

The subjective, effort-based reward structure has several consequences that enhance organizational learning. First, by decoupling rewards from absolute output performance, managers are shielded from the variability in outcomes due to an uncertain environment. Information is not used to set absolute performance targets that may subsequently become unattainable owing to changing conditions. Information about changes in the environment is shared more readily since individuals are sure that their personal rewards will not be threatened.

Second, a natural consequence of rewarding effort is the desire of subordinates to make their efforts visible. Managers do this by creating an agenda with superiors that focuses on their actions and plans in response to changing business conditions. Incentives are provided for managers to inform superiors of actions taken to deal with unforeseen opportunities and problems and thereby demonstrate their competence.

Finally, rewarding effort requires more knowledge by superiors than rewarding performance on the basis of output. To assign subjective rewards to operating managers engaged in complex tasks, senior managers must understand changes in the competitive business environment, potential opportunities and constraints, and the range of action alternatives available to subordinates. The efforts of subordinates can be accurately evaluated only in these contexts. Thus, subjective evaluation reinforces information gathering and organizational learning.

The decision environment must be conducive to interactive control. Normative decision theory cautions against unwavering consensus in complex decision settings (Janis 1982). Empirical evidence suggests that diversity in managerial perceptions of the environment is positively related to performance (Bourgeois 1985). At Johnson & Johnson, managers uniformly report that they do not feel threatened by their involvement in the interactive control process. Freedom exists to challenge and defend unconventional points of view. Risk taking is not only tolerated but encouraged. A popular question at Executive Committee and other senior management meetings is, "Are we taking enough risk?" Failure seldom surprises since senior managers are involved early if problems arise in meeting commitments. Managers report that control system information is not used to punish or chastise; failure is treated as an opportunity to learn how to do better.

Programmed control at Johnson & Johnson. As in most large-scale organizations, many control procedures at Johnson & Johnson are programmed: controls are delegated by operating managers to subordinates and staff specialists for codification, implementation, and maintenance. Operating managers do not involve themselves in these programmed control processes unless outcomes are not in accordance with desired specifications.

Many accounting-based programmed controls are administered centrally by the Johnson & Johnson corporate controller department to obtain reasonable assurance that resources are secure and properly accounted. Examples include periodic inventories of fixed assets, stipulated approval procedures for resource spending, and the maintenance of detailed formalized manuals for financial procedures and internal controls.

At the operating company level, a variety of programmed controls are used throughout the organization to provide assurance that operating tasks are performed efficiently and effectively. Procedures are used to hire and train qualified individuals, route information and work through the organization, provide task descriptions, and provide various types of feedback on task effectiveness (Simons 1982).

Which controls are appropriate to delegate? When is programmed control preferable to interactive control? At Johnson & Johnson, I have postulated that controls are interactive when learning needs are high; i.e., when tasks are nonroutine and when significant parts of the organization are affected. Therefore, programmed controls may be suitable when these conditions do not hold. That is, programmed controls may be appropriate for decision situations encompassing routine tasks, with low learning needs that affect discrete parts of the organization.

To gain more understanding of how programmed controls are used at Johnson & Johnson, we can illustrate how two types of accounting-based programmed controls are implemented: financial reporting standards and transfer pricing.

Financial reporting standards are detailed in the Johnson & Johnson financial procedures manuals. These procedures are implemented to produce reliable reports and to satisfy external audit requirements. An internal audit department of seventy professionals travels worldwide to conduct audits of internal controls and financial reporting procedures.

These programmed controls are not allowed to constrain managerial prerogatives. For example, an Executive Committee member described how the procedures are implemented in a newly acquired subsidiary:

On a new acquisition, we don't try to change the financial system. We don't want to arrive with three books of financial corporate procedures. Even if they allocate expenses differently between cost of goods sold and commercial expenses than Johnson & Johnson, we don't ask them to change. It is not material to us and it is too disruptive for them. We do not want to break the momentum—that is the reason we bought them. However, we do try to get them to change things that are important to Johnson & Johnson. For example, we may ask them to implement procedures and report on equal opportunity activities, fire inspections, toxic waste handling, and the implementation of procedures to satisfy the F.D.A.

Similarly, the controller of one operating company noted that, for accounting reports, satisfying the external auditors was sufficient in terms of corporate procedures. No directives are provided by corporate headquarters on how to allocate costs or develop standard costs. These decisions are delegated to staff accounting specialists at the operating company who report to the operating company management.

The second example involves transfer pricing. The internal transfer of products among the many business units of Johnson & Johnson are accounted for at cost or cost plus a small (ten to twelve percent) markup. Similarly, transfers between departments within an operating company are at standard cost. Thus, according to the corporate controller, marketing departments enjoy the bulk of company profits and are motivated by growth objectives. Manufacturing is held accountable for achieving standard costs.

The corporate controller's office never becomes involved in the rare transfer-pricing disputes. Unresolved issues must be aired directly before the Executive Committee. Because of this procedure, operating company managers always resolve disputes themselves rather than burden the Executive Committee.

Transfer pricing in Johnson & Johnson has been designed as a programmed control. Procedures are formalized and delegated to staff specialists. Managers are not actively involved in the process because transfer pricing at Johnson & Johnson is a routine task that does not affect significant portions of the organization. In fact, operating companies at Johnson & Johnson are relatively independent, and with one or two exceptions, the transfer of products among the many operating companies accounts for less than ten percent of total sales.

Organizational learning needs in regard to the transfer of products between operating units in Johnson & Johnson are low because of a relative lack of interdependencies. In other firms, conditions may require much more interactive transfer-pricing processes. Significant interdependencies may require transfer prices to be based on outside market prices or renegotiated between operating managers on a periodic basis (Eccles 1985).

These two examples of financial reporting standards and transfer pricing illustrate programmed control in action at Johnson & Johnson. The following features are in evidence:

1. The role of staff specialists in preparing and interpreting information is pivotal;

2. The process involves operating managers infrequently and on an exception basis;

3. Data are transmitted through formal reporting procedures; and

4. The process accomplishes predetermined outcomes.

DISCUSSION

The findings of this study suggest a new interpretation of the role of formal planning and control procedures in modern, large-scale organizations. The legacy of Burns and Stalker (1961) is a widely held belief that formal controls are inappropriate in uncertain environments. Empirical studies based on incomplete evidence have allowed this hypothesis to survive. Van der Ven, Delbecq, and Koenig (1976), for example, reported that as task uncertainty increases, coordination is achieved through the use of personal, lateral communications rather than by rules and standard operating procedures. Argote (1982) concluded that programmed control (rules and procedures) is more effective with low task-uncertainty than with high task-uncertainty; nonprogrammed control (autonomy and mutual adjustment) is more effective in conditions of high task-uncertainty than low uncertainty. McCulloch (1978—cited in Argote) associated task uncertainty with increased monitoring of inputs and behaviors and less monitoring of outputs.

These studies have clearly demonstrated that simple rules and procedures are inadequate tools for planning and control in uncertain environments. The studies reported to date, however, have failed to provide guidance as to what should replace "formal controls" in conditions of high uncertainty. Concepts such as "autonomy" and "mutual adjustment" offer scant help to either scholars or practitioners on how to best structure the flow of information in the firm. If environmental turbulence and dynamism require increased information processing (Lawrence and Lorsch 1967; Galbraith 1973; Tushman and Nadler 1978), what is the appropriate role for formal planning and control systems?

Structural solutions have been suggested by accounting researchers. Gordon and Miller (1976), for example, hypothesize that accounting information systems can be designed to cope with environmental uncertainty by incorporating more nonfinancial data, increasing reporting frequency, including more forecast information, and tailoring reporting systems to local needs. Similar conjectures have been offered by MacIntosh (1981) and Ansari (1977).

This study indicates that formal planning and control systems have a critical role in large organizations operating in uncertain environments. While previous work points to the relevance of structural information systems design in conditions of high uncertainty (Gordon and Miller 1976; Gordon and Narayanan 1984), this study suggests the importance of understanding the *process* of using planning and control systems in uncertain environments.

Organizations do not abandon their formal planning and control procedures in conditions of high uncertainty. Rather, programmed controls become transformed into interactive controls as managers become personally involved in control procedures. As previous studies have suggested, uncertain environments require more information sharing and personal exchange. The sharing and exchange process, however, does not occur in the absence of formal control procedures. Rather, it is the consequence of interactive planning and control processes. In conditions of uncertainty, planning and control processes can be more important than in highly structured environments (Simons 1987; Kamm 1980; Khandwalla 1972).

When and why do organizations choose to program control procedures? In the absence of high organizational learning needs affecting significant segments of the business, organizations can be expected to program control procedures for reasons of efficiency and cost. In the pure form, this is the machine bureaucracy described by Mintzberg (1979a) or the mechanistic firm of Burns and Stalker (1961). Codifying and routinizing control procedures for routine tasks allows controls to be applied in a cost effective manner. Delegating the design and implementation of these procedures to staff specialists allows systems to be designed and operated efficiently using current information techniques and control procedures. Both of these forces free the attention of operating managers, one of the firm's scarcest resources, to concentrate on meeting business objectives.

NOTES

1. Comprehensive theories and reviews of the concept of environment have been provided by Aldrich (1979), Pfeffer and Salancik (1978), and Starbuck (1976).

2. By selecting a well-managed company and studying its planning and control processes, I am implicitly assuming a causal link between good management practice and a firm's performance. This is a compelling assumption that, in a less functionalist (Burrell and Morgan 1979) view of the world, may not be supported. Nevertheless, as researchers, we must strive to understand and develop practices that are likely to yield benefits to the firm (Merchant and Simons 1986).

3. Managers interviewed included the president of Johnson & Johnson (who chairs the Executive Committee), a member of the Executive Committee with responsibility for sixteen companies worldwide, the presidents of four operating companies, the corporate controller, and financial and marketing executives in four operating companies. Interviews were generally two hours in length and were relatively unstructured. Discussions focused on planning and control procedures and the reasons, benefits, and problems associated with their use.

REFERENCES

Aldrich, Howard E. 1979. *Organizations and Environment.* Englewood Cliffs, NJ: Prentice-Hall.

Ansari, Shahid L. 1977. "An Integrated Approach to Control Systems Design." *Accounting, Organizations and Society* (No. 2): 101–12.

Argote, Linda. 1982. "Input Uncertainty and Organizational Coordination in Hospital Emergency Units." *Administrative Science Quarterly* (September): 420–34.

Argyris, Chris, and Schön, Donald A. 1978. *Organizational Learning: A Theory of Action.* Reading, MA: Addison-Wesley.

Bourgeois, L. J. III. 1985. "Strategic Goals, Perceived Uncertainty, and Economic Performance in Volatile Environments." *Academy of Management Journal* (September): 548–73.

Burns, T., and Stalker, G. 1961. *The Management of Innovation.* London: Tavistock.

Burrell, Gibson, and Morgan, Gareth. 1979. *Sociological Paradigms and Organisational Analysis.* London: Heinemann.

Child, John. 1972. "Organization Structure, Environment and Performance: The Role of Strategic Choice." 6 *Sociology:* 1–22.

Daft, Richard L., and Lengel, Robert H. 1986. "Organizational Information Requirements, Media Richness and Structural Design." *Management Science* (May): 554–71.

Duncan, R. B. 1972. "Characteristics of Organizational Environments and Perceived Environmental Uncertainty." *Administrative Science Quarterly* (September): 313–27.

Eccles, Robert G. 1985. *The Transfer Pricing Problem: A Theory for Practice.* Lexington, MA: Lexington Books.

Emery, F. E., and Trist, E. L. 1965. "The Causal Texture of Organizational Environments." *Human Relations* (February): 21–32.

Galbraith, Jay R. 1973. *Designing Complex Organizations.* Reading, MA: Addison-Wesley.

Gordon, Lawrence A., and Miller, Danny. 1976. "A Contingency Framework for the Design of Accounting Information Systems." 1 *Accounting, Organizations and Society* (No. 1): 59–69.

Gordon, Lawrence A., and Narayanan, V. K. 1984. "Management Accounting Systems, Perceived Environmental Uncertainty and Organizational Structure: An Empirical Investigation." 9 *Accounting, Organizations and Society* (No. 1): 33–48.

Hedberg, Bo. 1981. "How Organizations Learn and Unlearn." In *Handbook of Organizational Design*, edited by Paul C. Nystrom and William H. Starbuck. New York: Oxford University Press.

Hopwood, Anthony G. 1986. "Management Accounting and Organizational Action: An Introduction." In *Research and Current Issues in Management Accounting*, edited by M. Bromwich and A. G. Hopwood. London: Pitman.

Janis, Irving L. 1982. *Groupthink: Psychological Studies of Policy Decisions and Fiascoes.* 2d ed. Boston: Houghton Mifflin.

Kamm, Judith B. 1980. "The Balance of Innovative Behavior and Control in New Product Development." Harvard Business School. DBA diss.

Kaplan, Robert S. 1984. "The Evolution of Management Accounting." *The Accounting Review* (July): 390–418.

Katz, Daniel, and Kahn, Robert L. 1978. *The Social Psychology of Organizations.* 2d ed. New York: Wiley.

Khandwalla, Pradip N. 1972. "The Effect of Different Types of Competition on the Use of Management Controls." *Journal of Accounting Research* (Autumn): 275–85.

Lawrence, Paul, and Lorsch, Jay. 1967. *Organization and Environment.* Boston: Harvard Business School, Division of Research.

Leifer, Eric M., and White, Harrison C. 1986. "Wheeling and Annealing: Federal and Multidivisional Control." In *The Social Fabric*, edited by James F. Short. New York: Sage.

MacIntosh, Norman B. 1981. "A Contextual Model of Information Systems." 6 *Accounting, Organizations and Society* 6 (No. 1): 39–53.

McCulloch, Donna. 1978. "The Structure and Performance of Institutional Review Boards: A Contingency Perspective." University of Michigan. Ph.D. diss.

Merchant, Kenneth A., and Simons, Robert. 1986. "Research on Control in Complex Organizations: An Overview." 5 *Journal of Accounting Literature:* 183–203.

Miles, Raymond E.; Snow, Charles C.; and Pfeffer, Jeffrey. 1974. "Organization-Environment: Concepts and Issues." *Industrial Relations* (October): 244–64.

Miles, Raymond E., and Snow, Charles C. 1978. *Organizational Strategy: Structures and Processes.* New York: McGraw-Hill.

Miller, Danny, and Friesen, Peter H. 1982. "Innovation in Conservative and Entrepreneurial Firms." 3 *Strategic Management Journal:* 1–27.

Mintzberg, Henry. 1979a. *The Structuring of Organizations.* Englewood Cliffs, NJ: Prentice-Hall.

———. 1979b. "An Emerging Strategy of 'Direct' Research." *Administrative Science Quarterly* (December): 582–89.

———. 1975. *Impediments to the Use of Management Information.* New York: National Association of Accountants.

Mintzberg, Henry; Raisinghani, D.; and Théorêt, A. 1976. "The Structure of 'Unstructured' Decision Processes." *Administrative Science Quarterly* (June): 246–75.

Pfeffer, Jeffrey, and Salancik, Gerald. 1978. *The External Control of Organizations: A Resource Dependence Perspective.* New York: Harper & Row.

Porter, Michael E. 1980. *Competitive Strategy.* New York: Free Press.

Simons, Robert. 1987. "Accounting Control Systems and Business Strategy: An Empirical Analysis." *Accounting, Organizations and Society.*

———. 1982. "Control in Organizations: A Framework for Analysis." Proceedings of the 1982 Canadian Academic Accounting Association.

Starbuck, William H. 1976. "Organizations and Their Environments." In *Handbook of Industrial and Organizational Psychology,* edited by Marvin D. Dunnette, 1069–1123. Chicago: Rand McNally.

Thompson, James D. 1967. *Organizations in Action:* New York: McGraw-Hill.

Tushman, Michael L., and Nadler, David A. 1978. "Information Processing as an Integrating Concept in Organizational Design." *Academy of Management Review* (July): 613–24.

Van der Ven, Andrew H.; Delbecq, Andre L.; and Koenig, Richard, Jr. 1976. "Determinants of Coordination Modes Within Organizations." *American Sociological Review* (April): 322–38.

Weber, Max. 1947. *The Theory of Social and Economic Organizations.* New York: Collier Macmillan.

Weick, Karl E. 1979. *The Social Psychology of Organizations.* 2d ed. Reading, MA: Addison-Wesley.

Contributors

RAJIV D. BANKER is professor of accounting and public management at Carnegie-Mellon University. He received his bachelor's degree in mathematics and economics at the University of Bombay and a doctorate in planning, accounting, and accountability systems at the Harvard Business School. He has received many academic awards. Banker is currently a co-editor of the *Journal of Productivity Analysis*. His current research focuses on the design of productivity accounting systems, evaluation of organizational and industrial efficiency, and analysis of managerial decision making. He has recently been commissioned by the American Accounting Association to write (with Srikant M. Datar) a monograph on "Productivity Accounting for Performance Evaluation."

WILLIAM J. BRUNS, Jr., is professor of business administration at the Harvard Business School, where he has taught in the MBA program and educational programs for senior executives. He earned degrees at the University of Redlands (BA), Harvard University (MBA), and the University of California, Berkeley (PhD). Before accepting his current appointment, he taught at Yale University and the University of Washington. He is the author of several books, including *Case Problems in Management Accounting* with M. E. Barrett; *A Primer on Replacement Cost Accounting* with R. F. Vancil; and *Introduction to Accounting: Economic Measurement for Decisions*, as well as numerous articles which have appeared in professional journals.

ROBIN COOPER is an associate professor at the Harvard Business School. A member of the faculty since 1982, Mr. Cooper received a BSc degree from the University of Manchester, England, and MBA and DBA degrees from Harvard University. He is a Fellow of the Institute of Chartered Accountants in England and Wales. His current research focuses on the strategic importance of product costing. For the last several years he has been studying the design and introduction of innovative cost systems.

SRIKANT M. DATAR is an associate professor of industrial administration and public policy at Carnegie-Mellon University. He received his AM, MS, and PhD degrees from Stanford University. Professor Datar's research interests are in the areas of information economics, agency theory, auditing, productivity measurement and accounting, and accounting for manufacturing systems. He is currently working on methods to measure and improve software productivity. Professor Datar has recently been commissioned by the American Accounting Association to write (with Rajiv D. Banker) a research monograph on "Productivity Accounting for Performance Evaluation."

JEREMY F. DENT is lecturer in accounting at London Business School and a Fellow of the Institute of Chartered Accountants in England and Wales. He received his BSc. degree from the University of Southampton and undertook his doctoral research at the University of London. His accounting training was obtained with Peat, Marwick, Mitchell & Co. Before joining the faculty of London Business School in 1982, Mr. Dent was a lecturer at the University of Southampton. In 1985, he was visiting professor at the Copenhagen School of Economics and Business Administration. Mr. Dent has published a variety of articles on organizational and cultural aspects of control systems design and is the author of a forthcoming book, *Accounting Systems and Organizational Change: A Comparative Study in Three Organizations.* His current research focuses on the relationship between control systems design and organizations' strategies.

JULIE H. HERTENSTEIN is an assistant professor at the Harvard Business School where she has taught courses in management control and resource allocation. Professor Hertenstein received her B.S. in mathematics from The Ohio State University in 1969; her subsequent work experience included six years at Pacific Telephone and Telegraph where she managed a long-range planning project for interdepartmental computer services. Professor Hertenstein received her M.B.A. and D.B.A. degrees from Harvard University in 1979 and 1984, respectively. Her current research interests focus on the design of management control systems to allocate capital and other long-term expenditures.

H. THOMAS JOHNSON is the Dwight J. Zulauf Alumni Professor of Accounting at Pacific Lutheran University in Tacoma, Washington. A graduate in economics from Harvard College, he received his MBA from Rutgers University and his PhD in economic history from the University of Wisconsin. He was employed as a public accountant with Arthur Andersen before entering an academic career in 1964. He has held appointments in economics at the University of Western Ontario and in accounting at Western Washington University and the University of Washington. He was also chairman of the Department of Accounting at Washington State University and dean of the School of Business at the University of Puget Sound. In 1981, he received the Academy of Accounting Historians' Hourglass Literature Award and, in 1978, a Newcomen Award for the outstanding article in the *Business History Review.* A past president of the Academy of Accounting Historians, Dr. Johnson was selected by the University of Glasgow as the 1983 Arthur Young Distinguished Lecturer in Accounting. He has served on the editorial boards of several leading academic journals and is presently a member of the University Review Panel (Cost Management Project) of Computer-Aided Manufacturing, International. He has authored or co-authored four books—the latest, *Revelance Lost: The Rise and Fall of Management Accounting* with Robert S. Kaplan—and more than thirty articles for monographs and leading journals in accounting and economic history. His current research interest is the design of strategic cost management systems for service enterprises.

ROBERT S. KAPLAN is the Arthur Lowes Dickinson Professor of Accounting at the Harvard Business School and a professor of industrial administration at Carnegie-Mellon University. From 1977 to 1983 he served as dean of the Graduate School of Industrial Administration at Carnegie-Mellon, where he has been on the faculty since 1968. He received a BS and MS in electrical engineering from MIT and a PhD in operations research from Cornell University. He received the AICPA Accounting Literature Award in 1971, and in 1984, the McKinsey Award for an outstanding article in the *Harvard Business Review.* His textbook, *Advanced Management Accounting,* was published in 1982 and his 1987 book, *Relevance Lost: The Rise and Fall of Management Accounting* (co-authored with H. Thomas Johnson), was the cover story of the January 1987 issue of *Management Accounting*. A former vice president of the American Accounting Association, Professor Kaplan currently serves on the Executive Committee of the CAM-I Cost Management System Project, the Manufacturing Studies Board of the National Research Council, and the Financial Accounting Standards Advisory Committee.

MICHAEL W. MAHER is professor of accounting at the University of Michigan and visiting professor of accounting at the University of Chicago, where he teaches managerial and cost accounting. He received his BBA from Gonzaga University in Spokane, Washington, and his MBA and PhD from the University of Washington. A CPA, he previously was an auditor with Arthur Andersen in Portland, Oregon. He has written extensively on accounting and management accounting and controls, and is currently studying the causes of division and corporate fraudulent financial reporting. He received the American Accounting Association Competitive Manuscript award in 1980 and the AICPA Notable Contribution to the Literature Award in 1982 for his research on internal controls. In 1984, he received the American Taxation Association Manuscript Award for an article on inflation and taxes published in the *Journal of Accounting Research*. His books include *Cost Accounting* (with E. Deakin, 1987), *Managerial Accounting* (with Sidney Davidson, Clyde P. Stickney, and Roman Weil, 1985), and *Management Incentive Compensation Plans* (with Stephen Butler, 1986).

KENNETH A. MERCHANT is an associate professor at the Harvard Business School. He has degrees from Union College (NY), Columbia University, and the University of California, Berkeley and is a certified public accountant (Texas). He worked for Texas Instruments and Ernst & Whinney prior to joining the Harvard faculty in 1978. He is the author of *Control in Business Organizations* and a number of articles in journals such as *The Accounting Review, Accounting, Organizations and Society,* and *Sloan Management Review*. Professor Merchant's research interests are in the area of management control.

KRISHNA G. PALEPU is an assistant professor at the Harvard Business School. Mr. Palepu obtained his MBA from the Indian Institute of Management and his PhD from MIT. Prior to his doctoral work, he was a management consultant specializing in the design of financial control systems. Since joining the Harvard Business School faculty in 1983, he has taught in both Executive Education and MBA programs. Professor Palepu's research deals with issues in financial reporting and financial statement analysis and he has published a number of papers on these topics in academic journals. He is a member of the editorial board of *The Accounting Review*.

JAMES M. PATELL is a professor of accounting and associate dean for academic affairs at the Graduate School of Business, Stanford University. Professor Patell earned his bachelor and master of science degrees in engineering from MIT and a PhD in industrial administration from Carnegie-Mellon University. He has taught at Stanford since 1975; in 1981–1982 he was a Ford Foundation visiting associate professor at the University of Chicago. His research has centered on empirical investigations of the effects of financial disclosures on the stock and option markets and it has been published in the *Journal of Accounting and Economics, Journal of Accounting Research, Journal of Financial Economics, Journal of Legal Studies,* and *The Accounting Review.*

HEIN SCHREUDER is professor of business economics and organization at the University of Limburg, Maastricht, the Netherlands. He is also a fellow of the European Institute for Advanced Studies in Management, Brussels, Belgium. After graduating from the Erasmus University in Rotterdam he worked for the Netherlands Economic Institute, was director of the Economic and Social Institute of the Free University of Amsterdam, and visiting scholar at the University of Washington in Seattle. His main publications include three (Dutch-language) books dealing, respectively, with the usage of corporate financial reports, the predictability of sales and earnings (both with Jan Klaassen) and corporate social responsibility and reporting. He has edited volumes on European contributions to accounting research (with Anthony Hopwood) and on economics and business administration (with Joan Muysken). He was selected as the 1985 Distinguished International Visiting Lecturer by the American Accounting Association.

ROBERT SIMONS is an assistant professor at the Harvard Business School, where he teaches management control courses in the MBA and Executive programs. A Canadian chartered accountant, Simons received his PhD from McGill University with a joint concentration in accounting and control and in business policy. His current research focuses on how management control systems can be designed to fit a firm's business strategy, and he has written several papers on this topic. Simons is also a consultant to a number of large corporations, assisting in the design and implementation of strategic planning and corporate control systems.

JEROLD L. ZIMMERMAN is deputy dean and Alumni Distinguished Professor at the University of Rochester William E. Simon Graduate School of Business Administration. He holds a BS degree from the University of Colorado and a PhD from the University of California, Berkeley. He won the American Accounting Association Manuscript Award and, for two papers co-authored with Ross Watts, received the American Institute of Certified Public Accountants Notable Contribution to the Literature awards. He and Watts published *Positive Accounting Theory* and his articles have appeared in the *Journal of Accounting and Economics, Accounting Review, Journal of Business, Journal of Law and Economics, Journal of Accounting Research,* and *Management Science.*

Index

A

Accountability. *See also* Controllability principle
  cost and, 331, 332–333
  uncontrollable factors and, 318, 329, 330–333, 335
Accountability structure
  charge-back system and, 68–69
  control system design and, 122–123, 133–134, 137
  matrix organization and, 60–62
  under multidimensional accounting system, 129–130, 133–135, 137
Aldrich, Howard E., 360
Ansari, Shahid L., 359, 360
Antle, R., 296–297, 312, 313, 314
Authority structure. *See* Organization structure

B

Baiman, S., 318, 336
Baker, Gil, 59
Baker Corporation, 99, 102–104
Baker Corporation, Baker Division
  Accounting Resource Committee, 108–110, 112–113
  embedded accounting system at, 104–105, 107
  materials planning system at, 113
  need for new system at, 107–112
  new cost accounting system at, 112–117
  product flows at, 106
  reorganization at, 105–107
  "The Effectiveness Program" at, 103, 105
Ball, R., 93

Banker, R. D., 176, 180, 193, 200, 201
Baran, A., 45
Batch manufacturing. *See* Lot sizing
Beaver, W. H., 45, 46
Berliner, R. W., 45, 47
Bessent, A., 193, 202
Bessent, W., 193, 202
Bingham, C. W., 60, 67–68, 71
Boatsman, James, 45
Bonus system. *See* Incentive system; Management compensation plan
Bourgeois, L. J., III, 354, 360
Breden, Denise, 45
Budgeting procedures, 123
Bureaucratic organization
  formal control systems design and, 120–122, 142
  uncertain environments and, 341
Burns, T., 121, 143, 144, 341, 358, 359
Butler, S., 314

C

Capital charge, inflation accounting and, 26, 28
Capital-intensive companies, inflation accounting and, 43–44
Caves, D. W., 201, 202
Chandler, Alfred D., Jr., 70, 138, 144
"Charge-back" system, 50–51, 54. *See also* Strategic information procedures
  accountability and, 68–69
  operation of, 64–67

Charnes, A., 193
Christensen, L. R., 201, 202
Christenson, L. W., 72
Clark, K., 11–12, 117
Cohen, Michael D., 162
Competition
  analysis of, 310–311. *See also* Relative perform-
    ance evaluation
  interdepartmental, 135–137
Computer companies. *See also* Formal control sys-
    tem design; Hewlett-Packard Personal Office
    Computer Division
  accountability and performance measurement
    at, 129
  compensation schemes and, 130
  control system design and, 131–137
  divisionalization and, 138
  just-in-time manufacturing and, 229–266
  organization in, 127–128
  organization structure and, 142–143
Conglomerates. *See* Diversified firms
Conrad, R. F., 193, 202
Contingency theory
  formal control system design and, 120, 123–
    124, 125
  structure vs. process and, 125
Controllability principle, 316–337. *See also* Per-
    formance evaluation
  comparative implementation of, 330–331, 335–
    337
  with multidimensional accounting system, 133,
    140–141
  non-implementation of, 329–330
  partial implementation of, 327–328
  rationale for, 317–318
Control processes
  accounting data and, 41–42, 176, 356–358
  interactive vs. programmed, 345, 353, 358–360
  at Johnson & Johnson, 344–351
  MIS implementation and, 157, 161
  uncertainty and, 341, 358
Control system. *See* Formal control system design
Cooper, R. C., 70, 72, 93, 173
Cooper, W. W., 193, 201, 202
Copeland, Ronald, 12
Corporate overhead. *See also* Cost accounting;
    Overhead costs
  indirect approach to, 50
  strategic cost accounting and, 70
Cost accounting
  passive labor vouchering and, 246–248
  perpetual work orders and, 244–246
  sales costs and, 238
Cost accounting reports
  direct labor and, 275–277
  indirect expenses and, 275–277
  internal management and, 279–281
  part/product, 278–281
Cost accounting system. *See also* Full-cost ac-
    counting; Variable-cost accounting; *under spe-
    cific companies*
  change in, and embedded structures, 99–117
  consistency among measures and, 33

controls and, 176, 251–252
fixed vs. variable costs in, 205–206, 263–264,
  275–277
at Hewlett-Packard POD, 238–252
internal user needs and, 108–109, 110
job order system and, 273–275
just-in-time manufacturing and, 229–267
lag in development of, 97–98, 116–117
product costs and, 204–228
quality assurance and, 261–263
reasons for changing, 98, 107–112, 115
Cost allocation
  control system design and, 134–135
  cost drivers and, 225
  dual application rate for, 242–244
  fixed vs. marginal, 213–216
  machine hours and, 216
  material dollars and, 216
  multiple bases in, 215–216
  performance measurements and, 125–126
  for support departments, 242–244
  transaction-related bases and, 220–222
  two-stage system for, 212–213, 215–216
  volume-related bases and, 218–219, 220
Cost by Process diagram, 240–242
Cost drivers, 222. *See also* Product mix
Costing systems. *See* Marginal costing; Process
    costing; Product costing systems; Transac-
    tion costs
COSTIT system, 242, 263
Cost-plus pricing, 211
Cross-subsidization, 218–219, 224

D

Data envelopment analysis (DEA), 192–198
Datar, S. M., 177, 200, 202
Davis, Stanley M., 71
DEA. *See* Data envelopment analysis
Dearden, John, 70
Debt covenant requirements, 76, 87, 88, 90, 92–
  93
Debt/equity ratio, 76, 81
Decentralization. *See* Divisional organization
Defect Analysis Matrix, 252–253
Delbecq, Andre L., 358
DeMichiel, Robert, 45
Deming, Professor W. E., 150
Demski, Joel S., 267, 337
Depreciation
  change in estimation of, 85
  inflation accounting and, 24, 25, 26
Depreciation method, 85
Direct labor
  components of, 185
  cost accounting reports and, 275–277
  JIT cost accounting and, 246–248
  overhead allocation and, 212, 215–216, 242
Diversified firms, 50, 51–54. *See also* Divisional
    organization
  cost of complexity and, 217

distorted product costs and, 207
lot-sizing decisions and, 268–291
market contracting and, 63–64
RPE and, 299, 300–302
Divisional organization. *See also* Multidivisional organization
alternatives to, 138–139
controllability principle and, 319–337
implementation of MIS and, 155–157, 158, 161
inter-unit competition and, 135–137
performance evaluation and, 297, 298
at Weyerhaeuser, 62–69

E

Eccles, R. G., 313, 337, 358
Economic factors, accountability and, 331–332, 333–335
Economic order quantity (EOQ) models, 269
Economies of scope, 51, 55, 56, 59. *See also* Diversified firms
"Efficient market" hypothesis, 75, 91–92
Effort-based reward structure, 351, 354–355
"80/20 rule", 209
Eiler, Robert G., 117
Environmental context, 124
Environmental dynamism, 340–341
Environmental uncertainty, 339–360
EOQ models. *See* Economic order quantity (EOQ) models

F

"Failure-analysis laboratory", 252–253
"Failure-analysis shopfloor tracking" system (FAST), 253–260
barcode-reading system, 261–262
Falk, Haim, 12
FAST. *See* "Failure-analysis shopfloor tracking" system
FAS 33 (Financial Reporting and Changing Prices), 17, 45
Field research
biases in, 288–290
generalizability and, 290–291
issues in, 11–13
limitations of, 288–290
methodology, 1–13, 288–291
partial analysis and, 290–291
replication and, 289
vs. case studies, 8
Financial measures
ambiguity of, 10–11
inflation accounting and, 33, 39
Financial planning system
interactive control and, 349–355
organizational rewards and, 351
Financial reporting
accounting system change and, 9, 73–93
inventory reduction and, 265

JIT inventory reduction and, 265
linkage with managerial accounting, 87, 88–89, 92
Financial reporting standards, 356–357
Finley, Macon, 266
Fixed costs, 275–277. *See also* Full-cost accounting
discretionary, 217–218
failure of allocations and, 215–218
"Flattening", 61
Food products industry, performance evaluation in, 304–306
Formal control system design
alternative theory and, 120–122, 142
bureaucratic principles and, 120–122, 142
competition and, 135–136
criteria for appraisal of, 119
elements in, 122–123
environmental uncertainty and, 359–360
interactions and, 125–126, 132–135
management control and, 119–145
qualitative research and, 126–127
situational variables and, 123–124
structure vs. process focus in, 125
theoretical approaches to, 119–122, 142
Fosmire, Fred R., 71
Foster, George, 8
Friesen, Peter H., 98, 103–104, 115, 118
Full-cost accounting, 205–206

G

Gain-sharing program, 177–184
assumptions in formula for, 184–185, 189, 192, 193–194
computation method and, 173, 178–179
direct vs. indirect labor and, 185–186
implementation of, 178
indirect labor and, 179
problems with, 172–173
product-mix effects and, 173, 182–183
quality control and, 179–180
volume effect and, 172–173, 180–182
Galbraith, J. R., 123, 138–139, 340
Garrett, Linda, 266
Geertz, Clifford, 162, 165
Geneen, H., 316–317, 337
Gheyara, Kelly, 45
Goessel, William, 83
Goletz, Walter K., 117
Gordon, L. A., 121, 359
Grade, Jeffrey, 83
Grinyer, P. H., 121
Guetzkow, Harold, 118

H

Haka, S. F., 121
Harnischfeger, Henry, 83

Harnischfeger Corporation
  accounting change at, 85–86
  background on, 77–81
  corporate recovery plan at, 83–85
  Heavy Equipment Group, 77, 81
  impetus for accounting change at, 86–90
  Industrial Technologies Group, 77, 81, 84
  1982 financial crisis at, 81–83
Harrison, J. Michael, 266
Hayes, R. H., 72, 117
Healea, Gary, 72
Healy, P., 93
Hertenstein, Julie, 8, 44, 47
Heterogenity, uncertainty and, 340
Hewlett-Packard Personal Office Computer Division, 229–267
  background on, 230–232
  cost accounting at, 238–252
  just-in-time manufacturing at, 232–238
  standard setting at, 240–242
Hildenbrand, W., 201
Hofstede, G. H., 165, 319, 337
Holmstrom, B., 297, 313, 314, 336, 337
Holthausen, R. W., 76, 93
Honeywell, relative performance evaluation at, 307–313
Hopkins, Donald J., 71
Hopwood, Anthony, 9, 361
Horizontal integration, 51
Horngren, Charles T., 70
Human factors, MIS implementation and, 160
Hunt, Rick, 266
Hurwicz, Leonid, 266–267

I

Incentive system. *See also* Management compensation plan
  conflicting objectives and, 282–283
  division management and, 282–283, 300, 321–324, 325–328
  effort-based organizational rewards and, 351, 354–355
  financial performance and, 300
  inventory reduction and, 279
  lot-sizing decisions and, 270–271
  manufacturing complexity and, 270–271
  new product development and, 309
  queuing externality and, 270
  RPE and, 308
  top management and, 328–329
  uncontrollables and, 321–324
  workers and, 281–282, 285
Indirect expenses
  cost accounting reports and, 275–277
  performance evaluation and, 280
Indirect labor, 179, 185
Inflation accounting, 17–48
  adoption of, 35–39
  asset management and, 26
  capital charge and, 26, 28
  cost of goods sold and, 24, 25
  depreciation and, 24, 25, 26

distribution of data from, 26, 30
elements of system, 24–26
external reporting requirements and, 17, 45
financial performance and, 27, 44
fixed assets and, 24, 25
holding gains and, 24–26
implementation stages for, 33–35, 37–38
inventories and, 24, 25
investment base measures in, 29
management control and, 14–48
management systems and, 31
measures of return, 26, 28
monetary gains and, 24–26
morale and, 39
motivations for adopting, 26
negative effects and, 39
operating performance and, 26, 28, 32, 36–39, 41–42
as primary vs. supplementary method, 22, 23, 42
use of data from, 26–27, 31, 42–43
Informal communications, 132–135, 139–140
Information systems/technology (IS/T). *See also* Management Information System
  organizational ambiguity and, 161, 162–163
  organizations and, 148–149
Interactive control. *See also* Control processes
  at Johnson & Johnson, 345–351
  long-range planning system and, 351–355
  relevant situations for, 352–355
  transfer pricing and, 357–358
Inventories, inflation accounting and, 24, 25
Inventory control, 235–236, 238, 251–252
Inventory reduction, 265–279

J

Jaouen, Pauline R., 266
Jensen, M. C., 12, 71
JIT manufacturing. *See* Just-in-time manufacturing
Johnson, H. T., 9, 13, 70, 72
Johnson & Johnson
  background of, 342, 343
  control process at, 344–351
  programmed control at, 355–358
Just-in-time (JIT) manufacturing, 229–266
  accounting and, 244–251
  fluctuating demand and, 264–265
  inventory control and, 238, 251–252
  monthly report package and, 260–261
  process costing system and, 244–251
  quality control and, 252–260

K

Kahn, R. L., 121
Kanban card system, 235–236, 251
Kaplan, R. S., 13, 72, 93, 97, 117, 118, 170, 173, 198, 200, 202, 233, 298, 314, 361
Katz, D., 121
Keegan, Daniel P., 117

Kekre, S., 177, 200, 292
Kelvin, Lord, 199
Kennington, J., 193
Kinney, W., 314
Knowledge-intensive industry, control system design in, 137–138
Koenig, Richard, Jr., 358
Kozmetsky, George, 118
Kunkel, J. G., 313

L

Labor productivity, 169–201
  accounting system and, 171–172
  data envelopment analysis and, 192–198
  defined, 172
  product mix and, 189–192
Lawrence, P. R., 71, 143, 361
Leftwich, R. W., 76, 93
Leifer, E. M., 353
Lev, B., 93
Line-of-business (LOB) organization, 105, 110–112
  parts manufacturing and, 287–288
LOB organization. See Line-of-business organization
Loewe, D. A., 65, 72
Long-range planning
  fixed horizon and, 346–347
  information debate and, 347–349
  interactive control and, 351–355
Lorenz, C., 117
Lorsch, J. W., 143, 361
Lot sizing, 268–291
  computer models and, 283–284
  EOQ models and, 284
  internal accounting and, 270–271
  queuing externality and, 269–270

M

McComas, M., 199, 203
McCulloch, Donna, 358, 361
Maciariello, J. A., 317, 337
MacIntosh, Norman B., 359, 361
McKenney, James L., 71
McQuire, C. B., 267
Magee, R. P., 313, 317
Maher, M., 314, 337
Maindiratta, A., 193, 201, 202
Make-or-buy decision, 156–157
  cost accounting and, 288
  decentralization and, 285
  inventory holding costs and, 285–287
Management
  accounting system change and, 87, 88–89, 115, 116, 117
  risk and, 318, 324
Management and Labor New Style, 150
Management compensation plan, accounting procedures and, 75, 76, 90–91, 92–93, 130
Management Information System (MIS)

design problems with, 146
factors in non-implementation of, 155–160, 163
at Hewlett-Packard, 238–240
implementation of, 158–160, 163–164
nontechnical factors and, 148–149
organizational characteristics and, 157–158, 163
types of information and, 158–160, 161–162, 163–164
Management style, interactive control and, 353
Managerial accounting. See also Cost accounting
  ambiguity of measures and, 10–11
  linkage with financial reporting, 87, 88–89, 92
Manufacturing accounting system, 173–177
  productivity and, 170, 198–199
Manufacturing performance
  evaluation of, 280
  nonfinancial factors in, 176–177. See also Productivity
Manufacturing process, accounting reports and, 279–281
Manufacturing profit and loss (MP&L) statement
  cost efficiency and, 175–176
  productivity trends and, 174–175
March, James G., 162
Marginal costing, 213–215. See also Variable-cost accounting
Market contracting, diversification and, 63–64
Markus, M. Lynne, 164, 165
Materials managers, costs information and, 110–112
Matrix organization
  MIS implementation and, 156, 161
  problems with, 59–60
  at Weyerhaeuser, 54–55, 57–62
Mayers Tap
  background on, 207–208
  cost system concerns at, 212
  margin policy at, 211
"Mechanistic" hypothesis, 75
Merchant, Kenneth, 47, 315, 317, 361
Merz, C. Mike, 266
M-form organization. See Multidivisional organization
Miles, R. E., 121, 145
Miller, Danny, 98, 103–104, 115, 118, 165, 359
Miller, J. G., 225, 227
Mintzberg, Henry, 145, 146, 165, 362
"Minutes of output", 281
MIS. See Management Information System
MP&L statement. See Manufacturing profit and loss statement
Multidivisional organization, 52, 54–55. See also Divisional organization

N

Neuman, John L., 70
Neumann, Bruce R., 266
Noel, J., 318, 336
"No Invoice/Debit Memo" procedure, 249–251
Nolan, Richard L., 70
Nonroutineness, 124
Norburn, D., 121

O

Ohlson, J. A., 93
Operating performance, inflation accounting and, 26, 28, 32, 36–39, 41–42
Organizational change
  embedded obsolete systems and, 104–107
  planning and, 43
  revolutionary quantum view of, 98, 103–104, 115
Organizational learning, interactive control and, 352–353
Organization structure
  ambiguity of, 161, 162–163
  authority vs. responsibility and, 10, 137
  environmental uncertainty and, 340
  formal control system design and, 123–124
  information-processing model of, 340
  matrix form, 52–53, 62–63, 67–68
  M-form, 52, 62–63, 67–68
  overhead cost and, 49–72
  size and, 124
Ouchi, W., 314, 315
Overhead costs. See also Fixed costs; Support department costs
  allocation of, 242–244
  Cost by Process Diagram and, 240–242
  cost drivers for, 225–226
  organizational design vs. strategic information procedures and, 49–72
  transactions and, 54
"Overhead creep", 49–50

P

Paperwork reduction, 249–251
Part/Product Cost System, 278–281
Parts manufacturing, 287–288
Passive labor vouchering, 246–248
Pay increase assumption, 86
Pearcy, J., 45, 48
Performance evaluation. See also Controllability principle; Relative performance evaluation
  absolute vs. relative, 301–302, 312–313
  controllability and, 298
  division management and, 296, 297, 299–313
  effort levels and, 354–355
  financial measures and, 300–301, 309–310
  financial targets and, 300, 302–303, 311–312
  in health care industry, 306
  in heavy equipment industry, 302–304
  net income and, 325
  new product development and, 306
  nonfinancial, 302–303
  subjectivity and, 324, 327, 334
  top management and, 296–297, 301, 304, 312–313, 321
  under multidimensional accounting system, 129–130
  unprofitable contracts and, 309, 310
Perpetual work orders, 244–246
Pfeffer, Jeffrey, 165, 360
Pharmaceutical business, uncertainties and, 344

Pinches, G. E., 121
Planning system. See also Formal control system design
  accountability and, 133–134
  complex operations and, 132–133
  environmental uncertainty and, 339–360
  purpose of, 131–132
Political costs, accounting change and, 76
Porter, Michael E., 226, 340
Positive accounting theory, 90–91
  accounting change and, 75–76
Price-level adjustments
  general vs. specific, 23
  inflation accounting and, 41
Price war, controllability principle and, 323
Pricing, dual approach to, 211
Process costing, 244–251
Product-costing systems, 211
Product costs
  design changes and, 242
  distortion of, 204–228
  lot-size diversity and, 223–224
  misclassification of, 225–226
  pricing and, 210–211
  short-term focus for, 225
  short- vs. long-term measures of, 205–206
  transaction costing and, 219–222
Product decisions
  full vs. marginal cost and, 214–215
  product discontinuance, 209–210, 214
  product introduction, 209, 210
Production
  nonuniform, 284–285
  part/product cost report and, 278–281
  uniform and batch manufacturing, 269
Productivity. See also Gain-sharing program
  computation method and, 173
  factors in, 170
  improvement program for, 169, 171
  labor productivity in, 177–178
  prodution volume effects and, 172–173
  trends in, and MP&L statement, 175–176
Productivity measures
  DEA technique and, 192–198
  product mix and, 189–192
Product mix
  gain sharing and, 173, 182–183
  productivity measures and, 189–192
Professional businesses, uncertainties and, 343–344
Profitability
  accounting change and, 88
  inflation accounting and, 37
  management of diversity and, 52
  strategic cost analysis and, 220
Programmed control, 345, 355–358. See also Control processes

Q

Quality control
  barcodes and, 254–260
  cost accounting and, 261–263
  gain sharing and, 179–180

HP150C Process Sheet and, 255–256
JIT manufacturing and, 234, 252–260
measurement and, 252–260
process flow chart and, 256–257
production process and, 255–260
Quantum structural change, C_1 vs C_2 costs and, 98, 103–104
Queuing delays, 268–269
Queuing externality, 269–270

R

Radner, R., 267
Rate of return assumption, 85–86
Reagan, B., 193
Relative performance evaluation (RPE), 295–313
    in conglomerate, 301
    controllability principle and, 318–319
    in diversified industry, 304, 306
    long-term strategy and, 306
    in nondiversified industry, 303, 304, 305–306
    top management and, 305
Research methods. *See also* Field research, methodology
    traditional, 2
    validity and, 3–4
Resource allocation
    inflation accounting and, 27–32, 33, 35, 36, 37–38, 40–41
    procedures for, 53–54
Responsibility structure. *See* Accountability; Controllability principle
Responsibility vs. authority, 10
Reward structures, 123. *See also* Incentive system; Management compensation plan
Rhodes, E., 193
Risk, general managers and, 318, 324
Ro, Byung T., 45, 48
Rockford
    background on, 208–209
    cost allocations at, 212
    cost system concerns at, 211
    margin policy at, 210–211
RPE. *See* Relative performance evaluation

S

Salancik, Gerald, 360
Schön, Donald, 4–5, 14
Schonberger, Richard J., 266
Schrader Bellows
    background on, 208
    cost system concerns at, 212
    diseconomies of scope at, 224
    margin policy at, 210
    strategic cost analysis at, 219–222
Schuyler, Robert, 67
Seed, Allen H., 45, 48
Setups
    lot sizes and, 285
    number of, 219, 268, 283
    time in, 219, 283

Shank, John K., 12, 13
Simon, Herbert A., 118, 165
Situation variables
    formal control system design and, 123–124, 139
    interdepartmental competition and, 136
Smith, S., 296–297, 312, 313
Snow, C. C., 121, 145
Social factors, in MIS non-implementation, 157
Solomons, D., 337
Specialized firms, corporate overhead costs and, 53
Stalker, G. M., 121, 143, 144, 341, 358, 359
Starbuck, William H., 145, 360, 362
Stock market, accounting change and, 74–75, 87–88, 91–92
Strategic information procedures
    inflation-adjusted data and, 33, 40
    overhead cost and, 49–72
Strauss, R. P., 193, 202
Supplier relations, 248–251
Support-department costs
    allocation of, 242–243
    as fixed, 217–218
    nonvolume-related and, 222–223
    transaction costing and, 219–222
    volume-related bases and, 218–219
Swieringa, Robert J., 12, 13

T

Takeover specialists, internal performance assessment and, 63–64, 66
Task unpredictability, 124
Teece, David, 71
Transaction costs, 218–222
    cost accounting and, 225–226
    volume-related systems and, 220–222
Transfer pricing, implementation of, 357–358
Tyndall, Gordon, 118

U

"Unbundling", 49, 61
Uncontrollable factors, 277
    accountability and, 318, 329, 330–332
    management bonuses and, 321–324
    results of accountability for, 332–335

V

Vancil, Richard, 48, 126, 145, 319
Van der Ven, Andrew H., 358
Variable-cost accounting, 205–206, 212–213, 275–277
    long-term costs and, 222–223
Varian, H., 201, 203
Vertical integration, 51. *See also* Diversified firms
    Baker Corporation and, 99
Vollmann, T. E., 225, 227
Volume effects, productivity measures and, 172–173, 180–182, 185–189

Volvo Car B. V.
  background of, 147, 149–150
  information systems at, 150–154
  management accounting system at, 147, 151
  MIS and, 155–160, 161–162
  research activities and, 154–155
  Volvo Car New Style, 150, 157, 158

                      W

Watts, R. L., 93, 94
Weick, Karl E., 164, 362
Welch, B. L., 201, 203
Weyerhaeuser, George, 72
Weyerhaeuser Company, 49–72
  charge-back system at, 50–51, 54, 64–67, 68–
    69
  Customer Service Centers at, 61–62
  decision to diversify at, 54–57
  divisional organization at, 52, 54–55, 62–69

  economies of scope and, 55, 56, 59
  High Yield Forest program at, 56–60, 71
  Information Systems Department at, 65
  long-term planning and, 56–57
  matrix organization at, 57–62
  Timber Asset Management Department at, 56
White, H. C., 353
Williamson, Oliver E., 52, 70, 71, 165
Winward, Herbert C., 71
Wolfson, M., 313, 315
Wyatt, A. R., 93, 94

                      Y

Yin, Robert K., 48, 230, 266

                      Z

Zimmerman, J. L., 93, 318, 338